Ethnic Identity

Creation, Conflict, and Accommodation

Third Edition

■

Lola Romanucci-Ross
George A. De Vos
Editors

ALTAMIRA PRESS

A Division of Sage Publications, Inc.

Walnut Creek ■ London ■ New Delhi

For information address:

AltaMira Press
A Division of Sage Publications, Inc.
1630 North Main Street, Suite 367
Walnut Creek, CA 94596

SAGE Publications Ltd.
6 Bonhill Street
London EC2A 4PU
United Kingdom

SAGE Publications India Pvt. Ltd.
M-32 Market
Greater Kailash 1
New Delhi 110 048 India

Printed in the United States of America.

Library of Congress Cataloging-in-Publication Data
Romanucci-Ross, Lola.
Ethnic identity: creation, conflict, and accommodation /
Lola Romanucci-Ross, George A. De Vos.
p.cm.
Includes bibliographical references and index.
ISBN 0-7619-9110-7 (cloth : acid free).—ISBN 0-7619-9111-5
(pbk. : acid free)
1. Ethnicity—Congresses. 2. Ethnopsychology—Congresses.
3. National characteristics—Congresses. I. De Vos, George A.
II. Title.
GN495.6.E87 1996 95-32537
305.8—dc20 CIP

Editing and Production: Carole Bernard, ECS
Book and Cover based on a design by Kathleen Szawiola

Contents

About the Authors

GEORGE A. DE VOS, a psychologist, is emeritus professor of anthropology, University of California, Berkeley. He is the author of over fifteen books and numerous articles documenting his forty-five years of cross-cultural field experience and research in the United States, East Asia, and Western Europe. From his unique comparative perspective he has integrated a European-derived sociological approach with psychoanalytically oriented American anthropology and psychology.

He has advocated the use of psychological tests cross culturally (*Oasis and Casbah: Algerian Culture and Personality in Change* [1960]; *Symbolic Analysis Cross Culturally: The Rorschach Test* [1989]). He has written extensively on Japanese cultural psychology (*Socialization for Achievement* [1973]); religion (*Religion and the Family in East Asia*, [1986]), social problems, including delinquency (*Heritage of Endurance: Family Patterns and Delinquency Formation in Japan* 1984], alienation (*Social Cohesion and Alienation* [1991], and minority group issues (*Japan's Invisible Race* [1966] and *Koreans in Japan* [1981]). More generally, he has written and edited *Responses to Change: Society, Culture and Personality* [1976]; *Culture and Self: Asian and Western Perspectives* [1985]; and *Status Inequality: The Self in Culture* [1990]).

MARY KAY GILLILAND is on the anthropology faculty of the University of Arizona, Tucson. She has done fieldwork in Yugoslavia over the last ten years. Proficient in Serbo-Croatian, her research interests include family, gender, marriage, the cultural construction of identity, and ethnogenesis in the Balkans, focusing on what she calls "reclaimed lives" in this region.

STEVAN HARRELL, professor of anthropology, University of Washington, has done field research in Taiwan and southwest China. He has written *The Human Family* (forthcoming 1996) and *Being Ethnic in Southwest China* (forthcoming 1996) and edited *Cultural Encounters on China's Ethnic Frontiers* (1995), *Chinese Historical Micro-Demography* (1995), *Cultural Change in Postwar Taiwan* (with Huang Chun-chieh, 1995), and *Chinese Families in the Post-Mao Era* (with Deborah Davis, 1993). His next project is an interactive, hypertext, multimedia CD-ethnography.

ÉVA V. HUSEBY-DARVAS teaches in the Department of Behavioral Sciences at the University of Michigan, Dearborn, and at the Center for Russian and East European Studies at the University of Michigan, Ann Arbor. She has a Ph.D. in cultural anthropology from the University of Michigan and has published on topics of nationalism, ethnicity, gender, women's roles through the life cycle, identity, and socialist/postsocialist Hungary. She is studying and writing on long-distance nationalism among Hungarian-Americans, and on identity among village women in northeastern Hungary between 1945 and 1995.

CHARLES KEYES, professor and former chair of anthropology at the University of Washington was director of the Northwest Regional Consortium for Southeast Asian Studies that links Southeast Asian studies programs at the Universities of Washington, Oregon, and British Columbia. Keyes has done field research (totaling over eight years beginning in 1962) in Southeast Asia, primarily in Thailand, but also in Burma, Laos, Cambodia, and Vietnam. His books include *The Golden Peninsula: Culture and Adaptation in Mainland Southeast Asia* (1977; reprinted 1995) and *Thailand: Buddhist Kingdom as Modern Nation-State* (1987; 2nd edition in process). He edited *Ethnic Change* (1981), *Reshaping Local Worlds: Formal Education and Cultural Change in Rural Southeast Asia* (1991), and (with Laurel Kendall and Helen Hardacre) *Asian Visions of Authority: Religion and the Modern States of East and Southeast Asia* (1994) and is the author of over seventy articles.

MARGARET MEAD (1901-1978), internationally acclaimed anthropologist, author, and educator, has left the world a legacy of consciousness of culture. In a career spanning half a century, h er fieldwork in Samoa, New Guinea, and Bali stimulated her theories on topics of concern in the United States and many other countries. From her most scholarly writing (*Kinship in the Admiralty Islands*), to her controversial *Coming of Age in Samoa*, to her numerous articles in popular magazines, she always accomplished what meant most to her—leading the reader to understand the determinancy of culture in human behavior.

CZESLAW MILOSZ is a member of the American Academy of Arts and Letters. He won the Nobel Prize for Literature in 1980. His books of poetry in English include *Bells in Winter*, *The Separate Notebooks*, *Unattainable Earth*, *The Collected Poems: 1931-1987*, and *Provinces*.

GANANATH OBEYESEKERE, professor of anthropology at Princeton University, also taught at the University of California, San Diego, the University of Washington, and the University of Sri Lanka at Peradeniya. His recent books are *The Work of Culture: Symbolic Transformations in Psychoanalysis and Anthropology* (1990) and *The Apotheosis of Captain Cook: European Mythmaking in the Pacific* (1992).

LOLA ROMANUCCI-ROSS, a cultural and medical anthropologist, is a professor in family and preventive medicine, School of Medicine, at the University of California, San Diego. She has spent over a decade doing fieldwork in Mexico, the Admiralty Islands (Melanesia) in the South Pacific, and Italy, and has written numerous research articles about these areas. Her books include *Conflict, Violence and*

Morality in a Mexican Village; *Mead's Other Manus, Phenomenology of the Encounter*; *One Hundred Towers, an Italian Odyssey of Cultural Survival*; and *The Anthropology of Medicine, from Culture to Method.*

EUGEEN ROOSENS is professor and head of the Department of Anthropology at the Katholieke Universiteit of Leuven, Belgium. He has taught at Leuven since 1965 and at universities in the United States, Canada, and Zaire. He was P. P. Rubens Professor at the University of California, Berkeley (1989-1990). Roosens has done fieldwork among the Yaka in Zaire, with the Huron Indians in Quebec, and in Geel, Belgium. Since 1974 he has directed the project "The Cultural Identity of Ethnic Minorities," a long-term fieldwork project by a team of scholars that operates in five continents. He directed the anthropology team for the Geel project, which concerned community placement of the mentally ill in a Belgian town. His book on Geel has been translated into English, French, German, and Japanese. Roosens has written half a dozen other books and monographs on Africa, ethnicity, and immigration.

THEODORE SCHWARTZ has been professor of anthropology at the University of California, San Diego, since 1969. He has a Ph.D. from the University of Pennsylvania (1958) and was a founder of and has served as president of the Society for Psychological Anthropology. Schwartz is author of *The Paliau Movement in the Admiralty Islands* (1963) and has written articles on ethnicity for *Anthropological Forum.*

CAROLA SUÁREZ-OROZCO, Ph.D., a clinical psychologist, is a research associate at the Harvard Graduate School of Education. She completed a clinical internship in psychology in the Department of Psychiatry at the University of California, San Diego. She is the author of a number of publications, including (with Marcelo Suárez-Orozco) *Transformations: Immigration, Family Life, and Achievement Motivation among Latino Youth* (1995). Currently, she is studying school failure in a large urban high school.

MARCELO SUÁREZ-OROZCO is professor of education at Harvard University. Educated in Latin America and at the University of California, Berkeley, he has taught at various campuses at the University of California as well as in a number of European universities. He is the author of many books and essays published in the United States, Europe, and Latin America. Among his recent books are *The Making of Psychological Anthropology* (1994), with George and Louise Spindler, and *Status Inequality: The Self in Culture* (1990), with George A. De Vos.

VICTOR C. UCHENDU was the first director of the Center for African Studies at the University of Illinois. He has done research in Zaire and Nigeria.

LOLA ROMANUCCI-ROSS
GEORGE A. DE VOS

Preface: 1995

This is the third, completely revised edition of our volume, *Ethnic Identity*, first published in 1975 and reissued in 1982. This present edition reflects the changes occurring worldwide since our original editions, which resulted from a Wenner-Gren conference on ethnicity held at Berg Wartenstein, Austria, in 1970. We have added seven new chapters, and due to the exigencies of space, we have been constrained to drop some original chapters. The remaining chapters have been completely revised by the authors to reflect more recent events, personal fieldwork, or research. What we deem remarkable is that the original volume was predictive with respect to the greater saliency now given to ethnic problems and conflictful political events by social scientists.

Participants at the initial conference were especially partisan to ethnographic field research materials subjected to psychocultural forms of analysis. We considered ethnicity to be best understood by an approach that takes into account the experiential, subjective forces underlying ethnic identity and its maintenance; macrocultural forces alone (social structure and culture history, for example) are inadequate to ensure complete understanding of the nature of ethnic persistence. Our emphasis did not gainsay the political, economic, and other social features of the history of ethnic belonging or contrastiveness among people. However, it asserted that relative priority must be given to the emotional, even irrational psychological features underlying one's social identity. In the contemporary world of complex societies, identity is increasingly expressed in ethnic terms. We have insisted that ethnicity be considered by both emic as well as etic approaches. In other words, the *perspective* of the groups and individuals observed and analyzed should not be overwhelmed and engulfed by the perspective of the observer/analysts. There is a psychological as well as a social level of analysis, and it is irrational and emotional as well as rational and analytic.

The social sciences have identified many forms of classification within societies, from the kinship systems of simple preliterate, preindustrial societies, to the stratified economic classes of complex, industrial states. Ethnic divisions have always been present, but until recently have been relatively neglected as sources of instability, metastability, and social change.

A more dynamic point of view emphasizes that in almost every social organization there are tensions that result from pressures to unify versus pressures to maintain differences. This seems reminiscent of Nietzsche's discovery (as he describes it in his "Birth of Tragedy") of the relationship between the Apollonian and the Dionysian in the culture of ancient Greece. Nietzsche says this is a tension between measured, harmonic stasis and frenzied system perturbation that the human spirit needs. In fact, most social systems give evidence, mythological or otherwise, of some stubborn survival of alien traditions. We would therefore contend that the "normal" condition of many social systems is one of tension and intermittent conflict, of "system perturbation," rather than placid homeostasis. Such a view directs attention to the complexities arising out of conflicting, centrifugal tendencies in any society. It frustrates any desire to simplify theoretical explanations by stressing only the integrative, unifying processes of a social system.

In our concluding chapter we note the increased political, economic, and social centrality of events that fragmented previous multiethnic hegemonies and raised general international consciousness about the saliency of ethnicity as a contemporary social force. The more recent inclusions have greater emphasis on how ethnicity as a potentially conflictful form of social loyalty is constantly being newly created and developed, with both positive and negative social consequences.

In our original introductory chapter we sought to establish several essential issues to which the arguments of the book's contributors drew special attention.

The first effort was directed toward distinguishing ethnic identity from other forms of social segmentation. The anthropologists who then participated were, in most instances, members of an ethnic constituency themselves and they examined their social belonging from within. The general conclusion was that to understand ethnicity as a vital social force one had to consider subjective feelings related to group belonging more than to objective cultural criteria.

An abiding argument was that ethnic loyalties were a more governing, always potentially conflictful social force than social class loyalties in considering past or present social and political history. Marxist theorists have now retreated from preoccupation with class analysis toward espousal of ethnic problems as sources of social unrest and overt conflict. The Soviet Union as a multiethnic imperial state is gone. A diminished Russia has lost its most restive ethnic components but is still bedeviled by conflict between various ethnic constituencies within its borders and in the surrounding, now independent, territories. Yugoslavia has been destroyed by conflictful ethnic partisanship. Remaining Communist or leftist parties elsewhere cannot now unite their followers under any unifying banner of class warfare. Now, anti-imperialism makes a better rallying cry.

It is evident that espousing the saliency of ethnicity over class loyalty as we did in 1970 is no longer as contentious as it then was. Moreover, contrary to what some would still insist as to the goal-oriented nature of ethnic striving, social belonging is not based simply on rational, instrumental considerations. There are emotional considerations involved that may at times go counter to the rationally considered benefits of asserting, maintaining, or denying an ethnic allegiance.

The second argument that permeated our volume was that ethnicity was a subjective sense of loyalty based on imagined origins and parentage rather than something to be measured by objectively visible present cultural criteria or historical facts. This argument also remains.

What we have made more explicit in the chapters now added are the processes whereby there can occur a more-or-less deliberate creation, or even fabrication, of an old ethnic past for emotional as well as new political motives or social-economic gain. New forms of group affiliation, or bolstered self-esteem and group prestige gained from a refabricated or embroidered ethnic past, may in some instances exceed any hoped-for instrumental economic or political gains.

The present edition has, therefore, reorganized a few of the previous chapters and added new ones to highlight the processes actually involved in the creation and maintenance of an ethnic identity. Part I repeats some of the original conceptual chapters by De Vos and Schwartz; those by De Vos and Romanucci-Ross have been completely revised with addition of new materials.

Part II considers two new instances of how new ethnic definitions come into being, forming new ethnic group definitions in comtemporary China and Zaire. Part III looks at the formative processes of ethnic allegiance emerging in the development of ethnic majorities in politically independent national states, namely, Africa generally, modern Thailand, and Hungary. Part IV presents two instances of unresolved conflict that occur where exclusory ethnic and religious definitions of a national state gain an irreconcilable ascendancy. Here, we illustrate the destructive interactions presently occurring within Sri Lanka and the former Yugoslavia.

Part V discusses processes of change in the inclusion or exclusion of particular minority groups in Lithuania, the United States, and Japan. We have also added a chapter with a more direct consideration of generational changes in ethnicity that occur in Mexican-Americans. What happens in this migratory situation is not simply "acculturation," as has been predicted in the past by anthropologists or sociologists, but a more complex development of new forms of specific group identity within the surrounding multiethnic environment of a modern state.

The conclusions reiterate and again formulate what we consider the complex parameters involved and the psychocultural dynamics comprising an ethnic identity.

PART I ■

Concepts of Ethnic Identity

GEORGE A. DE VOS ■

Chapter One

Ethnic Pluralism: Conflict and Accommodation[1]

The Role of Ethnicity in Social History

A sense of common origin, of common beliefs and values, and of a common feeling of survival—in brief, a "common cause"—has been important in uniting people into self-defining in-groups. Growing up together in a social unit and sharing a common verbal and gestural language allows humans to develop mutually understood accommodations, which radically diminish situations of possible confrontation and conflict. In mammalian societies generally, ordered systems of individual dominance are a major accommodative device. Given the human capacities for cultural elaboration, we go further. Humans can, on the basis of *group definitions of belonging*, develop complex formal systems of individual and group social stratification. These systems are found in many so-called primitive societies as well as in technologically advanced modern states (see De Vos 1966; De Vos and Suárez-Orozco 1990).

The cultural bases for social groupings in society are varied. Some groupings, such as lineage systems, are defined reciprocally and horizontally. Kinship networks, a major form of grouping, very often operate horizontally as forms of reciprocal marital exchange. Other groupings, such as class and caste, are stratified vertically, with emphasis on the status of an individual or a group with respect to other persons or groups. Another form of group separation—the subject of this volume—is found most frequently in composite societies and results from the inclusion of groups of supposed different cultural, or "ethnic," origin (De Vos and Suárez-Orozco 1990).

Ethnicity can be a source of considerable conflict, since in many instances ethnic groups do not remain in a fixed position within a stratified system. A separate ethnic identity, when it persists in a group, tends to maintain boundaries, to use the perspective of Fredrik Barth (1969:15). Like Barth, I think that in the study of ethnic relations, one must first understand how and why boundaries are maintained, rather than simply examine the cultural content of the separated group. We both contend that boundaries are basically psychological in nature, not territorial. They are maintained by ascription from within as well as from external sources that designate membership according to evaluative characteristics.

It seems necessary, in discussing ethnicity, to start from a theoretical position that regards some form of *conflict* as a normal or chronic condition in a pluralistic society. Social tensions are manifestly different and less readily soluable in pluralistic societies than they are in stratified societies composed principally of an ethnically homogeneous populace.

Ethnically plural societies have occurred throughout human history, most often involuntarily as a result of imperial conquest. Today, however, ethnicity has become an important issue in modern states because of the ethnic interpenetration that has resulted from increasing social mobility (related to individual achievement) and from increasing geographic mobility (due to shifting labor markets).

We are also witnessing a revolution in the recording of social and cultural history. Today's ethnic minorities are not content to remain mute; they, too, seek to be heard. The defeated and the oppressed, now literate, are themselves contributing their interpretations to the writing or rewriting of history, adding their own and, where facts fail, creating or deepening their own sustaining mythologies. Social classes or pariah outcastes relatively invisible in earlier unrecorded histories are emerging as figures in a larger history of conflict or as new subjects in historical approaches that deal more directly with stratification in societies. The Marxist philosophy of history has deepened the perception of modern historians generally, enabling them to recognize the existence of historically oppressed groups. Like Freud's approach to personal history, a conflict approach to social history reveals the continuing influence of repressed forces—forces that do not disappear simply because they have been omitted from the official history written by the politically and socially dominant group.

Another social process is also continually at work—the creation of newly salient identities and group loyalties defined as ethnic in nature that are, actually, based on a past only recently fabricated, which comes to justify a presently sought-for, selectively contrastive social belonging. Ethnic identity, as we shall observe in several of the following chapters, is a continually evolving social process, sometimes occurring within a single generation.

Ethnic minorities have been present as long as sovereign political states have existed. However, ethnic conflict has usually been treated from the standpoint of political struggles for territory rather than from the psychocultural viewpoint of what occurs within individuals when they are confronted with the necessity of changing allegiance to a new master, adopting a new religion, or even acquiring a new language in order to participate in a dominant political society that is ethnically alien.[2]

Until recently, social science theorists have paid little attention to enduring ethnic or cultural identity as a primary social force comparable to territorial nationalism or class affiliation. Its role in past and present conflicts within complex societies was often neglected by social scientists, who usually concerned themselves with the relations between ethnically different but politically autonomous groups. Once a group has been conquered or absorbed politically, the assumption seems to have been that its existence in a new political state was of less concern than the state's external relations. From the earliest history of the state, however, many forms of intrasocial tensions arose from ethnic diversity. Such conflict has not been limited to empires that acknowledged political hegemony over ethnically heterogeneous groups. It is still apparent in states that seek to extend a uniform culture to all its members.

To maintain its focus, this discussion does not deal with conflict between independent cultures; instead it is restricted to a preliminary and partial overview of the nature of ethnic conflict in established pluralistic societies. In this introductory chapter, I shall briefly examine how ethnicity can be used both *expressively* and *instrumentally* within a pluralistic society and how it may or may not contribute to social instability.

Certain peoples insist on maintaining symbolic forms of cultural differentiation for centuries, despite a lack of political autonomy or even of a particular territory. Given the present abundant opportunities to observe groups firsthand, there is no excuse to neglect the question of how ethnic identity functions psychologically as well as socially in a complex, stratified social system.

One cannot fully understand the force of ethnicity without examining in some detail its influence on the personality of minority group members. It is insufficient to examine ethnic group behavior directly, from only the vantage point of social structure or social processes. The discussion of ethnicity and social stratification that follows relates conflict over allegiance and belonging not only to one's place in the status system, but also to internal conflicts over the priority to be given to past-, present-, or future-oriented forms of identity in "self" consciousness.

In a primary sense of belonging, an individual can lean toward one of three orientations: (1) a present-oriented concept of membership as a citizen in a particular state or as a member of a specific occupational group; (2) a future-oriented membership in a transcendent, more universal religious or political sense; or (3) a past-oriented concept of the self as defined by one's ethnic identity, that is, based on ancestry and origin. We contend that the maintenance of this latter form of identity is as powerful a force as a present or future allegiance in shaping human social history. The Marxist theory of class consciousness or class conflict tells us much less about human history than does a historical examination of ethnic consciousness.[3]

Ethnicity Broadly Defined

There is as yet no acceptable single word in English for the phrase "ethnic group," no one word equivalent to "class," "caste," or "family" to describe a group self-consciously united around particular cultural traditions, although French anthropologists have suggested the word *ethne* for technical usage. An ethnic group is a self-perceived inclusion of those who hold in common a set of traditions not shared by others with whom they are in contact. Such traditions typically include "folk" *religious beliefs* and practices, *language*, a sense of *historical continuity*, and *common ancestry* or place of origin. The group's actual history often trails off into legend or mythology, which includes some concept of an unbroken biological-genetic generational continuity, sometimes regarded as giving special inherited characteristics to the group. *Endogamy* is usual, although various patterns for initiating outsiders into the ethnic group are developed in such a way that they do not disrupt the group's essential sense of generational continuity.[4]

Some of the same elements that characterize ethnic membership seem to characterize lineage group or caste membership in some societies. The subjective definitions differ, however, as do their functions. A lineage group or caste perceives itself as an *interdependent* unit of a society, whereas members of an ethnic group cling to a sense of having been an *independent* people, in origin at least, whatever special role they have collectively come to play in a pluralistic society. Thus, caste definitions explicitly point to a present system of formal stratification, whereas ethnic definitions refer to a past cultural independence. In contrast, groups formed around universalist religious or political ideologies are oriented to a future society with less explicit or more satisfactory forms of status stratification. Individuals presently dissatisfied with the social status accorded them as members of a minority group may seek to leave their group. They may choose either to adopt a future-oriented religious or political ideology, thereby gaining admission to a new group, or they may emphasize their ethnic past and exert pressure to change the collective relative status of their group. (I shall presently illustrate instances of an attempt to escape caste definitions in India and the United States.) An alternative to any change in collective status is a change in individual status, which may involve "passing," as I shall also discuss later.

"Racial" Uniqueness

Some sense of genetically inherited differences, real or imagined, is part of the ethnic identity of many groups, as well as being one of the characteristics about an ethnic minority held by those dominant groups that wish to prevent assimilation. The relationships between caste, ethnicity, and racial definitions are complex in many pluralistic societies. A willingness to acculturate completely on the part of a racially defined ethnic minority, not only in comportment but also in actual identity, may not be acceptable to the dominant group. A system of stratified exclusion can be better maintained on the basis of genetic heritage, which implies that such backwardness is not to be overcome.

A socially defined racial minority wishes to assimilate but finds that intermarriages or other forms of integration are withheld on the basis of race; the group is forced to select another alternative. It can accept an inferior caste status and a sense of basic inferiority as part of its collective self-definition, or it can define the situation as one of direct political and economic oppression. Another alternative is to deliberatively redefine itself symbolically, creating a positive view of its heritage on the basis of cultural and racial distinctions, thereby establishing a sense of collective dignity. This separate in-group ethnic sense can be used in an attempt to escape caste stratification. Thus, an ethnic self-definition by a group in an already ethnically plural society such as the United States can heighten the relative status of a group vis-à-vis other groups also defined in ethnic terms.[5]

Territoriality

Most ethnic groups have a tradition of territorial or political independence, even though the present members have become part of another, or sometimes several, political entities. In comparing ethnic groups, however, one notes highly different patterns related to the possession of territory as a means of maintaining group cohesion. At one extreme are groups such as the Japanese, with their own separate origin myth, occupying an entire nation-state; at the other extreme are minorities such as the Jews, who had been without a territory for centuries, but now again, on the basis of an origin myth, claim the territory of Israel. In numerically large, politically independent groups, ethnic identity tends to be coextensive with national or regional identity. Social and political problems resulting from continual attempts by groups to extend their territory account for much of the world's political history.[6]

Strictly used, nationality is indistinguishable from ethnicity. But in a looser sense, the words "nation" and "nationality" often also encompass diverse groups that have achieved political unification but still consider some territorial base, actual or desired. It can be argued that for many people, national identity and subjective cultural identity cannot be distinguished, especially when ethnic identity and a national territorial identity have been united historically.[7] Otherwise, ethnic identity is either a more specific or a broader identity than national identity.[8] Identity may take on a local territorial flavor, so that a person defines him- or herself as Breton rather than as French, or as Roman rather than as Italian. However, a "German" identity can include Austrians as well as inhabitants of a present-day German state. Local identifications may or may not entail some feeling of continuity with the past.

Some ethnic minorities maintain themselves, at least partially, by sustaining hope for political independence or for the recapturing of lost national territory. Native American groups are designated as nations even though many have lost their territorial base. The most striking example of such thinking has been the Jewish vision of reestablishing Israel. Other groups, such as the Kurds in Iran, consider themselves as a nation and still hope to reassert their special autonomy by recapturing or maintaining a political territorial base. Some such groups inhabit territory that is difficult to penetrate and that therefore enables them to maintain a measure of local autonomy. Tibetans have thus resisted becoming "Chinese" nationals.

Some ethnic minorities have been partially incorporated into larger national units; Scottish and Welsh incorporation into Great Britain fall into this category. The Soviet Union was an example of a state with continuing tensions resulting from territorial expansion and the incomplete incorporation of widely divergent groups such as the Latvians and Estonians in Europe and numerous Moslem Turkic groups in Asia. They made very complex usage of distinctions between groups considered ethnic minorities and/or nations.

Thus, symbolically or actually, territory may be central to maintain ethnicity, it may be minimal or even nonexistent (the Rom, the wandering Gypsies of Europe, are an extreme example). The degree to which some territorial concept is necessary to the maintenance of ethnic identity, symbolically or actually, must be considered in relation to the salient use of nonterritorial definitions of ethnic uniqueness and in relation to economic, religious, linguistic, or other social activities.

Economic Bases

Economic factors contribute in a complex manner to ethnic definitions and identity maintenance. An ethnic minority can be well dispersed within another population and still defend itself from assimilation by maintaining a certain amount of economic autonomy. Specific occupational minorities such as particular Parsis in India, Jews of Europe, and overseas enclaves of Indians and Chinese manage to remain ethnically distinct, at least partially because their community organization has a secure subsistence base anchored in special occupations that they can pursue from one generation to the next. There is, however, a great deal of political ambivalence in some areas about allowing quasi-independent, economically secure ethnic enclaves to persist. The often ambiguous political role of overseas merchant Indians in Africa and Chinese in Southeast Asia are cases in point.

Hagen (1962) finds that a minority group may compensate for a prior downward shift in status by innovative economic activities that lead to a consequent resurgence benefiting the relative status of their members. Such an examination of the relationship between ethnicity and economic power is particularly revealing of the means by which group shifts occur in social position.

Religion

Religious conversion can be a means of abandoning one's ethnic identity by adopting a transcendent worldview or it can be used to maintain a separate identity. In their studies of revivalist cults among politically subordinate groups, anthropologists have found that religion can be used to mobilize members of a group to deal with a perceived threat to their continuing existence or, more directly, to attain a promised change of status through a religiously oriented social revolution.[9] Folk religion often takes the form of myths about the uniqueness of the group or its genesis. Nativism in medical practices—resistance to scientific definitions of disease and a tenacious clinging to traditional curing practices—is another means of maintaining ethnic identity (Romanucci-Ross 1977; Crandon-Malamud 1991).

A written tradition of sacred texts defining the religious faith can also be a strong force in maintaining a sense of identity in each succeeding generation. The Hellenic Iliad, the Bible of the Jews, and the Kojiki of the Japanese are three notable examples. The use of religion to support ethnic identity is clear in the case of folk beliefs and practices. But universalist faiths such as Buddhism, Christianity, and Islam can also contribute to ethnic group cohesion when special sectarian differences become important as a matter of group loyalty and identification in specific contrastive or conflictful social settings as occurred in Iraq and Iran or in Sri Lanka.[10]

Religious or ideological conflict in society often has more to do with increasing the power of one's own group than with extending the benefits of one's religion to converts. In fact, throughout history states have exploited religious differences to enhance their power. For this reason, religions have often been nationalized so as to diminish problems of divided loyalty.[11] For some groups, religious beliefs about their historical origin and past tribulations provide the vital definition of who they are. When a native religion is destroyed by the imposition of a conquering people's beliefs, the group identity, if it survives at all, receives a severe blow. There can be widespread loss of morale. The status role of adult males in particular can be affected by attacks on the indigenous religious system. When sustaining beliefs are undermined by this type of cultural contact, the individual and collective will to survive is weakened, leading to collective anomie.

Members of some groups, such as Native Americans, are unable to believe in themselves, because they have lost faith in their own religious system and its symbols of dignity and status. At the same time, they cannot draw sustenance from the religion of their conquerors without giving up their own identity. For many African-Americans, the Christian tradition remains a strong integrative force. But the preacher or minister, always a social leader, now finds the requirements of his role shifting from accommodation toward confrontation and protest. And some militant blacks today define Christianity, and sometimes Judaism, as white racist religions. They have turned instead to Islam, which they see as less racially discriminatory. As an African as well as Asian religion it is not associated with European political oppression, whereas Christianity, in Africa and elsewhere, had been introduced during colonial occupations and used to induce psychological and social accommodation to an oppressed status. To forge a new identity, some African-Americans have joined new groups such as the Black Muslims, or affiliated directly with an established Arab Muslim sect. Implicit also in this pro-Arab movement is an anti-Jewish feeling based on the ghetto experience of many blacks, who perceive Jewish merchants as using sharp practices to take advantage of them.[12] Other blacks, though not adopting Islam, find it psychologically easier to identify with their African heritage by simply foregoing Christianity. Their sense of ethnic identity takes precedence over even a universalist definition of Christianity or the secular universalist outlook of Marxism.

Aesthetic Cultural Patterns

Particular cultures afford particular patterns related to aesthetic traditions used symbolically as a basis of self and social identity. Tastes in food, dance traditions, styles of clothing, and definitions of physical beauty are ways in which cultures identify themselves by aesthetic patterns.[13] In times of ethnic resurgence, greater emphasis is put on aesthetic features related to communication and social communion. The "soul" concept of African-Americans is a case in point. Their patterns of communication form a basis for mutual acceptance and identity and include a vocabulary of gestures and formal language characteristics. A new holiday can be fabricated or new styles of dress can be defined as ethnic to signify an ethnic belonging based on "authentic" African culture. The religious, aesthetic, and linguistic features of ethnic identity are related to questions of artistic creativity examined in psychocultural terms. Modes of ethnic persistence depend on the capacity to maintain art forms distinctive of a group rather than of an individual.

Language

Language is often cited as a major component in the maintenance of a separate ethnic identity, and language undoubtedly constitutes the single most characteristic feature of ethnic identity. But ethnicity is frequently related more to the symbolism of a separate language than to its actual use by all members of a group.[14] The Irish use Gaelic as a symbol of their Celtic ethnicity, as do the Scots, but speaking Gaelic or Scottish is not essential to group membership in either case. Where languages have transcended national frontiers, as have English, French, and Spanish, ethnicity is not necessarily broadened to include all speakers of the language, any more than it encompasses all believers in a common faith or all people with similar life-styles.

Group identity can even be maintained by minor differences in linguistic patterns and by styles of gesture. There are many ways in which language-patterning fluency or lack of fluency in a second language is related to identity maintenance. Changing patterns within groups are related to the sanctioning, positively or negatively, of specific dialects. Reassertion of local versus central political controls is sometimes symbolically indicated by the degree to which local dialect patterns are maintained. This is apparent in European countries such as Italy, and has strong influence in such pluralistic states as Indonesia. There is reemphasis, for example, in England on maintaining local speech patterns. Political and economic sanctions against "improper" English have lessened in Britain, so much so that it is no longer necessary to adopt standard speech or intonation to apply for a particular job.[15]

The manipulation of language as a status marker can also be used by individuals aspiring to change how they are defined ethnically. Roosens cites how the Yaka of Zaire drop their traditional language when moving to urban settings so they will not be seen pejoratively by others.[16]

The Invention of Ethnicity as an Advantageous or Deliberately Marketable Identity

When particular ethnic groups or nationalities are examined historically one becomes aware that the evolution of ethnic consciousness in many instances was not a slow crescive one. It does not necessarily develop slowly or spontaneously out of a growing awareness of differences from other contrasting groups of different origin. A new ethnic loyalty can be created as deliberatively as can a fabricated or adhanced mythology of origin. Belonging to a specific group with a genuinely unique past, or, if need be, a fabricated one, can become a conscious advantage to be manipulated by at least some members of a social or territorial group.

Some special members can designate themselves as scholars examining the supposed heroic past. An origin myth can be created to justify a contemporary political loyalty or new sense of contrastive status enhancing social identity. Some of the newly added chapters discuss how ethnic identity is fabricated and for what purposes. There are several reasons for invention—notably, consolidation and legitimization of political power; enhanced social status; or economic advantage. For example, Keyes who coins the appropriate term "marketable identity," discussed in Chapter 7, notes how a particular group of so-called Lue market "authentic" ethnic "native" wares to Chinese tourists.

A striking example of fabricated identity is described in detail by the historian Schama (1987). He describes how, in the sixteenth century, certain dedicated Calvinist scholars helped create, for inhabitants of the provinces of the newly independent northern Dutch Republic, a single mythological origin involving a folk hero and his followers coming west to build dikes against the North Sea from Batavia, a small isle lying between the Rhine and the Waal rivers. This "Batavian" identity helped mark off the Dutch and justified for them a special religious-political-economic destiny that distinguished them from the linguistically related southern, yet captive provinces of the Netherlands (principally Flanders and Brabant), which remained under the control of Spanish occupation forces. The new capital of the Dutch colonial empire in the Indies was appropriately named "Batavia," to symbolically mark the administrative seat of their expanding manifest destiny in Asia.

Ethnicity: A Subjective Sense of Continuity in Belonging

In brief, the ethnic identity of a group of consists of its *subjective*, *symbolic*, or *emblematic* use of any aspect of a culture, or a perceived separate origin and continuity in order to differentiate themselves from other groups. In time, these emblems can be imposed from outside or embraced from within. Ethnic features such as language, clothing, or food can become emblems, for they show others who one is and to what group one's loyalty belongs. A Christian, for example, wears a cross; a Jew the Star of David.

An extreme case, but useful for illustration, is that of the modern American Jew. There is a considerable body of literature written by Jewish intellectuals throughout their history in Europe and in the United States about what it is to be a Jew, and how one reconciles one's sense of ethnicity with citizenship, power, and social status in a prevailingly Christian society. Some contemporary writers fear that with the attenuation of social discrimination, modern American Jews may soon lose their sense of Jewishness. Already, some individuals who consider themselves Jews have no remaining special linguistic heritage; they no longer adhere to any of the beliefs of Judaism nor to any customs peculiar to Jewish culture, and they do not believe that Jews comprise any special or distinct racial group. How, then, can they continue to feel that being Jewish is important to their sense of social self or ethnic identity? Apparently it is a difficult task, for today some Jewish youth, although children of nonpracticing parents, study Hebrew, visit Israel, join an orthodox synagogue, and reinstitute the rituals of the Sabbath in order to "find themselves."

This example illustrates dramatically the need for a psychological or emic[17] approach to the question of ethnic identity. As a subjective sense of belonging, ethnicity cannot be defined by behavioral criteria alone. Ethnicity is determined by what one feels about oneself, not by how one is observed to behave. Defining oneself in social terms is a basic answer to the human need to belong and to survive.

In a simple independent culture the sense of self is relatively uncomplicated. One's instrumental goals and expressive needs are inseparable. One's sense of belonging and social meaning—past, present, and future—are defined without contradiction in a unified belief system. This unified sense of belonging is disrupted, however, when the state emerges as an institution for governing—when several ethnic groups are coercively unified within a single political framework. Social allegiance is further complicated when future-oriented revolutionary ideologies appear. These are often religious movements that offer a transcendent form of identity more encompassing than currently available definitions.[18]

As indicated earlier, religious movements can appear as revivalist cults or as a newly fabricated ethnicity that reinterprets symbols of the past so as to reestablish the group, using the old patterns to evoke an image of a better future for its members. Ethnicity, therefore, is, in its narrowest sense, a feeling of continuity with a real or imagined past, a feeling that is maintained as an essential part of one's self-definition. Ethnicity is also intimately related to the individual need for a collective continuity as a belonging member of some group. The individual senses some degree of threat to his or her own survival if the group or lineage is threatened with extinction. Ethnicity, therefore, includes a sense of personal survival through a historical continuity of belonging that extends beyond the self. For this reason, failure to remain in one's group leads to feelings of guilt. It is a form of killing inflicted on one's progenitors, including one's parents, who still "live" as long as some symbols of their culture are carried forth into the present and future, out of the past. In its deepest psychological level, ethnicity is a sense of affiliative survival. If one's group survives, one is assured of survival, even if not personally.

Transcendental religions or universalistic ideologies offer an alternative form of survival by affording a new identity and a new form of continuity. The reasons for rejecting the old in embracing the new are varied and complex. Entering a new religion or leaving the family are marked by symbols of death and rebirth in many forms of initiation ceremonies, such as baptism. These symbolic rituals testify to a transition in identity and are a source of security about survival, whatever the threat of death may be in relinquishing an old identity. Broadly, universalistic ideologies and ethnically oriented social definitions are contrastive and alternative patterns that introduce conflict in complex societies.

Basic Types of Group Allegiance

Problems of Priority

In a complex society, the body to which an individual gives greatest commitment depends on whether one is oriented primarily to the past, the present, or the future (see Figure 1). With a present orientation, one's primary loyalty can be directed toward a country of residence. Patriotism can become a powerful emotion, making people willing to sacrifice their lives for the "fatherland" or "motherland." Here, survival of the nation is more important than personal survival. Although this strength of emotion can bind citizens together, it may, but does not necessarily, involve any concept of past common origin. The emphasis is on present participation. French citizenship and American citizenship are assimilative legal concepts defining vital and continuing national identities.

A less general and sometimes conflicting form of present-oriented social belonging is identity through participation in an occupation or profession. This identity may conflict with a national identity. When an individual acquires competence in a skill or a profession, his or her primary commitment shifts to the mastery of a specific skill, or more generally to the social class of that profession. A person may identify him- or herself by status as a noble or a commoner; or by occupation, as a merchant or a worker; or more specifically as a scientist, a physician, and so on. This identity may be much stronger and more compelling than any national or ethnic allegiance. However, in time of conflict, ethnic or national allegiance may assume priority, as happened with some German and Japanese social scientists who distorted professional knowledge in the direction of ethnic-national ideologies in World War II. Present occupation and past ethnic identity can, in addition, sometimes represent caste allegiances.

Individuals who are dissatisfied with the past and the present may adopt a future orientation, attaining a sense of social belonging by identification with a cause or a revolutionary movement. These movements may be directly generated by a religious or politicosocial ideology. Individuals whose sense of social self is related

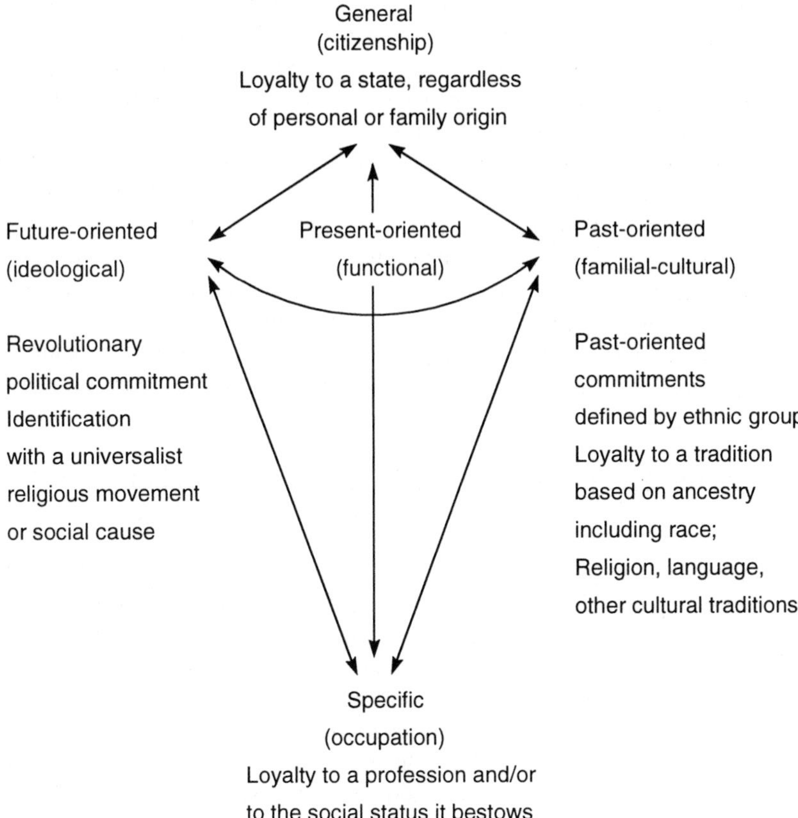

Figure 1. Priority in belonging: directions of conflict and accommodation between types of group allegiance.

to a perceived exploitative, unjust, or immoral present social system may develop a sense of identity that brings them into political conflict with their society. Unrest on the basis of religious or political beliefs may develop in individuals or in whole social groups. Sometimes an ethnic minority will seem to use a future-oriented movement as a vehicle for protest, but in such cases the actual motivation of participants must be carefully examined. Russians in World War II, for example, are reported to have fought more to defend their ethnic homeland than to defend the ideology of international communism.

In contrast to present- or future-oriented sources of social identity, ethnicity is oriented to special past heritage. It may be congruent with present citizenship in some states, or be quite unrelated to citizenship in others. It may overlap with a future-oriented identity when the two are seen as mutually supportive. But ethnicity, as defined here, is primarily a sense of belonging to a particular ancestry and origin and of sharing a specific religion or language. This primary sense of belonging may or may not be related to political or geographical units, and may or may not bring the individual into conflict with the larger society.

The history of minority peoples and organizations has in general, however, been an unhappy series of conflicts and accommodations arising from the coercive pressures that politically dominant groups exert on their subordinates to gain and to maintain loyalty. Some members of subordinate groups may seek to change their assigned or ascribed lower-status positions to more congenial past or future definitions of self and group. This pressure for change causes instability in stratified societies. They often respond with suppressive measures, seeking sometimes to assimilate the group, causing it to disappear rather than according it more autonomy.

Ethnic Pluralism as a Means of Changing Relative Social Status

The conceptual scheme just presented helps explain why social movements based on group belonging take the particular form they do in given cultural-historical situations. The change of status demanded by black Americans from their reluctant white compatriots is a good example of how ethnic membership shapes social movements. Gerald Berreman (1967) and others have advanced cogent arguments defining how caste concepts govern social relationships not only in India, but in the United States between blacks and whites. In assessing the status of the Burakumin, the former pariahs of Japan, Wagatsuma and I came to a similar conclusion (1967). Those groups of Native Americans, ethnic Americans, and Japanese who have been treated as members of outcaste or pariah groups show numerous similarities in their collective attempts to overcome the effects of caste.[19] However, the differences are striking and reflect overall differences in cultural history and present social structure. They influence the method taken to change one's status individually and collectively in each instance. The directions taken by their social movements differ depending on the inherent difficulties faced in reconciling class, caste, and ethnic identities.

Both caste and class definitions of self are explicitly related to a system of formal stratification, whereas ethnic definitions imply some less explicit hierarchy, hence are more open to change with shifts of economic or political power. Both ethnic and class self-definitions can constitute a challenge to the state, since loyalty to either one may transcend national boundaries. International communism, for example, threatened the state by emphasizing the solidarity of the world's working classes, whereas ethnic groups may threaten by a struggle for political separation.[20] Some of the present caste groups in India were originally non-Hindu tribes, but they cannot draw on this past to change their present relative status. Some of these groups, however, have in recent times reconstructed their history to create, in effect, a myth of a past higher status (Rowe 1960, 1964). Since caste rank is strongly internalized as part of an Indian's identity, freeing oneself from it is very difficult. A socially mobile group in India must, therefore, constrain others to recognize its right to a higher rank, rather than trying to escape from the caste system altogether.

Harijans, or former untouchables, are attempting to escape caste by converting from Hinduism to Buddhism, but with questionable success. A universalistic faith, Buddhism was born in India partially as a revolutionary attempt to overcome caste. When caste-oriented Hinduism prevailed, Buddhism was forced to retreat from India. Now, again, Buddhism is being used for the same revolutionary task that it failed to accomplish in the past. Many Hindus consider Buddhism ethnically alien, just as some Shintoists in Japan have been anti-Buddhist, resenting its universalistic elements. Although Indian state policy has taken steps toward establishing noncaste criteria for social ranking, caste remains the most potent influence on social status. Since ethnicity is not an effective means for changing relative status within Indian society, some territorial-ethnic groups such as the Assamese are seeking political autonomy instead.[21]

The United States, on the other hand, is a mixed class-ethnic society with caste-race features. In order to resolve the caste-related conflict, as well as other social and ideological inconsistencies, the United States is attempting to eliminate caste-race categories in favor of an overall ideology of ethnic pluralism. There is, as a result, a reduced commitment to assimilation and a greater emphasis on religious, cultural, and even linguistic pluralism.[22]

Black Americans are redefining themselves in ethnic terms. Among blacks brought in as slaves, African ethnic traditions only persisted as submerged fragments. Now, however, black Americans are reaching back to a pan-African heritage to create an ethnic tradition of their own, separate from that of Europeans and Asians. They are trying to recreate their identity on the basis of cultural continuities rather than on the simplistic caste-racial criteria used in oppressing them. Blacks are seeking means of amplifying all the criteria comprising ethnicity. Territorial origins in Africa; and territorial and economic strongholds in present American settings; old folk and religious practices; and features of life-style, family relationships, and artistic traditions are being scrutinized for their Afro-American flavor.

As with all groups concerned with origins as a source of social meaning, where history is insufficient, myths are created. Some blacks, reversing the pejorative connotations imposed by Europeans, consider "soul" or "negritude" biologically inherited and the source of special folk features supposedly shared by all of African heritage but not in Europeans or Asians. The search for origins goes back to a black history that preceded slavery. The slave past is not denied or hidden but is seen as a transitory stage of exploitation of black Africans as a people, not as an occupational class. This ethnic definition is presently more powerful than any occupational or social class as a means of overcoming the disadvantages of caste definitions since such affinities, where they exist, do not as yet cross the caste barrier among white, European-derived, working-class Americans.

Hence, by using an ethnic definition of themselves to change their relative status, blacks are pursuing a characteristically American path. Ethnic relationships remain as potential sources of identity and of social participation in America. They cut across patterns generated by the various levels of social class positions and occupations that stratify the society economically and socially. It is a way to change relative status that works for the blacks, who have now taken the initiative in defining themselves by means of confrontation and militancy.

Whites of various ethnic backgrounds, especially on the working-class level, are being forced either to fight back or to find some accommodative redefinition that makes sense to them and that they can accept, while still not admitting blacks totally as in-group social participants. Retreating from overt racist positions, some American urban groups are seeking defensive accommodations or are launching counteroffensives on the level of ethnic groupings. Third-generation working-class Jews and Italians in New York and Poles in Pittsburgh, Chicago, and Milwaukee are rekindling a sense of ethnic belonging, restoring definitions that had become attenuated by attempts to pass as nonethnic Americans.

A pattern of a dual ethnic-social class identity is found in many so-called hyphenated Americans—e.g., Italians, Jews, Irish, Poles, Lithuanians, Armenians, Mexicans, Chinese, Japanese—who are sprinkled throughout various occupational-social class levels in American society and who may or may not maintain overt continuity with their ethnic group as a feature of their social life or as a part of their self-identity. Nathan Glazer and Daniel P. Moynihan, in *Beyond the Melting Pot* (1963), offer many examples of the persistence of such ethnicity despite the American ideology of assimilation.

Much American conformity behavior and concern with loyalty is a reflection of uneasiness over the legitimacy of a claim to be American on the part of second-generation ethnic immigrants. Many ethnics still pass by moving to a suburb. A widespread phenomenon is presently taking place among the third-generation children born in these suburbs. Now attending American universities, they are searching for ways to gain a feeling of some past ethnic identity, which their parents failed to transmit to them. Majority white young people, of various European lower-status origins, seek out some former ethnic identity as a counterpart to the soul espoused by their black classmates. Children of parents who carried little ethnic baggage in their search for upward mobility deeply miss the expressive emotional satisfactions of some form of ethnic belonging.[23]

At this point in American history, past-oriented ethnicity is more appealing to American blacks as a means of reordering their status than is a future orientation, such as a universalist religion or self-definition as a member of an exploited proletarian class. Black workers are aware that emotionally expressive caste attitudes remain a strong part of the spontaneous relationships of the other workers. Many of these white workers are still prejudiced ethnics to some degree. One recognizes that Irish get certain jobs, Poles others, and that they, too, live in special neighborhoods. These American realities are more visible than is any supposed alliance among workers to remove discrimination.

Discussed below, one finds similar caste discrimination in Japan. Despite their Marxist militancy, the former Japanese pariahs get little support from majority group Japanese workers. Worker unity, emotionally at least, does not seem to cross their caste barrier (Totten and Wagatsuma 1967).

In socially pluralistic America social primary group participation is becoming more ethnic oriented, while ways are being sought to eliminate occupational discrimination. The processes occurring in combating the force of caste as a social institution in America are far different from those in India. Out of this use of a new ethnic definition by black Americans a shared social self-identity is emerging that is internally and externally overcoming the negative social definitions that have been internalized by many people in the past.

Ethnicity and Individual Social Mobility

Complex cultures contain differential patterns with respect to how upwardly mobile behavior is learned and how culture is or can be diffused. For example, in Japan, until the 1960s, patterns for diffusion of status behavior were related to apprenticeship experiences of men and women, who in their youth, had worked several years for individuals or families of higher status. Women from lower-status positions were apprenticed in the houses of upper-status persons and learned patterns of acceptable behavior with which they at least partially identified and which they used to evaluate the behavior of members of their own social class. Such judgments then created internal tensions in lower-status persons, inducing them to acquire the more highly valued traits. Earlier, status emulation was apparent in the diffusion of warrior or samurai traits into the Japanese population at large, especially when the samurai were abolished as an exclusive official class after the restoration of the central status of the emperor in 1868.

With the development of mass communication media in Japan, these patterns of diffusion have been radically altered. The source of models for emulation is shifting from immediate personal contacts with people of higher status to an extracultural or extranational frame of reference for all segments of the population. The effects of modern mass media on cultural identity should be thoroughly examined for their influence on evaluative patterns related to ethnic behavior and to other forms of social mobility. As the late Hiroshi Wagatsuma suggested in our later chapter, much of this behavior is a change of reference group rather than of ethnic identity. Modern Japanese youth are Japanese even though they wear "mod" clothing or sing country and western music.

In some instances, there are reverse romanticizations of submerged ethnic minorities; that is, behavioral traits can be borrowed from more active, less rigidified lower-status groups. In California, for example, some Japanese-American militant youth, in the 1970s, seeking an ethnic pattern of confrontation seemingly lacking in their parental tradition, borrowed the black dialect and its rhetorical inflections directly from members of the black power groups with whom they associated.

Very often, upward mobility weakens ethnic priorities in loyalty and behavior. Maintenance of ethnicity in some societies is obviously more characteristic of non-socially mobile lower-status individuals who have few other sources for self-acceptance to fall back on. Thus, one's ethnic background can be important in proportion to the number of other sources of status (occupational accomplishment, economic success) that are available.

Crises in Alienation

The alienation felt by some successful upwardly mobile individuals may be the result of their having cut so many ties with the past that they have lost a deeper sense of meaning, although the loss may not be apparent to them at the time. The sense of anomie in American society that is commonly attributed to social mobility may often have more to do with the loss of ethnic inheritance than with the simple movement from a lower to a higher class. When occupational success moves a person into an alien group, what is alien is often the change in ethnic behavior required, rather than new status behavior as such.

Jews are an ethnic group that has accommodated well to living within another culture while maintaining internal integrity. Even the resultant psychological problems do not, in the main, interfere with social adaptation. Many occupationally successful Jews have adapted to shifts in social class status without feeling any loss of their ethnic integrity. In fact, Jewish culture looks upon successful individuals as heroic figures. There are many tales of how Jews who were successful in the alien Christian world were able to maintain ethnic integrity and benefit the community, rather than using success for selfish personal reasons. As I shall discuss with respect to patterns of group expulsion as well as passing, other ethnic groups, such as Mexican-Americans, have no similar tradition that individual success should benefit the ethnic community, since their culture is so often characterized by deprived social status.

A major source of ethnic identity is found in the cultural traditions related to changes in the life-cycle, such as coming of age, marriage, divorce, illness, or death.

It is particularly in rites of passage that one finds highly emotional symbolic reinforcement of ethnic patterns. Erik Erikson has delineated well the problem of identity commitment in modern complex societies (1968). Adulthood is particularly problematic for younger members of minority groups, because of possible difficulties with what Erikson termed "identity diffusion."

The situations and the time of life in which members of particular ethnic minorities are subject to alienation probably vary from group to group. A Mexican-American male child may experience a social crisis involving potential alienation early in his formal school experience when he is torn between the conflicting demands of the school and the peer group. Either he sides with the peer group, which may lead him into a career of social deviance during adolescence, or he chooses to conform to the role of a good pupil. The tensions of minority status are visible in some good students, whose conformity to mainstream expectations may lead to a deep sense of personal alienation.[24] In some minorities, peer group conformity induces one toward a socially deviant career, whereas in other groups tensions lead to internalized forms of psychopathology that are not visible to the casual observer (De Vos 1965:328-356).

Patterns of Passing

It is readily observable that in most societies where upward mobility is possible, ethnic minorities continually lose members to the politically, economically, and socially dominant segments. Such mobility not only provides the individual with a means of resolving his or her social and psychological problems, it also maintains the stability of the society. Individual "evaporation" takes the pressure out of potential social protest movements of dissatisfied groups. When a group is totally blocked in an otherwise mobile society, however, pressure can build to explosive proportions as it has among some racial minority groups in the United States. As we discuss in a following chapter, the Koreans and Burakumin in Japan, who are denied many openings to ordinary careers, are overrepresented in organized as well as in individual criminal activity, similar to what we find for some ethnic minorities in the United States (De Vos and Mizushima 1967:289-325; De Vos and Wagatsuma 1969; Lee and De Vos 1981).

The term "passing," used in race relations literature, is usually applied only to situations in which an individual of partial black African ancestry disappears from a black social classification and reappears as white, if appearance permits. By disguising origins one passes unnoticed, in some forms of participation at least, into white society. Wagatsuma and I (1967) studied this phenomenon in Japan, where members of a former pariah caste cut off all visible contact with family and friends of similar origin, as part of individual attempts at social mobility. In this instance, the issue was racial only in that members of this caste are generally but erroneously considered to be biologically, hence racially, different from other Japanese.

Passing is not simply a procedure used for direct social advantage; it also has expressive emotional meaning. A variety of intrapsychic as well as external behavioral maneuvers are involved, which can in turn lead to different types of internal tensions related to alternatives in reference groups and alternatives in degree and pattern of partial incorporation of alien elements into the self. In some situations individuals reidentify with their ethnic origins, having found the alienation and malaise involved in maintaining a new identity too great a strain (De Vos and Wagatsuma 1967).

Since passing is usually effected through self-conscious manipulation of behavior, it requires maintaining a facade. To the degree that the facade is not part of oneself there is often an internal duality involving a partially pejorative self-image. The self is thought to have been stigmatized by one's parents, in Goffman's sense of the term (1963), with some resulting elements of self-hate, or hate of one's progenitors. In psychotherapy, however, the sequence uncovered is often found to be the reverse. *First* a primary pattern of hate starts within the family, which in turn produces an ambivalence about the self. The individual may *then* seize upon an available pattern of class differences or ethnic pluralism and use social mobility to attempt a resolution of psychological distress.

It is not possible to discuss here the role of conscious and unconscious psychological mechanisms in the original psychosexual identification processes that underlie those later processes that form the total social self-identity, of which ethnicity is a central component. I cannot do more now than introduce the topic of individual passing and its personal motivations as a general phenomenon that cannot be ignored in studying social stratification. Suffice it to say that people often need to escape what is perceived to be a negative social self-identity. Most individuals who pass are, in this sense, prejudiced against their group of origin.

Physical appearance in the direction of favorable stereotypes may provide reinforcement for change. A person whose appearance is not conducive to passing may view his or her own appearance as an irremovable stigma passed on by one's group. Obvious physical differences make passing difficult but not always impossible, at least from a subjective standpoint. Some black Americans "become" Hindus. There was a period when some Mexican-Americans believed they were socially better off if they passed as Italians. But in any case, the absolute black-white racial distinction is only an extreme among various modes used by class- or race-oriented societies to prevent individuals from passing upward.

Some of the most poignant incidents related to us about the passing among Japanese outcastes were situations in which the individual deliberately exposed his or her stigmatized outcaste origin. We presume this was out of a need to escape the intolerable burden of continual disguise. Many individuals sooner or later find it psychologically more tolerable to drop their facade, to "come in from the cold." Some like to avoid identity ambiguity. Instead of exposing themselves to possible social trauma related to a disguised identity, they use an overt, unmistakable symbol or emblem of identity that signals to others their origins and their continued ethnic or class allegiance. Some militant Korean women, for example, wear Korean dress in Japan (Lee 1981). Such usages resemble what Erving Goffman would consider the flaunting of a stigma.

Withdrawal and Expulsion

Social mobility does not invariably involve passing as we have described it. Much more often, one finds gradual withdrawal from previous social participation. Economically successful upwardly mobile individuals, or members of their family, may no longer feel comfortable with people they know from childhood. New experiences develop social perceptions and needs that move the individual out of the former group. The social alienation is probably mutual in most instances. There may be no shift in identity or disguise of one's past, rather a shift in acceptable life-style.

Sometimes the individual is ostracized by members of his or her own social group. In Mexican-American or Native American groups, for example, to be successful economically, or to participate socially with dominant-status whites, is by definition to be a "falso," a deserter (De Vos 1982). To maintain individual wealth without sharing can be considered a reason for social exclusion.

A social group that has experienced evaporation can be particularly sensitive to the first signs of a member's behavioral emulation of traits of an outside group. From early on, members may be prevented by group sanctioning from taking on other linguistic or social usages. The individual is made well aware of the threat of expulsion; hence, there can be a self-fulfilling prophecy that those who learn Anglo behavior, for example, are not to be trusted.

The child of a mixed union is almost always put into an ambiguous role, a complex topic that cannot be pursued in depth here. Where racial differences in appearance make some social affirmation of identification important, there can still be room for ambiguity in definition of individuals of mixed ancestry. In Brazil, if light-skinned Afro-Brazilians are socially presentable, they are, in a sense, given the choice of passing if they so desire, with passing being treated rather lightly. In the United States, on the other hand, where maintaining the "purity" of the white group has been important, passing is a serious issue for those whites who fear "tainted blood." It is also a serious concern to the black group, which would like to assert sanctions to keep their own members loyal. This is a particular point of tension in contemporary American society, not only from the standpoint of subjective self-inclusion as an American of African ancestry, but also because the word "black" has become symbolic of ethnic membership (as contrasted to the word "Negro," which is seen as indicating excessive accommodation to the culture and viewpoint of the dominant white population). Thus, the role of light-skinned persons of mixed white-black ancestry has become more difficult, especially since the threat of expulsion has increased with attempts to establish a militant black solidarity.

Sanctions of belonging start very early and cannot be separated from the development of the sense of self. The conscious processes involved in the later stages of identity formation are preceded by earlier, automatic processes. The self, as it develops in a human being, is innately social—it is related to the primary community belonging. Experiences in the family develop a sense of self, but peer group experiences in childhood are also important. In some societies, in fact, peer groups are much more important than the family as a principal mediator of social identity. The peer group is certainly a most exacting socializer, which demands continual symbols of allegiance from those participating. Although childhood gangs in many cases are transitory, they are instrumental in setting standards for language usage, and even for modes of thinking, which may in some instances run counter to parental patterns.

In acculturative situations such as those in New York or Chicago in the early twentieth century, primary social identities reflected more the effect of the peer group than of the home in self-definition, especially with regard to language. American-born ethnics of that generation identified themselves as Americans linguistically, by refusing to speak the language of their parents, and attitudinally, by rejecting many of the expressed values of their parents. Instead, they adopted the values presented by the mass media and the school, as well as by the predominantly American peer group. Social mobility was part of a positively sanctioned American identity. These children accepted without question the characteristics of those who are today viewed with much more ambivalence—the white Anglo-Saxon Protestants who, as many children in New York learned, all came over on the Mayflower.

Why was American education so successful in overcoming linguistic pluralism, when other countries encounter so much difficulty in changing the language of minority groups? The explanation may lie in the influence of the peer group at school. Since the school was a meeting ground of peers from different language groups, English became its lingua franca in the early 1900s. No European ethnic minority children could hold out for a language that separated them from the others at school. In other words, the peer groups were broadly American in orientation. The sense of self that developed out of this experience in the sons and daughters of immigrants was of being American rather than simply remaining Italian—or Jewish, or Irish—in a new setting. Being American was extremely important for the American-born children of immigrant parents at the turn of the twentieth century.

Compared with the experiences of the waves of European immigrants, there seems today to be more difficulty in educating children of Mexican-American,

Puerto Rican, African-American, or Native American background. It is evident, to me at least, that for these children to be amenable to learning majority norms, the counterinfluence of their minority peer groups against such norms must be overcome (De Vos 1992). Threats of expulsion from the ethnic peer group are a strong force against the formal educative processes in the schools. Scattered informal evidence suggests that European schools—for example, in Switzerland, France, or Belgium—are beginning to encounter similar difficulties in educating ethnic minorities, including the children of migrant workers (De Vos and Suárez-Orozco 1990).

For some minority groups, the majority-oriented school cannot provide the means of acquiring occupational mobility. The status of the group as a whole tends to remain depressed, offering no variation in class position or social-occupational models with which members of the group can identify and still retain a sense of belonging. By contrast, some groups, such as Jews and Japanese, severely sanction those who do poorly in school. The conforming attitudes of their peers reinforces in these children the need to learn at school (Caudill and De Vos 1972; De Vos 1975).

Although this topic has more dimensions than it is possible to consider here, we can say that from a social structural standpoint at least, early sanctioning to maintain ethnic integrity can cause certain ethnic groups difficulty in changing status through formal education. Within-group self-perpetuation is a partial cause as much as external social discrimination. In some groups, such as Jews and Japanese, there is sufficient support from within to push those who remain identified with their groups toward occupational mobility, whereas in other groups, such as Native Americans, group identity tends to prevent economic or social mobility.

Accommodation to Minority Status

The notion that externally accommodative behavior on the part of people of subordinate status reflects the true social self-identity of the group's members is not acceptable. Nor is the converse Hobbsian notion that a stratified system that often includes ethnic minorities remains stable simply by the threat of force. Some forms of psychological internalization are found among those forced for any period of time into accommodative behavior.

According to George Herbert Mead, in acquiring a sense of self, one "internalizes a generalized other" (1934:152-164). Approaching identity formation from this theory, one would expect a subtle but significant psychological difference between the social internalization of low-status individuals who are members of ethnic groups and those who are not. A lower-status member of a stratified society cannot resist internalizing a negative self-image as a result of the socially prevalent explanations for his or her group's relative occupational and social inferiority. Remaining oriented to a pattern of evaluation originating in one's ethnic group helps an individual avoid the internalization of attitudes toward the self pressed on him or her by outsiders. Nevertheless, ethnic identity is of itself no assurance that a negative self-identity can be avoided, if the negative aspects are continually reinforced by discriminatory social attitudes. Ethnic communities must be examined individually to ascertain how they protect or damage the self-evaluation of their members.

To illustrate briefly, the majority population on the West Coast expected second-generation Japanese-Americans to fulfill certain stereotypes: they would become ideal houseboys or gardeners, etc., emulating the lower-status accommodative occupational roles permitted their parents. In California, where the social discrimination was the strongest, there were even attempts to use legal as well as social means to limit the occupational roles open to Japanese. Such social pressures did not prevent the nisei (the American-born generation) from attaining educational and occupational goals defined by their own families and communities rather than by the outside society (Caudill and De Vos 1972). The period of low-status accommodation to social discrimination in the United States has been relatively short. But even more important is that those emigrating to the United States brought with them their own sense of self-respect and cultural attitudes that were useful in overcoming the severe racism of American society.

An estimated 85 percent of Japanese immigrants were from rural areas, but they were not former serfs or peasants in the European sense. In Japan, farmers were a respected class, ranking only after the samurai and ahead of merchants and artisans, regardless of economic fluctuations. The Japanese communities in the United States accorded status to their members that had little or no correspondence to their jobs outside. They did not evaluate themselves on the basis of American attitudes toward them as peasants, or immigrant workers, or "yellow" Asians. Moreover, they brought with them a future orientation, ready to postpone immediate gratification and to endure adversity. Characteristically, a person would submit to an apprenticeship, with the goal of acquiring status through competence (De Vos 1973), just as in a traditional Japanese society one was expected to submit to a long apprenticeship, anticipating status acquired by compliance to a mentor. Japanese also avoided confrontation in working out differences with American discrimination—direct confrontation was only used as a last resort. In their recent history, governmental authority, both legally and socially, has tended to be paternalistic but responsible, making it possible for them to think of the government as interested in the welfare of the people, rather than hated or feared as exploitative. Compliance was rewarded.

These and other interrelated cultural features help explain the relative lack of confrontation and conflict both in the United States, where West Coast Japanese were put in guarded camps, and in Japan, during several years of postwar occupation. A traditional Japanese does not feel it socially or personally demeaning to be in a subordinate position while he or she is learning. A sense of integrity is not destroyed by adversity. Japanese immigrants to the United States imparted to their nisei children a respect for authority, even the authority of an alien society—they were to become loyal citizens. This was not inconsistent with Japanese concepts of loyalty to organizations once one became a member (Nakane 1971). Children were taught to conform to regulations imposed in school. Improper behavior would bring injury and shame to parents and to Japanese generally. To be Japanese was a matter of deeply felt pride on the part of the immigrant issei, whatever attitudes they met on the outside. They therefore imparted an accommodative but future-oriented concept of success. This pattern is less understood by some third-generation, or sansei, youth who are impatient with what they considered the complacency and conformity with which their parents met social discrimination

The indirect nonconfrontational methods of Japanese community leaders in dealing with the racist attitudes of white Americans is illustrated by an incident in Chicago in 1949. The well-known news commentator Drew Pearson learned that cemeteries in Chicago were refusing to bury Japanese, even if they were Christians. He wished to make a public issue of this act of social discrimination, but members of the Japanese community asked him to refrain, saying that they did not want "dirty publicity"—they would find indirect means of resolving the problem.

Given the terrible problems of dislocation of Japanese families in California, our research team failed to find any but a minimal use of public welfare agencies. The Japanese solved their social problems within their own community. The fact that they did well in American schools attests to group consistency with respect to what was expected. Parents were cohesive reinforcers of tightly sanctioned values with regard to education, and the community itself heavily sanctioned conformist behavior in the schools. The Japanese peer group left no alternative to studying hard in the American schools. Conversely, parental pressures to learn Japanese in Japanese language schools were notably unsuccessful. The peer group pressure was in the other direction, toward an American identity. The written Japanese language was not learned. The response of Japanese children in refusing to learn Japanese was in no way different from that of the children of European immigrants who refused to learn Italian or Polish.

The contrast with the ethnic adaptation of Mexican-Americans is striking. Since Mexico is directly south of the United States, the continuous in-migration encourages the persistence of Mexican ethnicity, including language, a persistence that is not found in those coming from Europe. Nevertheless, the Mexican-American ethnic minority, in contrast to the Japanese, manifests a relative lack of cohesiveness both in the community and in family life. While young Mexican-Americans are seeking a positive ethnic identity, the traditions available are sometimes conflictful and nonsupportive with respect to economic and occupational mobility.

The Mexican traditions of status and class are complex (Romanucci-Ross 1986), but in general there are wide status disparities and mutually alienating feelings among Spanish-speaking Americans. Some parts of Mexico have the highest homicide rates in the world because of violence between individuals (Romanucci-Ross 1986:132-134). American territorial aggrandizement at the expense of Mexico incorporated into the United States Mexican minorities with a variety of internal class and status conflicts that later immigrants have reflected.

The class, racial, and ethnic cleavages are noticeable: those who identify with a Spanish background look down on the Indian culture and people. Others conceive of Mexican ethnicity as membership in "la raza," a special blend of European and Indian. There has been severe exploitation of peons, a depressed peasantry that has known only a society marked by extremes of poverty and wealth. The history of government authority is suspect (Romanucci-Ross 1986). A Mexican male feels a need to defend himself from being "taken" or penetrated (Paz 1961). Even within his immediate community he must defend himself against the easily aroused, malevolently perceived envy of neighbors. Social and personal distrust are part of the community life of many. Traditionally, it is difficult to think of the economic success of one person without seeing it as taking something away from others. There is, in fact, a widespread belief in what George Foster terms "the limited good" (1967).

Within the family, one frequently finds distrust between marriage partners. In some lower-status Mexican families the mother expects the child to take her side against a father who is depicted as drunken, unfaithful, and financially irresponsible (Lewis 1959). The mother pictures herself as keeping the family together for the sake of her children and as lacking rapport with her husband. This contrasts with the Japanese family, where cohesiveness is based on the mutually supportive status that each parent accords the other. Discord within the Mexican family makes it more difficult to inoculate Mexican children against the discriminatory practices and attitudes of the majority group. Thus, Mexican youth, in many cases, are alienated not only from the majority society but from their own parents in such a way that their personal development is debilitated. They find themselves performing inadequately both in school and at work. The peer group for growing boys becomes an escape from family tensions. It is oriented against authority and discipline: it often takes on a delinquent character. It becomes the principal reference group until marriage, which may, in turn, lead to the repetition of an unhappy domestic pattern.

To make my point, I have stressed the negative aspects of Mexican-American ethnicity that contrast in my mind with features of Japanese community and family life. The vast differences in individual and community response of Mexicans and Japanese both to social discrimination and to occupational opportunity depend very much on class and ethnic identity as well as on differential socialization, expected role behavior, and the effect of the reference group. These differences are most graphically seen in patterns of school performance and differential rates of delinquency (De Vos 1992).

Amelioration of the effects of social discrimination of Mexican-Americans depends not only on changing the social attitudes and practices of the majority, but on strengthening the positive integrative function of the family and community. As we have seen, for some Mexican-Americans an ethnic background has not helped maintain a positive social self-identity against majority Anglo attitudes. The Chicano movement is an attempt to develop community pride and cohesiveness in order to give Mexican identity a more positive meaning.

Among Americans of African ancestry, the relative number of individuals suffering from personal debilitation as a result of past as well as present American racism is considerable. The "mark of oppression," as Kardiner and Ovesey (1962) termed it, is widespread, whether one uses indices of addiction to drugs, brittle and unsatisfactory heterosexual relationships, delinquency and crime, or hospitalization for mental illness. The cases cited by Kardiner and Ovesey or the writings of Malcolm X (Haley 1966) are full of evidence about the psychological problems attendent upon the internalization of a negative self-image. It has been difficult for some black families to provide sufficient psychological and economic security for their young. For too many, racial oppression penetrated into basic child-parent relationships to the degree that a negative self-image was passed on from parent to child, without the child's even having had any direct contact with the outer white society.

Unfortunately for those who seek to change the effects of discrimination by changing laws or social attitudes, a personal sense of failure among some blacks is not due solely to the force of external discrimination but to a generational internalization of traits debilitating to intellectual functioning and to the will to achieve. Malcolm X discusses with great integrity and candor the self-degradation of his generation, of "Negroes" who internalized concepts of physical beauty that flattered the white and degraded the black. It is very often the black man's own mother who "puts him down," causing self-hatred and self-rejection.

In our book, *Japan's Invisible Race* (1967), Wagatsuma and I describe similar processes involving unconscious negative self-images that helped debilitate the former Eta, or pariahs, of Japan and still lead to their relative failure in the economically competitive contemporary Japanese society. These internal processes are never separate from the external forms of discrimination that deepen and intensify the inner difficulties experienced by members of disparaged groups.

Conclusions

I have contended here that ethnicity or ethnic identity is as important as social class or class consciousness in social theory, that a psychocultural approach to social belonging and to defensive or hostile contrastiveness is necessary for understanding social behavior. I have also suggested that a conflict approach to society is more productive in understanding change than one based on formal structure analysis alone.

Change as a result of interethnic conflict is a reality of human history. Seen from one perspective, the history of social life in a culture is a continual rhythm of conflict and accommodation between groups, both external and internal (De Vos and Suárez-Orozco 1990). Stratification allows for some form of accommodation. Those coming to power continually seek a more stabilized allegiance from those subordinate to them. Some theorists who emphasize conflict and coercion in political matters forget, however, to examine the forces of belonging that unify individuals into the groups that then struggle with each other for power. Hobbes, in his discussion of the state, leaves us dissatisfied when he sees coercion as the only force keeping individuals united.

Durkheim, in his *Elementary Forms of the Religious Life* (1947), pointed toward the proper direction for such understanding. He saw humans as social animals who achieve both real and ideal concepts of self partially out of a sense of belonging to a group. In a primitive, occupationally undifferentiated society, there is little tension between a sense of social identity with the political community with its primary form of citizenship, and the "church," a sacred representation of primal folk ethnicity. The political and the spiritual communities are one. Within such a community the relatively undifferentiated occupational system affords little basis for divergent concepts of belonging. Hence, it is only in more complex social units—with their occupational divisions and their amalgamation of groups maintaining a sense of diverse origin—that tension develops in the overall sense of belonging. But, depending upon the vagaries of their history, not all societies develop chronic tensions resulting from political incorporation. In some instances of recorded as well as unrecorded history, initially separate ethnic groups have indeed disappeared into a unified nation-state, just as nation-states have disappeared by incorporation or dissolution.

In members of more simple communities one usually finds much less evidence of any form of identity crisis as a part of social maturation. The present widespread existential search for meaning suggests the presence of conflicting alternatives. Modern conceptual systems attempt to relate past cultural traditions to ideological alternatives about the future direction of society and to questions about the degree of allegiance to be paid to the different social units in the system. Those who see individualism as the highest goal sometimes mistakenly assume that individuation or autonomy means a lack of allegiance to any group. They fail to see that individuals today are also searching for meaningful and ultimate units of social belonging and a sense of survival through such belonging.

Problems of choice related to occupation or identity occur only in flexible societies with a great deal of internal social mobility. In rigidly stratified societies, the individual's occupation tends to be predetermined, inculcating early a sense of belonging to a primary occupational group. Even this situation may not be completely free of conflict, since the state may apply pressure concerning religious and political adherence, leading to conflicts over loyalty.

Seen from this perspective, human history shows numerous combinations of tension, conflict, and accommodation related to conflicts between loyalty to a past ethnicity, a present status, or a future idealized concept of society. Sections of this chapter discussed only a few of the topics related to ethnicity and social stratification, and even they need much more detailed examination than was possible here. Other complementary approaches to ethnic identity appear in subsequent chapters.

Especially to be noted in what follows is how new ethnic groups are continually created for expedient economic or social reasons as well as to resolve an inner existential need to belong. The collective fabrication of a mythical past may prove to be as socially efficacious as actual history.

In emphasizing the need for social belonging, perhaps I have not sufficiently pointed up the social and psychological uses of contrastiveness and difference in human interaction. As social animals, we are combative as well as affiliative. Ethnicity can be very negative and destructive in its intent. I may have touched too briefly here on a number of specific psychodynamic reasons for contrastive conflict. The following chapters will, however, illustrate several instances of the destructive use of contrastive ethnicity. Psychodynamically, ethnicity as any other form of Otherness, can be an excuse for collective projection of a dehumanizing nature. Such hostile contrastiveness is clearly seen in the chapter by Gilliland describing Serb-Croat-Bosnian relationships in the former Yugoslavia.

There is continual flux in the saliency of an ethnic identity used negatively in response to changing social conditions. Ethnic definitions are projected upon others, who, out of loyalty, cannot escape being partially or wholly identified with their group of origin. A hostile contrastive use of an ethnic definition can be forced upon those whose ethnicity had for them no particular relevance. The sad case of the resurgence of ethnic conflict in the former Yugoslavia points up how the duress of economic stress can rekindle a hostile-defensive ethnic contrastiveness in some, whose abusive acts then provoke a general rupture between the many who are forced to choose sides again, despite living together in previously harmonious relationships.

Projective dehumanization of another group is a too readily available collective psychological mechanism. If a group allows itself to be susceptible by condoning the irrational acts of any of its members, any past difference can be used as sufficient justification for renewed hostile contrast. The use of anti-Semitic explanations for economic-social malaise has again reappeared as a threatening specter in

Eastern Europe despite the now generally acknowledged catastrophic madness of Germany's recent Nazi past. This reappearance should remind us how easy it is to use one's ethnic identity to project negatively into others. When there is inner need to project or dehumanize, self-righteous ethnicity becomes a potential for mutual destruction.

Finally, for the future, we must seek out some collective transcendence of past ethnicity to achieve present social harmony as well as savoring the past to give flavor to human experience.

NOTES

1. This revised chapter adds references to my subsequent writings and footnotes that update some issues raised initially by events that have transpired since the first edition. A number of contentions asserting the saliency of potentials for ethnic conflict over those of social class loyalty have been borne out most forcefully since the initial writing.

2. In the past we have had relatively little concern, for example, with reconstructing the internal crises faced by individual Gauls as they resisted or accepted Roman or Christian influence. Today, however, there is growing interest in those who resisted. It is a sign of the times that the most popular comic book hero in France (from the 1960s to the 1980s) was Astérix, a counterculture Gaul whose Druidic potion gives him superhuman powers to help his tiny band of countrymen resist the establishment Romans.

3. This assertion has been reaffirmed in the last twenty-five years by the collapse of the Soviet Union.

4. See Roosens's discussion in Chapter 5 of how this is done among the Luunda of Zaire.

5. This is occurring in the self-definitions of a separate ethnicity being adopted by many African-Americans.

6. Such is the political history of Serbs in the former Yugoslavia. Gilliland in Chapter 9 gives a careful discussion of the interpenetration of meaning between the terms "nationalism" and "ethnicity."

7. This is most noteworthy in contemporary Eastern Europe.

8. See the discussion in Chapter 8 by Huseby-Darvas concerning Hungary.

9. See Schwartz's (1976) extensive discussion of these phenomena and the conflicting theory of Lanternari (1963).

10. Obeyesekere in Chapter 10 provides a severe illustration of this process at work in postcolonial Sri Lanka.

11. In this context, it is interesting to note that until recently, disputes between Marxist-oriented socialist states markedly resembled past sectarian conflicts within Christianity or Islam. Religious adherence on the part of an ethnic group may also become a symbol of resistance to the dominant group, thereby, regardless of personal belief, reducing religious affiliation to simply being a means of asserting ethnic identity. Thus, many secularized intellectuals in Poland attended church to mark symbolically their allegiance to an independent Poland. (They now no longer find it necessary to do so.)

12. Over the past twenty-five years there has been an increase of anti-Semitic activities among a number of different black organizations and a curious inability by more moderate African-Americans to directly attack such movements, even in university settings.

13. Harrell describes how differences in dress continue to operate as part of the ethnic distinctions separating the Chinese minorities he discusses in Chapter 4.

14. See the detailed discussion of the uses and distortions of ethnic definitions related to language in the chapters by Harrell and Keyes.

15. This trend is now apparent on BBC radio and television in the United Kingdom.

16. See Chapter 5.

17. An emic approach is an attempt of the scientific observer to understand the conceptual system of the observed and to state one's observations as best one can within the conceptual framework of the observed. This is opposed to an etic approach, which analyzes an observed situation in terms of the external system of the observer.

18. As Roosens discusses in Chapter 5, ethnicity itself can be newly created. In this process, a self-constituted group can give itself a mythological past justifying its present cohesion.

19. See further discussion of the adaptation patterns of Japanese minorities in Chapter 12.

20. Events since our initial edition demonstrate clearly that ethnic loyalties have prevailed in all instances over any form of class alliance.

21. The Sikhs' seeking of political autonomy has become a serious political movement since our initial writing.

22. This movement is presently producing serious sources of new conflict in universities as well as in American urban settings.

23. These paragraphs written in 1970 have become even more cogent in the 1990s. The sense of alienated loneliness found in many youth from so-called old American backgrounds has become even more pronounced.

24. The autobiographical volume, The *Hunger of Memory*, by Richard Rodriguez, exemplifies this process. However, a shift toward acceptance of the successful seems to be moving faster in the Mexican-American than in the African-American poorer communities.

REFERENCES

Barth, Fredrik. 1969. *Ethnic Groups and Boundaries.* Boston: Little, Brown.

Berreman, Gerald. 1967. "Structure and Function of Caste Systems" and "Concomitants of Caste Organization." In *Japan's Invisible Race: Caste in Culture and Personality*. George A. De Vos and Hiroshi Wagatsuma, eds. Pp. 277-307. Berkeley: University of California Press.

Caudill, William, and George A. De Vos. 1972. "Achievement, Culture and Personality, the Case of the Japanese Americans." In *Socialization for Achievement: The Cultural Psychology of The Japanese.* George A. De Vos, ed. Pp. 220-250. Berkeley: University of California Press.

Crandon-Malamud, Libbet. 1991. "Phantoms and Physicians: Social Change through Medical Pluralism." In *The Anthropology of Medicine; From Culture to Method.* Lola Romanucci-Ross, Daniel E. Moerman, and Lawrence Sancredi, eds. Pp. 85-112. New York: Bergin and Garvey.

De Vos, George A. 1965. "Transcultural Diagnosis of Mental Health by Means of Psychological Tests." In the Ciba Foundation Symposium on *Transcultural Psychiatry.* A. V. S. de Reuck and Ruth Porter, eds. Pp. 328-356. London: Churchill.

De Vos, George A. 1966. "Conflict, Dominance and Exploitation in Human Systems of Social Segregation: Some Theoretical Perspectives from the Study of Personality and Culture." In *Conflicts in Society.* A. V. S. de Reuck and J. Knight, eds. Pp. 60-81. London: Churchill.

De Vos, George A. 1973. *Socialization for Achievement: The Cultural Psychology of The Japanese.* Berkeley: University of California Press.

De Vos, George A. 1992. *Social Cohesion and Alienation: Minorities in the United States and Japan.* Boulder, CO: Westview Press.

De Vos, George A., and Keiichi Mizushima. 1967. "The Organization and Social Functions of Japanese Gangs." In *Aspects of Social Change in Modern Japan.* R. P. Dore, ed. Pp. 289-326. Princeton: Princeton University Press.

De Vos, George A., and Marcelo Suárez-Orozco. 1990. *Status Inequality: The Self in Culture.* Newbury Park, CA: Sage Publications.

De Vos, George A., and Hiroshi Wagatsuma. 1967. *Japan's Invisible Race: Caste in Culture and Personality.* Berkeley: University of California Press.

De Vos, George A., and Hiroshi Wagatsuma. 1969. "Minority Status and Deviancy in Japan." In *Mental Health Research in Asia and the Pacific.* William Caudill and Tsing Yi-Lin, eds. Pp. 342-357. Honolulu: East-West Center Press.

Durkheim, Emile. 1947. *The Elementary Forms of the Religious Life.* J. W. Swain, trans. Glencoe, IL: The Free Press.

Erikson, Erik H. 1968. *Identity, Youth and Crisis.* New York: Norton.

Foster, George. 1967. "Peasant Society and the Image of Limited Good." *American Anthropologist* 69:293-315.

Glazer, Nathan, and Daniel P. Moynihan. 1963. *Beyond the Melting Pot.* Cambridge, MA: MIT Press.

Goffman, Erving. 1963. *Stigma: Notes on the Management of Spoiled Identity.* Englewood Cliffs, NJ: Prentice Hall.

Hagen, Everett E. 1962. *On the Theory of Social Change.* Chicago: Dorsey.

Haley, Alex. 1966. *The Autobiography of Malcolm X.* New York: Grove Press.

Kardiner, Abram, and L. Ovesey. 1962. *The Mark of Oppression.* Part One: The Concept of Ethnic Identity. New York: World.

Lanternari, V. 1963. *The Religions of the Oppressed: A Study of Modern Messianic Cults.* New York: Knopf.

Lee, Changsoo, and George A. De Vos. 1981. *Koreans in Japan: Ethnic Conflict and Accommodation.* Berkeley: University of California Press.

Lewis, Oscar. 1959. *Five Families.* New York: Basic Books.

Mead, George Herbert. 1934. "The I and the Me." In *Mind, Self and Society.* Charles Morris, ed. Pp. 276-292. Chicago: University of Chicago Press.

Nakane, Chie. 1971. *Japanese Society.* London: Weidenfeld and Nicolson.

Paz, Octavio. 1961. *The Labyrinth of Solitude: Life and Thought in Mexico.* New York: Grove Press.

Romanucci-Ross, Lola. 1977. "The Hierarchy of Resort in Curative Practices: The Admiralty Islands, Melanesia." *Journal of Health and Social Behavior* 10(30):201-210.

Romanucci-Ross, Lola. 1986, rev. ed. *Conflict, Violence and Morality in a Mexican Mestizo Village.* University of Chicago Press.

Rowe, William L. 1960. "Social and Economic Mobility in a Low-Caste North Indian Community." Ph.D. diss., Cornell University.

Rowe, William L. 1964. "Myth as Social Charter: The Assignment of Status in Hindu Caste Origin Stories." Paper presented at the 63rd Annual Meeting of the American Anthropological Association, Detroit, November 20.

Schama, Simon. 1987. *The Embarrassment of Riches: An Interpretation of Dutch Culture in the Golden Age.* London: Fontana Press.

Schwartz, Theodore. 1976. "Cargo Cult: A Melanesian Type Response to Culture Contact." In *Responses to Change: Society, Culture and Personality.* George A. De Vos, ed. Pp. 157-207. New York: D. Van Nostrand Company.

Totten, George, and Hiroshi Wagatsuma. 1967. "Emancipation: Growth and Transformation of a Political Movement." In *Japan's Invisible Race: Caste in Culture and Personality.* George A. De Vos and Hiroshi Wagatsuma, eds. Pp. 33-67. Berkeley: University of California Press.

THEODORE SCHWARTZ ■

Chapter Two

Cultural Totemism: Ethnic Identity Primitive and Modern

The point of departure for this paper is my conception of cultural totemism, which can be shown to embrace a broad range of processes that contribute to the identity of individuals and groups. Students of culture from Tylor (1958) to Lévi-Strauss (in his recent reconsideration of totemism [1962]) have understood its bearing on the problem of identity. In the classic anthropological sense, totemism linked humans into groups under the emblem of common totemic species (animal or plant usually, but sometimes also objects, places, and natural phenomena) and set them apart from groups claiming common substance or origin under other species.

It is true that Lévi-Strauss declared totemism an illusion on the ground that no single set of attributes would fit all cultures that hold a belief in some special relationship between individuals or groups and natural species. As Goldenweiser noted (1937), beliefs concerning descent from the totem; taboos on killing, eating, or using the totem; a "ritual" attitude toward the totem considered as sacred; and a rule of exogamy imposed on all having the same totem did not invariably constitute a complex but could occur separately and in quite different combinations in those cultures where they occurred at all.

Illusion or not, totemism remains the theme of much of Lévi-Strauss's recent work. He maintains, as others (Durkheim and Mauss 1963) had maintained, that totemism constitutes a system of classification of human groups, with natural species providing a set of convenient labels. But for Lévi-Strauss it is more than this, it is also the perceptible similarities and differences of one natural species contrasted with another. Not only could species be used as arbitrary labels, they could be used to represent the relations among human groups. He sees the natural species as suggesting a mode of thought to humans: ". . . natural species are chosen not because they are 'good to eat' but because they are 'good to think'" (1962).

It can be argued, as Durkheim's school maintained, that the social order is primary, that the assemblage of totems is either arbitrary or reflects social order through attributes and dimensions of contrast chosen from many possible ones to reflect changing relations between social groups. The reader may find the Lévi-Straussian interpretation disappointing and ask, "is that all totemism is?" The interpretation amounts to intellectual reductionism of a phenomenon that seems more than a calculus of categories. Totemism is that, but it is apparently also a religion, a world view, a theory of origins, a theory of relation of humans to nature.

Durkheim thought that humans at a primitive stage of cultural development could not have arrived at a complex system of categories without an external model. For Durkheim, that model was the social order itself. And though Lévi-Strauss sees himself as not disparaging but as defending the intellectual capabilities of "savage" humans, newly emergent but still near to nature, he, too, seems to argue that the mode of thought must be derived from an external model—the relations among natural species. I maintain that the social order or the natural species are domains to which the human intellect (the culturally implemented intelligence) is applied. The "mode" is humanity's. The model is a human construction, but it is under the adaptive constraints of an external reality. A model of one domain may be mapped onto another. In suggesting a cultural totemism, I wish to *add*, not substitute, another domain—that of the perceived similarities and differences among human cultures themselves, the ethnic groupings conceived of by people as if those groupings were species.

Humans generally discovered (as anthropologists did much later) that cultures, too, are "good to think." There would be sufficient interest in considering culture as one among the many domains to which humans in all societies, primitive and modern, turn their minds. But the phrase "cultural totemism" may suggest even more than simply the comparison between thinking about culture and thinking about natural species.

De Vos has commented that "ethnicity is like religion, people seem to need it." I would speculate that in order for people to "have ethnicity" they must have at least two (and usually more) ethnic groups. The same may be true for religion, where the point may be as much to differentiate oneself from others (infidels or sects) through the object or manner of one's worship, as it is to worship at all. If this were true, then religion would be (among other things, of course) an "ethnognomonic trait" illustrative of what I mean by cultural totemism. That is, it would be a cultural trait characteristic of one group in contrast to others, at once emblematic of the group's solidarity and of the group's contrasting identity and relation to the groups within its ambit of comparison.

Religion is only one among the features of an identified or self-identifying group that could be taken by members of that set of ethnic groups as ethnognomonic. Other likely candidates are variations in physical appearance, language, hairdo and body ornamentationrabaul, costume, the shapes of artifacts such as houses and weapons, and ecological type such as farmer, fisherman, or pastoralist. Not surprisingly, a classification based on such traits might not be that different from the classification an anthropologist would arrive at. Anthropologists do purposively and methodically what people have always done intuitively, often unconsciously. They perceive a degree of order and predictability as well as similarities and differences in the behavior of other persons, and they characterize or represent this behavior to themselves in various ways. Their formulations are analyses molded to their interests under the constraints of an external reality. Such cultural analyses are fairly adequate for their purposes, being neither wholly objective nor wholly capricious. To such fields as ethnobotany or ethnoichthyology, then, we could add ethno- ethnography and ethnolinguistics (in the sense of folk taxonomy and characterization of languages and cultures). They constitute part of what one might call the self-reflexive portion of a culture.

After describing the field experiences that suggested this analogy between totemism and ethnicity and the idea of a totemism of cultural differences, I will discuss some of the ways in which cultural totemism operates as a component of individual and group identity. I must admit that having been raised on the classical ethnographies in graduate school, I was thrilled to find, during my first fieldwork in 1953 in the Admiralty Islands (Manus) of Melanesia, people who told me

> I am a descendant of the crocodile. I must not kill the crocodile of a particular river where my ancestor came from nor eat the meat of any crocodile. If I do I will get sores, my teeth will fall out and I will age quickly. My wife is descended from the *chauka* bird and our children will inherit her taboo. They and their children will have to watch out for mine too, but after that it will have no effect. I must be careful also to burn no wood of this tree called "crocodile." I think it is all right for me to marry a woman with the crocodile taboo though some say it is not, but if I did we would check very carefully to be sure we are not closely related. If I went to another village [back in the days of intervillage warfare], I could ask if there was a child of crocodile in the village. He would protect me, feed and house me and assure my safe departure even if he was a complete stranger to me and we could trace no other relationship.

This is a condensation of the general formulation of totemism among the peoples of the interior and fringe islands of the Admiralties. The Manus of Melanesia, a fishing, seafaring people who formerly lived over the lagoons and the in-reef waters, have food taboos. Their taboos are similarly inherited, but without the rationale and elaboration of the other groups. The Manus tie into the totemic system through a certain small percentage of cross-ethnic marriages with mainland and island women. They formerly exploited these ties, utilizing the privilege of supposedly safe conduct to make "roads" for trade.

In view of my Admiralty Island experience and in spite of the deficient totemic package of the Manus seafaring people, I find it difficult to view totemism as an illusion. All such cultural categories could be pronounced illusory if we expected to find them comprised of precisely the same set of traits wherever found in the world. To apply this criterion of uniformity, as of identical discrete sets, would strip us of all of our hard-won conceptual tools. Rather, we expect to find a situation of "family resemblance" à la Wittgenstein, among varying packages of traits comprising the cultures we study and the conceptions we form of them. Of such "things" are cultures made.

Ethnic Interpenetration and Separation in the Admiralties

Totemism was only one of the systems segmenting the population of the entire archipelago in various interlacing ways. In a previous article (Schwartz 1963) I attempted to break away from the more usual anthropological practice of taking cultures one at a time, often as represented in a single village at a single point in time. There were at least twenty locally recognized linguistic groups in the Admiralty Islands, each associated with cultural differences other than language. I believed that I was dealing with a single areawide culture of the Admiralty Islands, the components of which were the many mutually identifying ethnic groups.

I distinguished this kind of "areal culture" from the more familiar "culture area." The cultures making up a culture area need only be historically related. In an areal culture such as that of the Admiralties, direct and indirect interaction links all groups, making events in any part relevant to the whole. The area was tied together through networks of trade and markets, ceremonial exchange, totemic relations, marriage, and warfare.

The languages were related and structurally similar. But they were at the least as different from one another as, say, Spanish and Portuguese and, at the most, as different as Portuguese and Italian. No lingua franca had developed rather, multilingualism was prevalent. Many adults spoke the languages of all groups with whom they had regular contact. Minimally, each could speak one's own language to the other, having learned to understand neighboring languages. Cross-ethnic marriages were relatively more common (under polygyny) in families of relatively higher prestige. It could happen that one's parents spoke different languages. The grandparents of one important man each spoke a different language.

Language merely illustrates the more general point that difference within the areal culture was not based on separation or communicational gaps. I began my areal study puzzled about the proliferation of languages and cultures in spite of propinquity in the whole of Melanesia, in contrast to some other parts of the world, such as Polynesia. I saw that there were mechanisms that maintained, if proliferated and amplified, "ethnic" differences. There were cultural attitudes or sets toward the perception and emblematic use of cultural differences (including language, of course) that were characteristically Melanesian, although I have no doubt they could be extensively demonstrated elsewhere.

The area that I am describing is organized as a stateless society. Headmanship, for example, did not formally extend beyond the village, although a "big man" may have been influential within the aura of his renown. The area is well characterized (prior to European administration) as politically atomistic with extreme local particularism. Even villages, the maximum effective public of a big man (aside from his diffuse network of cooperating affines and allies) were unstable, often splitting along clan lines. It could be reconstituted from clans and village fragments that had been autonomous for a time.

The clans themselves split along lineage lines, not automatically on the basis of size alone but with the occurrence of rival aspirants to leadership. Many were motivated to strive for independent status as big man. To have a "name" required that one have a "place" and public of one's own, however small, if one's feats of warfare and exchange were not to redound to the credit of another.

I stress the prestate level of Melanesian cultures because it might be thought that ethnicity and its implied problematics of identity could exist only in complex, pluralistic societies that unite different ethnic groups on a territorial basis under state control, in contrast to the supposedly more primitive isolated cultures. Much of the primitive world must have been like Melanesia before the establishment of large-scale states. Each group experienced its social environment as a mosaic of groups manifesting, even consciously "instancing" to use Devereux's term (1982), certain similarities and differences. They were different, not out of lack of awareness of the behavior patterns of others, but in spite of and by means of such awareness.

I am not attempting to nullify the effect of geographic barriers and sheer distance. Rather, I am asserting that interaction and communication-generating differences and similarities must have always depended greatly on cultural definitional boundaries. The "speciation" of cultures is largely a cultural process.

The Manus, who were the most widely dispersed and largest linguistic-ethnic group of the Admiralties, intermarried and maintained a high degree of linguistic and cultural commonality. At the same time, they maintained their differences from the bush villages within a mile or two of them, while they engaged in trade, markets, ceremonies, and war with these neighbors. On the other hand, the Manus, like all other linguistic-ethnic groups in the Admiralties, illustrate the difference-amplifying effect of formally recognizing incipient cultural differences that would seem very small to the outsider, while overlooking (in some contexts) massive commonality.

The Manus see themselves as divided into two main named dialect groups on the basis of a single phoneme shift, /r/ to /l/. They also recognize a considerable number of differences in vocabulary based on substitute terms rather than on sound shifts. In all cases my informants could state, "We say this, but they say that," specifying the corresponding terms. To a remarkable extent, people of all ethnic groups could demonstrate their knowledge of linguistic and cultural differences for many or all of the recognized Admiralty Island groups. I found that languages and, at times, the collectivity of their speakers were referred to by one or more of four common words that occurred frequently in speech. These were the demonstrative pronoun meaning this, here, today, or now (sometimes the same as the word for this), the word for brother, and the word for speech or language. Thus, the Manus were often referred to as the *titan* (that) or as the *ndrasi* (brother), or as speakers of the *angan* (language). These terms contrast with *ario* or *mepo* (this, today), or *nali* (brother) or *nongan* (language) by which their closest mainland neighbors were known. This minimal lexicographic list sets apart the languages of the Admiralties while indicating some of the degree of relationship between them.

On the cultural level, the picture is at once more complex and in some ways simpler. All Admiralty Island groups divide the area's peoples into three gross ecological types that correspond to the most fundamental cultural differences. These are the Manus, the fishing, trading, lagoon-dwelling people with whom Margaret Mead's and Reo Fortune's studies are largely concerned (Mead 1934; Fortune 1935); the Usiai (gardening, nonseafaring peoples of the mainland's interior); and the Matankor (of the fringing islands, practicing mixed fishing and gardening and noted for specialized manufactures). All ethnic groups were entirely contained within one or another of these ecological types. The Manus are a single ethnic group, whereas the Usiai and Matankor are subdivided ethnically. The major difference between high island Matankor and low island Matankor is not part of the native set of categories. Intraethnic relations are always intraecological. The most economically important cross-ethnic relations are those that are cross-ecological. Cross-ethnic relations within the same ecological grouping tend to resemble intraethnic relations in that the exchange is between groups commanding similar resources. This arrangement has important consequences for the structure of the areal culture (Schwartz 1963).

Not all culture traits serve as ethnognomonic features. Some basic institutions and modes of organization—for example, village social and political organization and ways of thinking about marriage and ceremonial exchange—are uniform throughout the Admiralties. Other traits—myths, for example—circulate freely throughout the Admiralty Islands. It is usually said that they have been brought in from somewhere else within the archipelago. Original provenience is almost impossible to establish. In contrast, manufactured objects such as pots, carved beads, lime spatulas and gourds, basketry, and spears are completely characteristic of particular ethnic groups. Furthermore, to the connoisseur they are characteristic of their village of origin, and often their maker.

Song styles can be broadly grouped according to the three ecological types, but further subdivisions are possible (although the Usiai ethnic groups tend to fall together on this and a number of other features). Songs can be readily assigned to particular ethnic groups among the Matankor without using language as the indicator. Their songs are as distinctive as bird calls. Distinctiveness may be one of their functions, whatever else they also convey. Dance styles, on the other hand, tended to be much the same throughout the Admiralties until the effect of recent outside influences that now produce "native" dances that have little to do with traditional Admiralty Island forms.

Village particularism, schismatic leadership, and the competitive prestige motive make for patterns of diffusion of other major traits, such as ritual innovations, that tend to cut across and weaken the ethnic groupings. Diffusion of such innovations and their further elaboration take place within the entrepreneurial framework of aspirant leadership. The competition for reputation is undertaken especially with reference to other leaders of one's own ethnic group. This means that because one leader becomes associated with a given innovation, some of the other leaders of the same ethnic group will not adopt it. They will assert the superiority of previous forms or they will create or import a competitive innovation. Such innovations may be minor, perhaps a change in the design of the men's house or of canoe prows, or they may involve a major block of culture, such as a new form of ceremony in affinal exchange with associated paraphernalia and perhaps a mythological rationale. The spread of the cargo cults that I have described elsewhere was affected by this pattern of competitive diffusion (Schwartz 1962).

However, to say that the ethnic group was weakened by such cross-cutting diffusion might give the impression that they were ever otherwise than those who shared a presumed common origin, blood, or substance and who were marked by common language and an assemblage of culture traits that were their "property." Ethnic groups often had myths of origin that accounted for their descent from particular persons in a specified place and for the present location of their members. At present this accounting is generally fragmentary, vague, and seemingly unimportant to members of the ethnic group. The myths characteristically take account of no group on the island other than their own. Even the few hundred people of the two neighboring islands of Hus and Andra off the north coast, although obviously closely related, look upon themselves as separate ethnic groups and do not consider each other's existence in their origin myths. The larger, multiple village ethnic groups seemed to have no social or political function as such, other than endogamy and exophagy.

By exophagy ("eating out") I mean the prohibition on eating a member of one's own ethnic group who is killed or taken in warfare. The prohibition resembles the totemic taboos prohibiting one from eating one's own substance. Cannibalism but not autocannibalism was practiced by all groups except the Manus, who traded any bodies that came their way to members of other ethnic groups. Although warfare was not infrequent within ethnic groups, exophagy may have prevented vendettas leading to decimation. To return a fallen body to the enemy was an act of peace; to eat him was the gravest insult.

Ethnicity and Endogamy

Ethnic endogamy did not operate on the basis of any explicit rule but followed established customs. Marriages were investments between sponsors or financiers of the marriage who were preferably in a relation that could be classed as that of cross-cousins. The sponsors should be matched in status and able to meet their exchange partner's show of wealth in a long series of transactions that would exceed their own lifespans.

I do not wish to elaborate the relevant ethnography here more than is necessary (Mead 1934). Obviously, ethnic matching in such complex interactions makes for trust and reliability. I have mentioned that cross-ethnic marriages were more prevalent in families of highest status, who both competed and cooperated across ethnic lines, dependent on each other as trade and exchange partners in the sharp ecological complementarity of the Admiralties. In warfare and reputation they required each other as worthy adversaries.

Another factor that reinforced ethnic endogamy was fear of the magic and sorcery of "foreigners." Any stay among other ethnic groups in their own place must have been an uneasy one. The primary circle of trust was one's lineage. Trust within the ethnic group as a whole was weaker than the lineage but much greater than between ethnic groups. Under colonialism and, as mobility of Melanesians within the country grows, more and more people spend time away at work or at school among foreign natives. There is some evidence that the attribution of serious illness to sorcery is increasing in response to the levels of anxiety occasioned by this dispersion (Romanucci-Ross 1966). Away from the Admiralties, any Admiralty Islander is a relatively welcome associate, as if all are Manus—a single ethnic group when viewed from this new level of contrast. Where possible, however, urban associations are with others of one's own ethnic group.

In Admiralty Island cultures, the female is the exogam. She must leave her lineage and clan to live among those who, as persons suitable for marriage, are by definition people of a different substance. They are people whom she has been taught to avoid and before whom she feels shame, but at least they speak her language. Even without cross-ethnic marriage she would be regarded with some distrust, as representing or even spying for her brother's clan or village. Distrust is endemic and pervades the ethnic group as well, but it is exacerbated in cross-ethnic relations (Schwartz 1973).

Another contributing factor to endogamy is the effect of disparagement between ethnic groups. In some ways, all groups felt superior. The Usiai disparaged the landlessness of the Manus who "lived like fish" and who were dependent upon the Usiai for all cultivated foods. Although the Usiai collectively outnumbered the Manus, the Manus despised them as "landlubbers" who worked in dirt, had skin diseases, and "lived like animals," even making their house floors of bare dirt.

Manus men occasionally married Usiai, gaining a woman who would live among them, bringing her kinship ties with her in a relation in which the Manus, on the groom's side, could give valuables in exchange for the consumables they desired. I have mentioned the totemic connections gained through the woman. A Manus woman, however, would be demeaned and in danger living among the Usiai. The Usiai, on their part, displayed the adaptations of an entrapped, disparaged minority even though they were, in fact, the majority. They were both hostile to and respectful of the Manus. They internalized the Manus disparagement. The coastal strip became a no-man's land where markets could be held at river mouths, but where trade always tempted ambush by one side or the other. The Matankor were intermediate in the scale of respect. The Manus generally disparaged them as little better than Usiai and made their ventures away from their immediate coasts high risk operations.

During the period of continuous colonial control (since the establishment of the German colony in 1884), the Manus continued to dominate. The Admiralties were eventually pacified by about 1912, ending the marauding of the Manus. But the Manus became the favorites of the Europeans, though they were considered "cheeky" types. They were quite open to change as a result of culture contact, although in their seeming openness they were being and preserving themselves. They became an overrepresented group in ship's crews, in the native constabulary, and later in the new, English-educated civil service. During this period, which lasted into the 1950s, they served as the mediating model of acculturation for the Usiai. They formed the core of the Paliau Movement (Schwartz 1962), although its leader Paliau was a Matankor only weakly supported by his own ethnic group on Baluan Island.

Manus dominance began to decline soon after partly because of the Paliau Movement, which they supported. With the end of native internal warfare, villages began moving from their less accessible defensive locations to the beaches, and gardening peoples walked inland as often as necessary to attend their gardens. They began to use seagoing canoes, although they generally did not move beyond the shallow, safer waters within the reefs. To the extent that cash-cropping, native plantations, and agricultural programs became important, the Manus, still effectively landless, were left out. The Manus were successful in converting their ethnic self-confidence into scholastic achievement, but Usiai and Matankor children raised entirely within the postwar contact culture in beach villages are now doing as well.

The Paliau Movement represented a turning point in the totemic perception that emphasizes difference. Paliau belittled differences. He saw through to the basic institutional similarity of Admiralty Island and, more generally, of all Melanesian cultures. He called for the end of all major lines of division within native society. He set himself against the ecological split and tried to bring Usiai and Manus to practice mixed economies. This met with little success among the Manus, except for their recent acquisition of European coconut plantations. Paliau was especially concerned about ending the sharp ethnic separation of the Admiralty Islands people. He promoted the move to the beach and in many locations brought villages of diverse ethnic membership together to form larger, composite villages.

In spite of "integration," my 1967 survey showed that the relations of Manus to Usiai and Matankor remained much as before. In Bunai village, where since 1948 various Manus villages had united with five main Usiai villages, twenty years had produced only three intermarriages between Manus and Usiai, two of which were explained away by physical or moral defects of the Manus bride.

Ethnicity was and remains an important component of the identity of individuals and groups despite the informality of the ethnic group, its few social and political functions, and its relative lack of economic importance due to the isoecological position of villages of the same ethnic group. What I have called "ethnic groups" would sometimes be called "tribes" (Sahlins 1968). The term "tribe," however, already seems to be extended too far from its established traditional sense to be applicable to these politically and socially unorganized groupings based on presumed common descent, blood, and culture. Under the influence of new and broader forms of political leadership within the imposed and assimilated state, some of the ethnic groups may become tribal in the more prevalent political sense. Tribalism of the sort described in Africa is a specter much feared in Melanesia as independence approached these groups. Hostility and distrust remain. Here and there violent encounters occur. The rubric of ethnic relations serves us better if it is free of the connotations of tribe.

Melanesian Ethnicity and Cultural Totemism

Thus, the existence of ethnic groups and ethnic relations is an important part of the areal society and culture comprising the whole of the Admiralty Islands. The differentiation and maintenance of difference among these groups depends on self-

and mutual definition. That is, the groups are distinguished by selected ethnognomonic traits emblematic of the separate identity and community of substance of each group. In my studies of the Admiralty Islanders (Schwartz 1962, 1963) I found they had an attitude toward culture that made them hypersensitive to selected cultural and linguistic differences but relatively blind to the similarities between groups they defined as different. I have called this subgrouping of a society according to diagnostic cultural traits "cultural totemism." In other words, I am comparing it with the coding of social structure in terms of natural species, the attribute relations among which provide an analogue for relations among social groups. Culture provides its own analogue.

Social structure is a cultural artifact like anything else to which humans impart form, select, and categorize. Cultural differences reflect the social differentiation and grouping that they are used to map and label. But the relation is not merely one of passive reflection. I believe that the totemic attitude, natural or cultural, promotes differentiation and fragmentation of a certain order characteristic of Melanesia, and perhaps of many primitive societies.

The totemic attitude, which I perceived in 1963 and later related to totemism (1968), I considered to be an explanation for the proliferation of languages and cultures in Melanesia, specifically in the Admiralties. This attitude cannot be left unexplained as if it were a prime mover rather than a link in a nexus of intercausality. I suggested that it derives historically from the original multiethnicity of Melanesia, resulting from migration and settlement patterns that brought already differentiated Austronesian and non-Austronesian-speaking peoples into contact. Diversity became a way of life, an adaptation to this ethnic mosaic. The overall system of areal integration combines political atomism with economic-ceremonial integration. Fragmentation provides more people with the opportunity to be big men to numerous small publics. Yet leadership that promotes political fragmentation must manifest itself in exchange and network building, reintegrating the fragments in a nonpolitical mode. The participant in such a system is attuned to relatively small group differences. As a kind of consciousness of culture, cultural totemism apparently amplifies differences. Natural totemism would not seem to have this effect. To seize upon incipient differences for their emblematic value appears to cause, as much as to reflect, social differentiation. Such differences, overly attended, can define the lines of further differentiation.

Under cultural totemism, anything that is recognized as culturally distinctive is regarded as the property of a group (or individual). It is a property in the dual sense of an attribute and of a possession or a patent. Thus, in spite of mutual knowledge of each other's manufactures and special practices, these properties cannot simply be imitated without securing the right to them through kinship, marriage, or some form of purchase or licensing. Diffusion is not automatic on exposure, as we sometimes imagine. At best, we have thought of selection on the part of the recipient.

For the cultures in question here, the owner of cultural property has rights of control over its diffusion. I am aware of instances of native warfare over violations of such rights as ways to ornament a canoe prow. Cultural totemism would have the effect of defining new social divisions, of amplifying differences, and of maintaining differences in the face of contiguity and communication. Cultural totemism is not only a form of ethnic recognition and categorization, it is an ethnicizing process, a mechanism of cultural speciation.

Further reflection subsequent to my 1963 paper led to some revision of the above emphasis on the amplification of differences. Is the recognition of incipient difference the start of a schizmogenic process (Bateson 1936)? Does the difference, once noted, act like the beginning of a furrow on a rain-washed embankment, which, as it continues to deepen, channels an increasing volume of water that works to deepen it even more? If so, why are the differences kept within the recognizable outlines of Admiralty Island cultures? They are limited, of course, by the general evolutionary level of these cultures on a given technological base, but this base has supported far greater diversity than is manifested in the Admiralties. The very isolation of selected traits by people interested in finding and maintaining such differences allows the massive similarity of all else to go unnoticed. This aspect of cultural totemism has implications as important to the general understanding of ethnicity as the difference-amplifying aspects.

Anthropologists also alternate between these aspects of our own cultural totemism. At times we are intent on differences, which have great value to us in expanding our awareness of the range of possibilities in human cultures. They may also, perhaps, reward us with a differentiated "property" that becomes our particular stock in trade. At other times we allow ourselves to perceive the commonalities that, on a given level or type of culture, extensively underlie the differences. There would seem to be good bases in information theory for the behavioral tendency to perceive and react to differences as stimuli. Their magnitude need not be great. They may be the "just perceptible differences" of psychophysical research fame. Information requires difference: more accurately, information is about difference. The sameness of difference-manifesting objects is of indefinite extent, hence not determinately describable until we shift to a higher level of contrast at which this former sameness then becomes one side of a difference.

On their own level, Admiralty Island cultures could keep generating differences that are usable for social differentiation without the area really becoming much more culturally varied. In this light, the totemism analogy becomes striking. The differences are real, but most often (outside of the ecotypic division) are instances of ethnicity having an identificational, bounding function. Much more in culture might be of this order than we think. Sectarian distinctions that seem very important to insiders, dividing them into passionate factions, may seem like the merest variations on a theme to outsiders. The similarities revealed by external contrast are, perhaps, more remarkable. As I argued earlier, similar basic institutional designs prevail throughout the Admiralty Islands, and some of them throughout Melanesia, in spite of the dramatic contrasts of ecological areas and the different historical provenience of peoples.

The above discussion seems to raise the question, "How great is a difference?," which sounds a bit like the children's conundrum, "How long is a piece of string?" Obviously, once the difference and the objects in the implicit comparison are specified, the anthropologist can answer this question in many ways. He or she might ask, "How many people are affected?" Or "How much system accommodation does the difference set in motion?" Or "How much would communication by people on either side of the difference be affected?" Much but not all can be learned by ascertaining the insider's construction of the matter.

Regarding languages, it is clear to the Manus that some are more distant from their own than others and therefore more difficult, or "dear" (costly) as they sometimes put it in Pidgin English, to learn. Such inquiries reveal that even where the differences between groups are many, only a few need be taken into account, and these need not be the etically (descriptively) major ones. The brief lexicographic list of language designations is a case in point. Another, for example, is the difference in carving styles among the Matankor. It is enough to say, "This is a carving from Pak Island. They make noses that way." This ignores as unnecessary, for ethnic assignment, the many other differences perceptible to the outsider whose comparisons among the objects of Admiralty Island cultures are affected by innumerable external contrasts registered in past experience. The outsider's interests are not confined to ethnic assignment alone but to the overall characterization of style. The insider's is largely the cultural totemic view.

It has perhaps been formative of the distinctive Manus ethnic culture and ethnic "personality" (in Devereux's sense [1982]) that the Manus alone, of all Admiralty Island ethnic groups, are set off from others at the level of their ecotype, which they alone occupy. By contrast, all the Usiai ethnic groups within the Admiralty Islands comprise a single ecotype, as do the Matankor ethnic groups, so that they must distinguish themselves from each other at a different level of ethnognomonic detail.

Ethnic Groupings in Relation to Other Groupings

Thus far I have described the segmentation of the Admiralty Island areal culture at the ethnic level. The actual situation is more complex. The ethno-ethnography contains multiple, hierarchic, cross-cutting taxonomies that must be taken into account for a more complete picture of the overall identificational matrix. Natural and cultural totemism are two such cross-cutting taxonomies. As an initial crude approximation I could characterize cultural totemism (membership in the ethnic group and its subdivisions) as patrilineal, and natural totemism as matrilineal. Given the combination of the two I could speak of dual descent, but either the uni- or the duolineal characterization would somewhat exaggerate the difference between Admiralty Island and other primitive cultures.

All unilineal societies pay some attention to relations with the descendants of their exogamic members, such as, in the Admiralties, the women who marry out and their descendants. Lifelong exchange with one's affinal allies follows the path of the out-marrying women. Their children are the cross cousins and future exchange partners of the men who remain in the village or clan. The grandchildren of the exogam will again seek wives from their grandmother's clan. The progeny through the out-marrying sex are regarded as having residual rights in the patrimony of the clan. They are potential recruits to the clan, should its numbers dwindle.

Therefore, whether one speaks of dual descent or of complementary filiation (Fortes 1949), the unilineal idea, applied flexibly to local group composition, is always accompanied by a more or less formal accounting for relations through the opposite sex. This accounting is formally marked in the Admiralty Islands in various ways, including the lines of descent that make up the natural totemism. (It is also marked by the Crow-type kinship terminology, which, as I have argued [1963], reflects not some culminative development of unilineality but rather an emphasis on the crosscutting ties centering on the solidarity of siblings of opposite sex and the continued relation of their progenies.)

The natural totems and associated taboos comprise a flat taxonomy. They do not divide into subtotems. They do not map a hierarchic structure comparable to that of the patrilineally organized, coresidential or coterritorial ethnic groups, villages, clans, and lineages. The tree formed by these entities is not simply a downward radiating genealogy, real or assumed, but has different bases for membership on each level. The ethnic group is assumed to be a community of substance, even though members are aware at times that members of other ethnic groups have been assimilated, for example, as captives. One Matankor village is now largely descended from an Usiai taken captive several generations ago, with no apparent cultural or linguistic effect and no sense of ethnic discontinuity.

Full membership in the ethnic group is patrilineal in native theory. The child of a woman of the ethnic group is said to be a "lateral," to supply a gloss for native terms, which they translate as "half-caste" in Pidgin English. Inquiry evokes the names and territories of quite a few ethnic groups, of which it is said only half-castes remain. The same conception applies at the clan and lineage levels.

Clan membership is also patrilineal in the above sense, but clans are subject to splits along lineage lines. In such cases the clan name is often retained by one of the products of fission, together with a clan location and territory. A clan is thought of as a "place." It has a location in a village and territorial resources, land, fishing areas, sago swamps, reefs, and cultural properties such as types of fish nets or particular ceremonies. Clans consist of one or more patrilineages. In all other groupings, lineages are the units of composition most firmly rooted in genealogical relations, either known or stated as if known. They are named for the nodal ancestor from whom they trace descent. The level of mutual trust is strongest within the lineage, in consonance with the assumption of the closest community of substance. One or more lineages can become clans by splitting off and becoming associated with a place of their own. Many clans, however, are quite old and consist of lineages that cannot trace their relations to one another. They assume that such relations exist and that the lineages of a clan have always been associated with one another.

Villages may split and recombine along clan or subclan (that is, lineage) lines. The political association that a village represents may be disrupted by quarrels or by rivalry. The split can be violent or merely one of spatial separation. At times, a move of even a few hundred yards will suffice. The lineage and the ethnic group thus resemble one another, in contrast to the clan and village. They are not directly territorial. The ethnic group is associated with a territory over which its members are spread, but it is the clans and villages that hold and defend the territory. Both lineage and ethnic group are communities of substance like the natural totemic lines, in contrast to the clan and village, particularly the latter, which are political associations. The village is a purely political, unstable assemblage of a selection of clans from within the pool bounded by the ethnic group.

An ethnic group, like a lineage, stresses substance rather than place. Like totemism, such groups are useful for broad or fictive association on a scale for which political organizational means does not exist. Village and clan membership, on the other hand, implied a kind of citizenship in a microstate. Clan and, to a greater extent, village cohesion was consensual, dependent on the current prestige and vigor of their leaders and always limited by the potential exercise of the sanction of withdrawal or separation. It is often asserted that the assumption of common substance is the basis for food taboos (including ethnic exophagy), as well as lineage, clan, and broader rules of exogamy. But this assumption must also be one of the bases of ethnic endogamy, even though the latter is a result rather than a rule and lacks the kinds of sanctions attached to incest or totemic taboo violation.

Lineage and its extensions seem to define an inner circle, whereas ethnicity defines an outer circle. Within the inner circle, incest is prohibited. But between the inner and outer circle there is an area of relatively safe incest in the sense of copulation with one defined as of the same blood or substance. Any excursion beyond the outer circle is at the venturer's risk, in much the same degree as interethnic trade or warfare.

One effect of colonial administration and of the models of the new amalgamated communities has been to inhibit, but not eliminate, the processes of split and merger. Ethnic groups tend to be represented in fewer separate communities. In some cases they have coalesced into a single community. Some leaders of the Manus group have had the fantasy of reversing the Manus diaspora, which they trace back in myth to a single founder village. They dream of bringing all of the ten or so current Manus villages together into a single Manus town based on the acquisition of a sufficiently large European plantation. Certain ethnic groups may yet become coordinated in the context of modern political action.

Ethnic Traits as Emblematic Property

Ethnic group, village, clan, lineage, and individuals comprise a hierarchy of material and nonmaterial property-bearing entities. Admiralty Islanders have terms such as the Manus word "*kaye*," which, applied to any of these levels, means any and all of the following: way, manner, kind, fashion (the actual Pidgin English gloss), property or attribute, and inherent characteristic of that object. The *kaye* was conceived of as inherent but not in the same way as a physical property such as skin color. For such attributes the person is taken as an object, and I have never heard *kaye* applied to objects. A ceremony, a way of fighting, a trait of touchiness about status, a style of canoe construction or a love of canoe racing, an individual's lack of generosity—any of these and all collectively would be referred to as the *kaye* of that individual or group. Statements using the term are often comments intended as explanations: they are behaving in a certain way because it is their *kaye*—"That's the way they are." Although the conception is different, it tends to cover what we mean by culture, when applied to groups, or personality, when applied to individuals.

If one asked what are the *kaye* of a particular ethnic group, village, clan, or lineage, one would elicit not an exhaustive characterization, of course, but a brief set of group properties or distinctive traits, not necessarily selected for contrast on the same attribute dimensions as those mentioned for other groups. It is assumed that all groups will manifest some behaviors by which one can identify them. These are the behaviors by which they express their group membership. Many other behaviors, if they are distinctive of the person or group to which they are attributed, will be recognized as *kaye*, but they will not be the ethnognomonic traits that come most readily to the informant's mind. The extension of cultural totemism to individuals, in the same terms and conventions of discourse as apply to groups, is logically consistent for the Admiralty Islander and parallels my own preferences in modeling the relation of culture and personality (Schwartz 1972, 1973).

The totemic attitude is still with us. As Lévi-Strauss argues, it is not a distinguishing characteristic separating primitive people from modern or civilized ones. Linton's parable of the Rainbow Brigade in World War I illustrates beautifully the assimilation of the primitive into the modern. Totemism is a mode of human thought that has certain effects, and perhaps shortcomings, that are important to conceptions of ethnicity and the behavioral implications of these conceptions. These effects were discussed in relation to the possible difference-amplifying effects of according emblematic significance to seemingly slight or incipient cultural differences. At the same time, it became noticeable that what was being multiplied was not the degree of difference or overall cultural variation among all groups of this interactive areal culture, but only the number of distinctive groups. This increase in groups means that the number of domains increased within which entrepreneurs could separately reckon their own prestige. *Since similarities pass unnoticed when attention is focused on the emblematic differences, it would be possible for cultural diversity to diminish even while ethnic diversity increases.*

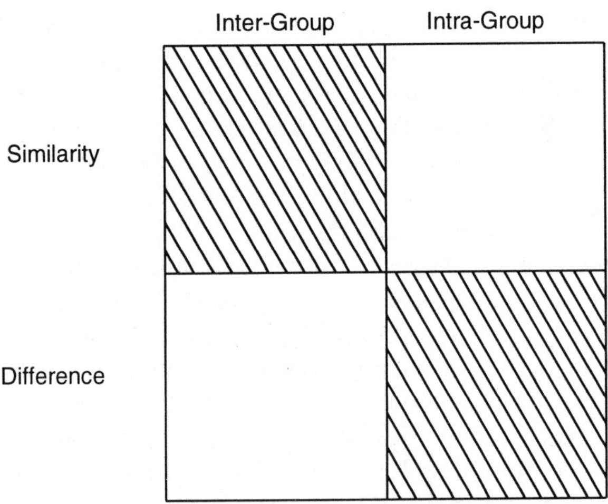

Figure 1. Differentiating groups by distinctive traits.

Figure 1 illustrates the totemic attitude and its effect. This attitude clearly leads to the use of only one of the diagonals in selective perception and neglects or overlooks the other. In differentiating groups from one another by a set of distinctive traits, it emphasizes the similarity or solidarity within each of the distinguished groups and the dissimilarity between the groups. As De Vos (personal communication) expressed it in speaking of ethnicity, "It takes care of belonging and distantiation at the same time." What are ignored are the variations within each group and the similarities between them. Also ignored are all similarities and differences on noncriterial traits.

The totemic attitude involves the perceptual speciation of all known humankind. The premises of natural totemism seem to enjoy a primacy that goes beyond its value of totemism as a classificatory analogy. Groupings based on any criteria—genealogical, cultural, territorial—either assume a set of specieslike qualities or remain weak, conflictful, and schismatic assemblages. Upon this mosaic of little "species," individuals further impose their rankings of respect and disparagement, which become embodied in patterns of domination and counterdreams of revindication.

Christian Conversion and Religious Ethnicity

The tendency to convert groups not based on genealogy and not initially taken as ethnic into quasi-ethnic "species" may be illustrated by the effect of the conversion of Admiralty Islanders to various Christian missions. The process began in the 1880s and was largely completed in the 1930s, when the Manus became Catholic en masse. The Usiai and Matankor had been split into several groups by Catholic, Lutheran Evangelical, and Seventh Day Adventist missionaries.

The conversion of the Manus to a single sect both reflects and reinforces their ethnic unity and seems to have had little effect on their internal relations. Other small ethnic groups went to one or another of the sects, whereas many were split between two or more. The Seventh Day Adventists sometimes were able to gain converts from other missions, dividing some ethnic groups. In the 1940s, the Paliau Movement led to a break between its adherents and the Catholic and Protestant missions to which they had belonged, although the Seventh Day Adventists seemed immune to such defections. Once again the Manus, though the largest and most dispersed spatially of the Admiralty Island ethnic groups, went en masse into the Paliau native separatist Christian church. Other ethnic groups were divided by recruitment to this church. The Paliau Church was split episodically by splinter cults dividing even the Manus ethnic group.

I cannot assess as yet the effect of the more recent segmentation of the Admiralties by religious and political affiliations. The initial pattern of mission recruitment, however, had a drastic effect on the ethnic groups that were partitioned by it. The mission sects became themselves similar to ethnic groups and took on some of the totemic features already discussed. They soon became virtually endogamous. Where nearby villages of the same ethnic groups had formerly been the principal sources of spouses for one another, this relation ceased if they came to belong to different missions. Marriages predominated between villages of the same ethnic group and mission, but many cross-ethnic, intrasect marriages were formed. The Paliau Church, sometimes known as the Baluan Church, began to have the same effect. Each group had its own taboos and new ethnognomonic traits.

Members of other sects looked with awe upon the transformation of behavior effected by Seventh Day Adventists and their considerable success in tabooing the most highly valued oral pleasures: betel nut, tobacco, pork, and alcohol (recently become available to natives). The distinctive Sabbath day and use of English as a liturgical language heightened the sense of belonging among Seventh Day Adventist converts and their sense of distance from non-Adventist groups. Their belief in an imminent apocalypse also helps account for the strength of their new "ethnicity" and the commitment that made them immune (until 1967, at any rate) to the attractions of other cults. The other missions, churches, and cults were less impermeable during the period under observation, but at their height they showed similar characteristics.

The members, encouraged by their leaders, have come to think of themselves as different or new kinds of men. They wear the new (or relatively recent) identities conspicuously. During periods of strong group feeling they have tended to act as political blocs, putting forward their own candidates in territorywide and local elections. Since some church groups require the nonmember spouse to join the church, endogamy results partly from rules. In most church groups, however, it operates like that of the old ethnic groups, informally as an effect of attribute clustering, preference, and the operation of community pressures as well as the effect of network involution on the likelihood of inside and outside contacts of potential sponsors and spouses.

The heterogeneous members of the new sects seemingly could not claim common origin, yet they develop an identification with the origin myths of their sect as well as with its unique correctness and the special benefits promised to them as the elect. They feel tied, as well, to the countries of origin of their sects. It is another source of strength for the Seventh Day Adventists that their sect is of American origin, given the prestige of America, which had an enormous military base in the Admiralties in World War II. I found that their members believed that most Americans are Seventh Day Adventists, even though the other sects are also represented by American priests and missionaries who have largely replaced the earlier German ones. Although they are in many ways deeply separated from one another by their different religious memberships, converts are linked, albeit somewhat remotely, to organizations of worldwide scope. On the local scene, however, I believe my comparison of the sects to the old ethnic groups is justified.

In the towns, at boarding schools and work centers, and in the civil service, individuals of ethnic groups derived from all parts of the mainland and islands of Papua and New Guinea now intermingle. And there is now a higher level of contrast in which Admiralty natives are classed together as a unit, in comparison with other equally broad groups whose ethnic differentiation becomes irrelevant at a distance. In the towns, attribute clustering takes place to the greatest possible extent. The more specific the shared attributes, the more likely an intimate association. Manus in Rabaul, for example, will first associate with their own kin if any are present, second with members of their own village, third with other Manus, and fourth with other Admiralty Islanders of their own locality, religious background, and so on through a series of increasingly general attributes. The ethnic enclaves or networks of ethnic associations in towns are not merely indifferently ethnic but ethnolocal. African urban studies indicate the same pattern. For example, a Yoruba's ties in town are not with just any Yoruba, but primarily to those of his home locality (Plotnikov 1969). Jacobson indicates this is more true of nonelite than of elite urban workers (1973).

Sexual Attraction and Ethnic Contrast in Pluralistic Situations

In Melanesia this picture of ethnic clustering may hold somewhat more strongly for ties with persons of the same sex in towns, schools, and work centers than for persons of the opposite sex. Admiralty Island parents are disturbed at the frequency with which their sons and daughters marry or become romantically and biologically involved with young women and men of the most diverse origins—New Guineans, Trobrianders, Solomon Islanders—when they are away from parental supervision. Many cross-cultural marriages are occurring. The greatest concern of the Admiralty Island parents is that a daughter will go to live with strangers and be subject to dangers that this entails beyond the reach of their protection. Romantic sexual attraction not only does not respect ethnic lines, it may be stimulated by the very distancing that ethnic contrasts guarantee, since it may depend to some extent on contrast, on mystery, and on the assumption of an informational gradient.

Within the ethnic group the incest taboo provides a line between the familiar and the sufficiently distant insider. Our thinking about incest usually focuses on it as a prohibition that compels men to marry out, as if without it their natural tendency would be to couple with whomever were closest at hand. The incest taboo could be seen as a guarantee of a marriage that is sufficiently distant by definition for an adequate initial potentiation before it too becomes affectively and institutionally familiar.

To the extent that the mating is distant (but still "inside"), it is approved. To the extent that such a mating is approved, it becomes less distant. If there is anything to this speculation, why would incest taboos have to be stringently sanctioned if attractiveness is lessened with familiarity? For one thing, the effect on intrafamilial attraction may not be wholly nullified. An attraction may exist at one stage of life that in the presence of the incest taboo would be repressed later or redirected as part of the basis for the potentiation by distance. But aside from that, I hypothesize that a taboo requires enforcement because it exists. The incest taboo itself provides distance to a disapproved coupling that counteracts, to some extent, the effect of familiarity. In sum, with respect to sexual attraction, close familiar relations are less potent sexually but are made more so by their distancing illegitimacy. Permissible, enjoined, or prescribed relations are, by definition, sufficiently distant but made less so by their legitimacy and institutionalized familial status. Under past circumstances, as well as the present situation of a mingled ethnic setting, the cross-ethnic liaison between young people is still more distant, less incestuous, in that the partner is unlike one's familiars in more ways. In addition, such a liaison is formally legal but disapproved by one's home community and family. The resultant marriages usually gain approval after the fact, but they are regarded as potentially unstable and dangerous.

Conclusions: Cultural Totemism and Identity

I have taken the concept of totemism as the starting point of this paper and have attempted, by way of the notion of cultural totemism, to extend it to ethnic relations in a primitive areal culture. I have argued that ethnicity is decidedly relevant to primitive societies when they are taken not as isolates, either culturally or socially, but as we usually find them, part of a complex of communities. In these stateless societies the boundaries between ethnic groups are neither political nor necessarily natural boundaries but are instead defined within the areal culture. These definitions are subject to both gradual and relatively sudden changes, even within the relative stability and relatively slower rate of change that characterizes societies at the preurban, preindustrial level.

Nor are such changes simply the result of passive drift of cultural differentiation. Human beings themselves cannot help but treat human behavior as they do all other phenomena. They form constructs of the phenomenal fields that are derived from it and imposed upon it. In this case, the constructs of the field of cultural variation and similarity form a part of the system of constructs orienting the very behavior that is being perceived. I have asserted that this perception is selective, attending most sensitively to certain key differences, and I have described schematically what I have called the totemic attitude or mode of perception. Implicit in the totemic mode is that the resulting social segregates are conceived of as species, each united in substance and origin, each manifesting its species-specific behavior. The fact of interethnic marriage and assimilation of persons and behavioral properties is not missed, but the analogy to a species remains, enhanced by ethnic endogamy and myths of origin and continuity. For the Admiralty Islands, I have compared the cross-cutting relations of natural and cultural totemism.

Totemism, even in this extended sense, remains a matter of classification, as so many have established. But as others have sensed, it is more than this. The classification is a means of reciprocal identification of individuals and groups. It provides both a key and a model, perhaps corresponding to Devereux's (1982) ethnic identity and ethnic personality or to a status system and a role system.

Any status system is not merely a set of labels corresponding to a set of relative social positions. It must also specify how individuals or groups are to be assigned to these statuses by providing a set of qualifying attributes. We often believe we can decide on the position assignments without necessarily considering what behaviors will be expected of the persons occupying such positions. We cannot always find exclusively nonbehavioral criteria. Furthermore, nonbehavioral criteria, other than marked racial or sex differences, are not visible, not supportive of the species analogy.

Cultural totemism applies where certain particularly attended behavioral differences are the bases for the assignment or validation of ethnic status. Manifesting or, as Devereux (1982) puts it, "instancing" the role, validates the status. Such instancing, singly or collectively, is very much the concern of members of the mosaic of ethnic groups that I have described. One proves as much to oneself as to others who one is, or one seeks to discover who one is, by displaying various behaviors—trying on identities.

In what I have described, as well as in the details of individual behavioral stances that I could not deal with here, I posit that there is evidence that identity is always problematic and consequently dynamic, not only in modern, rapidly changing societies but in primitive ones as well. It becomes problematic in new ways under culture contact, domination, and acculturation, but it is not created anew.

Much of culture and personality is adaptive to the problem of identity, which is never completely resolved in a given culture or personality. Individuals or groups seem always to confront the question of their identity—of what that identity implies and of what they must do to validate their own and others' sense of that identity. Against what counterassertion is directed the assertion of identity in myth, in ritual and religion, in institutions, in the flow of behavior itself? Why is all this necessary? What is the problem? Perhaps all we need posit to begin to answer this question is the existence of more than one individual and, beyond this, more than one distinguished group of people. We would then have to explore the individual and cultural ontogeny of how identities are established and maintained. Much of psychoanalysis is concerned with this question, most explicitly in the work of Erik Erikson.

Any status is a part of identity, and for most societies ethnic status (like sexual status but perhaps with an even greater priority) is one of the bases upon which identities are constructed. It establishes a relative ranking for all other statuses that are added on for the individual or group vis-à-vis the corresponding statuses of others. Thus, it would follow that if white is higher than black, a white doctor is higher than a black doctor.

But ethnic statuses are often so displaced in rank that the lowest-ranked secondary statuses of one are above the highest ranked of the other. Probably the weight of ethnic status as a component of identity is correlated to the degree of status ranking on that basis. Where it is not so used (as within a given ethnic group), sex or occupation or age may act as the basal status that calibrates the relative standing of the rest and upon which identity is constructed. Under such circumstances sex, occupation, age, or other statuses may be ethnicized, cleaving the social spectrum into groups of persons manifesting the emblematic traits of sexual, class, age grade, or generational identities.

The weighting of a basal status in the construction of identities depends on their use in ranking individuals and groups in institutionalized patterns of dominance. A basal status such as ethnicity would become even more salient when ranking becomes unstable. In an assimilating environment, ethnicity itself is thrown into question as a significant basis of identity and some alternative basis such as class or nationalism is asserted (and may take on ethnoid or specioid characteristics as a result).

Ethnicity is most prominent when the rank order rather than the ethnic basis is under attack. Where ethnicity and rank are fused, the relative movement of any one person sets all into movement. The relativity of such a basal status system is highly problematic unless it is based on an overwhelming domination, which even then will not stifle all fears of revindicative movement from below. In the Admiralty Islands, the two situations combine. The Usiai can rise in relative status through assimilation without asserting Usiai ethnicity, which was always plural rather than a strong collective identity. The Manus, on the other hand, have no power to prevent the Usiai from overcoming their precontact inferiority and they are, partly by the very strength of their own singular ethnicity, less able to assimilate because they lack the land base with which to do so. For them, the reference group is European; for the Usiai, it is both Manus and European.

As culture change has accelerated, time makes an increasing difference in defining the identity of individuals. They are grouped by the totemic perception in time and change as they once were in space. It is increasingly true that cultures are bounded more in time than in space. The result differs greatly from the age grading which has been a feature of all cultures to some extent. Although one now becomes a member of the adult age grade, it is part of a culture that differs from that to which one's father belonged. Somewhere one's identity becomes anchored in time as part of a generation in the cultural sense. But this generation does not extend throughout the lifetime of the individual. One's generation is attached to a certain period of one's life—in America, late adolescence and young adulthood, perhaps—the age at which one has one's war, learns the songs and dance styles that are especially one's own, receives the most formative occupational training, and so on. One survives through the successive generations of others in more or less useful ways.

This longitudinal effect of cultural acceleration creates a new kind of plurality of identities that are, like geographically separated ethnic groups, sharply set apart by the totemic perception. Our societies are pluralistic with respect to these time limited cultures as well as with respect to the older types of culturally differentiated segments. And with this new multiplicity, identity becomes all the more problematic. Riesman (1963), Mead (1956), and Toffler (1970) have done interesting explorations in these time-limited cultures and have been concerned about the problem of identification when one lacks exact precedents in identity but must extrapolate to something new. Many have written about peer group modeling as one response to this situation.

The difficulty of finding an identity without precedent is not completely solved by adopting a contemporary precedent. The signs of search seem even more evident and more frustrating than before. Migrants of identity wander the land, trying on this or that identity, never sure, and perhaps, under the circumstances, unable to attain familiar forms of authenticity of identity. To terminate any search requires that, whatever one is seeking, one must recognize it when it is found. It must also be acceptable, if the masquerade is to be ended. The search for another or a new identity is a contradiction in terms.

My further research among the people of the Admiralty Islands will be particularly concerned with where they find themselves in time and change, with the state of their present self-recognition, and with the conception of themselves and of their elders formed by the young, who have been raised and educated wholly within the post-World War II contact culture and who are taking their places as mature adults. What do the old bases of identity now mean to them? What has been the fate of the old ethnicity? How "modern" have they become? Although identity has always been problematic in primitive and modern cultures alike, we may yet find that there has been a change, from the question "Who am I?" to "Who am I really?"

REFERENCES

Bateson, Gregory. 1936. *Naven*. Cambridge: The University Press.

Devereux, George. 1982, 2d ed. "Ethnic Identity: Its Logical Foundations and Its Dysfunctions." In *Ethnic Identity: Cultural Continuities and Change*. George A. De Vos and Lola Romanucci-Ross, eds. Pp. 42-70. Chicago: University of Chicago Press.

Durkheim, Emile, and Marcel Mauss. 1963. *Primitive Classification*. Rodney Needham, trans. and ed. Chicago: University of Chicago Press.

Fortes, Meyer, ed. 1949. *Social Structure: Studies Presented to A. R. Radcliffe-Brown and D. Forde*. Oxford: Clarendon Press.

Fortune, Reo F. 1935. *Manus Religion*. Philadelphia: American Philosophical Society.

Goldenweiser, Alexander. 1937. *Anthropology*. New York: Crofts.

Jacobson, David. 1973. *Itinerant Townsmen: Friendship and Social Order in Urban Uganda.* Menlo Park, CA: Cummings.

Lévi-Strauss, Claude. 1962. *Le totemisme aujourd'hui.* Paris: Presses Universitaires.

Linton, Ralph. 1943. "Nativistic Movements." *American Anthropologist* (new ser.) 45(2):230-240.

Linton, Ralph. 1945. *The Cultural Background of Personality.* New York: Appleton-Century.

Mead, Margaret. 1930. *Growing Up in New Guinea.* New York: William Morrow.

Mead, Margaret. 1934. "Kinship in the Admiralty Islands." *Anthropological Papers of the American Museum of Natural History* 34(2).

Mead, Margaret. 1956. *New Lives for Old.* New York: William Morrow.

Mead, Margaret. 1970. *Culture and Commitment: A Study of the Generation Gap.* New York: Natural History Press.

Plotnikov, Leonard. 1969. *Strangers in the City.* Pittsburgh: University of Pittsburgh Press.

Riesman, David. 1953. *The Lonely Crowd A Study of the Changing American Character.* Garden City, NY: Doubleday.

Romanucci-Ross, Lola. 1966. "Conflits fonciers a Mokerang, village Matankor des iles de l'Amiraute." *L'Homme* 6(2):32-52.

Romanucci-Ross, Lola. 1969. "The Hierarchy of Resort in Curative Practices: The Admiralty Islands, Melanesia." *Journal of Health and Social Behavior* 10(3):201-209.

Sahlins, Marshall. 1968. *Tribesmen.* Englewood Cliffs, NJ: Prentice-Hall.

Schwartz, Theodore. 1962. "The Paliau Movement in the Admiralty Islands, 1946-1954." *Anthropological Papers of the American Museum of Natural History* 49(2).

Schwartz, Theodore. 1963. "Systems of Areal Integration: Some Considerations Based on the Admiralty Islands of Northern Melanesia." *Anthropological Forum* 1(1):56-97.

Schwartz, Theodore. 1972. "Distributive Models of Culture in Relation to Societal Scale." Burg Wartenstein Symposium No. 55, Scale and Social Organization. New York: Wenner-Gren Foundation.

Schwartz, Theodore. 1973. "Cult and Context: The Paranoid Ethos in Melanesia." *Ethos* 1(2):153-174.

Toffler, Alvin. 1970. *Future Shock.* New York: Random House.

Tylor, E. B. 1958. *Primitive Culture.* New York: Harper.

LOLA ROMANUCCI-ROSS ■

Chapter Three

Matrices of an Italian Identity

Past as Prologue

The Italian experience of group and personal identity is a distillate of millennia of the fusion of cultural traits in group definitions of "belonging" and occasional fissioning in cultural differentiation. I will focus here on the Piceno as one variant of the historical and cultural processes that could apply to a number of Italian regions. The Piceno is one of the truly ancient regions; others are Apulia, Campania, Latium, Lucania, and Umbria. Until relatively recently (the last century), there was no Italian nation-state, and some Italians like to quip that there really isn't one now. The humor in such remarks barely masks the always more deeply ensconced attachment to regional affiliations, as I will indicate in this chapter.

By way of introduction, a profusion of languages and cultures "became" Italy. Origins are sought in remnants of dialects as well as in archaeological and paleontological discoveries. The Italic dialects are described by linguists as a subdivision of Indo-European languages. Only Latin, spoken by a tribe in the lower regions of the Tiber, survived; the rest can be only reconstructed and surmised. Upon this fundamental cultural stratum there came a wave of invasions from all quarters, and we find evidence of these occurring even prior to the Neolithic. Eventually, because of the differing origins of linguistic groups that invaded and/or settled, one can determine a definite split between the northern and southern dialects in Italy. These differences were further amplified by the introduction of Slovene speakers in the Udine and Gorizia areas, Albanian speakers in the south-central region, Greek-speaking villages in Calabria, and French Provençal speech in the north.

In prehistory, we can infer only that "warrior elements" came from central Europe, bearers of the "bell beaker culture" from Spain, founders of the Terramara culture from the north, and the Villanovan culture, which appeared in the Iron Age. The Iron Age also saw the Illyrians cross the Adriatic to join the inhuming Apenine culture to dominate the Picenum (the place and people described in this chapter).

Etruscans (of Greek origin?) tried but failed to unite the peoples of Italy. The Romans later succeeded in this for a time, politically at least. The Romans bound them together through administration and a network of permanent highways. Medieval Italy saw a new period of invasions by Goths and Longobards; the latter brought a permanent settlement of Germanic peoples into Italy (including the Piceno area, as we shall see). Next to cross the Alps were the Franks, with a legacy of cultural features often referred to as Carolingian Italy. Meanwhile, the Arabs had begun the conquest of Sicily in 827 and also began to settle in various places on the mainland. About two hundred years later the Normans, having come to destroy Byzantine power in the service of the church, were given incentives to begin permanent settlements in Sicily and nearby regions.

In the eleventh century, this welter of cultural overlays began to conform to a new sorting device, that is, to be expressed as "communes," which later became city-states. This fissioning along geographical descriptors could occur because some Italian towns had reached a level of prosperity and size that allowed development of local self-governments that asserted themselves and rose up to rebuff challenges to their authority. Venice, for example, elected its own dukes (doges), Amalfi and other cities their own magistrates. At times such communes were opposed by the pope (as in the Piceno area). Such polarization of town-and-ecclesiastical-gown was expressed in conflicts in many city-states and often spread into wider areas under an encompassing leadership for each side, as in the battles between the Guelphs and the Ghibellines.

In addition to attaining independence, city-states or *comuni* had two other politicocultural agendas: to make war upon each other and to conquer and absorb the *contado* (countryside) into their immediate environs; what follows is a discussion of these relationships in the Piceno as a paradigm for other regions of the whole later-to-be nation-state of Italy. The paradigm could apply, for example, to Sicily, where the earliest indigenous Indo-European speakers were joined, either through invasion or settlement, by Phoenicians, Greeks, Carthaginians, Romans, Vandals (in the Byzantine period), Arabs, Normans, Spaniards, Savoyards, and Austrians. Markers of these conjoinings in Sicily are found in the dialect, art, architecture, music, historical dress, cuisine, gender relations, family structure, healing and curing rituals, and so on. Regional histories in Italy have similar patterns if not similar content.

In Italy, a regional culture, it seems, can be thought of as an array of elements in a space, out of which determinants of configuration characterize and distinguish it from other regional cultures. Invasions came as ocean tides, disturbing the set or array of elements. In the ebbing of the invasion force, either by expulsion or withdrawal, the invaders left their mark. Sometimes they rearranged somewhat the elements in the cultural matrix, sometimes they changed the determinants, and sometimes they remained as long-term settlers to become the people they had conquered (Pulgram 1958; Musa 1964; Barzini 1965; Balena 1970; Dundes and Falassi 1975; Petrusewicz 1978; Treggiari 1991).

Relating Time and Space

The city of Ascoli Piceno predates its encounter with the Romans. Not only the city's inhabitants but those in the towns and villages in its province are aware of their long traditions and unique characteristics. Ascoli Piceno lies along the ancient Via Salaria, the Roman "salt road," to the Adriatic Coast, five hundred feet above sea level among the wooded hills of oak and chestnut where the Tronto and Castellano rivers meet. In this chapter I examine the self-conscious self-perceptions that are the products of behavioral strategies the Ascolani developed over long periods of time while interacting with other ethnic groups that came to claim their precious and limited geographical space.

Time and space relations are a crucial element in the creation and preservation of ethnic group identity (Romanucci-Ross 1985:xi). For Europeans who came to many parts of the American continent, space was vast and historical time-in-residence was relatively brief. For the English, French, Spanish, and others, "colonization" after several centuries was complete, and an identity (carried from home and slightly modified) was formed. This group identity was based on enduring conquest with accompanying acquisition of land and resources, and an indigenous work force in some cases; it was not interrupted by meaningful historical moments of loss of control.

In a nation-state such as Italy, however, the time-in-residence of ethnic groups reaches back through the millennia (modified though these groups might have been by incursions of some new genes and assimilated cultural traits). Origins of language, "race," and cultural traits disappear in prehistory, and the territory on which all this occurred was relatively small. Therefore, it is in the long stretch of historical time that ethnic enclaves in Italy produced the diversities that determined group identities. To the outsider, these are readily recognized as broad-stroked *regional* differences; to each *ethne* the distinctions are finer. But it is recognized that all areas of Italy have shared the historical experience of constant invasions and incursions from political or military representatives of other "countries," even though regionally these were usually not the same specific and particular versions of the countries and cultures that left their mark. What was shared was the manner of conquest or persuasion, the occasional revolts, and often the unique feature of the conquerors who came and stayed long enough to blend into the culture and become bearers of the culture they found, even while retaining parts of their own. How did this happen?

Philosophers critical of the school of phenomenology dwell upon the difficulties of reconciling the "internal discourse" (that is, the "I" of solitary discourse, see, for example, Jacques Derrida [1967] or Dilthey [see Hodges 1952], among others, who have written on the history of human consciousness). Such critics feel there is no persuasive model to indicate that a phenomenological (solipsistic?) worldview can ever be shared. Yet, we do have the legacy of George Herbert Mead (1934), which is an attempt to describe the socialization process of the child and the manner in which it becomes a group member. The fieldwork of Margaret Mead (1930, 1975) is an example of an anthropologist recording the process of socialization in the South Seas, in Bali, and in New Guinea, and there have been other commentaries on such a process (Romanucci-Ross 1985). With such foundations, it is remarkable that (as De Vos indicates in Chapter 1) the psychocultural aspects of ethnic identity have not been explored as much as the descriptive dimensions such as class, caste, and other modes of stratification and differentiation.

Since we begin with the relationship of time and space coordinates, I suggest at the outset that peoples who feel part of the Americas model (still exemplified in large portions of the western United States or Argentina) are likely to see themselves more in relation to the *landscape* and less in the view of the Other. People of the Italian model (small space, long time span), on the other hand, have identities more likely to be formed as reflections of the self in the eyes of others.

Accepting Devereux's (1982) definition of ethnic identity as a "sorting device," I describe here the creation and preservation of an ethnic group identity in the nation-state (though many Italians would say "geographical expression") that is Italy and how the notion of group identity is transmitted culturally. Considered, in belonging, are the structure of the family (and the exoticization of romantic love), the mythologized family and other religious symbols, use of language and dialect, conflict resolution strategies, models of behavior, ethics or the creation of ethnic character, aesthetics in the creation of ethnic personality, and how these models are actualized through work and play and the negotiating of exchanges of goods, or services, or persons (as in marriage). All are conjoined in a semiotic complex in which all actions of persons and interactions between persons are embedded.

The People of the Piceno

The area of the Piceno encompasses the city of Ascoli Piceno and the small towns and villages in the countryside that, circumscribed, constitute the province similarly named; it is all now considered administratively part of the larger region of Le Marche (in central Italy), surrounded by Tuscany, Umbria, Lazio, Abruzzi, and the Adriatic Sea.

Much of the province of Ascoli Piceno is agricultural. Its produce consists of cereals, grapes, fruits, vegetables, and products of animal husbandry. However, the area from the city toward the Adriatic to the port city of San Benedetto is becoming increasingly industrialized.

Though it has long been fashionable to write and think in terms of rural/urban dichotomies and all that implies for behavior and life-style, it is important to be aware that such a dichotomy is tenuous at best in this locality. In the early nineteenth century, we find a great intensity of urban-rural homogeneity; 70 percent of those allowed to call themselves Ascolani worked in the countryside (Fabiani 1967:225-235). From the earliest historical times, there has been a constant movement of individuals and families from the city to the country and from the country to the city. Sometimes temporary, sometimes permanent (at least for several generations), the reasons for these migrations may have been political (refugees from the groups in conflict), economic (inability to live off the land or to survive in the city), or to reestablish family ties (there are villas owned by the well-to-do who have estates outside the city; there are also small cramped apartments in certain sections of the city for the marginal people who come and go). In the village of "Malva," in which I have conducted many intensive periods of fieldwork over a twenty-year period (Romanucci-Ross 1991), male heads of families (and wives) who work in the city and commute "home" outnumber those who live only off their crops or their crops and their pensions. Nor is this atypical.

How does an ethnic group interpret and memorialize its own history, and how does the consciousness of it come to be used as an identity marker? Various historical events are remembered in the plan or layout of the city (or piazzas in small towns and villages) and its streets, buildings, and monuments. Some are recalled in monuments or in festivals, some of which call for the dramatization of a period complete with costumes, food, music, and games of that era. There is also the ongoing artistry and trade of "pictorializing" (on canvas, ceramics, metals, clay, stone, marble, or through photography) ancient bridges, cathedrals, convents, moats and fortresses, churches, monasteries, designs of portals, and house doors. There are also continuous critiques of the originals and of their representations; no one ever seems to tire of any of these activities.

Therefore, the historical events I chose to note have been chosen for me; they are commonly noted events, almost universally known and referred to with some frequency by certain segments of the population. As an example, life in *il cinquecento* (the 1500s) is celebrated on the days of the *Quintana* (the *palio* horse-racing event) during the first week of August. This is when much of the city "becomes" sixteenth-century Ascoli, many citizens joining the parade clad in period costumes. This historical period is very important to the Ascolani as they celebrate annually the transfer of the "keys of the city" from civil magistrates back to the church. The ceremony is conducted in front of the cathedral of Saint Emidio, named after the city's German-born patron saint; he was Ascoli's first bishop and has protected the city from earthquakes and invasions since his death, so it is believed.

If you ask the Ascolani or Piceni (the countryside people) about their origins, you will be offered, in a modality that does not distinguish between history and mythology (since to them the word "origin" does not call for that distinction), a set of probable and not necessarily exclusive accounts. The descendants of Peucetios and his friends came from the Aegean seventeen generations before the Trojan War; or perhaps they were those Achaeans (in the Iliad) who came as pirates after defeating the Minoans; or Mycenaeans who emigrated to Italian shores after the destruction of Troy; or those called the Pelasgians. Who knows with certainty? "Certainly it was one or more of these groups. Look it up in the archaeological museum."

They like to tell the story of King Pico, the Italic, and his beloved Pomona, the goddess of gardens and fruit. Circe, jealous of such passion by the king that was not directed toward her, turned him into a woodpecker (*picchio*). In the guise of that transformation he led the homeless Sabines from upper-central Italy somewhat south and east of the Ascoli Piceno site. These Sabines were the "chosen" of the *ver sacrum*, also called *primavera Italica*, a ritual moment in which one-tenth of newborns were sacrificed (i.e., selected for a later social death) by a promise their parents had to make that in early adulthdood they were to leave for a new land. This is the favored later cultural origin story, considered supplemental to any one of the early Greek migration origin stories (Romanucci-Ross 1991).

We know that the Greeks knew of the people of Ascoli, for they referred to them as Askilaioi, and the Etruscans called them Asklaic. Linguistically, it appears that the Piceni were related to the Aegean-Anatolian area peoples by the end of the third millennium B.C. (Pulgram 1958:164). There is an oral tradition that passes on a folk explanation of the evolution of language and dialects using bits of archaeology, mythology, and phonology, which in some instances is not too far off the mark from what we know today from scant evidence (Lehman 1993).

In recorded history, Ascoli Piceno was once an ally of Rome and as such was encouraged to fight off the Gauls for Rome. Resenting the nature of such an alliance and the presence of Roman garrisons in their city, the Ascolani severed relations and by 269 B.C. they were at war. Losing the war, Ascolani became a vassal state, but, being considered a *civitas foederata,* it had the right to bestow military and political honors. By 90 B.C. the two cities were at war again, and acorn-shaped missiles with inscribed invectives can still be found in the museum. Any schoolchild knows about these events and will tell you "We never caved in to Rome" and were "never truly conquered." They further point out that Spartacus and his former slave gladiators defeated Roman soldiers very close to Asculum Picenum (as it was then known). It was on "that very slope" that leads down to the Tronto River, then known as the Truentum, that in 49 B.C. Julius Caesar himself stopped at the *Castrum Truentum* (camp of the Tronto); and it was there he said, "The die is cast."

The Ascolani may never have been truly conquered for a significant period of time, but their city and its environs became quite Romanized during the long period of nonconquest; the city was considered one of the best organized in Italy. It is not without pride that you will be shown the two ancient Roman bridges (one still in use), the Roman theater, and parts of the Roman wall that once surrounded the city.

Ascoli's height of involvement with Christianity occurred in 300 A.D., when Saint Emidio was its bishop. In 476 A.D.–though Rome had fallen–Christianity remained, since it had been (among other things) an anti-Roman sect. This period is memorialized in the Baptistry, still standing, and in statues of persons (found in the lower floor of the cathedral of Saint Emidio) who preferred death to renouncing Christianity.

Invaders came from the north: Goths, Franks, Vandals, and Longobards; the latter successful as the others were not in overrunning Ascoli. The Longobards left many marks to which the language, dialect, and remains will attest, and they stayed for centuries, the best example of becoming the people they had conquered. Circa 368 A.D. they captured the city already defeated by hunger and disease. Even some personal names (especially those of women, e.g., Isolina) are traceable to this cultural source. One can still find traces of Longobard necropoli in the countryside, and some Longobards are buried in the cathedral of Saint Emidio.

During the reign of the Longobards the papacy became powerful in a political sense and lands around the city were acquired by the church, often as gifts. Centers of monastic life had already taken root in the hills surrounding the city. These were contemporaneous with other characteristically medieval events, such as sending men off to the crusades, conflicts between noble families–which often symbolized church against state–and attempted invasions of the Adriatic Coast by Turks and others. "Better families" took refuge during these crises, in what are still called "Longobard towers." Everyone knows the names of some of the noble families, whether they sided with Guelph or Ghibelline, who took turns in power and control, for such names are still found on streets and buildings as well as in the local telephone directory.

These events are recalled as examples of the courage to perdure as a city-state, but so is the establishment of the commune of Ascoli Piceno, first organized legally in 1253. This was an interesting experiment in democratic governance even though it lacked representation for those who had neither property nor money (Fabiani 1957-1959, 1967). But it is important to note, in connection with repulsion of concepts for social reform, that the working class doubled as urban *and* rural workers. They did repair work, ran errands, and transported building materials and all manner of other objects for their employers. Their wives and children helped out with chores, they gave gifts (*regalia*) to the patrons (*padroni*) on certain holidays, and even "worked silk" for them in their leisure hours.

By the end of the eighteenth century, the army of Napoleon Bonaparte had reached Le Marche, which fell under French "protection." Some Ascolani had become—not knowing what it meant—"Republican." But because of their revolutionary ideals, the French had insulted religion and attacked the class structure by declaring their intent to abolish all titles of nobility; two unfortunate decisions to rich and poor alike in the city and the country.

The Neapolitans, too, under Spanish rule were beginning to attack nearby ports, and the spectacle of Spanish and French persons wandering in and out of the city brought on a great wariness and deep distrust of all protectors, governors, and governments. This led to a pervasive cynicism that is still the major influence on attitudes toward "the vote," now part of the democratic process. "France or Spain, as long as we eat" is often brought into a conversation on current political choices—meaning that it makes no difference who takes control—if only one can survive. The present "democracy," it is felt by many, merely facilitates corrupt practices and political favoritism.

Brigandage

Even prior to the purchased freedom from the French, this area of Italy shared the pan-Italic experience of brigandage. A locally born man called "Sciabolone" (brigands all had nicknames) hated the Jacobins; he and three hundred men ambushed a group of French soldiers and killed all of them. This ragged band took the city of Ascoli Piceno, as they shouted "Ave Maria." However, the French regained it—this time looting, burning, and killing. Nevertheless, they eventually had to ask for peace from the *briganti*; these were true early guerrilla fighters who took to the hills and attacked constantly.

After blows from the guerrillas, together with financial incentives (payments of large sums of money to France after Napoleon's defeat in 1815), the French left the city, helping themselves to precious manuscripts, paintings, sculptures, and other treasures as they left. Ascoli then became once more a papal state, leaving the people with little desire to join the new Italian nation.

In 1849, anti-Roman Republic brigandage was quite concentrated in Ascoli. In fact when the Piedmont army (of Italian unification) arrived in a village in the Piceno area on January 28, 1861, they were ambushed by guerrilla fighters. As the Piedmontese army fought with orders to "smash the Sacerdotal Empire" (Balena 1970:315), many Ascolani took to the woods and hills to fight again for the pope. The poor often joined the brigand leaders in hopes of getting land and rights of which they had been deprived. When combating the Roman Republic, brigands followed their leader, a young mountaineer called Giovanni Piccioni. He was the leader who, with his men, confronted General Pineili and the troops of Victorio Emanuele II. In every instance they were inspired and driven to fight foreign governments in the name of the Catholic faith, and Piccioni had a deep hatred for the troops of the future king of Italy, referring to them as "the anti-Christ."

Brigands were not always Robin Hoods or primitive rebels as some would have us think (see Hobsbawm 1959), but often worked for powerful patrons (Davis 1988:72). These romanticized figures operated with a sociopolitical background of food riots, tax riots, attacks on public officers, cattle rustling, kidnapping, and murder. Many women rode with their men and some were brigands in their own right. Brigands were common and are remembered in central Italy; *L`albero dei Piccioni*, the tree in which Piccioni and his men hid, still stands and carries his romanticized name.

More accurately, brigands were entrepreneurs who shifted alliances, but did not disdain help even from those with more noble motives or from the poor, who from time to time joined the sorties of brigand leaders. Brigand leaders conjured romance in their exploits and had names such as "Crocco" or "Serravalle." Nevertheless, they provided occasions for other significant events to co-occur—women as equal partners (if in crime only), the struggle for social justice (even as an epiphenomenal event), and the expulsion of the French (even if for less than purely patriotic motives).

From 1863 to 1865, brigandage died out in the Ascoli Piceno area. The brigands are remembered for driving out the French, although that was not the only reason for the French retreat from this area. The local assessment of the attempted importation of the ideals of the French Revolution were expressed as follows in dialect and in semijest: "Libertà e uqualianza! La moneta va en Franza e `*Ndri-ndri'* fa la panza" (Liberty and equality! The money goes to France. Rumblings of hunger in the belly).

More recently, there has been great pride over a group of young men bayoneted to death on September 12, 1943, a result of the resistance (*i partigiani*) bringing the battle to Ascoli and drawing German troops into the city. These men were thought valiant, but Saint Emidio was given the full credit for sparing the city from German assault and German bombs (presumably meant for Ascoli but dropped by mistake on nearby Macerata).

Recounting this "historical past remembered" is kept current in the names of the streets, or persons, through statues and the plan of the city; the architecture of the buildings, too, is a mnemonic device signaling these important identifying events. The city plan is an urban expression of the cosmology of the times, reflecting the ideal "Heavenly City." A resident, medieval painter Alemanno, portrayed Ascoli as such. The so-called Longobard towers remind them of the conflict and fractions led by noble families and the intruders from the north who came and stayed and became one people and one culture with them (red-haired, fair, and freckle-faced children often elicit Longobard invasion jokes). The modern buildings, mostly schools and offices, are reminders of the Fascist period of which only a few ever speak of at all—none with nostalgia (Romanucci-Ross 1991).

A First Reality

Events remembered are the first reality of an identity as a group that has a common experiential past. And part of this, in the heuristics of frequent recall, rests in the linguistic vein in the local dialect and its uses. Dialect is spoken primarily as an index of intimacy (family or close friends). Between associates it is a bid for trust, perhaps to establish a deal that can then be negotiated in politics or in business, or in the resolution of a conflictful situation. Shifting to the Italian language during such negotiations means "Are we coethnics or not? You begin to make me wonder."

No one seems to care very much about how the local dialect "*parlata Piceno*" (Piceno speak) really crystallized. Although, if asked, you will probably be told by many that it is presumed to be proto-Indo-European bandied about by Italics and Sabines, and maybe by the Volsci, Umbri, and Osci, all later considerably Latinized, as the archaeological evidence would suggest (Pulgram 1958). Interest peaks with discussion of Longobard words that entered not only the dialect, but the Italian language as well, parts of the vocabulary that deal mostly with the rustic life, a basic existence based on farming and hunting.

Longobard words are those for grains, birds, baskets, and mud (*bratta*). The Longobards, who lingered for centuries enriching and diversifying the genetic pool, also left words that described military events, artisan trades, body parts, and animal life (Romanucci-Ross 1991). The strata of cultural incursions are found in an archaeology of added vocabularies, including words they "know" as ancient Greek: the word for bread bin or kneading trough (*mattera*), or a "snotty-nosed child" (*mierceluse*), and the more recent and familiar Latin words for family members, roads, and the like. More pervasive and behavior determining than vocabulary, however, is the preserved conversational style, accompanied by the kinetics, or body language, regarded by many others in the rest of the world as incomparably eloquent and unique.

Although dialects might be more frequently used in rural areas in other countries, and in rural areas in other parts of Italy, this does not hold in the Piceno area. There it is emitted with ease and comfort in certain contexts, even from city dwellers, the affluent and the poor, the professional and the worker. There is, in fact, a current attempt to dignify and revitalize the dialect by journalists in newspapers, in tourist-attraction brochures, in recordings of songs of the past in the Piceno dialect, and by historical societies and literary groups. The aim is to create a new sense of ethnic belonging and to emphasize a uniqueness to be contrasted with other regions of Italy in a long history of a past rich in artistic and moral splendor and business acumen.

The Family

Formation of the ethnic personality, that part of the person that an individual presents to self and others, has a foundation in the historical memory of group identity, although this is perhaps not so manifest as the history of personal experience within that context. Both conditions are pathways of learning that are prescribed by ethnic belonging. The family has long been pronounced by culturologists as the prime instrument of acculturation; the individual's position in the constellation of family members is equally significant.

In contrast to American culture, in the Piceno area the strongest ties are not within the nuclear family of parents and children. In an emotional sense (and at times in a material way) such ties are fragile in comparison to the attachment to one's stem family. To understand the term "stem" as I have used it in kinship (Romanucci-Ross 1991:47-48), one has to recognize and give proper weight to the expression *il ceppo*, which is polysemic. It can mean the Christmas log that is meant to never burn out entirely, and from which a new log is lit, which in turn keeps alive the flame for its successor; in fact, *il focolare* (the hearth) is used as a synonym for family. *Il ceppo* may also refer to the male head of a family (at any point in time) who came to a *place* to begin a line of descendants. The literal meaning of trunk becomes the metaphorical trunk of the family tree.

This may not appear extraordinary, except that in this culture the *ceppo* may change over time depending on land ownership changes, or a venture that brings an accumulation of wealth from an unexpected quarter, or acquisition of a title (a remote possibility but not an inconceivable one). Psychological rather than strict genealogical forces in all such instances can be said to be the motivating principle in defining a new *ceppo* and the reckoning of a lineage. This is not to say that genealogical ties are denied or negated, but simply that in "the telling" or "writing," a person tends to select the *ceppo* of preference within the genealogy from his or her vantage point and to personal advantage.

Gendered spaces (i.e., where women may dwell and play a role) are crucially affected by ethnic belonging. If the groom has a widowed mother, the newlywed bride has a live-in mother-in-law whom she is expected to honor and obey as she does her husband. One does not hear complaints about this from young married women; it is accepted as the way things are and ought to be. Sometimes the eldest son is invited to bring his bride into the paternal home, where, according to local humor, one learns early who is to be in charge. At the wedding, someone (impersonating the groom's mother) will say "Enter my daughter—at this lintel you will leave all your bad habits and adopt all of mine."

The new bride knows she must never make public her husband's faults, but rather handle all the public relations aspects so as to hide them and publicize his virtues. She must uphold her husband's family's honor, even more than she did her own family's honor before the marriage (homicide for honor's sake was deleted from the Italian penal code as justifiable only in 1981) (Cantarella 1991).

In the parental role, neither parent is ever tempted to "be a friend" to the children. Parent-child bonds are strong, but they are always vertical and strengthened through discipline and a sense of social place and duty to honor, not friendship. As in Mexico (Romanucci-Ross 1986), mothers seek to bind their sons to them, knowing they will lose their daughters when they "marry out" of the family. This is not as neat and formulaic as it appears, however, for in the Piceno what married persons do in crucial or crisis moments manifests the very deep loyalties to the stem family of their birth. But even without crises, thoughts, acts, and financial resources are frequently directed toward members of the stem family.

Individuals play these roles within the family without too much analysis of them and without the agonistic displays that are sometimes seen in other parts of Italy or other cultures (Romanucci-Ross 1985). There is an awareness that at times the cost of certain ties is high and that perhaps it does not have to be this way, But if you ask how they feel about this, you are likely to be told of the advantages rather than the disadvantages of the cultural prescriptions and proscriptions concerning family duties and obligations.

It is interesting to observe and analyze how children are reared to become what they must be for their immediate and future family roles (see Romanucci-Ross 1991:56-63). My purpose here, however, is to indicate briefly that family membership and its expression is part of the ethnic personality within the context of ethnic identity.

Separation rituals (from the family) begin quite early, with baptism and the recognition of a unique soul. This is followed in prepubescence by communion and confirmation for membership in the wider family, i.e., the community of the Catholic church. The marriage rite is a presumed definite (but not always actual) separation from the family of one's birth. Godparenthood is a superimposition of the fictive family, a further affirmation of the parental concept but with an overlay of the notion that substitution *is* possible should it become necessary. *Comparaggio* (godparenthood) also strengthens bonds between biological and fictive parents, bonds that are often used in business deals, in conflict resolution, or in deciding where one goes for favors.

The Church Family

Immediately beyond the "family in this world" constellation is the apparitional family structure of the administrators of the spiritual realm: the fathers, sisters, mother abbesses, and brothers of the church. These are ideal behavioral models, considered just a bit above the grasp of ordinary persons without vocations. Beyond these, the saints are models of perfection in behavior, symbols of the possibility of transcendence "to real meaning" in worldly existence. Though very few can obtain sainthood, it remains a refulgent transforming goal to a God-like being, in this world and beyond.

The local saints are considered of great importance for the young to emulate: there is Santa Rita da Cascia, for example, who lived and died in a fifteenth-century village on the crest of the Apennines. Married to a drunk who was often brutal and was later murdered, she prayed that her two sons would die before they could avenge their father's murder. This they both did and she, as it is said, "regained her freedom" (De Marchi 1969:47-49) to join a convent, perform miracles, and become a saint. The lesson for local women? *Amor fati*, love your fate. Think only of pleasing the Lord.

Saint Serafino was so poor he had to work for a *contadino* (a sharecropper who already works for someone else). In Saint Serafino we find an illiterate who had a calling to preach and to spread the faith. Seeking out discomfort and humiliation, badly treated by everyone in his own family he, like Santa Rita, was eventually revered for his healing miracles. His behavioral model for young men: spurn the pursuit of wealth for it is harmful to the spirit.

Saint Francis preached in Ascoli, arriving in 1226 to establish his order. The church at that time was on one side of the *Piazza del Popolo*, and a thirteenth-century cathedral named after him still stands in that place. Ascoli has a convent of the Poor Claires, founded by his good friend, Santa Chiara (Giorgi 1968).

Fathers and sisters of the church offer models for taking vows of poverty and chastity. They, along with the saints, link "good sons and daughters" from secular families to the larger all-embracing spiritual family. The Ascolani have never relinquished that part of their identity that was shaped by the Catholic church. The urban center of about sixty thousand people has a great (some say inordinate) number of churches and several cathedrals, a fact constantly remarked upon by the residents to visitors and tourists. Without its being viewed as contradictory, even as contrapuntal, you will be shown the statue of Cecco d'Ascoli (Francesco Stabili), the scientist-magician, an original and free thinker who defied the church by lecturing and writing that all could be learned by studying nature and the stars. He was burned alive at the stake in Florence in 1327, along with all his writings. Other naturalist-astronomers such as Cecco are now seen as forerunners of modern science. It has been noted that others who expressed antichurch sentiments were not burned at the stake; but Cecco was arrogant, pouty, and never given to compromise, traits that made him thoroughly Ascolano, the ultimate *scontroso* (a pouting and sulky person). And for that, he is theirs (Crespi).

Time and Identity

In reckoning group identity, time is not only linear and vertical, as in historical remembering or genealogical reckoning, it is also horizontal in the sense that it is cyclical, repetitive, and predictable. From planting to harvesting of vegetables, cereals, and fruits; from hard work to festivals and joy in the countryside—the shared rhythms of labor and celebration of its rewards is an ever-renewing bond.

The men's heavy work of plowing, seeding, and planting in early spring leads to lesser but still demanding work (by men and women) in the fields and gardens. They plant tomatoes, peppers, beans, onions, lettuce, etc., in March and April, and continue to hoe and weed around the young plants as they grow. During the summer months fruits and vegetables are ripening while being attended by appropriate rainfall and constant care by the villagers who watch the progress with both apprehension and pride. If nature cooperates, collective expectations lead to the "beautiful" months of harvest.

Harvesting wheat and other cereals in July, gathering vegetables from June on, enjoying the sequence of fruits and berries all summer long, picking grapes in early autumn and shaking chestnuts and olives from the trees around November, along with cutting wood for winter—those who work the land like the repetitive cycle but fear the possible bitter surprises, or even disaster. One keeps an eye on the sky as one walks through the just-about-ready-to-harvest field of hay or wheat that can be ruined by a sudden cruel outburst of hail. An untimely frost can "burn" the tender buds on the fruit trees or young shoots of plants overnight, and one is forced to reseed if one can afford the expense; even ever-elusive money cannot save the crops that will rot if the fields are flooded. The suspense renders the harvest a blessing, and some villages have their village feast day in September, with a procession that begins in the church, led by the statue of the Madonna.

The blossoming of flowers reminds the person of love (in all its varieties, the constancies and betrayals, hopes, and desperate sense of loss). It is said that the appearance of each flower is a specific reminder. There are many feast days, in addition to universal Christian holidays; these include a special day to the Madonna, one to a saint to protect the farm animals, and to the purification period for Mary after the birth of Jesus. Feast days are also perceived as reminders of the need for protection from the unpredictable and for celebration of community.

Community and Conflict

In the community, village or urban, an individual is defined by many recognized hierarchies: occupation, status, gender, age, sex-role, and demeanor as to manner of dress, addressing others, and presenting the self. The urban center also has communities within it—the *sestieri* (sections of the city), which give an even more intimate sense of community. Residents of the various sections run *their* horse and jockey in the *palio*. For the sense of community does not mean equality or a sense of solidarity and certainly does not exclude rivalries and conflict in city or country. Patronage systems give rise to factions, and communal land, private landholdings, and collective land use create much to negotiate about—most often not harmoniously. Disputes over collective land use or water use were common historically in central Italy (Davis 1988) and the Piceno area was no exception. Disputes still arise over boundaries of even the smaller plots of land, over a "misplaced" fence line around the house, over seeding, over water use, over firewood, over rights to animal grazing, or even over the question of where and when a neighbor's chickens might wander.

In fact, conflict has the very important function of positioning a family or a lineage in the hierarchy of control and respect. In a village I focused upon for countryside ethnography, one conflict over water lasted many decades. It was settled only after the solicited intervention of magistrates and administrators from the *comune* and letters of admonition from a married couple who had gone to live in the United States (a couple that had united the two lineages in marriage). When I expressed relief that there might be peace now I was told, "Don't count on it. Those two families will always find something to fight over." Clearly that has proven to be the case, since I have found at least half a dozen other conflicts between them: about roads, night lighting, parking, and fences. One of these incidents merited a write-up in an Ascoli city newspaper, referring to the misplaced fence around a house in the village as the "Berlin Wall." Villagers noted that urban conflicts can occasionally be just as trivial. But placing the squabbles of this village in the history-writ-large context became a point for city laughter. As I drove up to the village with an Italian Ascolana friend, she said, "Who shall we visit first—the

Guelphs or the Ghibellines?" "They need each other," I replied, "that's how they know who they are."

And that appears to be the purpose of conflict; it rarely erupts into violence, murder, or destruction of property. To contain and *maintain* the conflict, to contain one's anger, to use the tort in presenting the self in other contexts demonstrates that one is evolved, civilized, and unlike, for example, the southerners who are considered emotionally incontinent about all things and in all events. It was actually a strategy at times to allow one's adversary to "win" (by not going-to-the-wall, so to speak), and then to assume a moral stance of "bearing it" without violence or recrimination. Such attitudes toward conflict and conflict resolution allowed these people to further contrast their behavior to groups in other regions of Italy and even other parts of the world, all of them "lesser breeds" without a moral law or knowledge of smart gamesmanship.

Other scholars have noted that one very important and neglected area in Italian studies is the working of the criminal courts and criminal law in Italy. I agree with Davis (1988:87) in noting that *any* knowledge, though not yet systematized, of this area demonstrates how deeply many of the more fundamental institutions of the state were (and are) rooted in the everyday experience of Italian life (Pompeiano, Fazio, and Raffaele 1985).

The Aesthetics of Shaping Ethnic Identity

In the years of Emperor Augustus, the Piceno area was known as the *Provincia Flaminia*. Fruits, cereals, "cooked wines," and stuffed olives were supplied to Rome. Biscuits known in Rome as *panis Picentinum* were singled out by Pliny as notable fare.

The ingestion of food, and the manner and timing of it, are linked to health and body image. "Well-upholstered" women and "padded" male bodies were considered healthy. These values were expressed in the context of possible disease states, "The fat ones only grow thin, the thin ones die." Foods are classified as heavy or light, with the designated need for balance. Where foods originate is very important; cultivation within the Piceno area is highly regarded, especially for certain crops such as olives and lentils. But even for other comestibles, there is the problem of how to know what the witches from other parts of Italy will do to their crops if they are thought to be for export.

In certain Italian contexts (illness or malaise) some foods are transformed into medicines. Decoctions or infusions of herbs grown locally are often sought by patients, even those from adjoining provinces who hope to find a cure they did not find at home. They come for this in conjunction with a search for intervention by special saints, both major and minor, who have shrines, monasteries, or churches named after them.

There is another long history of events that keeps reinforcing the ethnic bonds in the Piceno in the form of many miraculous cures effected in the area over the centuries. The trajectory of a person's experiences is, always and everywhere, in large part, a narrative of experiencing the world as the body allows, does not allow or "interprets," providing metaphors and nourishing the imagination (Romanucci-Ross 1991:136).

On beauty: the heavenly city was meant to be filled with beautiful people. Accordingly, the aesthetics of physical beauty include the ideal of Praxitelean symmetry for the body, facial grace of the Madonnas of Raphael or Sassoferrato for women, and Michelangelo's paintings and sculpture for men. Skin color should be very light, hair and eye color do not matter, shape of leg is very important, body contours crucial. Tall and curvilinear bodies are preferred, "*fatt'a pennello*" (fashioned by the artist's brush) is the supreme compliment for that. A surprising number of young people can be found who approach this, but the key word is "approach."

No sooner is one pronounced *fatt'a pennello* when a moment of silence occurs, followed by rapid critiques. I think of it as the search-and-destroy method of finding minor blemishes and slight asymmetries. What will be recalled of a young person in discussions of beauty (which are quite frequently topics of conversation) is that fraction of that year in which perfection was reached, after which the "sagging" began here and there. The person became *sciupato* (spoiled), like any fruit that is a bit overripe (though a woman's face may reapproach beauty during pregnancy—although perhaps only the first one).

The almost unattainable ideals followed by appraisals and the grading system soon reduce everyone to the same aesthetic rubble, which has the strange effect of converting physical beauty to something of little or no importance. (This is not unlike the "overfixing" of the outcomes of *palio* races, which has the final effect of their not being fixed at all.) If people of other parts of the world find these exercises comic, they are not considered so in the Piceno. It is *important* to know what beauty is in an ideal sense and to strive for it—in mating, if nothing else. It is important to think of all the possibilities in a game: both are survival techniques for one's progeny.

Ascolani distinguish themselves aesthetically from their neighbors, near and far. People from a northern province are said to have "crooked legs" (a spite song refers to them as such); a group to the south is said to be "too short" and "too robust," and many other points of differences are noted with other groups. The admonishment not to marry out of your city/countryside is meant also to prevent miscegenation with people from such groups. Yet, at the same time, one hears, "*Non è bello quel ch'e bello, è bello quel che piace*" (Beautiful is not beautiful unless it pleases one).

Why? Because true beauty is in gracious behavior. The child is taught to cultivate a pleasant-sounding voice and not to be *sgarbato* (lacking in grace and elegance, politeness, and correctness).

From Childhood to Adulthood

Because it is not believed that one is in control of one's own destiny, it is important that as the child develops, he or she be taught moral strategies. Ethics and aesthetics therefore appear to be one and the same when socializing and acculturating the child, and they are the source of the meaning of virtue. The goal of the effort, for parents and child, is to be thought by others to be a good person and not to "cut a bad figure" (*fare brutta figura*). (You exist in the gaze of the others, as I indicated earlier.) One must not lack in graciousness of manner or in dependability. People who don't behave ethically are *brutta gente* (ugly people).

One can do much to control the opinion that others will have of you. It is extremely important to negotiate every encounter, no matter how trivial, with that in mind: how do you handle the unwelcome caller, reciprocate a gift, and handle a rebuff, real or imagined? The child must learn to manage small encounters that require "exquisite calibration of boundaries of time, space and affect" (Romanucci-Ross 1991:177). Survival, the child is taught, will often be found to be in correct self-perception and self-correction. This area of development of the ethnic personality is frequently commented upon and contrasted to analogs in other parts of Italy. To the outsider, such preoccupation with this aspect of child rearing that follows one in adulthood may appear to be an obsession.

Romantic love is a dangerous game to play, and you will be told that "most people here" do not marry for "that kind of love." It was that kind of love that led to the great passions that destroyed Romeo and Juliet, Tristan and Isolde, Paolo and Francesca, and so on. A woman who loves her husband in *that* way is not to be trusted to handle his affairs, his business, his reputation. Her personal fantasies about him will render her irrational, and perhaps not even a good mother. Even extramarital affairs are never discussed in terms of romantic love. This does not mean that romantic love unions never occur; unquestionably a number do. What is important, however, in terms of child rearing and *expectations* is that romantic love is considered best left to other less prudent cultures, that is, exoticized.

There is constant instancing of bad outcomes that follow romantic love unions. The pragmatic approach to marriage is counseled: *moglie e buoi dei paesi tuoi* (wives and bulls should be from your region). There is a complex volitional interplay among relatives and friends as a young man (or woman) approaches the choosing of a spouse. Proper social contacts for appraisal are at times arranged by local priests at church functions, but most often by female relatives of both sides of the families who might be affected by such a union. Mothers of sons are always on the lookout for a suitable daughter-in-law who will bear their grandchildren. A father is concerned about the type of man to whom he will be bequeathing a daughter he loves and has reared. Such practices are very similar to customs in ancient Rome (Treggiari 1991). Thus, marriage rules, like food preferences, enjoy a robust cultural continuity in this area.

Ethnic Identity as Theatre

Some aspects of ethnic identity exemplify the radiation effect of similar historical events over a wide geographic area. No part of Italy, for example, escaped the reckless but regular intervals of invasions by expansionist groups seeking to extend their boundaries. Some armies, such as the French to the northwest and the Spanish from the south, covered wide regions, at times overlapping in the Piceno area. Arabic invaders from the southeast would hit the coastal area but were concentrated more to the south. All of them left cultural artifacts—material, linguistic, and artistic (visual and musical)—in their wake, as the waves of invasions retreated after periods of occupation. Some strategies for cultural survival, then, were pan-Italic and shared over a large area; among these, how to wait and how to perdure.

The manner in which many non-Italian historians write about such strategies, however, shows a lack of understanding. This is exemplified in the Elizabethan period in the perversion of Machiavelli's thought by English writers, turning this astute observer into a master of deceit. In fact, Machiavelli merely recorded his observations about what a wise prince *should* know (about human motivation and political strategies) if he wanted to maintain peace and retain power (Musa 1961); it was also about how to behave in the *polis*. This Elizabethan view of history was exacerbated in recent times by the Italian journalist, Luigi Barzini (1965), who found it amusing and profitable to *select* facts to fit his baroque portrait of "the Italians."

Among Piceno pan-Italic characteristics is the acceptance of conflict (perhaps even the necessity of it), the absolute need to contain it, and the strategies with which to accomplish the containment. Theatricalized (perhaps much as the ancient Greek plays were a community catharsis) in a yearly competition, the *Quintana* (or *palio*) of Ascoli Piceno pits the various sections of the city against each other in a horse race. Each of the sections sponsors its own horse and jockey. The winner gets the *palio*, the prized cloth given to the winner and his section to keep for a year (Zeigler 1994:163-166). This ritual and ceremonial celebration dates back to the twelfth century. By the fifteenth century its military aspect in Ascoli was replaced by symbolic combat in games that featured skill and grace within a framework of theatrical elegance. Several Italian cities featured such an event. The tradition in

Ascoli is very old, analogous to those of Siena, Asti, and Fermo, the rival city of Ascoli. (Fermo and Ascoli Piceno, neighboring city-states, had sought each other out for occasional small "wars," as was the custom in Italy; Firenze and Pisa and Perugia and Assisi were other examples of "warring pairs" in proclamations of distinctiveness.)

Dundes and Falassi (1975) have described in some detail and with interesting interpretation the *palio* of Siena. In what I consider a particularly insightful description of the preparations, they note that races are said to be "fixed," and also "counterfixed" with innumerable deals and planning. But this, as they note, guarantees it is so overfixed that it is not fixed at all. Although they drop the argument there, I should like to carry it a bit further, to consider as it would be used in the Piceno context. To the outsider it may appear to be an exercise in futility, amusing or comic to the extreme. But to the Piceni (and perhaps the Sienese?) it is an important exercise, a honing of skills, a game in which you must try to assess every possible strategy of the other and to know which negotiations might fail, and in what manner. After all, in Ascoli during the horse race, as each jockey races around the track he *also* "fights" a "Moor" with a lance once during each lap, needing to displace a wooden attachment to score a point. Skills against the Moor are sharpened in the practice of skills against each other.

The same "game theory" aspects can be seen in the strategies of the Italian soccer team. A sports writer for the 1994 International Soccer Competitions compared Coach Arrigo Sacchi's changing styles as an affront to the usual way soccer is to be played. For example, he would switch his lineup to 4-4-2, after everyone thought it would be 4-3-3. "They play defensively, just trying not to lose, and then—no one was ever quite sure how—they scored in the winning goal, apparently improvising, making things happen as they went along" (Zeigler 1994).

In making inquiries the sports writer was told: "This is a country of organized chaos. The old way or Italian soccer, called *cantenaccio*, mirrored Italian life" (Zeigler 1994). Sacchi agreed and admitted that Italian culture is not suited to his kind of soccer—to run constantly and always be in control of the ball. But the soccer players do not heed their coach; they decide what to do as they play. Sacchi and the "demigod" forward Baggio argued publicly about how the game should be played before the semifinals. Should they pass more and run less or vice versa? The coach finally exclaimed in desperation: "They ought to run more and talk less" (Zeigler 1994).

In the past thirty-one games, the Azzurri had thirty-one different starting lineups. They won the semifinals and faced Brazbyzanil for the World Cup, losing by one point in the penalty-kicking postgame, post-extra-time period. One can agree with some game theorists that the only certain way to win is to not know yourself what your next move will be, for then how can anyone strategize from these expectations? It may appear to the outsider as organized chaos. But it may have occurred to the observed that it is good for them that the observer should think that about such strategies.

To the Wall of Unintelligibility

The Piceno person is well adapted to his or her ethnic niche and has learned how to deflect intrusions into the many accommodations needed in daily living. When they go to other parts of Italy they often encounter many difficulties and, as Kertzer has noted, problems caused by the presence of a person from another region erase whatever bonds of solidarity may have accrued on the job or in a political party as far as relating to that person is concerned (1980:169-175).

Persons from the Piceno area who immigrated to the United States in the early decades of this century (during the great waves of European immigration) came to a country where there was one dominant cultural group. Like many other ethnic groups from European countries they learned that the strategies that worked so well at home had to be redefined and reevaluated. The new standards were the values of the English-speaking dominant culture, whose bearers had found the previous waves of immigrants (German and Irish) not totally to their tastes but more like themselves than the newcomers (Romanucci-Ross 1987).

The Piceni, like many groups from Italy, found themselves isolated and burlesqued; they were especially not accustomed to the latter, as they found themselves lumped with Neapolitans, Sicilians, and others. Many Piceni returned home. Those who stayed had to learn that the sorting devices of ethnicity in Italy had to be recalibrated in this new land, yet they did not feel comfortable with the southerners and felt closer to the Tuscans, even though these were thought to be too "cold and unfeeling," not religious enough, and irritating as they constantly quoted lines from Dante, always noting that *their* dialect had become the tongue of Italy.

There were radically different outcomes in such accommodations, depending on the section of the United States in which the immigrants settled (Rolle 1968). Throughout, all Italians were studied (as though they were homogeneous) to test hypotheses about cultural maladjustment. Most studies stressed lack of mobility and indicated that Italians "huddled" in extended family groups and in certain city neighborhoods. (Contemporary studies show that Mexicans and other recent immigrants also huddle in the same way.) Indeed, as should surprise no one (not even social scientists), those from certain regions of Italy tended to live in proximity to each other in certain neighborhoods, or in certain parts of the United States (Nelli 1970). Still, they all distinguished themselves from the culture of the host country, as well as the culture of ethnic groups from other regions of Italy. Each group still prefers its own cuisine, its own marriage customs, its own concepts of child rearing. However, culture has recursiveness as one of its major features; the children and grandchildren tend more and more to go to the country and region of their parents—to take vacations, to study, to write, to paint, to compose, and even in some instances to marry. And they often marvel that their parents had survived in America as immigrants without knowledge of language or custom.

But their parents and grandparents survived (Gambino 1974) because they shared a view of life that is "right out of Pirandello," the Sicilian playwright. Life is a series of layers of reality and fiction, and maneuvering in and out of these layers is the only way to get through it relatively intact. Such metaknowledge had served them well in the millennia filled with new invaders who culturally had little in common with their invading predecessors. What good to them, to spend your life accommodating to details of foreign cultural content?

People from the different regions who come from different *ethnes* were not unaware of the irony of all being labeled "Italian" (or by more indelicate references to mean "Italian" in some instances). But they retained the lessons learned in childhood: see yourself reflected in the eyes of others and do, or pretend to do, what is necessary for personal and cultural survival. Personal and cultural identity are one, for you cannot lose one without losing the other. Still, they did not hesitate to incorporate new strategies and retain former schemata with modifications in new accommodations. They were able to experience those things that may have required some flexibility but did not touch the sense of authenticity. At home or school, Italians know that when a situation is different, *they* must be different, as has happened many times over the millennia of their recorded history.

It is still difficult to assess accurately what happened to various ethnic groups in America (those who were already here, those who came of their own will, or those who were brought here against their will) in the relatively brief history of the United States. But the immigrant experiences of the people of the Piceno, those who return or their progeny who return to the old country, have a certain impact on their region. It has been further intensified by the new re-ethnicization of the world, but it had begun years before. There are many attempts within the Piceno area to reaffirm and revitalize ethnic identity. This is done through "celebration" of dialect, historical commemorations, food festivals, promotion of herbal and other alternative folk-healing methods (even by pharmacists), folk music, architectural restorations, and refurbishing of historic buildings and houses.

The Will to Identity

All of the above activities are reminders to group members of how they contrast with other groups. The Piceni did not—and they are adamant about this in prose and print—have an ethnic identity thrust upon them. It is theirs, fashioned by historic events to be sure, but events in which they made choices or, in other words, "chose to remain free." Free to be a papal state, or free to be a republic-city-state (with the countryside villages always at their side); free to celebrate the events that defined them. Importantly, they also felt free to reject the ideologies that did *not* define them, e.g., the ideals of the French Revolution such as "the tree of liberty" that French soldiers placed in their piazzas along with their ("foolish") ideas about liberty, fraternity, and equality. In the freedom to reject ideologies foreign to them or accept those to which they feel a congeniality, the referentials are the matrices, one within the other, of a long and rich historical past and the treasured values within it, families, worldly and spiritual concerns, and the ever-creating, ever-correcting self.

REFERENCES

Ariès, Philippe. 1960. *L'enfant et la vie sociale sous L'Ancien Regime*. Paris: Plon.

Balena, Secondo. 1970. *Ascoli nel Piceno*. Ascoli Piceno: G. Cesari.

Barzini, Luigi. 1965. *The Italians; A Full Length Portrait Featuring Their Manners and Morals*. New York: Atheneum.

Bateson, Gregory, and Margaret Mead. 1942. *Balinese Character: A Photographic Analysis*. Special Publications, Vol. II. New York: New York Academy of Sciences.

Cantarella, Eva. 1991. "Homicides of Honor: The Development of Italian Adultery Law over Two Millennia." In *The Family in Italy from Antiquity to the Present*. David I. Kertzer and Richard P. Saller, eds. Pp. 229-246. New Haven: Yale University Press.

Crespi, A. 1927. *L'Acerba*. Turin: no publisher.

Davis, John A. 1988. *Conflict and Control; Law and Order in Nineteenth Century Italy*. New York: McMillan Education.

De Marchi. 1969. *Santa Rita de Cascia*. Bari: Edizioni Paolini.

Derrida, Jacques. 1967. *La voix et le phenomène*. Paris: Plon.

Devereux, George. 1982, 2d ed. "Ethnic Identity: Its Logical Foundations and Its Dysfunc tions." In *Ethnic Identity: Cultural Continuities and Change*." George A. De Vos and Lola Romanucci-Ross, eds. Pp. 42-70. Chicago: University of Chicago Press.

De Vos, George A., and Lola Romanucci-Ross, eds. 1982, 2d ed. *Ethnic Identity in Cultural Continuity and Change*. Chicago: University of Chicago Press.

Dundes, Alan, and Alessandro Falassi. 1975. *La Terra in Piazza: An Interpretation of the Palio of Siena*. Berkeley: University of California Press.

Fabiani, G. 1957-1959. *Archivio Storico del Comune di Ascoli*, Vol. I:9-32. Ascoli Piceno: Società Tipolitografica.

Fabiani, G. 1967. *Ascoli nel Ottocento*: Ascoli Piceno: Società Tipolitografica.

Gambino, Richard. 1974. *Blood of My Blood: The Dilemma of Italian-Americans*. New York: Doubleday.

Giorgi, Raniero. 1968. *Les Clarisse in Ascoli*. Ascoli Piceno: Tipografia Fermo.

Hobsbawm, E. J. 1959. *Primitive Rebels: Studies in Archaic Forms of Social Movement in the 19th and 20th Centuries.* Manchester: Manchester University Press.

Hodges, H. A. 1952. *The Philosophy of Wilhelm Dilthey.* London: Routledge and Paul.

Kertzer, David I. 1980. *Comrades and Christians; Religion and Political Struggle in Communist Italy.* Cambridge: Cambridge University Press.

Lehman, Winfried P. 1993. *Theoretical Bases of Indo-European Linguistics.* London: Routledge.

Mead, George Herbert. 1934. *Mind, Self and Society.* Charles Morris, ed. Chicago: University of Chicago Press.

Mead, Margaret. 1930. *Growing Up in New Guinea.* New York: Morrow.

Mead, Margaret. 1975 (1st ed., 1956). *New Lives for Old; Cultural Transformation—Manus.* New York: Morrow.

Musa, Mark. 1964. *Machiavelli's "The Prince."* New York: St. Martin's Press.

Nelli, H. S. 1970. *The Italians in Chicago 1880-1930; A Study in Ethnic Mobility.* New York: Oxford University Press.

Petrusewicz, M. 1978. "Signori e Briganti: Repressione del Brigantaggio nel Periodo Francese in Calabria Caso Barracco." In *Storia e Cultura del Mezzogiorno: Study in Memoria di U. Caldora Cosenza.* Pp. 333-346. Press unnamed.

Pompeiano, D., I. Fazio, and G. Raffaele. 1985. *Controllo Sociale e Criminalità.* Milan: Mondadori.

Pulgram, Ernest. 1958. *The Tongues of Italy: Prehistory and History.* Cambridge, MA: Harvard University Press.

Rolle, Andrew, F. 1968. *The Immigrant Upraised; Italian Adventurers and Colonists in an Expanding America.* Berkeley: University of California Press.

Romanucci-Ross, Lola. 1985. *Mead's Other Manus; Phenomenology of the Encounter.* South Hadley, MA: Bergin and Garvey.

Romanucci-Ross, Lola. 1986. *Conflict, Violence and Morality in a Mexican Village.* Chicago: University of Chicago Press.

Romanucci-Ross, Lola. 1987. "Von ethnologoi: Die Erfahrungen das Einwanderers." In *Die wilde Seele: Zur Ethnopsychoanlyze von Georges Devereux.* Hans Peter Duerr, ed. Pp. 383-397. Frankfurt: Suhrkampf Verlarung.

Romanucci-Ross, Lola. 1991. *One Hundred Towers: An Italian Odyssey of Cultural Survival.* New York and Westport, CT: Bergin and Garvey.

Treggiari, Susan. 1991. *Roman Marriage: Iusti Congiuges from the Time of Cicero to the Time of Ulpian.* Oxford: Clarendon.

Zeigler, Mark. 1994. "Baggio Scores Twice as Italy Stops Bulgaria." *San Diego Union,* Section D, p. 8, col. 6, July 20.

PART II ■

Fabrication of New Ethnic Enclaves

STEVAN HARRELL ■

Chapter Four

Languages Defining Ethnicity in Southwest China

Liangshan, or "The Cool Mountains," is a region of rugged, often vertical topography sandwiched between the high plateaus of Tibet to the west and the gentle hills and fertile plains of central China to the east and northeast. Its people are as diverse as its landscapes—they inhabit a cultural and ethnic border region between the Buddhist civilization of Tibet, which has its most southeasterly influence here, and the imperial and postimperial civilization of China, whose westward expansion did not bring administrative control over Liangshan until the 1950s.

There are two main ranges in the Liangshan. Neither are inhabited primarily by Chinese or Tibetans, but by descendants of ethnolinguistic groups that lived in the region before the recent spread of Chinese and Tibetan influence and power. In the eastern range or Great Liangshan, the population is predominantly Nuosu, or Liangshan Yi. In the western, or Lesser Liangshan, the Nuosu are joined by the Qiangic-speaking groups formerly known as Xifan, or "western barbarians" and by various other Yi-speaking groups that have entered the area from neighboring Yunnan and Guizhou. There are a sizable number of Han Chinese, both long-term resident peasants and, recently, immigrant cadres and teachers, a few Hui, or Chinese-speaking Muslims—mostly traders originally—and pockets of Miao and Lisu who seem to have come as refugees from fighting in areas to the east or the west, respectively.

This chapter explores three kinds of languages used to speak or write about this ethnic mosaic and the relations among the people who comprise the mosaic. The first language is the scholarly one of *ethnohistory*—the geographic and temporal story of the location and movement of peoples, presuming for the sake of argument that there are such things as peoples, civilizations, and cultures. This presents the background necessary to understanding the next two languages.

The second language is that of the *state discourse of ethnic classification*, or *minzu shibie*, through which the Chinese authorities have identified every citizen of this area (and of the rest of the People's Republic) as members of one or another *minzu*, or ethnic category (Fei 1980; Lin 1987). All official communications use this language of ethnic identification.

The third kind of languages are those of *ethnic identity*—the ways in which local people communicate, to themselves and each other, their membership in ethnic groups that they themselves perceive and in terms of which they interact in everyday life. The languages of ethnic identity include both languages in the literal sense —the vernaculars in which local people speak and write—and other kinds of behaviors that communicate meanings concerning ethnic group membership and relations. These latter languages include what are often called "ethnic markers"—dress, food, marriage patterns, rituals, and customs generally (Schwartz 1975; Keyes 1981:7-10).

These three kinds of languages operate, in the first instance at least, on different levels. The first two are metalanguages—ethnohistory and ethnic classification are used to talk about ethnic relations. The languages of ethnic identity, on the other hand, are practical languages, used *in the practice of* ethnic relations. But the distinction between metalanguage and practical language is not absolute. People practicing ethnicity in their everyday life have occasion to talk about it—to discuss who is who, who marries whom, and who got here first—and outside analysts influence local practice, particularly when the analysts are representatives of a powerful state that distributes many resources according to official ethnic category membership. In real life, then, practical languages and metalanguages overlap.

There is, however, a much more important distinction between at least one of the metalanguages and the practical languages. The official metalanguage of ethnic classification assumes the equivalence of categories. Everyone is a member of a particular *minzu*, and all *minzu* are, theoretically at least, defined according to the same criteria—those set out by Josef Stalin in his essay on the Nationalities Question (Stalin 1935). What makes one *minzu* a *minzu* is the same thing that makes any other *minzu* a *minzu*. In the practical languages, by contrast, groups are not necessarily equivalent—they "speak" about themselves in different kinds of terms, using different criteria for membership, different signs of identity or separation, different degrees of clarity or fuzziness of boundaries, and different possibilities of discrete or overlapping group membership.

Because the metalanguage of ethnic classification and the practical languages of ethnic identity influence each other, real life in an ethnically diverse area such as Liangshan consists of interactions among groups that are like each other in one sense (they are all *minzu*, defined according to certain criteria) and different in another (they speak about themselves and others in various ways). This means that real life is complicated, and that ethnic relations take on a great variety of forms. I will illustrate that in this chapter with reference to ethnic groups inhabiting the Lesser (western) Liangshan area. I first give a brief account of this area in the metalanguage of ethnohistory. Then I describe the principles of ethnic classification followed by the Chinese state and recount how they were and are used to determine the *minzu* categories now operating in Liangshan. Finally, the bulk of the chapter consists of descriptions of the use of practical languages of ethnic identity by two groups—the Nuosu, or Liangshan Yi, who communicate their ethnicity in terms of sharp in-group/out-group boundaries, and the Prmi, whose ethnic identity is historically contingent and differs from place to place.

Ethnohistory

It is not clear who inhabited the Lesser Liangshan area in the pre-Imperial period (before 221 B.C.), but in the *History of the Latter Han Dynasty*, there is mention of a kingdom of Bailang in this area, whose king sent ambassadors to the Han court in Loyang, and some of whose songs were recorded by the court historians. Ethnolinguistic analysis by Chen Zongxiang (Chen and Deng 1979, 1991) and others suggests that the language recorded (in Chinese characters, of course) in that account is related to the modern Qiangic languages, spoken by the Xifan or Prmi people in this area. If so, the Prmi can claim to be, if not the original inhabitants, at least the earliest ones who are still there.

Better established is the fact that today's Prmi people speak one of the perhaps twelve or so languages belonging to the Qiangic subfamily of Tibeto-Burman (Matisoff 1991), and that the other languages of this small family are distributed along what is probably a historical migration corridor from the Qinghai or northeastern Tibet area south through the series of deep, north-south river valleys that parallel the eastern edge of the Tibetan plateau. This seems to indicate that speakers of this group of languages migrated southward along this route, culminating in the Prmi, who are the southernmost Qiangic speakers.

The Naze (or Mosuo), other early inhabitants of this area, also claim a northwestern origin. They may have come along the same route as the Prmi, or they may have entered from the southwest. The latter is where the Naze and their close linguistic relatives, the Naxi, initially established small chiefdoms during the middle Tang Dynasty (seventh and eighth centuries), which continued during the period of the hegemony of the Nanchao and Dali kingdoms, from the ninth to the thirteenth centuries (Shih 1993:25-26). Naze and Prmi have lived intermingled in this area for hundreds of years and intermarry freely in many areas.

From the fourteenth through the sixteenth century, Tibetan Buddhism began to spread into the Lesser Liangshan area. Monasteries of the red, or Karma-pa sect, were established as early as the fourteenth or fifteenth century. The Gelugpa, or orthodox Yellow sect, which assumed the government of Tibet in 1642 (Goldstein 1989:1), also began to build monasteries and to convert the population of Prmi and Naze peoples beginning in the mid-sixteenth century (Shih 1993:180-182). The Monk-ruler of Muli, whose kingdom was established at the beginning of the Gelugpa ascendancy over Tibet, spread his administration into what is now northern Yanyuan at that time. Most of the Prmi-speaking people under his rule appear to have converted to the Gelugpa sect during the seventeenth through nineteenth century. He was made a local official *tusi* of the Qing dynasty in 1729 (Fu 1983: 138), but it is unlikely that this changed his local political position or the ethnic composition of his domain.

Speakers of Yi languages, which belong to a different branch of Tibeto-Burman (Matisoff 1991), appear to have entered the area in three waves. The first Ming emperor, Taizu, in order to consolidate his rule over the area after his defeat of the Mongols in the 1370s, supported the establishment of local rulers at Puwei in Miyi. They came from northwest Guizhou or northeastern Yunnan and spoke languages of the Nasu group, a subgroup of the northern branch of Yi (Bradley 1987).

Meanwhile, the Nuosu, or Liangshan Yi, maintained a basically tribal political existence[1] in the Greater Liangshan well into the twentieth century, with Han civilization encroaching only around the frontiers of what came to be known in the West as "Independent Lololand." But because of intertribal warfare in Greater Liangshan, perhaps brought on by population pressure, Nuosu began to cross the Anning River and settle in the Lesser Liangshan in the early decades of the Qing period. This mass population migration continued into the mid-twentieth century, and Nuosu now constitute a majority of the population in Ninglang, over 40 percent in Yanyuan and substantial minorities in Yanbian, Muli, Mianning, and Miyi. In the process of this migration, Nuosu have displaced Prmi and perhaps Naze people in the peripheral areas of all these counties; it is unclear whether they have also displaced Han populations.[2]

The history of the migration of peoples in this area is thus exceedingly complex, and the resulting mix of local jurisdictions, languages, customs, and marriage alliances is as complicated spatially as is the temporal sequence. However, using the language of ethnohistory, it is possible to divide the current inhabitants into four sorts of people.

First, there are the early-resident groups, who were the basis of the *tusi* (native-ruler) political system of the area from the Mongol conquest in the fourteenth century until the 1950s. A few of these are Yi (such as the Nasu *tusi* at Puwei), but most of them are either Naxi/Naze or Qiangic speakers such as the Prmi. By the nineteenth century, many but not all of these people were adherents of one or another sect of Tibetan Buddhism, and many had picked up other Tibetan customs such as drinking yak-butter tea and barley beer. Therefore, the influence of Tibetan civilization in this area, although rather late historically, is nevertheless profound.

Second, there are the Nuosu. They are among the latest of arrivals, but because of the massive numbers of migrations they now form a demographic plurality in most parts of Lesser Liangshan. They have been remarkably resistant to acculturationist and especially to assimilationist pressures from Han or Tibetan civilization.

Third, there are small groups living in isolated enclaves. Some of these, the Miao and Lisu, maintain relatively sharp ethnic boundaries; others, mostly speakers of Yi languages other than Nuosu, are highly acculturated to Han customs, and in some cases are becoming assimilated to Han identity.[3]

Fourth, there are the Han themselves. They are a people living on the very remotest fringes of the world's largest civilization, a minority locally in many parts of the region, but attached by descent and culture to the billion-strong Han Chinese. They include both peasants, who have migrated here for many centuries, and educators and administrators who have come since the establishment of the People's Republic in 1949.

Ethnic Classification

Into this complex mosaic came the Chinese Communist Party in the 1950s, with the project of building "a unified country of diverse nationalities" (*tongyide duominzu guojia*). From the standpoint of Communist ideology, it was the party's mission first to find out who was living in the territories they now (sometimes tenuously) controlled and then to set about creating the conditions for these diverse peoples to participate in the socialist economy and polity that the Communists were constructing (see Heberer 1989; Harrell 1994).

The first step of the Communists in the Lesser Liangshan, as in all areas of the country inhabited at least partly by non-Han peoples, was to determine who the inhabitants were. To do this, they used a language of classification that was first set out in the works of Lewis Henry Morgan, Friedrich Engels, and Josef Stalin.[4] Stalin's language was a way of categorizing people, whereas that of Morgan and Engels was a way of ranking them on a scale of civilization.

According to Stalin, a "nationality" is a historically situated group of people who have four things in common: a common territory, a common language, a common economy, and a common psychological essence expressed in a common culture (Stalin 1935). In the 1950s the Chinese Communists took their administrative and academic cues primarily from the previous Soviet experience. So they set out to identify the minority peoples of the People's Republic in terms of these criteria set out by Stalin.

For the Russian term *nationalnost'* (nationality), the Communists chose the Chinese word *minzu*. This word, like so many other terms for political and social concepts, was a neologism of Meiji-era Japan, borrowed into Chinese. Its use, however, is multivalent and sometimes ambiguous. It can be used in a broad sense as *Zhonghua Minzu* (Chinese nation) or in a restricted sense to refer to one of the groups that were identified according to Stalin's criteria as being subgroups of the larger nation, such as the Han *minzu* or the Yi *minzu*. Official Chinese literature invariably translates *minzu* into English as "nationality," which seems to fit only the larger sense of "the Chinese nationality," or perhaps, though the Communists would deny it, some of the historical nations such as Tibet or Mongolia, part of whose population and territory are now under the rule of the Chinese government.

It is tempting to translate *minzu* as "ethnic group" instead, since *minzu* in the narrower sense tend to be minority local/linguistic/cultural groups within the larger population of the country. But *minzu* as used in China is not really an ethnic group. In Western anthropological literature, ethnic groups are usually defined as groups with ethnic identity, that is, groups that perceive themselves to have common ancestry and common cultural characteristics (Keyes 1976; Harrell 1990). *Minzu*, on the other hand, are defined according to Stalin's method by objective rather than subjective criteria. Ethnic groups are also usually seen as contextual and shifting, whereas *minzu* are fixed, at least across the shorter sweep of history. Finally, people can be members of nested or overlapping ethnic groups (one can be both French and Provençal, or both English and Jewish), but *minzu* are mutually exclusive categories, and one can belong to only one *minzu*, even if one's parents come from two different *minzu*. So I choose to leave the term *minzu* untranslated here.

In order to determine which *minzu* existed in China, the Communist authorities in the 1950s organized an immense ethnological project, known as *minzu shibie* or "ethnic identification." Local people all over the country were invited to apply for recognition as *minzu*; the authorities received over four hundred applications, mostly from the southwest. Then large research teams—about two thousand scholars and students of history, ethnology, and linguistics—were sent to investigate the claims of the groups that applied (Fei 1980; Lin 1987). By 1962, fifty-four minority groups had been recognized; a fifty-fifth, the Jinuo, was recognized in 1979; added to the Han this makes a total of fifty-six *minzu* in China. This number now appears to be fixed and not admitting of any further *minzu*, though there are groups that are still hoping for recognition, including a portion of the Naze in Yunnan.

Categorization according to Stalin's criteria was only half the project, however. *Minzu* also had to be ranked according to a scale of modes of production. The scale was based on Lewis Henry Morgan's evolutionary sequence from savagery to barbarism to civilization (Morgan 1985), sifted through Marx's more formal historical dialectics, and rigidified in the Soviet Union under Stalin. In this scheme, all peoples evolve through a fixed sequence of stages from primitive to slave to feudal (with two substages in China: manorial feudalism and the landlord economy) to capitalist to socialist. The possibility of skipping stages is sometimes entertained, as with the Nuosu, who were thought to be able to move directly from slavery to socialism, bypassing feudalism and capitalism altogether. Once the *minzu* were identified and ranked on the great scale of history, the projects of development and transformation could be undertaken in a rational manner, and all the peoples of China could march together toward the socialist future.

This language of ethnic classification produced a map of the peoples of the Lesser Liangshan that is somewhat at odds with that drawn in ethnohistorical terms above, and very much at variance with that described below, in terms of the practical languages of ethnic identity. In the Lesser Liangshan today, the following *minzu* are recognized: Han, Yi, Zang (Tibetan), Meng (Mongolian), Pumi, Naxi, Hui, Lisu, Miao, and Bai.

The *minzu* produced by the ethnic classification process are not the same as the ethnic groups defined in the practical languages of ethnic identity. These *minzu* categories, however, are far from irrelevant to people's daily lives. Censuses and social surveys, for example, often include data classified by *minzu* affiliation. More importantly, being classified as a minority of any sort, as opposed to a Han, brings with it certain affirmative action benefits. In the Liangshan Yi Autonomous Prefecture, which includes the municipality of Xichang and the counties of Yanyuan, Muli, and Mianning discussed here, rural minority families are uniformly allowed three children; rural Han can have only two. In Panzhihua Municipality, which includes Miyi, Yanbian, and Renhe, quotas vary from township to township, but townships with heavy minority representation tend to have higher birth quotas. There are special schools and classes for minorities throughout the area, and members of minority groups usually receive preference in applications for admission to regular schools.

Membership in particular *minzu* is also important. In the areas designated autonomous prefectures or autonomous counties, or in the smaller *minzu* townships, members of the locally predominant minority *minzu* tend to be appointed to positions of political power and authority in the four wings of the state bureaucracy: the party, the government, the legislature, and the People's Consultative Conference. In addition, where there are programs of bilingual education, members of particular *minzu* are often offered the chance to become literate in their *minzu* language as well as in the national language, Standard Chinese. For example, Prmi speakers in Muli, who are classified as Tibetans in a Tibetan Autonomous County, learn standard written Tibetan starting in the third grade, using textbooks composed and printed in Lhasa. Prmi in Yunnan, classified as Pumi, are educated in Chinese only.

The Communist civilizing project has thus created a map of China, including the Lesser Liangshan area, that uses the metalanguage of official ethnic classification and that channels administrative, educational, and developmental resources according to this map. In this sense, then, the map represents an important reality. It is not, however, quite the same as the reality of ethnic identity in the same region, to which I now turn.

Ethnic Identity

Whereas the various *minzu* identified in the metalanguage of ethnic identification are equivalent categories—each is defined as a group having a common territory, language, economy, and culture—the various ethnic groups spoken about in the practical languages of ethnic identity are not formally or logically equivalent. Their criteria for inclusion and exclusion, the clarity or fuzziness of their boundaries, their possibilities for belonging to overlapping or nested groups, all differ from one ethnic group to another. In this short chapter, it is not possible to write in detail about the languages of identity used by every ethnic group in the Lesser Liangshan region, but case studies of the Nuosu and Prmi illustrate these different modes of speaking.

Nuosu

Nuosu are not only the largest ethnic group in the Lesser Liangshan, with several hundred thousand people in the counties of Mianning, Yanyuan, Yanbian, Muli, Miyi, and Ninglang, they are also the most clearly defined and exclusivist. Ethnic identity is expressed in idioms of exclusivity and boundary maintenance. One is Nuosu or not, and the boundaries of this identity are sharp, clear, and relatively impenetrable at present.

To be Nuosu is, first, to be a member of a Nuosu clan, or *cytvi* (*jia zhi* in Chinese). Clans are patrilineal and exogamous, and are ranked into two strata, sometimes called castes: the *nuohxe*, or "black" aristocrats, and the *quhxe* or "white" commoners. Aristocratic clans often trace their descent back over eighty generations to the putative founders of the world, but even commoners can often recite a genealogy of twenty to thirty generations. All members of a clan call each other by kinship terms corresponding to those for primary agnatic relatives, and call members of affinally linked clans by the terms corresponding to close affines. When two Nuosu meet who do not know each other already, their first two questions are almost always about each other's clan affiliation and place of origin. In pre-1956 society, aristocrats were ordinarily local political leaders, and members of commoner clans were retainers of the aristocrats. Since the economic reforms of the 1950s, however, the economic positions are no longer important, but the strata remain endogamous. In a survey of over four hundred Nuosu marriages conducted in 1993, I found only two that crossed caste lines.

The system of clan membership, social stratification, and cross-cousin marriage is the strongest mechanism of ethnic boundary maintenance among Nuosu today. It precludes the blurring of ethnic boundaries, at least in rural society. (Urban, educated Nuosu sometimes marry Han or other minorities, but do not usually return to their rural communities when they do so). This system, in effect, assigns every Nuosu a social position in the cross-cutting web of clan and caste, excluding those who have no clan membership, except from the extremely undesirable status of *gasi*, a lower-caste group formerly consisting primarily of slaves.

The clan and caste system is, however, not the only idiom of separation between Nuosu and other people. Spoken language also plays an important part here. Even in the most acculturated Nuosu communities I have visited people are still bilingual. These are places actually bisected by the major interregional railroad in the Anning valley bottom, an hour or two bus ride from the primarily Han city of Xichang. People there have given up most of the other customs that serve as Nuosu ethnic markers, they no longer recognize the aristocrat-commoner distinction, and they are surrounded by Han in villages not 500 meters away. The Nuosu language borrows vocabulary freely from Chinese and occasionally Prmi or other local languages, but I have not encountered any Nuosu community where the language is lost. This is in stark contrast to every other ethnic group in the area. I have visited communities of many ethnic groups where the "native" language has completely or almost completely given way to Chinese or, in a few cases, to Chinese and Nuosu.

Nuosu also communicate in a language of exclusivity in several other aspects of life. For example, in the Lesser Liangshan Nuosu women, and often Nuosu men, wear ethnic clothing. Nuosu food is also characteristic—on formal occasions at least, Nuosu meals consist of boiled mutton, beef, pork, or poultry, eaten with the hands or with lacquered, long-handled spoons. Other ethnic groups uniformly eat what we would recognize as Chinese food out of bowls with chopsticks. Nuosu marriage and funeral rituals, their calendric holidays, and many other customs are clearly distinctive and separate Nuosu from other ethnic groups in the area.

It is also particularly striking that there is very little internal variation in Nuosu culture, even though the two and a half or three million Nuosu are scattered across a large area. The three local dialects of the Nuosu language are all mutually intelligible, and although dress styles for both men and women vary slightly from one area to another, they are all more like each other than any is like the styles worn by any other group. The same is true for food, rituals, and other cultural traits. Such uniformity across a broad area also helps to maintain the boundaries between Nuosu and others.

The sharp boundaries of Nuosu as an ethnic group do not preclude much cordial, everyday interaction with neighbors of other ethnic affiliations. In some areas, there is reported to be ethnic hostility, but where Nuosu live closely intermixed with Prmi, Naze, and Han, they often attend each others' weddings and funerals, play cards or pool together in their free time, buy goods from each others' stores, and attend classes at the same schools. They do not avoid each other in any sense, at least in mixed communities. Nuosu in the Lesser Liangshan almost uniformly are fluent in the local Chinese dialect as a second language, and many, depending on the area, speak Prmi or other local languages as well. Conversely, many Prmi and other local ethnic group members learn the Nuosu language, though there are considerable numbers of Han peasants who do not learn to speak Nuosu (and some who do).

Many Nuosu, however, particularly politicians and intellectuals, have a strong sense of ethnic pride, combined with resentment of Han people for what is seen as their incursions on Nuosu territory in recent decades, particularly since the Communist takeover in the 1950s. Local leaders, many of them members or even leaders of the Communist party, express great interest in using the economic reform policies implemented since 1979 to develop Nuosu areas by and for Nuosu people. In addition, many Nuosu people are offended by certain Han customs, such as polite dissimulation (Nuosu prefer straight talk, they say), eating foods the Nuosu taboo (such as dog and horse meat), or drinking contests (most Nuosu drink heavily, but do not play drinking games in the Han manner). I have been told by Nuosu intellectuals that only their language is really rich in vocabulary and symbolism, that Chinese is an impoverished tongue incapable of precision or subtlety of expression. Boundary maintenance is thus accompanied with a sense of ethnic superiority.

The sharp in-group/out-group distinction that is the basis of Nuosu ethnic identity, however, raises problems for the category of Yi, as formulated in the metalanguage of ethnic classification. Of the six and a half million Yi in China, probably slightly less than half are Nuosu and others are members of various groups scattered over Yunnan, Guizhou, and small sections of Guangxi. This is not a problem for peasants in Nuosu areas. Perhaps they have a common origin, but it is not of much concern to anyone. For two types of people, however, the category Yi is a real problem. Several of the smaller groups classified as Yi whom I have talked to do not like the classification. This was particularly true of the Shuitian people in western Renhe in 1988 (they seemed to have moderated their stance in 1994) and of the Yala people in Hengshan and Malong townships in Miyi in 1993. People in both communities indicated to me that they resented being classified as Yi and wished to be *minzu* in their own right. Certainly, they did not marry the Nuosu.

For Nuosu intellectuals and politicians, the category Yi raises a different kind of question. Many of these people feel a mission to record and celebrate the glories of Yi civilization, which to them may include not only all the people currently classified as Yi, but also Hani, Lisu, and other *minzu* whose languages and customs are similar to those of the Nuosu or other Yi. There is a large scholarly industry, supported by the national *minzu* bureaucracy, devoted to writing comprehensive Yi history. Many Yi intellectuals even claim that they were the first people in the world to invent writing, an invention that was later borrowed by the Han and then transmitted to other parts of the world. There has been no overt separatist activity like that in Tibet since the late 1950s, but there remains an overriding sense of ethnic nationalism among Nuosu intellectuals.

The Nuosu are thus the clearest case of an exclusive ethnic identity to be found in the Lesser Liangshan, or indeed probably anywhere in the southwest. Internal uniformity of language and customs, social-structural and cultural mechanisms for the maintenance of boundaries, and an intellectual class imbued with a strong sense of ethnic pride make it absolutely clear who is Nuosu and who is not.

Prmi

There were only about 57,000 Prmi in 1993, about half of them in the Lesser Liangshan counties of Yanyuan, Ninglang, and Muli (Wellens n.d.; Yan and Chen 1986). As mentioned above, in the official language of ethnic classification, those Prmi living in Sichuan are classified with Tibetans and other Qiangic-speaking or Xifan groups as Zangzu; those living in Yunnan are classified as Pumi (Harrell 1995). The Prmi are not only a much smaller ethnic group than the Nuosu; Prmi ethnic identity could also not be more different. The practical language of ethnic identity for Prmi in Lesser Liangshan has been historically contingent and shifting, full of local dialect differences and not sharply distinguished from others. This situation has permitted the Prmi to be given two different *minzu* identifications entirely, which have in turn reinfluenced practical ethnic identity. Ethnic boundaries, in terms of language, customs, social structure, and religion, have been fuzzy and permeable (Prmiable?).

To begin with, there seem to be no strong barriers to intermarriage between Prmi and outsiders in general, though there are local prohibitions against marriage with specific groups. Prmi in Muli laughed at the suggestion that anyone would even consider marrying Miao, and I know of very few marriages with Nuosu, but then Nuosu themselves prohibit intermarriage in most situations. Han people, on the other hand, never prohibit marriage with any other group, and whereas one Prmi community in Muli that I visited had never had any intermarriage with Han, in Yanyuan Prmi-Han intermarriage is quite common.

With other culturally similar groups, specifically Naze, intermarriage is free and frequent in every area I know about where the two groups live in close proximity. In these areas, where dress, religion, and other customs are nearly or completely identical between the two groups, *minzu* membership becomes more like simple descent-group membership than like an ethnic difference, except that Naze and Prmi are not the same languages. This is particularly true in the Lugu Lake/Yongning area, where Prmi have adopted the Mosuo custom of duolocal "walking" marriage, in which husband and wife continue to live in their respective maternal houses, the husband visiting his wife at night (Yan and Chen 1986:40-44; He Xuewen 1991; Hu Jingming, personal communication, 1993).

In contrast to the Nuosu case, the Prmi language varies widely in its usage; you do not have speak Prmi to be Prmi. In Muli, the Prmi language is spoken by the largest single ethnolinguistic group and is spoken widely by peasants and officials alike; the language is also flourishing in Ninglang. In Mianya Township, in Yanyuan, where the population is about 10 percent Prmi, people still speak Prmi. But in Baiwu Township, also in Yanyuan, where Prmi constitute only 5 percent, few young people can speak the language well; most Prmi there use a mixture of Han and Nuosu languages in their everyday conversation.

There is also much less local variation in the cultural traits that serve as ethnic markers than there is in those of the Nuosu. Prmi houses, for example, come in three styles that I have observed. In Muli, they have walls of stone, of stone and mud, or of wood in log-cabin style, and are centered around an interior room approached by a corridor from the front door. In the center of the room is a hearth, surrounded by mats, and sometimes by chairs and tables, for sitting and eating. Altars to spirits and ancestors are on the left-hand wall as one walks into the room, and Buddhist altars are directly above the hearth. Around Lugu Lake, they are built exclusively of logs, and the main room contains two hearths; one is in the corner opposite the door, where male hosts and guests sit on rugs, and the other is on a wooden platform on the left wall of the house, where men or women can sit around the fire on low stools or benches. In Yanyuan, the outer appearance is identical to that of local Yi and Han houses (i.e., it is built of mud walls), but the interior is easily distinguished by the altars to ancestors and sky spirits mentioned above.

Dress is similarly variable. In most areas I have visited, Prmi women's dress, with a pleated, single-colored skirt, an apron, and a plain black turban, distinguishes Prmi from Han, who never wear skirts, and from Nuosu, who wear a different kind of long, pleated skirt, with bands of alternating colors, no apron, and elaborate headdresses (rather than the simple turban). On the other hand, when Prmi want to emphasize friendship with Nuosu, they can haul out the proverb that "Everybody who wears skirts is one big family," thus including Prmi and Nuosu in one category that excludes the Han. And even though many Prmi in Muli consider themselves as belonging to the same Zang *minzu* as the Khamspa or Ba, whom the Prmi call Gami, and whom Westerners would consider Tibetans, their dress is completely different.

Dress thus distinguishes Prmi from others sometimes, but not other times. Prmi dress is identical to Naze dress in some areas, and in practical terms to Han dress (most of the time, at least) in others. And although Prmi are classified as Zang in Sichuan and as Pumi in Yunnan, local differences in Prmi dress do not coincide with the provincial border. Finally, those Prmi who are classified as Zang do not dress like the great majority of Zang, people whom Westerners would call Tibetans.

As with dress, also with religion. Prmi have two kinds of religious traditions. The first is Tibetan Buddhism; the second is the Dingba or Hangui religion, which has been defined by Chinese ethnologists and Pumi leaders as an indigenous religious tradition separate from Buddhism (Yan and Chen 1986:71-74; Hu Jingming, personal communication, 1993), a complex of folk beliefs and rituals that includes offerings to ancestors and nature spirits and may or may not include a written, textual tradition (Wellens n.d.). The degree of adherence to both of these religious traditions varies greatly among the Prmi communities that I have visited.

With regard to Buddhism, two examples will illustrate the range of variation. In the areas around the south shore of Lugu Lake in Ninglang County, as well as in most of Muli, most Prmi are devout Buddhists. Many families have formal shrines in their houses, complete with oil lamps burning constantly, pictures of the Dalai and Panchen lamas, and the custom of inviting monks to perform calendrical rituals and rites of passage. Many families have had members enter the monkhood, and there are monasteries populated primarily by Prmi in Muli as well as a large monastery with a mixed population of Prmi and Naze in Yongning, a township in the northern part of Ninglang.

In the Yuanbao township of Yanyuan, by contrast, all Prmi profess to be Buddhists, but no one there knows much about Buddhism. Families I talked to claimed to have Buddhist texts, written in Tibetan, but could not produce them for me to look at, and nobody could read the Tibetan-language inscriptions posted over some families' doors at Chinese New Year—they were written by a relative from a more devoutly Buddhist area, who had since returned home.

I know little of the Hangui religion. Mr. Hu Jingming, a Prmi leader from Ninglang and the vice-chair of the Ninglang County People's Consultative Conference, told me that the Hangui tradition is comparable to other non-Buddhist priestly traditions in the general area—the Dongba of the Naxi and the Daba of the Mosuo. The Hangui may have had written religious texts in the past—Mr. Hu has collected four texts probably written in the Prmi language, using Tibetan script, but as yet has found nobody who can read them. He says that in the southern part of Ninglang, near Yongsheng, the Hangui religion was traditionally more important, whereas in the northern part of the county, Buddhism has always predominated.

In Yanyuan, Prmi families ordinarily have two altars in their houses—a lower one that rises about three feet along the inner wall of the house above the hearth, where ancestors are worshiped, and an upper one, a shelf set high on the same wall, where they make offerings to a series of sky spirits, including Tsambela, Muneiguizhambala, and Bulenguizhambala. They also make offerings on the lower altar to Buddha (Han: *fo zu*). They used to write prayers in Tibetan, but now nobody knows Tibetan, so they write the prayers in Chinese.

Prmi religion of both kinds—Hangui and Tibetan Buddhist—acts as an ethnic marker, distinguishing them from both Yi and Han, neither of whom practice either of these traditions.[5] Other groups with whom Prmi come in contact, however, also practice Tibetan Buddhism. Naze in Ninglang and Yanyuan have shrines similar to those of the Prmi, and the Khamspa Tibetans in the remoter areas of Muli are almost by definition Tibetan Buddhists. (People in Yanyuan who think of the Prmi as Tibetan and Naze as Mongolian consider it paradoxical that the Naze—Mongols—are more religious than the Prmi—Tibetans.) I do not know if Hangui religion has ever served as a local ethnic marker to distinguish Prmi from either of these other Buddhist groups. But it is clear from this brief sketch that religious differences within the Prmi group are great. And although Tibetan Buddhism is the primary faith of Prmi, Naze, and Tibetans in this region, the religious and ethnic boundaries do not coincide.

As with Nuosu, Prmi intellectuals have great ethnic pride, and are beginning to assert this pride through projects of research and scholarship. In Ninglang County, for example, I learned in 1993 not only about the story of the king of Bailang in the history of the Latter Han Dynasty, but also of plans to establish a Pumi history and culture research center. But again, this pride seemed to accrue to the ethnic group, not to the *minzu* whose boundaries were defined by the ethnic classification project. I was told of the research center by a Pumi (Yunnan Prmi) cadre from Ninglang County in Yunnan, but the county magistrate of Muli, himself a Zang (Sichuan Prmi) from Yanyuan, took part in the same conversation and he told me he had agreed to contribute timber revenues from Muli's vast old-growth forests to help establish and support the research center.

To understand the nature of Prmi as a category, it is important to understand the process, alluded to above, by which the Prmi in Yunnan came to be Pumi and those in Sichuan came to be Zang. Before the ethnic classification project of the 1950s, boundaries were probably even fuzzier than they are now. People were identified culturally and linguistically as Xifan, called themselves Permi, Prmi, Pumi, or Primi (depending on the dialect), and saw their religious allegiance as being with Tibet, which was the spiritual and sometimes the political center to which they owed allegiance. They had, as it were, a multivalent identity, which was precipitated or crystallized by the classification project. After the ethnic classification project, people were Prmi or Zang or neither, where once they had been both, or Xifan as well, depending on the context.

We can therefore see a clear contrast between the Nuosu and the Primi. The Nuosu have a practical language of identity, with minimal local dialectal variation and sharp distinctions between Nuosu and others. The Prmi speak practical languages that have great local variation (both in spoken language and in the other ethnic markers) and they do not distinguish very clearly between themselves and others, drawing neither the cultural nor the intermarriage boundaries very sharply. In this sense, Nuosu and Prmi (much less Yi and Pumi) are not logically equivalent categories.

It would be a mistake, however, to surmise that Pumi and Zang are false categories, or that they bear no relation to ethnic relationships on the ground. Most Prmi I talked to on both sides of the border were perfectly content with their current classification and used it for some purposes. The most striking among these was that Prmi in Muli received Tibetan language instruction, whereas Prmi in Yunnan, not being Zangzu, of course did not. Once the categories were created in the metalanguage of ethnic classification, they became one more set of vocabulary items borrowed into the practical language of ethnic identity.

Discussion

The very complexity of the ethnic mosaic in Lesser Liangshan (and in southwest China generally) enables us to see, perhaps more clearly than in areas where there are fewer or more discretely defined groups, how ethnicity works as a system of communications. If, as Williams asserts (1989), ethnicity is the process by which small populations are incorporated, sometimes by actual or symbolic violence, into larger national structures, that process in this case is neither purely oppositional nor purely cooperative. There are minorities, such as the Nuosu, who may resent aspects of the imposition of state power—speaking about the Han or the Communists who have taken our land, our resources—but who do not dispute the rules under which the game is being played; they accept their designation as the basis of what at least some people see as a struggle of Yi people against outsiders. In this case, the vocabularies of the metalanguage of ethnic classification and of the practical language of ethnic identity are the same; the political question is simply one of cooperation or opposition.

In other cases, however, the vocabularies of the two kinds of languages differ. Various ethnic groups, e.g., Prmi, Naze, Yala, Nasu, and Tazhi, do not coincide with the official classification of any *minzu*. In some cases, there may simply be mistakes. Classifying Naze or Mosuo as Naxi is clearly incorrect, even in terms of the Stalinist vocabulary of ethnic identification (McKhann 1995). But misclassification is only a small part of the problem. As we have seen, the classification of some Prmi as Zang and others as Pumi has caused little strife or resentment; what it has caused is opportunistic manipulation of the system by those who are caught in it.

It is not necessarily wrong, in terms of the official criteria, to classify small groups such as Yala, Nasu, or Tazhi as a branch of the Yi *minzu*—they are certainly closely related historically and linguistically. But the criteria themselves do not connect with the meaningful divisions of local society. Even here, however, this is more of an issue for the Yala, who refuse outright to be Yi, than for the Tazhi and Nasu, who are ambivalent about this classification. And in none of these cases has the lack of coincidence between ethnic identity and ethnic classification caused much oppositional consciousness; far less, as a matter of fact, than in the Nuosu case, where everyone agrees on the categories.

In sum, state projects of nation building, involving multiethnic populations in a single nation, always do some sort of violence to the arrangements of cooperation or hostility worked out in local communities. But the two realms of discourse are not separate. Local communities and their leaders may work within or against the system established by the state.

NOTES

1. I am using "tribal" here in the narrow sense suggested by Fried (1967:170-174), that is, a secondary, semicentralized polity that arises on the periphery of, and, in response to, pressure from a state system.

2. Other Yi have come into the area in small numbers since the 1950s. They are related to people in central Yunnan and speak dialects of the central branch of Yi; they call themselves Lipuo. Finally, there are pockets of Yi speakers known as Yala, Shuitian, and Tazhi whose origins and linguistic affiliations still remain to be researched.

There are also enclaves of Lisu in Dechang, Miyi, Yanbian, and Yanyuan as well as Miao populations in Yanbian and Muli. Most are recent immigrants; some were settled there by the Qing government in the late eighteenth and nineteenth centuries after being involved in disturbances in other parts of the country (Ye and Ma 1984:111, 129).

3. I will treat these small groups more fully in my forthcoming monograph, *Ways of Being Ethnic in Southwest China.*

4. American lawyer and ethnologist Lewis Henry Morgan wrote the evolutionary classic *Ancient Society* (1877), which was in turn used as the basis of Friedrich Engels's *The Origin of the Family, Private Property, and the State*, a canonical text of Marxism used in all socialist countries.

5. There may be isolated Han Buddhists, but they ordinarily do not follow Tibetan conventions or rituals, observing instead Chinese Mahayana—primarily Pure Land—forms.

REFERENCES

Bradley, David. 1987. "Language Planning for China's Minorities: The Yi Branch." In *A World of Language: Essays Presented to Professor S. A. Wurm on his 65th Birthday*. D. Laycock and W. Winter, eds. Pp. 81-89. Canberra: Australian National University.

Brown, Melissa J. 1995. "On Becoming Chinese." In *Negotiating Ethnicities in China and Taiwan*. Melissa J. Brown, ed. Pp. 36-74. Berkeley: University of California Center for Asian Studies.

Chen Zongxiang. 1991. "Bailang Ge" Yanjiu (Research on "The Song of Bailang"), Vol. 1. Chengdu: Sichuan Renmin Chubanshe.

Chen Zongxiang, and Deng Wenfeng. 1979. "Bailang Ge" Yanjiu Shuping (A Summary and Critique of Research on the "Song of Bailang"). *Xinan Shifan Xueyuan Xuebao* 4:48-55.

Engels, Friedrich. 1985 (1884). *The Origin of the Family, Private Property, and the State*. Harmondsworth, England: Penguin.

Fei Xiaotong (Fei, Hsiao Tung). 1980. "Ethnic Identification in China." *Social Science in China* 1:94-107.

Fried, Morton. 1967. *The Evolution of Political Society*. Boston: Little, Brown.

Fu Yuyao. 1983. "Yanyuan, Muli Er Xian Minzu Shehui Lishi Kaocha Jilue" (Notes from Investigations of the Ethnology and Ethnohistory of the Two Counties of Yanyuan and Muli). In *Yalongjiang Xialiu Kaocha Baogao* (Reports on an Investigation along the Lower Reaches of [the] Yalong River). Li Shaoming and Tong Enzheng, eds. Chengdu: Zhongguo Xinan Minzu Yanjiu Xuehui.

Goldstein, Melvyn C. 1989. *A History of Modern Tibet, 1913-1951*. Berkeley and Los Angeles: University of California Press.

Harrell, Stevan. 1989. "Ethnicity and Kin Terms among Two Kinds of Yi." In *Ethnicity and Ethnic Groups in China*. Chien Chiao and Nicholas Tapp, eds. Pp. 179-197. Hong Kong: New Asia College.

Harrell, Stevan. 1990. "Ethnicity, Local Interests, and the State: Yi Communities in Southwest China." *Comparative Studies in Society and History* 32(3):515-548.

Harrell, Stevan. 1994. "Introduction: Civilizing Projects and the Reactions to Them. In *Cultural Encounters on China's Ethnic Frontiers*. Stevan Harrell, ed. Pp. 1-35. Seattle and London: University of Washington Press.

Harrell, Stevan. 1995. "The Nationalities Question and the Prmi Problem. In *Negotiating Ethnicities in China and Taiwan*. Melissa J. Brown, ed. Pp. 274-296. Berkeley: University of California Center for Asian Studies.

He Xuewen. 1991. "Yongning Mosuo Ren de hunyin ji qi xisu" (Marriage and Its Customs of the Mosuo People of Yongning). In *Ninglang Wenshi Ziliao Xuanji* (Selected and edited Historical and Literary Materials from Ninglang). Ninglang: Ninglang Zhengxie.

Heberer, Thomas. 1989. *China and Its National Minorities: Autonomy or Assimilation?* Armonk, NY: M. E. Sharpe.

Keyes, Charles F. 1976. "Toward a New Formulation of the Concept of Ethnic Group." *Ethnicity* 3:203-213.

Keyes, Charles F. 1981. "The Dialectics of Ethnic Change." In *Ethnic Change*. Charles F. Keyes, ed. Pp. 4-30. Seattle and London: University of Washington Press.

Li Haiying et al. 1983. "Yanbian Xian Hongbao Gongshe Miaozu Diaocha" (Investigation of the Miao in Hongbao Commune, Yanbian County. In *Yalongjiang Xialiu Kaocha Baogao* (Reports on and Investigation along the Lower Reaches of [the] Yalong River). Li Shaoming and Tong Enzheng, eds. Chengdu: Zhongguo Xinan Minzu Yanjiu Xuehui.

Li Liukun. 1992. "Miyi Baizu shi wei Yizu zhong de Baiyi kaozheng" (A Proof that the Bai of Miyi Are Really the Baiyi, a Kind of Yi). In *Miyi Wenshi Ziliao* (Literary and Historical Materials on Miyi County), Vol. 5, pp. 116-118. Miyi: Miyi Zhengxie.

Lin Yaohua. 1961 (1947). *The Lolo of Liang Shan*. Ju-shu Pan, trans., from Liangshan Yijia). New Haven: HRAF Press.

Lin Yaohua. 1987. "Zhongguo xinan diqu de minzu shibie" (Ethnic Identification in the Southwest Region of China). In *Yunnan shaoshu minzu shehui lishi diaocha ziliao huibian* (Collection of Materials from Historical and Sociological Investigations of Minority Nationalities in Yunnan). Kunming: Yunnan Renmin Chubanshe.

Matisoff, James A. 1991. "Sino-Tibetan Linguistics: Present State and Future Prospects." *Annual Review of Anthropology* 20:469-504.

McKhann, Charles F. 1995. "The Naxi and the Nationalities Question." In *Cultural Encounters on China's Ethnic Frontiers*. Stevan Harrell, ed. Pp. 39-62. Seattle and London: University of Washington Press.

Morgan, Lewis Henry. 1985 (1877). *Ancient Society*. Tucson: University of Arizona Press.

Peng Deyuan et al. 1992. *Miyi Minzu Zhi* (Account of the *Minzu* of Miyi). Miyi, Sichuan: Miyi Minzu Zhi Bianji Xiaozu.

Schwartz, Theodore. 1975. "Cultural Totemism: Ethnic Identity Primitive and Modern. In *Ethnic Identity: Cultural Continuities and Change*, 1st ed. George A. De Vos and Lola Romanucci-Ross, eds. Pp. 106-131. Palo Alto: Mayfield.

Shih, Chuan-kang. 1993. "The Yongning Moso: Sexual Union, Household Organization, Ethnicity and Gender in a Matrilineal Duolocal Society in Southwest China." Ph.D. diss., Stanford University.

Stalin, Josef. 1935 (1913). *Marxism and the National and Colonial Question*. Moscow: Co-operative Publishing Society of Foreign Workers in the USSR.

Wellens, Koen. n.d. "To Be or Not to Be Pumi: The Pumi Minority in Southwest China and State Monopoly on Defining Ethnic Identity." Unpublished paper.

Weng, Nai-chun. 1993. "The Mother House." Ph.d. diss., University of Rochester.

Williams, Brackette. 1989. "A Class Act: Anthropology and the Race to Nation over Ethnic Terrain." *Annual Review of Anthropology* 18:401-444.

Yan Ruxian, and Chen Jiujin. 1986. *Pumi Zu* (Pumi Nationality). Beijing:Renmin Chubanshe.

Ye Dahuai, and Ma Erha. 1984. *Yanbian Minzu Zhi* (Account of the *Minzu* of Yanbian). Yanbian, Sichuan: Yanbian Minwei.

Chapter Five

Subtle "Primitives": Ethnic Formation among the Central Yaka of Zaire

Situating the Case Study

This is ethnography from the past. The case study illustrated that some very isolated African populations that, some thirty years ago, had been barely in touch with the urbanized world, showed mechanisms of ethnic formation that come close to processes found in contemporary urban America, in what is called "symbolic ethnicity" (Wright 1994).

The Luunda, Suku, and Yaka of Central Kwaango in southwest Zaire, whose culture I studied between 1961 and 1965, had all been colonized by Belgium (Roosens 1971). The Baluunda, Basuku, and Bayaka—names used by the local population—were generally amalgamated as the "Yaka" or "Bayaka" in the ethnographic literature. This "tribe" or "people" was, in fact, a set of merged populations of diverse ethnic origin. At least the three ethnic categories mentioned above could be distinguished in the population of Central Kwaango. All were, within the traditional system, subjects of one king or ruler, the *kyaambvu* of Kasongo-Luunda, who presented himself as Luunda and traced his origins via his ancestors and predecessors back to Koola (a region in Shaba, Zaire), the country of the *mwaata yaambvu*, the prince of the Luunda kingdom.

The Luunda, in all probability, conquered the area in the seventeenth century. Using a strong assimilation and intensive intermarriage policy, they merged with the existing ethnic groups to the extent that the opposition of Luunda versus non-Luunda only survived in certain facets of the sociocultural reality, primarily in the opposition between the categories of "political chief" and "landowner" and in the ideology and rites expressing this political duality. A great deal of importance was attached to the latter political structure by the parties involved. The institution was clearly African and had survived throughout the colonial and postcolonial periods.

Like many populations of the south, the Yaka were oriented to economic development and to the acquisition of "modern civilization," albeit in a rather passive way. The Yaka of Muningulu I studied were separated from what is now Kinshasa by hundreds of miles of "savanna path," and had little or no acquaintance with the West, let alone with the broader world system.

In Kinshasa, where a large number of Yaka, mostly men, had settled as immigrants in squatting zones and where, in the 1960s, they formed a socioeconomic underclass, both the Luunda and the non-Luunda hailing from Central Kwaango tried to disappear ethnically. They were hiding their origin and only used Lingala, a local contact language, in public places.

"Primitive" Conditions?

The Yaka of Central Kwaango are a group that current stereotypes, even in 1995, would depict as belonging to the "best-conserved" peoples of Africa. In the 1960s the Yaka were often cited as an unknown, very primitive, and isolated group.

In professional circles, of course, there has long been awareness of how deceptive the word "primitive" is. But if it simply means very different from the West, which is often the case, or if it means having changed relatively little under the influence of external factors, then this hardly scientific concept is indeed applicable to the Yaka of the 1960s. For this reason, they are suitable for reflection on ethnic formation in an isolated region with a very low degree of technological development, especially, as it is often suggested that the present ethnic phenomenon is a kind of return to the preindustrial past. Some even see it as a dangerous and unproductive regression to something that should be gone for good, like religion (Patterson 1977).

The term "tribalism" is often used with pejorative connotations, implying a reversion to an earlier period in the evolution of humankind. Considered within this frame of reference, the Yaka should have provided a clear example of what a monolithic, seamless tribe looks like. The facts, however, were totally different. Ethnic formation among the Yaka appeared to be a subtle and complex process. In order to be able to work with first-hand data that I collected over several years of field research, I will limit the scope of this article to the Muningulu region, located in the central part of the Kwaango region.

Ethnic Structure: A Subtle Layering

Well before the 1960s, a few missionaries who were interested in the culture and the history of the people with whom they lived had wondered about the origins of the Yaka. But they found no clear answer to their questions. One thing emerged with relative certainty, however: the population that the colonial and the missionary organizations called the "Bayaka" was composed of different groups: the Luunda, the Yaka, the Suku, and probably other peoples. A colleague-anthropologist, who had done a great deal of work among the Suku, was, after a short visit to the eastern Yaka region, convinced that the so-called Yaka of the eastern zone of the Kwaango region were not at all Yaka "by origin," but genuine Suku. In other words, among the interested Europeans, the respective ethnic identities remained unclear and opinions divided. This division of the experts reflected, at first sight, a confused situation within the local populations themselves.

A closer look, however, revealed that this confusion only resulted from the way in which the Europeans formulated the problem. Europeans realized that some people from this region were identified as Luunda, others as Yaka, and still others as Suku, whereas in Kinshasa, all were indistinctly labeled "Bayaka" by members of other ethnic groups or categories. The assumption was that a given group of people had to be either Yaka, Luunda, or Suku by origin and filiation. It was not noticed, though, that mostly *the same people* identified themselves as Yaka under certain circumstances and called themselves Suku or Luunda in another context, whereas a small number of other inhabitants of the same region vehemently rejected the name Bayaka or Basuku and called themselves Baluunda only.

The older men and notables from the Muningulu region—actually the only ones who had the right to discuss the subject in the presence of an outsider—stated that the important people of the region were all Luunda. The political chiefs and their family members called themselves Baluunda, not Bayaka. They used Muyaka (sing.) as an abusive word for the least respected of their subjects. They said that their ancestors came from Koola, from the court of the *mwaata yaambvu* of Koola, a region of present-day Shaba. I was able to note the following, rather stereotypical texts about these origins.

The first text presents the arrival of the Luunda as a kind of idyllic event: a young woman, a sister of the *mwaata yaambvu*, went on a journey with her retinue to the region of the Kwaango River where she met a native hunter who soon became her husband. She gave him the power of Koola, and their descendants became the rulers of the region.

The Origin of Us, the Luunda of Kasongo-Luunda

We, we are descendants of Luunda, of Mwaadi Kamoonga, a sister of Koola.
She requested permission to go on a journey from her brother, the Mwaata Yaambvu of Koola.
She said: "I want to go on a journey. I am going to visit our vassals so that they will pay us the tribute of Luunda."
Her brother answered her: "It is fitting that you, my sister, lay out the fields (metaphor for "tend to the affairs of the kingdom"); afterwards come back where I, your brother, reside."
She took her brother Kihuunda Mangaanda with her and gave him the dancing drum, the signal drum, the *bisaandzi* (sing.: *kisaandzi*, a kind of instrument with tuned strips of iron), and the rattles.
Kihuunda Mangaanda was like someone who suffers from the neck disease.
Kihuunda Mangaanda went always further along very bad roads.
Phaangwa Mataku Mansandzi Kamoonga Lukawasa went along the road of Kwaango.
She was in the midst of singers in order to sing with the *bisaandzi* of Luunda.
There was a hunter who always killed wild animals. His name was Muta Kateela Khaandza Mudimi Kadimina Ndzala ("who shoots [hunting] shoots out of need [for meat]; who works the field, works it from hunger"). He observed that smoke from a fire began to rise.
Arriving, he saw a house surrounded with shrubs, as a plot for a house generally appears.
He came with the spoils of his hunt, laid them on the ground, and bowed to the earth to greet the queen.
He said: "Greetings, Deputy."
Kamoongo Luwakasa replied: "Greetings."
After they had acted thus, Kamoonga Luwakasa took her water pipe, and brought out tobacco and hemp.
She smoked; a part of it she gave to him, Muta Kateela Khaandza Mudimi Kadimina Ndzala.
Muta Kateela Khaandza gave some of his game to Kamoonga Luwakasa.
In the evening he left and went hunting again.
He came again, again with game.
Another day he appeared again with more spoils.
He came to Mwaadi Kamoonga Luwakasa.
He said: "Queen, today I sleep here because I am very tired from hunting."
Mwaadi Kamoonga Luwakasa said: "Very good."

> When night fell, this man, Muta Kateela Khaandza Mudimi Kadimina Ndzala spoke: "Queen, I am your vassal. It would be good if I were also your husband."
> Mwaadi Kamoonga said: "I, I may not marry you. If you want me to be your wife, let us then first send the matter to the residence of my brother, the Kyaambvu of Koola."
> Muta Kateela said: "Very good, Queen Kamoonga."
> Mwaadi Kamoonga sent a message to the Mwaata Yaambvu of Koola. He answered: "If you, my sister, have found a man that suits you, there is no objection. I send you a Luunda knife, a drinking cup from the chief, and a lion skin on which your husband, Muta Kateela Khaandza, can be enthroned. Let him live with you, our sister from Koola."
> She gave birth to their first child. They named him Pfumusaangu Mwaaku Kambumba Maafu Kambadika Thiinu Mudimi Ndzala.
> Then they lived many years the hunter and his sister (= of the Mwaata Yaambvu).
> When Kihuunda Mangaanda heard: "Your sister, Kamoonga Luwakasa has married a man," and when she already had given birth to two children and he saw her again, he asked: "What is this, my sister, you marry without informing me?"
> Mwaadi Kamoonga said: "You, my brother, have acted badly. You went wandering and left me behind alone. As matters now stand, my brother Kihuunda Mangaanda, it is no longer possible to grant you the investiture because I have given the power to my husband from Koola, Muta Kateela Khaandza Mudimi Kadimina Ndzala, and not to you, Kihuunda Mangaanda."
> Kihuunda began to wail, but in vain, since all questions about the power had already been settled.
> When Chief Khaandza died, he appointed his son, Pfumusaangu Mwaaku Kambamba Maafu Kambadika Thiinu Mudimini Kadimini Ndzala from Luunda, from Koola. (Here, usually follow the names of the *byaambvu* [plur. of *kyaambvu]* who succeeded each other.)

Another text, which is performed as a kind of song at feasts in the presence of the traditional political Luunda rulers and their suite and relatives, presents the dominance of the Luunda with much more cruelty.

> Great King, who draws all human life force to himself, who has masses of people destroyed.
> Muni Phutu Mangaanda, Mwaata Yaambvu (= names of prominent historical kings).
> Who walks on palavers (= is master over), who walks on disputes.
> Everywhere you take what you want.
> Who shall curse you (= kill you)?
> *N-syeenini phoombo* (= a kind of large tree), that one cannot climb.
> Descendant of Kamoonga Luwakasa (sister of the Mwaata Yaambvu, who came from Koola: see previous text).
> Who holds in his possession the foot ring of the chiefs, the foot ring of the Kyaambvu. (Note: ankle ring [*kazekele]* of the *kyaambvu*; whoever succeeds in stealing it has the power.)
> Who keeps watch over the maize, who supervises the wealth of people.

> The second wife is charged with the cooking, the first wife takes care of the *myoombo* (sacred trees).
> Who loves the *matuumba* drum (= a double drum carried around the neck), who loves the rattles (Note: these musical instruments are said to have been imported from Koola.)
> Washing out of the road (= who channels the rain water; fig.: the chief who organizes everything), who lets the fog rise (= who is the origin of all sorts of mysterious events, such as the death of particular people).
> The others sleep next to fire of dead wood; you sleep on the bones of sons of men. (Note: formerly, the body of the *kyaambvu* was lowered into his grave on the arms of two men who were forced to sit down in the grave with their wrists tied together.)

The older informants from the region explained the historical events in the line of these texts: the Luunda were conquerors who came to rule the people already settled in the Kwaango region. They came from the kingdom of the great *mwaata yaambvu* of Koola. Hence, the supreme authority of the Yaka, the *kyaambvu*, who lives near Kasongo-Luunda, considers himself the younger brother of the *mwaata yaambvu*, a metaphorical kinship term. This also explains that, up to the middle of this century, a kind of *missus dominicus* was sent on foot every year from the court of the *mwaata yaambvu* to the court of the *kyaambvu*. He reenacted the historical journey of the forefathers and would be welcomed enthusiastically everywhere on his route to the capital of the Luunda of Kwaango.

It was self-evident for the local population that the political chiefs were Luunda. The territory of the approximately three hundred thousand Yaka was divided into about ninety regions. Each region was governed by a political chief who regularly paid tribute to the *kyaambvu* and offered homage to this supreme authority in his residence near Kasongo-Luunda a few times a year. At the same time, all the informants agreed that the Luunda, who came from Koola centuries ago, married native women from the Kwaango region, generally daughters of the autochthon chiefs, and that this practice had been continued by their descendants.

Ethnic Descent: A Symbolic Construction

Whoever conceives ethnic belonging as a pure, monolithic reality faces a major difficulty. For it ought to be clear to everyone, and for the local population, that the descendants of the above-mentioned "mixed" marriages could at most be half-Luunda. Everyone realized that a kind of mixing had taken place, and this for generations. The informants even stressed the point: the Luunda had been using marriage as a kind of strategy, and they still did. A political chief of a region was generally polygamous and married women from several of his villages. Muningulu, for example, the chief of the Muningulu region, had in the early 1960s, about twenty wives among whom many were from various villages of his region. The children of these marriages, in turn, married young people from still other villages so that the political chief developed a very wide network of married relatives and descendants that made him a kinsman throughout his entire fief. In this way, Chief Muningulu was not only the lord of his region but also a relative in each of the village communities. At the same time, he was able to collect accurate information on his region and on the loyalty of his subjects.

Moreover, it was clear from the more than seven hundred family genealogies I recorded (Roosens 1971) that the Luunda of the 1960s related genealogically and biologically to the original Luunda immigrants from Koola only in the same "diluted" way as many Native Americans relate to their pre-Columbian ancestors.

When the aforementioned situation is analyzed in terms of the following theoretical assumptions, the questions of ethnic formation and structure become quite clear. (1) Ethnic identity is an ongoing process in which a feeling of belonging and continuity-in-being (staying the same person[s] through time) is generated and kept alive, resulting from an act of self-ascription, and/or ascription by others, to a group of people who claim both common ancestry and a common cultural tradition (De Vos and Romanucci-Ross 1983; Hutnik 1991; Roosens 1994). (2) In ethnic formation, reference to the "ancestors" (De Vos and Romanucci-Ross 1983)—the family metaphor—is at least as important as the maintenance of a sociocultural distinctions—the boundary metaphor (Barth 1969; Roosens 1989).

Among the Yaka of Muningulu, descent was reckoned in a double patrilineal manner: a person belonged at the same time to the patrilineage of his father and to the patrilineage of his mother. The paternal side did have a certain predominance, however. A man or a woman who had a Luunda father and a non-Luunda mother could readily call himself or herself Luunda and leave the other half of his or her ancestors in the background. Someone with a Luunda mother and a non-Luunda father could do the same.

Whoever was able to do so displayed the Luunda aspect of his or her ancestry. But not everyone with any Luunda ancestors was allowed to identify as a Luunda. A limited number of people of the region were constrained by the political system to display their non-Luunda origin, even if they had Luunda political chiefs among their direct ancestors. The people who were forced to identify as non-Luunda—as Suku or Yaka—were the *tulaamba* (plur. of *kalaamba*), the so-called landowners of the region. According to the collective representations of the Yaka, the Luunda chiefs were the most important men of the region, but they owned no land. The land was kept under the collective ownership of the ancestors of the *tulaamba*, the people who already lived in the region when the Luunda arrived. In the local ideology, these ancestors of the *tulaamba* formed a kind of absolute beginning: they were seen as the original and genuine owners of the land. Nobody could encroach on this collective ownership without compromising the fertility and the survival of the region. Should the political chiefs have passed themselves off as landowners, the population would have been afflicted by infertility and all kinds of other disasters. Thus, even the *kyaambvu*, in the conversations I had with him, stressed that he was not the owner of the land but that he did rule over the people, including the *tulaamba*.

One day, an argument developed in my hut between the Luunda subchief of the region (at the same time chief of the village) and one of the landowners of the region. The political chief called the *kalaamba* his slave (*mpika*). The latter replied that the Luunda would fare like the Belgians at the time of independence: the Luunda, too, would have to return to where they came from. This *kalaamba* who was called a slave in my presence, was the grandson of a political regional Luunda chief, but this aspect of his ancestry was totally ignored in the context of the discussion.

The opposition between the two functionaries—the political chief and the landowner—who each embodied a people was thus given form by their respective ancestry and by a few cultural traits. The distinction between the two figures and the differences between the rites they carried out were considered essential for the survival of the entire population. A binary opposition had developed in the Kwaango region between Luunda and non-Luunda. Both categories were eminently incarnated by particular figures who had a public function: the Luunda by the *pfumu mbeele*, or the political chief, and the non-Luunda (e.g., the Suku) by the *kalaamba*.

A Luunda chief was eligible for appointment to a political office by descent in the male line; the landowner inherited his office via matrilineal calculation: from a maternal uncle or from a maternal uncle of a maternal uncle. The "original" autochthons were thus placed in opposition to the Luunda by complementary functions that are occupied by virtue of a distinct ethnic belonging. The ethnic belonging of the functionaries, however, was presented as an intrinsic quality flowing from "pure," "full-blooded" descent, while every adult knew that pure, unmixed filiation on either side was out of the question. But this reality was simply not taken into account.

Those who were neither political chief nor landowner usually stressed their Luunda descent, displaying their belonging to the higher layers of the society. Almost everyone, except the landowners, could have ascribed themselves to the "better people." This explains that the above-discussed interpretation of the past and the legitimation of the political structure by the ruling Luunda were accepted by virtually everyone. That the inhabitants of Central Kwaango identified themselves as Luunda whenever possible was undoubtedly due to the relative prestige associated with this social identity within Yaka society. Moreover, the relationship and the historical bond with the *mwaata yaambvu* were felt to be a source of prestige, also to outsiders. Many residents of the region could just as well have been identifying themselves as Suku or Yaka, but they did not do so because it was contrary to their interest. As one can see, the social determination of ethnic identity can be far removed from the actual biological basis, even though this biological distance is publicly known.

Only in a few villages on the periphery of the eastern central area did the inhabitants mention to inquiring outsiders that they were, in fact, Basuku. In doing so, they presented themselves, at least verbally, as being independent vis-à-vis the ruling Luunda chief. But they did not display nor instantiate this position in daily routines, nor did they attempt to secede. Their ethnic self-definition reflecting the antagonism between the political Luunda chief and the descendants of the former original autochthon rulers only emerged in particular circumstances (e.g., when questions of ethnic origin were formally discussed with outsiders).

Becoming Invisible in City Life

Anyone from Central Kwaango who moved into Kinshasa in the 1960s was classified by city dwellers as a Muyaka. In Kinshasa, the term "Muyaka" sounded like an insult: it carried the connotation of being underdeveloped, being a peasant, a rural primitive, and so on. In the city, the Yaka had long been known as still untouched by modern times; as people who were willing to take care of the heavy, dirty, unskilled jobs for very low wages. The urban population did not make the subtle distinction between Luunda and non-Luunda. The Luunda of Kwaango had no status in the modern city and were even unheard of. Apparently, their status of conquerors coming from Koola was a local phenomenon, acknowledged only in the rural area of the Kwaango. In the city, Bayaka were only Bayaka: backward people from the wilderness.

In the city most Yaka tried to remain ethnically invisible outside their familiar surroundings. When they visited bars, markets, or stores, they spoke a version of vehicular Lingala, even among themselves. And many children of immigrants from the Kwaango did not learn the Yaka language, Kiyaka.

The ethnic identity of the Yaka was not a kind of tribalistic straitjacket. Neither was their ethnic group a seamless social texture left over from an original, primitive past.

REFERENCES

Barth, F., ed. 1969. *Ethnic Groups and Boundaries*. Boston: Little, Brown.

De Vos, George A., and Lola Romanucci-Ross, eds. 1975. *Ethnic Identity: Cultural Continuities and Change*. Palo Alto: Mayfield.

Hutnik, M. 1991. *Ethnic Minority Identity: A Social Psychological Perspective*. Oxford: Clarendon Press.

Patterson, O. 1977. *Ethnic Chauvinism: The Reactionary Impulse*. New York: Stein and Day.

Roosens, Eugeen. 1971. *Socio-culturele verandering in Midden-Afrika: De Yaka van Kwaango*. Antwerp-Utrecht: Standaard Wetenschappelijke Uitgeverij.

Roosens, Eugeen. 1989. *Creating Ethnicity: The Process of Ethnogenesis*. Newbury Park/London/New Delhi: Sage Publications.

Roosens, Eugeen. 1994. "The Primordial Nature of Origins in Migrant Ethnicity." In *The Anthropology of Ethnicity: Beyond "Ethnic Groups and Boundaries*. H. Vermeulen and C. Govers, eds. Pp. 81-104. Amsterdam: Het Spinhuis.

Wright, L. 1994. "One Drop of Blood." *The New Yorker*, July 25, pp. 46-55.

PART III ■

The Emergence of National States

VICTOR C. UCHENDU ■

Chapter Six

The Dilemma of Ethnicity and Polity Primacy in Black Africa

Of the many factors determining human action, two stand out in discussion of ethnic identity. The first factor consists of cultural values, which partly determine ethnic identity, its persistence, its change over time, and the "dilemma" of ethnic identity, especially in a plural social system. The second factor consists of the historical processes which tend to redefine a people's self-identity, to reinforce it, or to compel a search for a new identity. Among these historical processes two elements, imperial control and the demand for political independence, cannot be ignored, because of their pervasive influence on the identity of the black person in Africa. The background of ethnic identity, then, lies in contrasting value systems, contrasting social categories, and the dynamics of history.

We assume that ethnic identity is an imposed value over which its bearer has absolutely no control in his or her formative years, because of protracted dependence. Koestler (1969) argues that the "overwhelming capacity and need for identification" with a social group and/or a system of beliefs, which can even be "indifferent to reason, to self-interest and even to the claims of self-preservation," is a central feature of the human predicament.

This paper explores the predicament of ethnic identity in black Africa, especially in its political context, and puts the problems of ethnic identity in a wider sociocultural context. Among a human's unique qualities is the power to transcend the narrow bounds of an imposed social identity and thus compensate for the shortcomings of one's utterly helpless dependence on the early cultural environment. One also has the capacity to contract rather than to expand one's social frame of reference. When is it psychologically rewarding to maintain, expand, or contract the social frame of reference which confers a person's group identity?

Shils argues that the values or belief system of a society can be lived up to only "partially, fragmentarily, intermittently and only in an approximate way" (1957:130). He asserts that ideals and beliefs can only influence conduct "alongside of personal ties, primordial attachments, and responsibilities in corporate bodies." With respect to ethnic identification, Shils's arguments can be framed as three propositions, all depending on the "principle of choice," or cultural alternatives. First, ethnicity is impermanent in that individuals, communities, and territories change their identification over time. Second, members and nonmembers may use ethnic terms or labels differently, depending on whether the criterion of identity is self-identification or identification by others. Third, members of an ethnic group may not always use the same term for themselves. This introduces a segmentary or situational principle in ethnic identity.

Empirical studies of factors contributing to ethnic identity in black Africa are rare. Studies suggesting the problems which ethnic identity poses to political integration, while more frequent, are neither abundant nor definitive (Gluckman 1960; Wallerstein 1960; Mazru 1963). Although the question of ethnicity is academic in a stable, homogeneous social system, the recent social, economic, and political developments in Africa have so fundamentally shaken traditional African society that competing ethnic interests not only are asserting themselves but are violently striving for accommodation, sometimes domination.

Although recent works in psychiatry, social psychology and sociology have tended to ignore African ethnographic background, they are stimulating and contain many theoretical insights. We shall ignore much of the work by those psychologists and psychiatrists who have studied the acquisition, loss or severe disturbance of identity solely from the individual point of view. These limits are consistent with our limited goal of examining problems of ethnic identity in black Africa in their political context.

Psychologists have tended to regard the self as an independent structure, comparable to the ego but developed in adolescence. Eissler (1958), who subscribes to this view, believes that experiences of identity also occur during adolescence. This might well be true at the personality level, but at the group level, one's ethnic affiliation and identity might well be taken for granted long before adolescence (Proshansky and Newton 1968:184).

Erikson (1956), Wheelis (1958), and Lynd (1958) have tended to emphasize a sociological orientation to identity, an approach which Jacobson (1964:24-32) has criticized as unbalanced. Erikson's thesis is that identity formation is a "lifelong development." He uses the term "ego identity" to "denote certain comprehensive gains which the individual, at the end of adolescence, must have derived from all his preadult experiences in order to be ready for the task of adulthood" (1956:101).

Both Wheelis and Lynd view identity in terms of generalized group phenomena, pointing out that the search for identity is a general problem of structural change, especially rapid social change. This view is consistent with African data if we interpret structural change to be an increase in political scale which has created a polyethnic society. Whereas Wheelis (1958) tended to emphasize the disturbances in the feeling of identity caused by the "generation gap," especially the breakdown of the value systems of the past, Lynd (1958:215) attributes identity disturbance to social change processes which prevent a person from finding "aspects of his social situation with which he can clearly identify."

Emphasizing a psychiatric orientation, Jacobson stresses the continuity as well as the personality integration of identity formation. In her view, identity formation is "a process that builds up the ability to preserve the whole psychic organization—despite its growing structuralization, differentiation, and complexity—as highly individualized but coherent entity which has direction and continuity at any stage of human development" (1964:27).

Lichtenstein (1961) points out that in a dynamic world, an individual as a culture-bearing and culture-creating animal cannot take his or her identity for granted. He attributes the origin of identity formation to the earliest mother-child relationship and emphasizes the experience of continuity in the normal feeling of identity. In his view, the human quest for identity is unique. Unlike other animals, humans lack the preformed, adaptive identity which is guaranteed to animals by their genetic inheritance. On the other hand, because of their ability to profit by learning, humans inherit an existence with self-defined, self-created identity which they must struggle to maintain.

This brief survey indicates that ethnic identity lends itself readily to a psycho-sociological study in which individual identity and group identity can be related. A person's identity as it develops cannot be easily divorced from his or her cultural background or subjective experience. Positive group identification or group belongingness is not a problem for any social group that has status and power and enjoys prestige in a society. The problems of group identification arise for those who are deprived of these advantages and those in competition for them (Proshansky and Newton 1968:213).

Approaches to Ethnicity

The tribe, as an anthropological concept, derives from the premise that there are aggregates of people who essentially share a common culture (tribe), and that there are interconnected differences which distinguish one tribal culture from all other tribal cultures. Barth (1969) takes issue with this type of reasoning. He makes two observations which I consider relevant to ethnic processes in modern Africa.

First, he asserts that ethnic boundaries persist despite the interpenetration of cultures and that ethnic distinctions do not depend on an absence of physical contact. Rather, they entail social processes of exclusion and incorporation, whereby discrete categories are maintained *despite* changing participation and membership. The persistence of ethnic enclaves in urban environments in modern Africa lends support to this proposition. Second, he asserts that ethnic distinctions do not depend on absence of social interaction and acceptance; quite to the contrary they are often the basis on which embracing social systems are built. This indicates that cultural differences can persist despite interethnic contact and interdependence (1969:9-10).

Ethnic group boundaries are maintained by a limited set of cultural features. What are these features and how definitive are they? Naroll (1964) lists six criteria: trait distribution, territorial contiguity, political organization, language, ecological adjustment, and local community structure. In a critique of these criteria, especially of their diagnostic value, Moerman (1965:1215) argues that language, culture, political organization, etc., do not correlate completely, so that units delimited by one criterion do not coincide with the units delimited by another.

Barth (1969:10-38), who has grappled with the "defining characteristics" of ethnicity, suggests that when an ethnic group is viewed as a social organization, the critical feature becomes "the characteristic of self-ascription and ascription by others" 1969:13), a point also stressed by Moerman (1965:1219). When "self-ascription" is used as the critical mark of ethnicity, it becomes obvious that this definition imposes a series of constraints on the kinds of roles an individual is allowed to play, and the partners he or she may choose for different kinds of transactions. It is this self-definition, reinforced positively or negatively by the actions of other relevant social groups, that tends to perpetuate ethnic boundaries.

The Search For Cultural Roots

Membership in a traditional African ethnic group is a matter of social definition, the result of the interplay of members' self-definitions and the categorization and stereotyping by other groups.

In rural Africa, tribal identity persists because the colonial government gave it an institutional and political support and because the tie to the tribal, communal, or lineage land, often phrased in the idiom of filial loyalty to ancestors, is still an important social and economic asset. In the urban area, factors contributing [to] ethnic loyalty include the competition for jobs, the uneven distribution of government patronage, and the insecurity of urban employment. There is also an element of "ethnic patriotism"—an important value which conflicts with a wider national loyalty.

If tribal Africa took its identity for granted, the developments of the last seven decades—especially the fact of colonialism and the presence of white minority governments in Africa—have dictated a search for identity. Whether the frame of reference is at the continental, regional, national, or ethnic level, political considerations overshadow the recent search for identity in black Africa. This factor also illustrates a critical principle in the problem of African identity its segmentary or situational orientation.

The search for identity in black Africa can be considered from four perspectives. First, there was the demand for a "political kingdom," which compelled a search for continental identity. Continental identity became an instrument for decolonization and a weapon for postindependence international diplomacy. Second, there is the search for black identity which is motivated by racial pride—a search which makes it meaningful to speak of three Africas: Arab Africa, black Africa, and white minority Africa. Third, there is the search for national identity. And finally there is the demand for ethnic identity within the polyethnic state system. Whatever its immediate concerns, the search for identity in black Africa has always faced a dilemma in its choice of symbols. Which symbols should project continental, racial, national, or tribal identity?

Lacking a written culture, black Africa was not heir to any great traditions. Since what could be considered "great traditions" in black Africa enjoyed no higher status than the "little traditions," ethnic patriotism compelled African scholars and social thinkers to adopt continental identity. Nkrumah's "African personality" and Senghor's "negritude" are identity labels that are pan-African, transnational, and transterritorial. Similarly, the demand for political independence had a pan-African ideology. Nkrumah set the tone by declaring that he would not consider Ghana as truly independent until all Africa was liberated. This new emphasis in continental identification is a radical departure from an early outlook which regarded Egypt as the fountainhead of all African civilization. As Kopytoff (1967:55) points out, "this scientifically untenable interpretation of Egypt's role in world history" was first used to deprive black Africa of all credit for indigenous achievement, and is at present used "by some Africans to bolster the historical importance of Africa as a whole."

Mazrui (1963:88) has called attention to the dilemma of continental identification in Africa. He asserts that Africa has "a negative common element . . . [that Africans] are like one another to the extent that they are collectively different from anything in the outside world." Arguing that the continental feeling built up by colonialism was more emphatic in black Africa than it ever was in Arab Africa or in Asia, Mazrui (1963:90) observes that "Nasser is an Egyptian in a deeper sense historically than Nkrumah is a Ghanaian, but he is an African in a shallower sense emotionally than Nkrumah is an African."

The dilemma of selecting an appropriate symbol of cultural identity is not restricted to the continental level; it also persists at the national level. Throughout black Africa, the policy of decolonization is accepted as a political imperative, although the speed at which this policy is implemented varies widely. On a fundamental question of decolonization, such as language policy, the challenge of choice is rarely faced. Tanzania seems to be the only exception, thanks to a colonial policy which encouraged Swahili as a lingua franca and to the political courage of the leadership in adopting this language. It is difficult to see any aggressive language policy emerging in many black African countries. Although the idea of an African language to act as the vehicle for the new political cultures which African political leaders envision for their countries is attractive, there is no "politically neutral" language in a polyethnic state. The dilemma is compounded when it is realized that in a polyethnic system, where the competing languages are almost equally "politically visible," the foreign language becomes the only "politically neutral" language that can command consensus.

Shifts in Ethnic Identity

What are the factors which tend to shift ethnic loyalties, and to what extent are they operative in black Africa? Obviously many factors are involved but two will serve to illustrate the role they play in ethnic processes—political integration and urbanization.

The expansion and contraction of political scale are important factors in ethnic processes. Until the independence movement, the peoples of black Africa were not "African" by self-identification; they were Igbo, Zulu, Akan, Yoruba, Hausa, Kikuyu, Ganda, Lunda, and so forth. In this time perspective, one's self-definition and ascription by others rarely coincided. Independence and national consciousness are gradually bringing about the convergence of the two criteria, especially among the elites of African society.

Ethnic identification, even in the political frame of reference, can be segmentary in articulation. Nigerian students in London or New York are more likely to identify themselves as African than as Nigerian unless the situation clearly indicates that identification of country is expected or required. To another Nigerian, they are most likely to identify themselves with state or region; if they are speaking to a coethnic, they are likely to name the provincial or administrative headquarters to which they belong. Thus, identity is likely to change as the frame of reference changes.

Economic development leads to increasing specialization of functions, one of the most dramatic being an ecological rearrangement. Students of the emergent urban cultures in Africa have noted the widespread shifts of loyalty among Africans. This "shifting loyalty" has been termed "detribalization." To me, the concept of detribalized people is the product of bad sociology and of Western ethnocentrism (Uchendu 1969:54). The concept implies the existence of a tribal order of society which was the desirable state. Its logical implication is that detachment from this tribal order results in normlessness. It appears to me that the image of the detribalized African—the counterpart of the marginal man—who stands in the corridors of two cultures but belongs to neither is an ethnographic myth. Tribal loyalty has a number of aspects: loyalty to the family or lineage, loyalty to the tribal community, and loyalty to the tribal chief or government, where one exists, may be isolated. As Wallerstein (1960:130) points out, "it does not necessarily follow that an individual who is no longer loyal to his chief has rejected as well the tribe as a community to which he owes certain duties and from which he expects a certain security."

Gluckman argues that the ethnic identity of the urban African is situation oriented. He asserts that "the African in rural area and in town is two different men: he tends to be 'detribalized' outside the tribal area, and 'tribalized' or 'deurbanized' when he leaves the town" (1960:55). The view that persisting loyalty to a tribe operates for a man in two quite distinct situations and that different "spheres of identity" can be segregated is an interesting hypothesis which seems to receive wide ethnographic support in black Africa.

It is in the urban environment that the expansion and contraction of ethnic identity is manifested. The fact that ethnic groups must have a minimum size to function in an urban environment forces individuals to expand the social frame of reference which confers to them an ethnic identity. The dynamics of Igbo Unions illustrate the operation of this principle. It is common knowledge that the Igbo of Nigeria have a strong in-group feeling which is manifested in their tradition of founding urban associations wherever they happen to be immigrants. The structure of the Igbo Union, like the traditional Igbo polity, tends to be segmentary. The Igbo from one village group are more likely to have an independent "family meeting" to which other coethnics are excluded if the number of this particular village group in the town justifies a viable, independent union. However, if the number of people is limited, the village group in question is likely to be absorbed by a larger social unit. In this context, ethnic identification is constantly redefined according to new criteria which might not be considered socially relevant in the rural areas. The tendency, especially in West Africa, to define ethnic groups in terms that are not necessarily traditional but rather reflect the urban social situation indicates that ethnic identity is not a fixed phenomenon.

In the African urban environment, two major trends reinforce ethnic identity and loyalty. The first is the persistence of ethnic enclaves and the second is the dramatization of joking relationships in a panethnic framework.

Especially in West Africa, "strangers' quarters" are an important feature of the urban ecology. Whether in the forest areas or in the savanna lands, towns are zoned into indigenous and strangers' areas. In the copper belts of Central Africa as well as the eastern region of Africa, residential segregation tended to follow racial lines, with Europeans in their own reservation, the Asian population in the commercial center, and the African populations at the periphery. This pattern of development has tended to promote greater ethnic interpenetration in Central and East Africa than in West Africa.

Ethnic enclaves in urban Africa have two basic characteristics: they are "poverty pockets," which resemble many parts of the rural environment, and they are relatively homogeneous ethnically. On the question of poverty, the Hannas (1967:5) argue that "the deprivational conditions found in large sections of most African towns are not created by urban-specific factors, but are imported to the town and clustered in . . . ethnic enclaves." Because Africans in towns tend to reside, associate, and work with their coethnics, ethnic enclaves are marked by "ethnic clustering." In this environment, rural occupational training, ascriptive hiring practices, and the desire to work side by side with coethnics lead to occupational clustering.

Tensions arising from ethnic group rivalry may be transformed into joking relationships. Mitchell (1956) provides a dramatic example of such tension management in his discussion of the Kalela dance in the copper belt of Central Africa. Performed by teams of Africans who come from single tribes, the Kalela dance is probably the most popular entertainment in the copper belt. During the dance, a team of tribal dancers deride other tribes, alleging that the target tribes have, among many unpleasant habits, loose and even perverted sexual lives. The team praises the virtues of its own tribe. There is no ill-feeling provoked and everybody enjoys the performance. Gluckman (1960:63-64) suggests that the Kalela dance reflects the persisting significance in towns of tribal allegiance. In this particular context, ethnic identification in town operates as a primary mode of classifying into manageable categories the heterogeneous masses of people a person meets. Ethnic identity in urban Africa is in this frame of reference a social category by which people group one another.

Conclusion

Ethnic groups are social categories which provide a basis for status ascription. Because the factors which lead to status ascription are not static, the social frame of reference which categorizes ethnicity is subject to expansion and contraction. We cannot understand the dynamics of contemporary ethnicity in black Africa unless we take the political environment into consideration. Political competition, especially in the urban areas, tends to upset the criteria of ethnic definition which might be socially relevant in the rural areas. Ethnic identity is least segmentary in a homogeneous society and most segmentary in a heterogeneous society. In a small, homogeneous society, the criteria of "self-definition" and the "definition by others" tend to coincide. This is not so in an urban environment. Although ethnic groups tend to shed some of their cultural peculiarities in town, their ethnic identity—which is often expanded to make political competition effective—is perpetuated through common residence and common political interests.

The boundary-maintaining mechanisms which perpetuate ethnic identity in urban areas are embarrassing to political elites, who find themselves in role conflicts as national leaders and cultural brokers for their ethnic groups. This is the dilemma of ethnic identity: how to "keep faith" with competing loyalties.

Politics and tribe play an important role in the identity of black Africa. At the macro-level, it was colonization, based on power polities and superior technology, that imposed on Africa a negative self-identity. The expansion in political scale, which followed imperial expansion, created modern states such as Kenya, Uganda, and Nigeria. Reaction against imposed national labels also created modern Ghana, Zambia, Malawi, and Tanzania. The struggle for independence in parts of southern Africa finds expression in new national identities, of which Namibia and Zimbabwe are notable examples. The ambivalence toward anthropology as a scientific discipline in Africa is not unrelated to the early association between colonial administration and anthropology, and the wholesale imposition of pejorative terms such as "noble savage," "primitive," and "preliterate" on non-Western peoples.

At the national level, politics and tribe are still important in self-definition. In precolonial Africa, the national society tended to coincide with the tribal society. Because of the ramifying role of kinship and the absence of a written language, clear-cut class stratification did not emerge. In areas where immigrants were in political control (as in parts of the interlacustrine Bantu), a polyethnic social system became the pattern of the social structure. Here the polity was the integrating factor under a power system dominated by immigrant rulers but large areas of cultural diversity were left in religious and domestic spheres. In such a polyethnic system, ethnic identity was not coterminous with the political society. The traditional Rwanda society composed of three hereditary groups—the Batwa, Bahutu, and Bututsi—is a classic example.

The inclusiveness of the kinship system and the extended family obligations created an estate rather than a class system. It is not surprising that African leaders, who emphasize the continuity of traditional African past, resent the idea of a class society, which they view as highly divisive. Their ideology is one that seeks to create a nation of one extended family with which all must feel an equal identification.

This concept of a transclass society, in which hierarchy and rank do not create social distance and in which the extended family feeling is the center of identity, is the challenge of modern African society, and the contemporary dilemma of African identity.

REFERENCES

Barth, F., ed. 1969. *Ethnic Groups and Boundaries*. Boston: Little, Brown.

Eissler, K. R. 1958. "Problems in Identity." *Journal of American Psycho-analytical Association*, pp. 131-142.

Erikson, E. H. 1956. "The Problem of Ego Identity." *Psychological Issues Monograph* I.

Gluckman, M. 1960. "Tribalism in Modern British Central Africa." *Cahiers d'Etudes Africaienes* 1:55-70.

Hanna, William, and Judith William. 1967. "The Integrative Role of Urban Africa's Middleplaces and Middlemen." *Civilization* 17:1-16.

Jacobson, E. 1964. *The Self and the Object World*. New York: International Universities Press.

Koestler, A. 1969. "The Urge to Self-destruction." *The Observer*. London, September 28, p. 11.

Kopytoff, I. "Socialism in Traditional African Societies." In *African Socialism*. W. H. Friedland and C. G. Rosberg, Jr., eds. Pp. 53-62. Palo Alto: Stanford University Press.

Lichtenstein, H. 1961. "Identity and Sexuality: A Study of their Inter-relationships in Man." *Journal of American Psycho-analytical Association* 9:179-260.

Lynd, H. M. 1958. *On Shame and the Search for Identity*. New York: Harcourt Brace.

Mazrui, A. A. "On the Concept of 'We Are All Africans.'" *The American Political Science Review* 57(1):88-97.

Mitchell, J. C. 1956. *The Kalela Dance: Aspects of Social Relationships Among Urban Africans in N. Rhodesia*. Rhodes-Livingstone Paper No. 27.

Moerman, M. 1965. "Ethnic Identification in a Complex Civilization." *American Anthropologist* 67(5):1215-1230.

Naroll, R. 1964. "On Ethnic Unit Classification." *Current Anthropology* 5(4):283-312.

Proshansky, H., and P. Newton. 1968. "The Nature and Meaning of Negro Self-Identity." In *Social Class, Race and Psychological Development*. M. Deutsch and I. Katz, eds. Pp. 178-218. New York: Holt, Rinehart and Winston, 1968.

Shils, E. 1957. "Primordial, Personal, Sacred and Civil Ties." *British Journal of Sociology* 8:130-145.

Uchendu, V. C. 196. "The Passing of Tribal Man: A West African Experience." *Journal of Asian and African Studies*, pp. 51-65.

Wallerstein, I. "Ethnicity and National Integration in West Africa." *Cahiers d'Etudes Africaienes* 3:129-139.

Wheelis, A. B. 1958. *The Quest for Identity*. New York: Norton.

CHARLES F. KEYES

Chapter Seven

Who Are the Tai? Reflections on the Invention of Identities

Introduction

The category "Tai"—referring to peoples in mainland Southeast Asia, southern China, and northeastern India who are presumed to share not only related languages but also some essential "ethnic" characteristics—has been posited as a product of scientific (historical, linguistic, and ethnographic) research. I maintain that, in fact, it is a product of a politics of culture closely linked to the building of modern states and the shaping of national identities.

It is necessary first to comment briefly on the words "Tai" and "Thai." In English, "Tai" (although not necessarily pronounced with an unaspirated /t/) is used to refer to peoples found not only in Thailand but also in Laos, Burma, southern China, northern Vietnam, and northeastern India who speak languages belonging to the same language family (sometimes called "Daic"). "Thai," in English-language literature, refers to peoples who are citizens of the country of Thailand. In the Thai language, the two words are pronounced the same, but written differently.

The study of Tai peoples (*chonchāt Thai*) has significantly increased in Thailand over the past decade and a half. Much recent work has been carried out under the auspices of a Thai government agency, the Office of the National Cultural Commission, through a project on "The Study of the Culture of Tai Peoples." The significance of this project is indicated by the fact that a conference held in September 1993 at which participants reported on studies of various Tai groups was chaired by HRH Princess Galyani Vaddhana, the elder sister of the king, and was attended by over eight hundred people.[1]

Drawing on recent theoretical approaches to the study of ethnicity and nationalism as well as my own researches in Thailand, Laos, and southern China, I argue here that the recognition of kinship among (some) Tai-speaking peoples is a product not of objective linguistic or ethnolinguistic characteristics but of ethnic and national processes activated first by the creation of modern nation-states and then by the recent intensified flows of people, goods, and information across the boundaries of nation-states. Contemporary ethnicity theory has made us attentive to how "state, civil society, and nationalist precepts constrain processes of ethnic identification" and "influence modes of ethnic organization" (Williams 1989:426).[2] As I have argued elsewhere (Keyes 1992), the "scientific" classification of the peoples into ethnolinguistic groupings constitutes a Foucaudian "technology of power" (see Cohn and Dirks 1988) associated with the creation of nation-states. I want to show here how this technology has been deployed in a debate in Thailand about "Thainess" (*khwāmpen Thai*) that subsumes a debate about "Who are the Tai." Premodern[3] Tai-speaking peoples lived in communities that, I also maintain, were not defined in linguistic or ethnic or national terms, but with reference to genealogies that had very different premises than those derived from modern ethnology or linguistics.

The development over the past fifteen years of theories about how ethnic and national communities are constructed permit us today to rethink the question of how to recognize distinctive cultural communities.[4] We now recognize that all communities have a "genealogy," to use Foucault's term, and that genealogy is not determined by nature—by biological descent, for example—but is culturally constructed and historically contingent.[5] For a genealogy to be compelling it must not only be expressed in a cultural form—myth, written history, ritual, pageant, play, painting, monument, or more than one of these—but also must be backed by authority.

Such authority may be that of tradition—the voices of the ancestors speaking in the present through customary practices that seem timeless. Traditional authority is so embedded in practice that it goes unrecognized (see Bourdieu 1977). Authority may be perceived as a palpable quality of an individual whose extraordinary behavior marks that person as charismatic. Charismatic authority poses a direct challenge to traditional authority because the charismatic leader offers a new conception of community that breaks with traditional practice. Authority may also be hegemonic, the product of invention by leaders of modern states who are able to use the "technologies of power" of the state to transform such products into everyday practice. Hegemonic authority is a modern phenomenon and is self-consciously deployed to discredit traditional practices that have not been given a place in the new genealogy and to supplant, co-opt, or suppress charismatic authority.

In the remarks that follow I will attempt to trace, rather schematically, some ways in which the genealogies of communities that have included and still include Tai-speaking peoples have been constructed.

Premodern Genealogies of Tai Communities

The Early Tai

The speakers of ancient dialects of Tai have left us traces of their genealogies in myths that were later written down. Among the most ancient myths are the stories of Thao Hung, or Thao Cheuang, known from Laos, and of Princess Cāmadevī from northern Thailand.[6]

Thao Hung/Cheuang is a hero whose success in battles against human, natural, and supernatural enemies marks him as the type of early Southeast Asian leader whom Wolters (1982:7-9) has termed a "man of prowess."[7] Such a leader's charismatic qualities made it possible for him to attract followings, mainly from extended kin, living in many different settlements. Whether the story of Thao Hung/Cheuang is based on the actions of a real person will probably never been known, but the story itself, recounted in poetic form, must have made it possible for many peoples living in settlements scattered over a wide area and over a long period of time to think of themselves as the inheritors of a common ancestral hero.

Chamberlain (1991a:120) believes the story can be traced to the area where the Tai languages may have originated, namely in an area of what are now northern Vietnam and southern Guizhou in China. He suggests that Thao Hung/Cheuang may have been the same as Phung Hung, whom Vietnamese legend makes the founding hero of Vietnamese civilization (see Taylor 1983:327ff), but it does not follow that the earliest Vietnamese were Tai. The story of Thao Hung/Cheuang is also widely known in oral forms among Austroasiatic-speaking peoples, especially the Khamu (see Smalley 1961), and Maha Sila believes Thao Hung/Cheuang was probably a "Khǭm," that is, a speaker of an Austroasiatic language (Chamberlain 1979:5). Chamberlain has observed that "the sharing of myths between Austroasiatic and Tai is not uncommon and is reinforced by a ritual interdependence" (Chamberlain 1980:7). The epic only became a Tai story when it was written down in the thirteenth or fourteenth century (Chamberlain 1991a:120). Those who claim the genealogy of Thao Hung/Cheuang belong to communities that are not linguistically defined.

A similar point can be made for the story of Princess Cāmadevī.[8] This story was recorded by Tai-speaking people in several different versions, one of the most important being the Pāli text, *Cāmadevī-vaṃsa* (the Lineage of Cāmadevī). Cāmadevī, who is placed in legend in the eighth century A.D., not only carries the authority of kingship inherited from her father, the king of Lavo (Lopburi), but is also a "woman of prowess." She triumphs through magical means over a local chief in the vicinity of modern-day Lamphun and there founds the kingdom of Haripuñjaya that is usually associated with the Mon, but must have included peoples who spoke a variety of Austroasiatic languages and, maybe, Tai languages as well.

Since Cāmadevī appears to have been a Mon, why is she important to the Tai who later establish a kingdom in northern Thailand with a capital at Chiang Mai, not Lamphun? I believe it is because those Tai who compiled the earliest written versions of the legend of Cāmadevī were concerned with establishing the genealogy not of an ethnic group but of a civilization. The founding of Chiang Mai did not rupture this genealogy; it carried it forward. The significant "ethnic" contrast in the story of Cāmadevī is between those who are civilized (i.e., both Mon and their successors, the Tai Yuan) and those who were preliterate peoples who followed local chiefs and who are subsumed under the rubric of Lawa.

As these examples illustrate, the earliest genealogical records we have relating to the Tai-speaking peoples living in what is today Southeast Asia do not situate them as members of communities defined as Tai. Rather, they shared the same genealogies with peoples who were speakers of languages belonging to the very different Austroasiatic-language family. The sharing of genealogies between some Tai- and Austroasiatic-speaking peoples continued even after Tai-speaking peoples acquired the ability to write their languages. Much has been written about the subjugation by Tai of the *khā*, that is Austroasiatic-speaking peoples who were deemed to be barbarians (see, for example, Condominas 1990). Less attention has been given, however, to the fact that the Mon and later the Khmer provided the charter myths for the civilizations of many Tai-speaking groups.

Literacy and New Types of Community among the Tai

A major change in genealogies of communities among Tai-speaking peoples came with the adoption by some of these peoples of writing systems for their languages. A written language—including the alphabetic ones used by most Tai-speaking peoples—can be read by people who speak very different dialects. Texts in the same written language can also link peoples who are not currently in direct personal contact with each other. In other words, a literature that is written with the same orthographic system can serve as the basis for people to imagine themselves part of the same community. This imagining can be reinforced when the literature is religious or when some of the texts serve to extend the power of a state.

A major contrast obtains between the nonliterate and the literate Tai.[9] Many Tai-speaking peoples—I am thinking especially of the Zhuang, found primarily in Guizhou Province of southern China, as well as a number of other Tai-speaking peoples in China and such groups as the Tho and Nung in Vietnam—did not acquire literacy until it was introduced in the nineteenth century by missionaries or later by agencies of modern states. Before this, their horizons were much more localized than were those of the literate Tai.

The premodern writing systems developed by Tai peoples are all ultimately derived from alphabetic writing systems originally devised in India, but none were adapted directly from Indian scripts. Rather, their proximate models were the Indian-derived scripts used by other Southeast Asian peoples, namely, the Mon and Khmer. Thus, in the writing systems we have clear evidence of the importance of historical relations between Tai- and non-Tai-speaking peoples.

Mon writing systems appear to be at the root of many of the writing systems subsequently used by Tai.[10] In the thirteenth century, Tai who had gained dominance in what is today north-central and northern Thailand, undertook to reform the proto-Thai script for reasons that are not entirely clear. The chief product of these reforms was the Sukhothai system that became the ancestor of the scripts that are used to write the national languages of Thailand and Laos today. It is important to note, however, that the orthography of Sukhothai was not the exclusive writing system of either the Siamese or Lao until modern times. During the Sukhothai and Ayudhya periods—thirteenth-eighteenth centuries—Khmer rather than Thai was often used as the written language of the court, and a Khmer-derived script known as *khǭm* was used to write Pāli and sometimes Siamese religious texts even through the nineteenth century.

Penth (1986:248) maintains that from about the beginning of the fifteenth century, another Mon-derived script was adopted by many Tai-speaking peoples living in what are today northern Thailand, the Shan state of Burma east of the Salween, southern Yunnan, and northern and central Laos. He refers to this system as *Tham* since it was first used primarily as a vehicle to convey the teachings of Buddhism in a form more accessible to Tai-speaking peoples. *Tham* is a Tai-ized form of the Pāli word *dhamma* (Sanskrit, *dharma*) that refers to the Way taught by the Buddha. *Tham* script was based on a Mon script used in the old Kingdom of Haripuñjaya (modern-day Lamphun in what is today northern Thailand). It was slightly modified for use by other groups, including the Khün of Kengtung (Chiangtung) state in Burma, the Lue of the Sipsǭngpannā (Xishuangbanna) in southern Yunnan, and the Lao. But the modifications were not so great as to preclude any of these Tai-speaking people as well as the Yuan of northern Thailand from being able to read texts written by any other of these peoples.

I would carry Penth's argument a step further and claim that from the fifteenth to the nineteenth centuries, there was an "imagined community" (to use Ben Anderson's term) constituted by those who shared the same texts (mainly Buddhist) written in one of the variants of the *Tham* script.[11] In other words, Yuan, Khün, Lue, and Lao (albeit with a qualification to be noted in a moment) constituted subgroups of a larger community. This community was shattered when these various subgroups were divided between four modern states—Burma, China, Laos, and Thailand.

The Lao were different from other groups in that they used two different scripts. In addition to *Tham*, used for religious texts, they also used a Sukhothai-derived script, called *Lao Wiang*, for secular purposes. It is this script, and not *Tham*, that became the basis for the orthographic system used for writing the national language of Laos today.

The Fate of Tai Writing Systems

Each of the modern nation-states in which Tai-speaking people live today have adopted language policies that have changed profoundly how writing systems and language more generally are related to identity. The governments of Burma, China, Laos, Vietnam, and Thailand have insisted that all citizens learn their respective "national" languages. A national language is standardized in both written and spoken forms and is taught in state-sponsored schools.[12] The Peoples Republic of China and the Socialist Republic of Vietnam both allow instruction in languages other than Chinese or Vietnamese for early or supplementary education but insist that the national language be taught to everyone and that it become the exclusive language for higher-level education. In both countries, attempts have also been made to standardize and "reform" the writing systems of those languages that are allowed to be maintained by minority groups. In Burma, Laos, and Thailand non-national languages can be taught only outside the formal curriculum of state schools.

Only two of the premodern writing systems of the Tai have become the basis for the writing of national languages—the Sukhothai-derived scripts used for Siamese (central Thai) and Lao. All other Tai-writing systems have been marginalized by national language policies. Some have, however, become the emblems of groups seeking to maintain distinctive identities within today's modern nation-states.

In the late nineteenth century, a print form of *Tham* script was devised by Western Christian missionaries for use in northern Thailand. But *Tham* was unable to compete with Thai when the control of the Siamese state was asserted firmly over northern Thailand. The use of *Tham* was strongly attacked by the government of Thailand under Prime Minister Phibun Songkhram in the early 1940s and although the effort to destroy all manuscripts in *Tham* was aborted after Phibun's fall from power, and not renewed during his second period as prime minister in 1947-

1957, *Tham* was still replaced by Thai as the language of literacy in northern Thailand. Even many who entered the *sangha* (Buddhist monkhood) never learned *Tham*, despite the fact that monastic libraries were stocked with palm-leaf texts written in *Tham*. In the 1970s interest in *Tham* was revived, mainly by a small number of intellectuals, and with the invention of computer fonts for *Tham* in the late 1980s, it has once again become possible to print works in *Tham*. Although most northern Thai will continue to acquire literacy in Thai rather than *Tham*, many point to the rich literary tradition that was produced using *Tham* as part of the cultural heritage of those who identify as Khon Mụang, the term used by northern Thai for themselves. *Tham* has thus become one marker for those who seek to assert an identity in Thailand as a Tai people who are distinct from the dominant central Thai.

The Communist government of China allowed the Lue writing system, a variant of *Tham*, to be perpetuated, but Chinese linguists working together with certain Lue undertook to reform it to make it more adaptable for printing by modern methods. The reformed Lue script has proven to be very unpopular, however, and since the Cultural Revolution the old script, which continues to be handwritten and taught in Buddhist monasteries, has gained new attention by the Lue. Probably only a small percentage of Lue in China are literate in Lue and most are literate in Chinese, but Lue still point with pride to their traditional writing system as a marker of their ethnic distinctiveness.

The Tai Nụa, who have been subsumed by official Chinese nationality policy as part of the Dai-zu that includes the Lue, appear to have been far less successful than the Lue in perpetuating their distinctive script, although it has not totally disappeared. It appears that in many Tai Nụa monasteries, Lue script is also used. Other Tai languages in China are written in Romanized forms devised by Chinese or Chinese-trained linguists; these forms do not appear to have the same ethnic significance as does Lue script.

Khün, the variant of *Tham* used by the Tai-speaking people living in Kengtung in Burma, has no official status, but it is allowed to be taught in Buddhist monasteries. Some monasteries, however, offer instruction in Shan rather than Khün, reflecting the official subsuming of Khün under the Shan rubric in Burma. David Bradley (1993), a missionary linguist, reports that Khün texts were being printed at presses in Kengtung in 1993. Because only Burmese is taught in the schools, literacy in Khün is probably no more common than is literacy in Lue in the Chinese Xishuangbanna (Sipsǭngpannā), and in Burmese Kengtung such literacy is a mark of ethnic distinctiveness.

Communities with Written Histories

Once various premodern Tai-speaking peoples acquired the ability to write their own languages, they could construct texts in which they could "remember" the past.

Charnvit Kasetsiri (1976:1-10, 1979) has identified three types of premodern histories written by Tai-speaking peoples. The first is the *tamnān*, a legend that is often (but not always) a chronicle of a particular Buddhist monument or religious order. *Tamnān* can also be non-Buddhist myths or stories about ancient places. *Tamnān* are the most widespread of premodern historical writings. The second type is the *phongsāwadān*, the annals of a dynastic line of a particular polity. *Phongsāwadān* appear to have been a seventeenth-century creation of the Siamese court of Ayudhya, although they became a model for historical writing among some other Tai-speaking peoples, most notably the Lao. The third, based on primary documents (*cotmaihēt*) and inscriptions (*cārụk*), is the *prawatsāt,* "modern" history, that traces the genealogy of ethnic or national groups.

Tamnān and inscriptions do not offer genealogies of any Tai people. Rather, the communities they make possible to imagine are ones that are religious or are politicospatial in character. Again, one finds in some of these works a basic contrast between the civilized and the uncivilized, but on both sides of this contrast that there are peoples whom today we would say belonged to different ethnic groups. The *phongsāwadān* identify major political domains outside the realm of the Tai domain whose ruling family is chronicled in the work with labels that at first blush seem ethnic or national. But labels such as *phamā* (Burma), *yuan* (Vietnam), and *cīn* (China) hide the fact that these domains, like those of the Tai themselves, include peoples of diverse cultural traditions. All three of these domains included large numbers of Tai-speaking peoples.[13]

In sum, neither premodern histories, nor the literary traditions of premodern Tai-speaking peoples, nor the myths and legends of preliterate Tai-speaking peoples divided communities according to ethnicity or nations. Both "Tai" and "Thai," I maintain, are inventions of quite recent vintage, a century old at most. They are products of a process of restructuring of communities under the hegemonic authority of modern nation-states.

Prawatsāt history was an instrument of this process. It was developed in Siam and subsequently became the model for histories written about the Lao nation and state and about the peoples living within modern states who seek to assert their own distinctive genealogies from those of others in the same states.

Modern Nation-States and the Invention of New Genealogies for the Tai

The Thai Nation

The construction of a nationalist genealogy for the peoples living within the boundaries of Siam was mainly a product of the late nineteenth and early twentieth centuries.[14] The roots of the process must, however, be traced back to a much earlier period in the century. It is now well recognized that a critical event was the discovery in 1833 of the inscription of King Rām Khamhāeng of Sukhothai by the princely monk, Vajirañāna, who would later become King Mongkut. In 1868, the year of King Mongkut's death, Prince Pavares, the Sangharāja (patriarch) of the *sangha*, wrote a memorial in which he described the discovery of the stele with the inscription as being miraculous. But the significance lay more in the fact that when the inscription was read it was found to record the invention of the Thai system of writing.[15] The debate about the Rām Khamhāeeng inscription (see Chamberlain 1991b) seems conclusive to me that the inscription was composed in the Sukhothai period and not, as Piriya Krairiksh has argued, in the nineteenth century by Prince Vajirañāna/King Mongkut. The fact remains that the discovery and interpretation of the inscription made possible a radical break in historiography. Rām Khamhāeeng became and has remained the apical ancestor not of a dynasty but of the Thai people.

The construction of a genealogy for the Thai nation was, in part, a concomitant of the creation in the nineteenth century of what Thongchai Winichakul (1994) has termed the national "geo-body" of Siam. Through being co-opted into the colonial project of mapping the boundaries between Siam and the colonial domains on which it bordered, the Siamese elite began to think about how the people within this geo-body were connected. In the late nineteenth century, the necessity of determining who belonged within the realm of the Thai kingdom became even more compelling. This was because the French, who posed the greatest threat to Siamese sovereignty, utilized a "racial" (what we would today term ethnic) justification for expanding their control over the "Lao" and "Khmer," whom they claimed belonged within French Indochina. "Colonialism defined Siam *racially*. Who are the Thai? . . . Who are the Lao? The Cambodian? With a kind of 'logic of race' delimited, colonialism also came to define Siam legally: Who was a citizen? A protegé? Who was a national? Who had what nationality?" (Streckfuss 1993:125).

Faced with such a "logic of race," King Chulalongkorn and his advisers advanced the claim that most peoples living within Siam belonged to a *chāt Thai*, a Thai nation, that transcended local linguistic and cultural differences. Prince Damrong Rajanubhab, the chief architect of the administrative reforms instituted under King Chulalongkorn and the father of modern Thai historiography, has summarized the evolution of political thinking during the reign of King Chulalongkorn that led to the redefinition of those who spoke Tai languages and lived in Siam as belonging to the Thai nation:

> [King Chulalongkorn] observed that the older system of administration, recognized as being an empire[16] (*prathēt rātchathirāt*), had domains (*mųang*) as dependencies (*mųang khūn*) with peoples of different ethnic groups (*chāt*) and languages (*phāsā*). . . . That system of administration had, however, become obsolete. If it had been maintained it would have harmed the polity. The [k]ing thus determined to reform the

system of administration, changing it into a kingdom (*rātcha-ānākhēt*),[17] an integrated Thai country (*prathēt Thai ruamkan*). [Damrong Rajanubhab 1971 (1935):319-320; my translation]

Although there were many different Tai languages spoken by peoples living in Siam—Lao, Kam Mụang (Yuan), Lue, Phuan, Yǭ, Phū Thai, Ngiao (Shan), Khün, and so on—these were not to be given any distinctive recognition. All of these had previously been subsumed under the single rubric "Lao" by the Siamese, but were now to be considered to be of the same *chāt* as the Siamese; all were *Thai* (Damrong Rajanubhab 1971 [1935]:319; cf. Streckfuss 1993:138-143).[18] The fixing of the boundaries of Siam by border commissions insisted on by the colonial governments of the French and the British determined which Tai-speaking peoples were Thai and which were not (see Thongchai Winichakul 1994).[19] Perhaps the most profound consequence was that most Lao, because they lived in what became northeastern Thailand rather than in what became French Laos, acquired Thai rather than Lao nationality.[20]

The Tai Peoples

While the Siamese elite sought to "forget" the differences between Tai-speaking peoples living within the border of Siam in the process of constructing a new genealogy for the Thai nation, Western scholars, missionaries, and colonial officials were beginning to discover that there were many different types of Tai. There were several reasons for the efforts by Westerners to identify and classify the diverse peoples of mainland Southeast Asia and southern China during the period from about 1880 until World War II. Where colonial rule had been established, governments sought to control the societies through "a comprehensive project of documentation and certification" (Foster 1991:245) of the peoples living within the colonial territory. Protestant missionaries were motivated by the belief that it was necessary to offer people the teachings of Jesus in their own language if they were to understand them and convert them to their religion. Missionaries undertook much of the pioneering linguistic research in Asia, as well as in Africa, Oceania, and Latin America. And scholars adopted a "logic of race," because it provided a seemingly scientific means for classifying the diverse peoples who were being encountered in the expansion of Western power and influence. It should be noted that Westerners in Asia tended to associate race more with differences in language and culture than with differences in biology because phenotypical differences were not so obvious as they were in other parts of the world. Ethnicity would eventually replace race as the dominant concept, but the logic remained.

The accounts by Westerners of the diverse peoples of Burma, China, Vietnam, and Laos multiplied rapidly in the period from about 1880 until the mid-1930s. This research became the basis for most subsequent efforts to classify the peoples of the region systematically into ethnic categories. Of this work, that of the American missionary scholar, William Clifton Dodd, was the most influential for subsequent work on the Tai peoples. Indeed, his book, *The Tai Race: Elder Brother of the Chinese*, can be said to have invented the Tai.[21] Although Dodd uses the term "race," the genealogical principle he used for grouping and dividing the Tai was spoken language. "[T]he Tai are not simply one tribe of a racial family: linguistically, racially they are a family in themselves, like the other three great families in the region, the Chinese family, the Mon-Hkmer family, . . . and the Tibeto-Burman family . . ." (Dodd 1923:45).

The culmination of the approach that makes language the primary criteria for classifying the Tai can be found, I believe, in *Ethnic Groups of Mainland Southeast Asia* (LeBar, Hickey, and Musgrave 1964), a work that although published in 1964 remains a major reference work on the peoples of Southeast Asia.[22] The book was issued by the Human Relations Area Files together with a map entitled "Ethnolinguistic Groups of Mainland Southeast Asia," that was based primarily on the work of the same authors (LeBar, Hickey, Musgrave, and Williams 1964). The map also continues to be consulted as a major reference work although made nearly three decades ago.[23]

In the preface to their book, LeBar, Hickey, and Musgrave set forward their reasons for using language as the basis for classifying ethnic groups in mainland Southeast Asia:

> Considerable thought has been given by the authors to the problem of the identification of units for purposes of ethnographic description and to the subsequent organization of descriptive summaries for representation in book form. After much casting about, it was agreed that *language*, although admittedly not always in agreement with the realities of cultural identification and cultural dynamics, nevertheless offered the only consistent and complete basis for the selection and arrangement of *units*. E. R. Leach, writing on the peoples of the Kachin Hills area of Burma, rightly points out the incorrectness of always assuming that the people who speak a particular language form a unique unit with a particular culture, i.e., a "*tribe*" or "*race*." Leach demonstrates very well how in a relatively small area in northern Burma common social and political structures crosscut the conventional, linguistically derived concepts of tribe and tribal culture. Nevertheless, Leach himself, as soon as his discussion leads him outside the confines of his definition of Kachin culture, uses the very terminology he decries earlier. . . . And this, of course, is the crux of the problem. *Until Leach or someone continues his type of analysis beyond the Kachin Hills, we are left with the conventional tribal units and subunits—defined in most cases largely on the basis of linguistic criteria, and adopted almost without exception throughout the existing literature.* [LeBar, Hickey, Musgrave 1964:v; emphasis added][24]

The privileged position that LeBar, Hickey, and Musgrave assign to spoken language has been followed by most other scholars; to this day the Tai peoples are usually classified by language. We can, as they do, begin by recognizing that there is a language family called "Tai" and that those who speak Tai languages can be differentiated linguistically from those who speak languages belonging to other families. This done, it becomes much more problematic as to how language can be used to divide Tai-speaking peoples into discrete ethnic groups.

If dialect differences are taken as significant, then the number of divisions of the Tai could be very much larger than the twenty-seven groups identified by LeBar, Hickey, and Musgrave or the twenty-five Tai groups and another twelve groups in related subfamilies identified by Clément, Clément-Charpentier, and Lévy (1985; also see Lévy-Ward et al. 1988) in a recent classification of Tai peoples derived from the one undertaken by LeBar, Hickey, and Musgrave.[25] Brown (1965) distinguished seventy-nine dialects of Tai languages spoken within Thailand alone, and Chamberlain (1975) would recognize over one hundred different Tai languages.

Linguists like Brown and Chamberlain, who seek to make fine distinctions between dialects and languages, are interested in historical connections between Tai languages, not in what constitutes speech communities, much less ethnic groups. People often recognize that their local languages (*phāsā phụ̄n mụang*) differ from other local languages. But because these differences often do not preclude communicative interaction with those speaking other local languages (see Hymes 1968) and because diglossia (competence in two languages) is common, people often imagine themselves as members of communities that do not divide along the lines of dialect difference. Diglossia is particularly common among peoples whose local language is not the same as the national language of the state in which they live.

It is also important to emphasize that historical connections between languages are not limited to those within the same language family. Matisoff (1983) has demonstrated that some important features of Southeast Asianicant. languages are shared because of long contact between those whose speech belongs to different language families rather than because of genetic relationships between their languages. Indeed, contact can produce linkages that outweigh those of genetic relationships. Siamese, for example, shares far more with Khmer, an Austroasiatic language, than it does, say, with Zhuang, the largest Tai-speaking grouping in China. For a variety of reasons Thai are, I suggest, more likely to feel kinship with Khmer than with non-Buddhist Tai living in China or northern Vietnam. The reasons include the borrowing of Angkorean ideas of statecraft by the rulers of Ayudhya; the presence in Thailand of many monuments belonging to Angkorean civilization; the sharing by Thai and Khmer of much of their Buddhist cultures; the remembering in historical narratives of many events when Siam and later Thailand were involved in Cambodian affairs; and the incorporation of at least a million people who speak Khmer or Khmer-related languages into Thailand.

Migration has also confounded the use of language as a criteria. In the nineteenth century the Siamese government encouraged or compelled the resettlement of large numbers of people from what is today Laos into what is today Thailand. Other migrants came to northern Thailand from southern China and Burma. And migration continues to the present day, with perhaps the most understudied Tai communities being those founded by migrants from Thailand and refugees from Laos in the United States, Australia, France, and Canada. Migrants sometimes give up speaking their original languages while still remembering their origins in story and legend. Such remembering makes possible the perpetuation of a distinct ethnic identity without maintenance of a distinct language.

Objective distinctions made by linguists between spoken languages or dialects are of value for tracing historical linkages between such languages and dialects. But they do not correspond to the communities whose members are united by shared competence in the spoken languages or assist us in determining what linkages between peoples speaking different languages are the most significant.

Although a linguistic approach to the classification of ethnic groups has proven inadequate, the idea that a "scientific" classification of ethnic groups can be made, including those that could be subsumed under the rubric of Tai, has a powerful appeal. The most elaborate projects of ethnic classification were undertaken in the Peoples Republic of China (see Tapp and Chien Chiao 1989; Harrell 1995; and Harrell's paper in this volume), the Democratic Republic of Vietnam and its successor, the Socialist Republic of Vietnam (see Evans 1985 and Phan Ngoc Chien 1993), and the Lao Peoples Democratic Republic (see Keyes 1992) where political leaders and scholars were influenced by Marxism-Leninism and especially by the nationality policies of Lenin and Stalin (see Connor 1984). The interest in classification has not been restricted, however, to those societies that have been organized according to principles of "scientific Marxism." As I have shown, a version of the project is still very much alive in Thailand.

The consequence of all such projects is the invention of ethnic groups, not their discovery. This is quite clear when we compare the different ways in which Tai-speaking peoples are classified in different countries. I have reviewed the processes of ethnic classification for China, Laos, and Thailand in another paper (Keyes 1992), so I will restrict myself here to a few related examples.

In China, Tai is not a general label for ethnic groups (*minzu*) speaking languages related to those of the dominant peoples of Thailand and Laos; rather those who speak what others would term Tai languages are considered in China to belong to the Zhuang-Dong language family. This family, and most of its constituent groups, are not construed in ways that would link them to the Thai of Thailand, or to the Lao of Laos for that matter. The one exception is the Dai *minzu*, whose name is a Chinese version of Tai. This *minzu* does not, however, correspond to a group that would be recognized in other systems of classification originating outside of China.

Dai include peoples—Lue and Tai Nụa in particular—who did not share the same premodern genealogies or writing systems. Dai is very much a Chinese creation.

In Laos, the Lue are recognized as a distinctive group, albeit one closely related to the Lao in contrast to those groups who are considered to be *phū Thai*—i.e., the Black Tai, Red Tai, and White Tai. Tai, in other words, is not the rubric in Laos for a general category of peoples, but is used to specify particular minority groups.

Distinctions between Tai-speaking peoples that were "forgotten" in Thailand while the Thai nation was being constructed were "remembered" in the 1930s when the country's leaders sought to reverse the process of colonialism. Luang Wichit Watthakan, director-general of the Department of Fine Arts and chief ideologue of the ultranationalist regime of Phibun Songgram in the late 1930s and early 1940s, drew on the writings of Western scholars to construct a new genealogy for the Thai nation by placing its origins in the migrations of Tai peoples from southern China. Tai became the rubric for those Tai-speaking peoples outside of Thailand who had historical linkages to peoples within Thailand or who were once under the Siamese empire.

This genealogical effort provided the basis for promoting a pan-Thai movement, or a *Mahā Ānachak Thai* (Great Thai Empire) as it was known in Thai, modeled on what "Hitler was doing with Germany in Europe" (Somkiat Wanthana 1986:271). This empire would unite "all the peoples of Thai stock, wherever they may be settled, into a single State with Siam [Thailand] as its nucleus" (Crosby 1945:13). Luang Wichit "is reported as having initiated the idea after he came back from a trip to Hanoi with a map showing that there were several groups of 'Thai' people outside Siam" (Somkiat Wanthana 1986:271).

Although the pan-Thai movement faltered after the end of World War II, Thai interest in the Tai did not disappear. Although the racist premises of pan-Thai-ism began to be challenged in the 1960s and 1970s by both radical thinkers (notably Jit Poumisak 1976) and more mainstream scholars (see Woodward 1965; Mote 1966), they are still incorporated in somewhat toned-down form in school texts. The recent interest among Thai in the Tai stems, however, primarily from very different motivations.

Beginning with the reestablishment of relations between Thailand and China in the mid-1970s and the subsequent rapprochement in the late 1980s between Thailand and Laos and Vietnam, it has become possible for Thai to travel to places where Tai-speaking peoples live in these countries. The expansion of the middle class in Thailand, with relatively large amounts of disposable wealth, has also made such travel feasible for a growing number of Thai. At the same time, the socioeconomic transformation of Thailand consequent on high rates of economic growth and the political upheavals beginning with the student-led uprising of 1973 and culminating in the successful challenge to renewed military rule in 1992 have brought Thai "national identity" (*ēkalak hāeng chāt*) into question.

For some Thai who have become deeply disturbed by life in a highly polluted and socially fragmented Bangkok, the interest in Tai-speaking peoples outside of Thailand stems from the desire to find those who have retained the "original" (*doem*) communal values of Thai/Tai society. This motivation has led to a romanticized interpretation of life among certain Tai-speaking peoples, an interpretation that perhaps is most conspicuous in some of the documentaries made for the National Geographic-like TV series, *lōk salapsī*, "Multihued world." Far more important than this nostalgia for the "original Tai" way of life, however, has been the development of a debate about Thainess (*khwāmpen Thai*), in which a discourse about the Tai is used to raise questions about what the essential characteristics of the Thai are.[26]

One perspective sees Thainess as rooted in both language and religion. Thus, the Tai who share the same Thainess with the Thai are those who not only speak a Tai language but also adhere to Theravāda Buddhism. This perspective is clearly enunciated by HRH Princess Galyani Vaddhana in her introduction to the book produced by members of a delegation who accompanied her in 1986 on a trip to Yunnan:

> I must believe that the Thai and Tai who speak the same language, have similar customs, and believe in the same religion used to be the same group (*phuak*), the same race (*phao*) at a time when the term "country" (*prathēt*) had little meaning and [the word] "people" (*chonchāt*) had greater meaning. It was not necessarily that they were forced to leave from elsewhere [i.e., forced to flee their homelands], but divisions occurred when it happened that different countries were created and boundaries were drawn about them. [Princess Galyani Vaddhana 1986:8; my translation]

Thus, it is hardly surprising that most writings in Thai about the Tai have concentrated on the Buddhist Tai—the Lao, Lue, and, to a lesser extent, the Shan. What makes the Thai different from the Buddhist Tai, however, is that the former have another "pillar" (*lak*) of identity—namely, loyalty to the Thai monarchy.

For an increasing number of Thai intellectuals, what is significant about the Tai is not what they share in common with the Thai but in how they are different. Research on non-Buddhist Tai has contributed to this perspective.[27] These intellectuals seek to show how the diversity among the Tai supports the proposition that the Thai are also diverse—in other words, that Thainess is defined not by a homogeneity of culture but by cultural pluralism. This perspective is most evident in those who argue that the Thai are those who live in Thailand, even if they cannot trace their origins to Tai-speaking peoples.

These intellectuals have offered answers to the genealogical question, "Where do the Thai come from?" (*khon Thai mā cāk nai?*) that have entailed deconstructing the hegemonic genealogy based on a putative common language and common religion.[28] In this view, those of Chinese descent in Thailand (*lūk cīn*) can and often do share more Thainess with others living in Thailand who can trace their descent to Tai-speaking peoples than do the latter with Tai-speaking peoples living outside of Thailand.

Conclusion

Tanabe (1991:3) in the introduction to his bibliography, *Religious Traditions among Tai Ethnic Groups*, has observed that "the ethnic identity of a particular group is constructed in a continual and complicated process not only by external forces and arbitrary labeling by outsiders but also by their own social process of creating a self-image." When we ask who the Tai peoples are, we cannot restrict ourselves to the ways in which they have been classified by others. The identities of Tai-speaking peoples are very much in flux as these people rethink their genealogies so as to situate themselves within worlds that have been radically changed by the intrusion of modern states into their lives; by their incorporation into global economies; and by the interest—sometimes positive, sometimes negative— shown in their cultural heritages by officials, tourists, or scholars.

We are not even on firmer ground when we push back in time to a period before the establishment of modern nation-states in mainland Southeast Asia, China, and India. As I have tried to show, a number of different principles underlie the construction of historical and prehistoric genealogies for communities that have included Tai-speaking peoples.

That identities are always historically contingent and are never unchanging essences means that we should be very wary of assuming that peoples who speak a common language, share many cultural practices, or even use the same name for themselves belong in fact to the same ethnic group. Let me give a few examples.

I have shown elsewhere (Keyes 1992) that people who might be considered Lue and who might actually accept this ethnonym for themselves can have very different identities. There are Lue who are Dai (in China), Lue who are Thai and northern Thai (in Thailand), and Lue who are Lao, but not Tai (in Laos). The Lue, then, are hardly a single ethnic group today. A similar argument could be made about any other putative people whose present-day representatives are found distributed among several different states.

The "Lao" provide a case in point. There are, for example, people who are Lao because they identify themselves as being the dominant people of the Lao Peoples Democratic Republic. This state also includes people who are classified as Lao nationals, but who are ethnically distinct from the Lao. Across the border in northeastern Thailand there is a far larger population of people who were once considered Lao by the Siamese and who sometimes today still call themselves Lao, but who are more commonly identified by others and by themselves as Khon Isan, people of the northeast (of Thailand). There are also people who migrated as refugees from Laos to the United States, Australia, Canada, the United Kingdom, and France whose descendants may call themselves Lao but who belong to minority ethnic groups within these countries.

Who are the Tai? They are peoples who have been invented by others and by themselves. It is the process of invention that we need to investigate, not the presumed essential qualities that make Tai different from other peoples.

NOTES

1. Versions of this paper were first presented in both Thai and English at this conference. I wish to thank the Office of the National Cultural Commission for making it possible for me to attend the conference. I want especially to thank Ms. Kulwadee Charoensri, then head of the Culture Authority Section of the ONCC, and Mr. Suriya Smutkupt, of Suranaree Technical University, for their help in preparing the Thai version. I have also benefited from discussing my ideas at a seminar on "Deconstructing Tai (Thai) Ethnicity," held at Australian National University in August 1994 (for a report on this seminar, see Wijeyewardene 1994).

2. Williams is, in the passage quoted, criticizing my (Keyes 1978, 1981) lack of attention to these issues in previous writing on ethnicity.

3. I use the word "premodern" here to refer to the period prior to the integration of Tai-speaking peoples within a modern state with its salient characteristic of precisely delineated territorial boundaries, centralized and uniform administration, and rationalized bureaucracy and fiscal management (including taxation). Although the foundations for modern states in Southeast Asia began to be laid following the British conquest of lower Burma in 1824-1826, the most intensive period of modern state building took place in the last decades of the nineteenth and the first decades of the twentieth centuries. Even then the process was incomplete; Laos cannot be said to have become a fully modern state until after 1975.

4. My thinking has been shaped, in part, by the work of Anderson (1991), Bentley (1987), Chaiwat Satha-Anand (1988), Cohen (1989), Cohn and Dirks (1988), De Vos (1975), De Vos and Romanucci-Ross (1975), Foster (1991), Gellner (1983), Hobsbawm (1990), Smith (1987), and Williams (1989). I am also building here on previous work of my own (see Keyes 1976, 1981, 1992, 1994).

5. Foucault's most succinct statement of his "genealogical method" is in his essay "Nietzsche, Genealogy and History" (1977:138-164). In thinking about this method, I have also drawn on Takashi Fujitani's insightful essay, "Inventing, Forgetting, Remembering: Toward a Historical Ethnography of the Nation-State" (1993). Note that the genealogical method makes "race" a cultural construct rather than a biological given.

6. These two stories do not, by any means, constitute the only ones from the preliterate past of the Tai. I have chosen to discuss these two because they are clearly among the most significant of the ancient stories. All of the genealogical traces relating to Tai-speaking peoples are similar in character to those discussed here.

7. Chamberlain (1986) has sought to identify the sources of Thao Hung/Cheuang story and has found it was once widely known among Tai-speaking peoples. The most complete version of the story comes, however, from the Lao Phuan of Xieng Khouang Province, northwestern Laos. Maha Sila Viravong, who until his death in 1986 was the foremost scholar of Lao literature, history, and culture, discovered the oldest manuscript version of the

epic in the National Library in Bangkok that had been taken by Siamese troops from Xieng Khouang in 1883 (Chamberlain 1986:57). Maha Sila transliterated this manuscript and published it in Thai in the early 1940s (Sila Viravong 1943). He also wrote about the text in an article in Lao originally published in 1953 and recently republished in volumes honoring him (Sila Viravong 1953; Sisana Sisane et al. 1990:194-215). This article, which Chamberlain (1979) has translated into English, provides the best summary of the epic. Chamberlain has undertaken to translate into English the version published by Maha Sila in 1943 (see Chamberlain 1980), but, to my knowledge, it has not yet appeared. I am also indebted for my understanding of the Thao Hung/Cheuang story to conversations with Douangdeuane Bounyavong, a daughter of Maha Sila who has followed her father in studying the cultural history of the peoples of Laos.

8. The legend of Princess Cāmadevī has been translated from the Pāli into Thai in two different versions (Bodhiraṃsi 1967 [orig. 1920], 1972) and into French (Coedès 1925). The story is also given in the Lamphun Chronicle that was originally written in Thai (see *Chronique de Lamp'un* [1930] for a French translation and Richardson 1837 for an early English summary). Condominas (1990) has discussed the contrast between the uncivilized Lawa and civilized Mon and Tai in the story of Cāmadevī.

9. Dodd (1923) was the first to draw attention to the significance of the contrast between the literate and nonliterate Tai.

10. Hans Penth, in a stimulating working theory, has argued that the Shan, Tai Nụa, Ahom, old Yuan (*fak kham*), and Black and White Tai orthographic systems all ultimately derive from "proto-Thai script" developed by about 1000-1100 A.D. by Tai-speaking peoples living in proximity to Mon located upcountry from the centers of Pegu and Lopburi (Penth 1986:246-247). Those who remained isolated from subsequent influences—most notably the Ahom (and the Tai Nụa and Black Tai)—conserved, he believes, the old system of writing.

11. In "Who Are the Lue? Revisited" paper (Keyes 1992:9-10), I characterize this community as one united by Buddhism and refer to it (following Dodd 1923) as "Yuan Buddhism" because of the centrality of Yuan of northern Thailand in its development. Here I stress the importance of a shared textual tradition through which Yuan Buddhism was known.

12. See, in this connection, the stimulating essay by Diller (1991) on the development of the Thai national language. Also see Smalley (1994).

13. When the premodern records deal with the domains of other Tai peoples, these are usually identified by names of the politicospatial *mụang* rather than by the names of the dominant people who live in these domains. Thus, one finds the names of Ayudhya, Sukhothai, Lānnā Thai (all today parts of Thailand), Sipsọngpnnā (Yunnan), Lan Xang (Lān Chāng; Laos), Kengtung (Chiang Tung) and Hsenwi (Sāenwī) (Burma), and so on. The only exception seems to be the Sipsọng Chū Thai, but even in this case the political domains located in what today are northwestern Vietnam and northeastern Laos included many different Tai-speaking peoples (the Black, Red, and White being the largest) and non-Tai Austroasiatic-speaking peoples as well.

14. That nations are "imagined communities" and national cultures "invented" are now well understood as a consequence of the influential writings of Benedict Anderson (1991 [orig. 1983]) and Hobsbawm and Ranger (1983; also see Hobsbawm 1990). The process of imagining nations has also generated the interest of political leaders and scholars in

determining what ethnic constituents make up nations and what linkages exist or might exist between ethnic or national groups in different states (see, in this connection, Williams 1989).

15. I here draw on Piriya Krairiksh's (1991) summary of Prince Pavares's *Rụang aphinihān kānprachak* (which Piriya translates as "An Account of Miraculous Happenings").

16. Prince Damrong used the English word "empire" as a gloss for the Thai *prathēt rātchathirāt.*

17. Prince Damrong himself uses the English word "kingdom" here as a gloss for *rātcha-ānākhēt*. For this reason, I prefer polity rather than kingdom, as Tej Bunnag (1977:146) has rendered it, as a gloss for *bān mụang* in the preceding sentence.

18. Although this is not the context to pursue the point, peoples living in Siam who spoke Khmer or Khmer-related languages (most notably Kui or Suai) also were considered to be Thai.

19. Although Wijeyewardene (1991) is somewhat critical of Thongchai's argument about the creation of the "geo-body" of modern Siam, he accepts that the mapping of the country entailed a radical "restructuring of the way in which the Bangkok court apprehended the territory and people it ruled" (1991:183).

20. For some reflections on the division of the Lao, see Keyes (1967, 1993, 1994).

21. This book was subsequently used as the basis by Luang Wichitmātrā (Sangā Kānchanākhaphan) for *Lak Thai* (The Roots of the Thai) (1963; orig. 1926), a work that laid the basis for the envisioning of a Thai nation that included many Tai peoples living beyond the borders of the country.

22. The book was compiled by Frank E. LeBar, an anthropologist who had done work in Thailand and Laos and who had worked on a number of U.S. government-sponsored handbooks; Gerald Hickey, an anthropologist who had spent much of his career working in Vietnam; and John Musgrave, a specialist on Burma and a senior bibliographer in charge of the Southeast Asian collection at the University of Michigan.

23. LeBar, Hickey, and Musgrave explicitly saw themselves as building on the work of John Embree and particularly on the draft study, *Ethnic Groups of Northern Southeast Asia*, compiled by Embree and William Thomas, published in 1950 (Embree and Thomas 1950; LeBar, Hickey, and Musgrave dedicated their book to Embree). The 1964 study was, however, far more systematic than the earlier work by Embree.

24. The reference to Leach is to his *Political Systems of Highland Burma* (1954).

25. The work of Clément, Clément-Charpentier, and Lévy and their associates in Thailand have refined the work of LeBar, Hickey, and Musgrave on the basis of new material, but they continue to use the same basic approach.

26. See, in this connection, Wijeyewardene (1990). I believe that recent Thai discourse and debate about Thainess is comparable to the Japanese discourse about *nihonjinron*, Japaneseness, which has been very significant in recent years. For a good introduction to the sociology of the Japaneseness debate, see Befu (1993).

27. See the studies of the Black Tai of northern Vietnam (Mǭ. Sībutsarā 1987; Srisakra Vallibhotama and Sujit Wongthes 1991), the Ahom of Assam (Chatthip Narthasupha, Renu Wichasilpa, Renu Arthamesr, and Nongnuj Chantharaphai 1991), and the Zhuang of

southeastern China (Srisakara Vallibhotama and Pranee Wongthes 1993).

28. See Kasetsart University, Department of History, Faculty of Social Sciences (1989), Srisakra Vallibhotama and Sujit Wongthes (1991), Sujit Wongthes (1986, 1987), and Terwiel, Diller, and Chonthira Satayawatthana (1990).

REFERENCES

Anderson, Benedict R. O'G. 1991, rev. and exp. ed. (orig. 1983). *Imagined Communities: Reflections on the Origin and Spread of Nationalism.* London: Verso.

Befu, Harumi. 1993. "Nationalism and *Nihonjinron.*" In *Cultural Nationalism in East Asia: Representation and Identity.* Harumi Befu, ed. Pp. 107-138. Berkeley: University of California Press.

Bentley, G. Carter. 1987. "Ethnicity and Practice." *Comparative Studies in Society and History* 29(1):24-55.

Bodhiraṃsi. 1967 (orig. 1920). *Cāmthēwīwong phongsāwadān mʉang Haripunchai* (Lineage of Cāmadevī, Chronicle of Haripuñjaya). Phrayā Pǫriyat Thammathādā (Phāē Tālalak) and Phra Yānwicit (Sitthi Lōcanānon), trans. Bangkok: Published on the Occasion of the 72nd Birthday of Mrs. Kimhǭ Nimānhēmin.

Bodhiraṃsi. 1972. *Khamplāē* Cāmthēwīwong phongsāwadān mʉang Haripunchai (Translation of Lineage of Cāmadevī, Chronicle of Haripuñjaya). Bangkok: Cremation Volume for Chat Dāēngdīlōēt.

Bourdieu, Pierre. 1977. *Outline of a Theory of Practice.* Richard Nice, trans. Cambridge: Cambridge University Press.

Bradley, David. 1993. "Kengtung in 1993: Languages in Use." *Thai-Yunnan Project Newsletter* (Canberra) 21:4-7.

Brown, J. Marvin. 1965. *From Ancient Thai to Modern Dialects.* Bangkok: Social Science Association Press of Thailand.

Chaiwat Satha-Anand. 1988. "Of Imagination and the State." In *Ethnic Conflict in Buddhist Societies: Sri Lanka, Thailand and Burma.* K. M. deSilva, Pensri Duke, Ellen S. Goldberg, and Nathan Katz, eds. Pp. 27-41. London: Pinter Publishers and Boulder, CO: Westview Press.

Chamberlain, J. R. 1975. "A New Look at the History and Classification of the Thai Languages." In *Studies in Tai Linguistics in Honor of W. J. Gedney.* J. G. Harris and J. R. Chamberlain, eds. Pp. 49-66. Bangkok: Centre of English Language, Office of State Universities.

Chamberlain, J. R. 1979. "A Lao Epic Poem: Thao Hung or Cheuang." Paper presented at the Symposium on Austroasiatic Languages, Helsingør, Denmark.

Chamberlain, J. R. 1980. "Translation of the Tai Epic Poem: Thao Hung or Cheuang." Proposal to the National Endowment for Humanities.

Chamberlain, J. R. 1986. "Remarks on the Origins of *Thao Hung* or Cheuang." In *Papers from a Conference on Thai Studies in Honor of William J. Gedney.* Robert J. Bickner,

Thomas J. Hudak, and Patcharin Pevasantiwong, eds. Pp. 57-90. Ann Arbor: University of Michigan, Michigan Papers on South and Southeast Asia, Center for South and Southeast Asian Studies, Number 25.

Chamberlain, J. R. 1991a. "Mène: A Tai Dialect Originally Spoken in Nghê An (Nghê Tinh), Viêtnam." *Journal of the Siam Society* 79(2):103-123.

Chamberlain, J. R., ed. 1991b. *The Ram Khamhaeng Controversy. Collected Papers.* Bangkok: The Siam Society.

Charnvit Kasetsiri. 1976. *The Rise of Ayudhya: A History of Siam in the Fourteenth and Fifteenth Centuries.* Kuala Lumpur: Oxford University Press.

Charnvit Kasetsiri. 1979. "Thai Historiography from Ancient Times to the Modern Period." In *Perceptions of the Past in Southeast Asia.* Anthony Reid and David Marr, eds. Pp. 156-170. Singapore: Heinemann Educational Books, Published for the Asian Studies Association of Australia.

Chatthip Narthasupha, Renu Wichasilpa, Renu Arthamesr, and Nongnuj Chantharaphai. 1991. *Mụang Nun Sun Kham* (Mụang Nun Sun Kham). Bangkok: Sāng San.

Chronique de Lamp'un, Histoire de la dynastie Chamt'evi. 1930. Camille Notton, trans. Paris: Charles Lavuzelle.

Clément, Pierre, Sophie Clément-Charpentier, and Annick Lévy. 1985. *Carte des Ethnies de Langues Thai.* Paris: Centre de Documentation et de Recherches sur l'Asie du Sud-Est et le Monde Insulindien.

Coedès, George. 1925. "Documents sur l'histoire politique du Lao occidental." *Bulletin de l'Ecole Française d'Extrême Orient* 25(1):1-202.

Cohen, Ronald. 1989. *Ethnicity, the State and Moral Order.* Cambridge: Massachusetts Institute of Technology, Center for International Studies, Working Paper.

Cohn, B. S., and N. B. Dirks. 1988. "Beyond the Fringe: The Nation State, Colonialism, and the Technologies of Power." *Journal of Historical Sociology* 12:224-229.

Condominas, Georges. 1990. *From Lawa to Mon, From Saa' to Thai: Historical and Anthropological Aspects of Southeast Asian Social Spaces.* Stephanie Anderson, Maria Magannon, and Gehan Wijeyewardene, trans. Canberra: The Australian National University, Research School of Pacific Studies, Occasional Paper of the Department of Anthropology (in association with the Thai-Yunnan Project).

Connor, Walker. 1984. *The National Question in Marxist-Leninist Theory and Strategy.* Princeton: Princeton University Press.

Crosby, Josiah. 1945. *Siam: The Crossroads.* London: Hollis & Carter.

Damrong Rajanubhab, Prince. 1971 (1935). *Nithān bōrān khadī* (Historical Anecdotes). Bangkok: Phrāe Phithayā.

De Vos, George A. 1975. "Ethnic Pluralism: Conflict and Accommodation." In *Ethnic Identity: Cultural Continuities and Change.* George A. De Vos and Lola Romanucci-Ross, eds. Pp. 5-41. Palo Alto: Mayfield.

De Vos, George A., and Lola Romanucci-Ross. 1975. "Ethnicity: Vessel of Meaning and Emblem of Contrast." In *Ethnic Identity: Cultural Continuities and Change*. George A. De Vos and Lola Romanucci-Ross, eds. Pp. 363-390. Palo Alto: Mayfield.

Diller, Anthony. 1991. "What Makes Central Thai a National Language?" *National Identity and Its Defenders: Thailand, 1939-1989*. Craig J. Reynolds, ed. Pp. 87-132. Melbourne: Monash University, Centre of Southeast Asian Studies, Monash Papers on Southeast Asia, No. 25.

Dodd, William Clifton. 1923. *The Tai Race: Elder Brother of the Chinese*. Cedar Rapids: The Torch Press.

Embree, John F., and William L. Thomas, Jr., comps. 1950. "Ethnic Groups of Northern Southeast Asia." Mimeo. New Haven: Yale University, Southeast Asian Studies.

Evans, Grant. 1985. "Vietnamese Communist Anthropology." Canberra Anthropology 8(1 & 2):116-147.

Foster, Robert J. 1991. "Making National Cultures in the Global Ecumene." *Annual Reviews of Anthropology* 20:235-260.

Foucault, Michel. 1977. "Nietzsche, Genealogy, History." In *Language, Counter-Memory, Practice*. Donald F. Bouchard and Sherry Simon, trans.; Donald F. Bouchard, ed. Pp. 138-164. Ithaca: Cornell University Press.

Fujitani, Takashi. 1993. "Inventing, Forgetting, Remembering: Toward a Historical Ethnography of the Nation-State." In *Cultural Nationalism in East Asia: Representation and Identity*. Harumi Befu, ed. Pp. 77-106. Berkeley: University of California Press.

Galyani Vaddhana, Princess, comp. 1986. *Yunnān*. Bangkok: Watthanāphānit.

Gellner, Ernest. 1983. *Nations and Nationalism*. Ithaca: Cornell University Press.

Harrell, Steven, ed. 1995. *Cultural Encounters on China's Ethnic Frontiers*. Seattle: University of Washington Press.

Hobsbawm, E. J. 1990. *Nations and Nationalism since 1780. Programme, Myth, Reality*. Cambridge: Cambridge University Press.

Hobsbawm, E. J., and Terence Ranger, eds. 1983. *The Invention of Tradition*. Cambridge: Cambridge University Press.

Hymes, Dell. 1968. "Linguistic Problems in Defining the Concept of Tribe." In *Essays on the Problem of Tribe, Proceedings of the 1967 Annual Spring Meeting of the American Ethnological Society*. June Helm, ed. Pp. 23-48. Seattle: University of Washington Press.

Jit Poumisak. 1976 (orig. about 1952; 2d printing, Bangkok: Duang Kamon, 1981). *Khwāmpenmā khǭng kham Sayām, Thai, Lāo lae Khǭm lae laksanā thāng sangkhom khǭng chụ̄chonchāt* (Origins of the Words, Siam, Thai, Lao and Khǭm and Social Characteristics of Nationality Names). Bangkok: Social Science and Humanities Textbook Project Foundation, Social Science Association of Thailand.

Kasetsart University, Department of History, Faculty of Social Sciences, comp. 1989. *Ekkasān prakǭp kānsammanā rụ̄ang "Khon Thai-nǭk prathēt phromdāen khwāmrū"*

(Collected Papers from a Seminar on "Tai Peoples Outside the Country—Frontier Knowledge"). Bangkok.

Keyes, Charles F. 1967. *Isan: Regionalism in Northeastern Thailand.* Ithaca: Cornell University Southeast Asia Program (Data Paper 65).

Keyes, Charles F. 1976. "Towards a New Formulation of the Concept of Ethnic Group." *Ethnicity* 3:202-213.

Keyes, Charles F. 1981. "The Dialectics of Ethnic Change." In *Ethnic Change.* Charles F. Keyes, ed. Pp. 4-30. Seattle: University of Washington Press.

Keyes, Charles F. 1992. *Who Are the Lue Revisited? Ethnic Identity in Laos, Thailand, and China.* Cambridge: Massachusetts Institute of Technology, The Center for International Studies, Working paper.

Keyes, Charles F. 1993. "A Princess in a Peoples' Republic: A New Phase in the Construction of the Lao Nation." Paper prepared for panel on "Minorities within Tai/Thai Political Systems: Historical and Theoretical Perspective," organized by Andrew Turton, 5th International Conference on Thai Studies, London, School of Oriental and African Studies.

Keyes, Charles F. 1994. "The Nation-State and the Politics of Indigenous Minorities: Reflections on Ethnic Insurgency in Burma." Paper prepared for the conference on "Tribal Minorities and the State," organized by the Henry Frank Guggenheim Foundation, Istanbul, February.

Keyes, Charles F. 1995. "Hegemony and Resistance in Northeastern Thailand." In *Regions and National Integration in Thailand, 1892-1992.* Volker Grabosky, ed. Pp. 154-182. Wiesbaden: Otto Harrassowitz.

Leach, E. R. 1954. *Political Systems of Highland Burma.* Cambridge: Harvard University Press.

LeBar, Frank M., Gerald C. Hickey, and John K. Musgrave, comps. 1964. *Ethnic Groups of Mainland Southeast Asia.* New Haven: Human Relations Area Files Press.

LeBar, Frank M., Gerald C. Hickey, and John K. Musgrave, comps.; Robert Le Williams, mapmaker. 1964. Map of "Ethnolinguistic Groups of Mainland Southeast Asia." New Haven: Human Relations Area Files.

Le Boulanger, Paul. 1931. *Histoire du Laos Français.* Paris: Plon.

Lévy-Ward, Annick et al. 1988. "Some Observations on the Map of the Ethnic Groups Speaking Thai Languages." *Journal of the Siam Society* 76:29-45.

Li, Fang-kuei. 1959. "Classification by Vocabulary: Tai Dialects." *Anthropological Linguistics* 1:15-21.

Matisoff, James A. 1983. "Linguistic Diversity and Language Contact." In *Highlanders of Thailand.* John McKinnon and Wanat Bhruksasri, eds. Pp. 56-86. Kuala Lumpur: Oxford University Press.

Mǭ. Sībutsarā. 1987. *Thai dam ramphan* (Black Tai from the Bottom of the Heart). Bangkok: Bannakhit Trading.

Mote, F. W. 1966. "Symposium on the Prehistory of the Thai People: The View from the Discipline of Chinese History." *Sangkhomsāt Parithat* (Social Science Review, Bangkok), *chabap phisēt kiaokap "prawatsāt Thai tām thatsanakhati samai patcuban"* (Special Issue on "Thai History in Contemporary Perspective"), pp. 24-31.

Penth, Hans. 1986. "Thai Scripts: An Outline of Their Origin and Development." In *Yunnān*. Princess Galyani Vaddhana, comp. Pp. 246-249. Bangkok: Watthanāphānit.

Phan Ngoc Chien. 1993. "Ethnic Identification of the Montagnards in the Central Highlands of Vietnam." Unpublished M.A. thesis, University of Washington.

Piriya Krairiksh. 1991. "The Date of the Ram Khamhaeng Inscription." In *The Ram Khamhaeng Controversy. Collected Papers*. James R. Chamberlain, ed. Pp. 257-272. Bangkok: The Siam Society.

Richardson, D. 1837. "The History of Labong." *Journal of the Asiatic Society of Bombay* 59:55-57.

Seidenfaden, Eric. 1958. *The Thai Peoples*. Bangkok: The Siam Society.

Sila Viravong, Maha, trans. 1943. *Thāo* Hung rų̄ Cų̄ang (Thao Hung or Cheuang). Ubon: cremation volume for Somdet Phra Mahā Viravong at Wat Boromniwat.

Sila Viravong, Maha. 1953. "Wannakhadī Lāo: Thāo Hung lų̄ Cų̄ang." *Wannakhadīsān* (Vientiane) 1(2):41-54, 1(3):56-60, 2(4):12-20.

Sisana Sisane (Sīsana Sīsān) et al. 1990. *Mahā Silā Wīlawong: Sīwit lae phonngān* (Maha Sila Viravong: Life and Work). Vientiane: Committee for Social Sciences.

Smalley, William A. 1961. "Ciang: Khamu' Culture Hero." In *Felicitation Volumes of Southeast Asian Studies Presented to His Highness Prince Dhaninivat Kramamun Bidyalabh Bridhyakorn*. The Siam Society, comp. Pp. 41-54. Bangkok: The Siam Society.

Smalley, William A. 1994. *Linguistic Diversity and National Unity: Language Ecology in Thailand*. Chicago: University of Chicago Press.

Smith, Anthony D. 1987. *The Ethnic Origins of Nations*. Oxford: Basil Blackwell.

Somkiat Wanthana. 1986. "The Politics of Modern Thai Historiography." Ph.D. diss., Monash University.

Srisakara Vallibhotama, and Sujit Wongthes. 1991. *Thai nǭi, Thai yai, Thai Sayām: Pramuan rųangrāo kiaokap "Khon Thai mā cāk nai?" phrǭm phāp chut 4 sīcāk mųang thāen (Dian Bian Fū) nai Wiatnām* (Thai Nǭi, Thai Yai, Thai Siam: Collected Essays Concerning "Where Did the Thai Come From?" together with a Collection of Four-colored Photos from Muang Thaen [Dien Bien Phu] in Vietnam). Bangkok: Sinlapawatthanātham, special Issue.

Srisakara Vallibhotama, and Pranee Wongthes. 1993. *Cuang: Phīnǭng phao Thai kao thīsut* (Zhuang: The Oldest Tai). Bangkok: Mahāwitthayālai Sinlapākǭn.

Streckfuss, David. 1993. "The Mixed Colonial Legacy in Siam: Origins of Thai Racialist Thought." In *Autonomous Histories, Particular Truths: Essays in Honor of John R. W.*

Smail. Laurie J. Sears, ed. Pp. 123-153. Madison: University of Wisconsin, Center for Southeast Asian Studies, Monograph No. 11.

Sujit Wongthes. 1986. *Khon Thai yū thīnī: Prawatsāt sangkhom lae wattthanātham khǫng chāo sayām nai mųang Thai* (The Thais Were Always Here: A Social and Cultural History of the Siamese People of Thailand). Bangkok: Sinlapawatthanātham.

Sujit Wongthes, ed. 1987. "Khon Thai yū thīnai bāng?" (Where Have the Thai Sometimes Lived?). Special issue of *Sinlapawatthanātham* (Art and Culture). Bangkok: Sinlapawatthanātham.

Tanabe, Shigeharu. 1991. *Religious Traditions among Tai Ethnic Groups: A Selected Bibliography.* Bangkok: Ayutthaya Historical Study Centre.

Tapp, Nicholas, and Chien Chiao, eds. 1989. *Ethnicity and Ethnic Groups in China.* Hong Kong: Chinese University Press.

Taylor, Keith Weller. 1983. *The Birth of Vietnam.* Berkeley: University of California Press.

Tej Bunnag. 1977. *The Provincial Administration of Siam, 1892-1915.* Kuala Lumpur: Oxford University Press.

Terwiel, B. J., Anthony Diller, and Chonthira Satayawatthana. 1990. *Khon hai (doem) mai dai yū thīnī* (The [original] Tai Did Not Live Here). Bangkok: Mųang Bōrān.

Thongchai Winichakul. 1994. *Siam Mapped: A History of the Geo-Body of a Naion.* Honolulu: University of Hawaii Press.

Wichitmātrā, Luang (Sangā Kānchanākhaphan). 1963 (1926). *Lak Thai* (The Roots of the Thai). Bangkok: Odeon Store.

Wijeyewardene, Gehan. 1990. "Thailand and the Tai: Versions of Ethnic Identity." In *Ethnic Groups across National Boundaries in Mainland Southeast Asia.* Gehan Wijeyewardene, ed. Pp. 48-73. Singapore: Institute of Southeast Asian Studies.

Wijeyewardene, Gehen. 1991. "The Frontiers of Thailand." In *National Identity and Its Defenders: Thailand, 1939-1989.* Craig J. Reynolds, ed. Pp. 157-190. Melbourne: Monash University, Centre of Southeast Asian Studies, Monash Papers on Southeast Asia, No. 25.

Wijeyewardene, Gehen. 1994. "Deconstructing Tai (Thai) Ethnicity: Seminar Report." *Thai-Yunnan Project Newsletter* 26:1-5.

Williams, Brackette F. 1989. "A Class Act: Anthropology and the Race to Nation across Ethnic Terrain." *Annual Review of Anthropology* 18:401-444.

Wolters, O. W. 1982. *History, Culture, and Region in Southeast Asian Perspectives.* Singapore: Institute of Southeast Asian Studies.

Woodward, Hiram W., Jr. 1965. "Who Are the Ancestors of the Thais?: Report on the Seminar." *Sangkhomsāt Parithat* (Social Science Review Bangkok) 2(3)88-91.

Chapter Eight

The Search for Hungarian National Identity[1]

Prologue: "And What about My Hungarianness?!"[2]

. . . My father was a very wise man. He died two weeks before the Germans came into Hungary. Over three hundred people attended his funeral in Zala—the mayor, the judge, the members of the appellate court from Pécs, the dignitaries from the bank; some even came from Budapest. Everybody who was anybody was there. The head of the bar association was the eulogizer, and after that other notables also addressed those who gathered on that cold and rainy day of March 4, 1944.

I always get very upset when I think of those times. Circumstances were disgraceful. . . . For example, when they rounded up all the Jews in 1942 a lot of second-generation Galicianers [Jews whose parents came from Poland], who already spoke only Hungarian were forcibly deported from this country. Heinous. . . .

. . . I am going to tell you something that may sound silly, but I know that you will understand. During my youth I fought eighteen duels: eleven sword fights and seven pistol incidents. Not that I was pugnacious youth, but I would never allow, not even in jest, stupid prejudiced remarks to be made in my presence. No, I never ignored stupid, demeaning comments. . . .

. . . My mother died in 1917, when I was sixteen. My father never married again. He made a vow after my mother died that never again. Why? Because theirs was a loveless marriage: my mother never loved him. Even as a small child I knew that, clearly felt it, and I was always on my father's side. I felt sorry for him. I don't really know why she did not love him.

Certain things were never talked about in our household. These issues were shady, but sometimes servants whispered. I still remember verses like "it was not only the candy-cane little Lizzy got from the big attorney. . . ." But the fact that my mother was fourteen when my father, an already successful, well-known attorney of thirty-four married her with special dispensation from the Ministry of Interior, indicates to me that something was definitely wrong. My father's apartment and his office were on the ground floor of Number 4 Erzsébet Square in Zala. The building was owned by my maternal grandparents, who also owned and ran a grocery store down the block in the heart of the city. So I am not sure what happened, how and when, but something surely did.

They married in 1896 and some months later my sister, Györgyi, was born. She had something like epilepsy, and did not live long. Then, two years later, my brother, Zoltán was born. Before he was a month old he died in sepsis as a result of having been circumcised. My father desperately wanted a child, a son, of course. So, when I was born in 1901, he did not allow me to be circumcised. He was unrelenting. He stayed unrelenting even after Rabbi Newmann threatened him and said that uncircumcised I could never be part of the covenant. To that my father reportedly replied with "and so what?!"

My father was never religious. . . . In fact, he was a member of the Free Masons. I remember that their lodge was on Rozgonyi Street, and he would attend the meetings late at night, on the sly, not so much because it was a clandestine association but mainly because his clientele, the mostly devout Roman Catholic gentry, would have never stood for it. Another attorney, I think by the name of Pál Aczél was the leader at the Zala Lodge. . . .

When I turned ten I began to attend the Piarist Gymnasium.[3] So I got a real, superior Piarist education. My teachers loved me and *ambicionálták* [they strove] that I become somebody who, until I got into their school, I was obviously not. When at the age of thirteen I converted and became a Roman Catholic, Sándor Gózon, the appellate court judge, became my godfather. From then on, I was raised as a real Magyar gentry. My godfather had a nephew, who was an officer in the Huszár [Hussar] Regiment and he married into a prominent gentry family. I was part of that circle. . . .

Then in my eighteenth year, when I moved to Budapest and started University, I legally changed my name from Klein to Huszár and chose to became Árpád Gyula

Huszár.[4] Understand, please: as a result of my upbringing, I not only became a gentry, but I became a genuine, grand Hungarian patriot. And never for a moment did I believe that my Jewish origins would block my way. Never. People of my circle never made me feel Jewish. And those others who dared to insult me so, I fought in a duel. . . .[5]

In '29—at that time I was already living in Budapest and was on my own as I had my doctorate in jurisprudence, my father lost everything, including our beautiful six-room house. The house was bought by the German, his name was Hild, the owner of Hild Mortuary. My father then moved into a small apartment on Sugar Street. . . . But life, our life like everybody else's, went on.

Everyone felt the Great Depression. But, starting in 1938, with the commencement of the so-called first Jewish Law things began to change. By the time they forced me into Forced Labor Battalion, I was made into a Jew again.[6] Yes, they made me into a Jew again, but they could not distance me from being a real Hungarian. . . .

What is a Hungarian, what is a real Magyar? It cannot be defined. But, say, I watch a Swedish-Portugal soccer game. I watch it because it is on TV and I like soccer. But my heart stays out of it. I don't really care. But if I watch our boys play I feel it in my very soul. It is a question of belonging. Being a Hungarian is not a physical state but an inner feeling, a condition here in your heart [he points to the left side of his chest] that I cannot really define. This is my big tragedy. Sometimes I curse those who did this to me. . . . Those who made a Jew of me again. When I really belong to the real Hungarians. . . . To say that your nationality is Israelite! What nonsense, here, in this context! Why it happened? How it happened? Take Chrudinak, the TV star. He writes his name with a "ch." Why is he a Hungarian? Why can all the Slovaks, Swabs, and Croats become Hungarians in a generation or two here? But what about my Hungarianness?!

. . . I am of the opinion that there are so very few in this little country who genuinely feel Hungarian, who really are dedicated Hungarians that [these new politicians today] should embrace us warmly, accept us with love, and without reservation. Yes, they should be glad that we, such a small remnant of an only too thoroughly exterminated people, are still loyal Hungarians in spite of all that happened in the past. There should be cohesion, they should aim for that above all.

Yet, I feel today again like I felt in the late 1930s. The same words are uttered by so many, by the people on the street, even by some politicians. The same graffiti appear on public walls. The same ominous threat hangs in the air. . . .

If I want to use a rational, cold mode of reasoning, I would have to say that those Jews who left Hungary were absolutely right. The ones who emigrated were smart to do so. But I can't think any way other than as a Hungarian and I can't live anywhere else but here. I know! I have been all over, even traveled to [North

America] twice. You know the saying, *extra hungariam non est vita* . . . [outside of Hungary there is no life, and if there is life, it is not life like this].

Still, if I try to look at this with a cold, rational head I know that there are a lot of Hungarians of Jewish origin who cannot think and do any other way but as Hungarians. Regardless of where they are. Look at Ágnes Heller, look at Ferenc Fehér, Ede Teller, and so many others! They left Hungary, but are still very much Hungarians. Wherever they went they did not turn into super Jews there, but remained deeply concerned with Hungarian-related issues. They did not turn out to be Jews but, regardless of their place of residence, *legalább féllábbal még benne vannak a magyarságban* [with at least one foot, they still remain firmly planted in Hungarianness].

The New-Old Question of Hungarianness, Or Who Is a "Deep Magyar"?

What is this Hungarianness? Dr. Huszár had a difficult time defining it. The aim of the foregoing prologue is to show, in the words and through the story of a single individual, struggles with this powerful construct. As Dr. Huszár's case illustrates, Hungarianness embodies Hungarian identity, ethnicity, nationality, and nationalism and the relationship between various groups during this century. There is no more faithful and ideal exemplar than a convert. This can be seen by Dr. Huszár's carefully studied and performed Hungarianness that was evident throughout all of our formal and informal conversations.

Why else have I begun this chapter with parts of a life history collected in Budapest in the early 1990s? Because this story gives us a diachronic glance into the very question of Hungarianness, while shedding light on a Hungarian system of national values and one individual's particular social portrait of our entire century.[7] People ultimately define themselves through their social relations as well as through the symbols they use.[8]

In Árpád Gyula Huszár's case his identity is overstated; since he was thirteen he tried to fit his persona into his godfather's social circle. His identity is exaggerated, made conspicuous not merely by clear signs but by glaring cultural markers. These markers include the immediately obvious, such as his mannerisms, his apparel, his carefully cultivated "Hungarian facial hair," and all three of his carefully chosen Hungarian first-, middle-, and family-names adopted at the age of thirteen. The markers also include less obvious, but still clear manifestations of Hungarian identity: the manner in which he tells stories with Hungarian emphases in style and content; his dueling and the scars of the duels; his habits of riding and hunting and related leisure activities; his education; the furnishings in his apartment; and how he communicates with his wife and others around him. These are all typical, rather stereotyped, behaviors that were, at one time, expected from members of Hungarian gentry. Not only is the past brought into the present as one person recalls his life, but the present, significantly, also becomes an integral part in the [re]construction of the past. It is important that the life history was recorded in the early 1990s because the Zeitgeist, the spirit of that historical moment, in a sense to helped recapture and frame the past.

Based on accounts, in the late 1860s Judaism was a less valued resource strategy than assimilation in Zala and its surrounding region. Unlike elsewhere in the Carpathian Basin, particularly in the eastern and northern regions of pre-Trianon Hungary, in secular, affluent, western Hungary the need to cultivate Jewishness, and to shape a distinct Jewish identity in contrast to the surrounding majority culture, did not seem as salient an issue as it did elsewhere. Rather, an exaggerated national identity, an overemphasized, all-encompassing Hungarianness was developed, manifested, and carefully nurtured, not only in the post-Trianon Treaty[9] frenzy of "No, No! Never!" but in decades earlier as well.

If we examine the case of Árpád Gyula Huszár through Barth's (1969) notion of self-ascription and ascription by others as the main factors of ethnic identity, the excerpts indicate clearly that an unbridgeable abyss grew between the self Huszár ascribed to himself and the way he was seen by others. This was particularly so during the critical period between the enactment of the first Hungarian anti-Jewish Laws in 1938 and the end of World War II.

Since 1989, once again, the difference between self-ascription and ascription by others is being felt strongly and increasingly. This tells us something of the general mood in Hungary today, an era filled with economic and political difficulties. Huszár's life story excerpts illustrate that now, as in all critical points in history, there is a search for scapegoats and politicians seek for ways to gain easy popularity. For Eastern Europe's small surviving Jewish populations, and for its large and growing Gypsy population, this is cause for special concern (Helsinki Watch, 1993; Hockenos 1993).

Chauvinistic nationalism in Hungary was internalized by large segments of all classes. This was an important factor in limiting the dissemination of international ideas of, among others, the Social Democrats, who, according to one historian, "underestimated the impact of nationalism in the working classes before World War I" (Bárány 1969:283). Today, as we approach the twenty-first century, I suggest that democratic ideas and ideals have a difficult if not impossible chance of taking root in Hungary, not only because these ideals are not indigenous notions in east-central Europe (with the debatable exception of the Czech Republic), but because the social and economic conditions are, again, ripe for evoking a specific, potentially very dangerous kind of Eastern European nationalism (Bárány 1969; Sugar and Lederer 1969; Ash 1989; Csepeli, 1990, 1992; Pataki 1990; Hockenos 1993; Sík 1992a, 1992b; Závecz 1992, 1993).

Among the fundamental elements needed to construct and maintain ethnic or national identity is the need for an Other, and in the multinational and multiethnic kaleidoscope of pre-Trianon Hungary, as in the entire Eastern European region, there was never a shortage of the perpetual Other against whom the often porous boundary of Hungarianness could be drawn and redrawn over and over. There is no question as to whether "passing" was possible. According to some observers (Telkes 1976), it was clearly invited. At times passing was not only overlooked but encouraged for Jews and others who claimed Hungarian as their native or primary language. This was particularly the case when there was a need to somehow prove that the Magyars were the numerical majority in the Hungarian part of the Dual Monarchy (especially between 1867-1914 when Magyars were not an absolute majority) and the criterion of ethnicity was language.

A Soviet ethnographer—who shall remain nameless here— asserted in the 1980s that "just like people in the Soviet Union, Eastern European people work in harmonious unison for building socialism while ethnic, national and class differences are rapidly fading away." When we observe the region in general, and Hungary in particular, it is obvious that these, in fact, did not fade away. After Albania and Poland, Hungary is ethnically the most homogeneous country in the general area. Yet, as I show in this chapter, the issue of "who is really Hungarian" became paramount in the post-Communist popular and political informal discourse. This issue has numerous undertones, including xenophobia, anti-Semitism, anti-Roma (that is anti-Gypsy), anti-immigrant, and antirefugee sentiments. Without a doubt, the question of national or ethnic identity is one of the most salient issues in Hungary since the collapse of the socialist regime in 1989. Although that regime kept the nationality and ethnic question artificially more or less dormant for over forty years, it is by no means a new question.[10]

Because of the particular national configuration of the peoples in east-central Europe in general and the Carpathian Basin in particular, the query "What and who is a Hungarian?" (*Mi a Magyar? Ki a Magyar?*) preoccupied generations since the early nineteenth century, when the young Hungarian political elite's misinterpretation of Herder's work on nations and national demise gave rise to similar issues. Although somewhat different, contemporary generations still appear to carry some vestiges of what Péter Hanák (1981:5) calls "Herderian gloom."

Today, amid radical and confusing political and economic changes in the difficult process of reconstructing much-battered ethnic identities and national self-images, a few politicians and people in academia and the media have begun to ask this "question of questions" once again. At the same time, they are searching for and trying to redraw the boundaries of Hungarianness. A struggle, similar in goal but different in motivation, can be observed among the various hyphenated Hungarians in Western Europe and North America, particularly since 1989.[11]

In a number of ways the many different kinds of revolution in Eastern Europe in 1989 signaled the restoration of a former situation. I am not only referring to the Hungarian elections in the late spring of 1994, which brought back many of the "old socialist faces" with personal histories well known during the pre-1989 socialist regime.[12] I am also referring to the fact that there are renewed overt ethnic and national conflicts throughout the region. In the ethnic conflicts we can all too clearly note the verbatim repetition of slogans, ideologies, prejudices, stereotyping, and scapegoating of the interwar period. Nowhere are these expressions manifested more bloodily and terribly than in the former Yugoslavia, with its so-called ethnic cleansing.[13]

Sources of Hungarian National and Ethnic Diversity

The history and the social and cultural relations of the Magyars are laden with internal and external conflicts. Some of these continue and are salient in the present. Domestically, particularly since 1989, there is often explicit discord between factions of the population and the Roma of Hungary, as well as increasing manifestations of popular, though not political and decidedly not official, anti-Semitism. Internationally, there is considerable friction between Hungary and the governments of Romania and the Republic of Slovakia over the treatment of the Hungarian minority populations in those countries. Rural-urban residence, social class, ethnicity, and nationality, among other factors, contribute significantly to social diversity in Hungary.

Demography

The total population of Hungary today is approximately 10,335,000 (KSH 1994); the nationality composition is about 96 percent Magyar, 0.5 percent German, 0.3 percent Slovak, 0.4 percent Croatian, with the rest composed of even smaller ethnic or nationality groups. In addition, since 1989 many refugees have entered the country; some either having settled permanently or having asked for political asylum in Hungary. The majority of refugees are from the former Yugoslavia and from Romania; smaller groups are from different parts of Africa; still others are from the Orient. For example, in the fall of 1991, with an estimated 30,000 to 40,000 Chinese living in Hungary, that country—which the Chinese call "Heavenly Castle of Eastern Europe"—had the most sizable Chinese population in east-central Europe (Nyíri 1994:50-84).

In addition to being a densely populated country (averaging three hundred persons per square mile), there are a number of existing and rapidly growing social problems. One problem is that more than one-fourth of the population is over the age of retirement. With a very low birth rate, one of the highest mortality rates in Europe for mature and middle-aged men, and the highest suicide rate in the world, Hungary's population has been decreasing since 1981 (KSH 1993). Citing World Health Organization and other data, recent studies show that life expectancy in Hungary is the lowest in the so-called developed and developing nations in the world (N.A. 1991; Eberstadt 1994). The average life expectancy is about sixty-nine years. The most shocking data were found among Hungarian men in the forties, whose death rate "fully doubled between 1966 and 1989" (Eberstadt 1994:203).

In part because of high out-migration from villages, the rural population has been continually declining since World War II. This is accompanied by the slackening of traditionally cohesive kinship, fictive kinship, and neighborhood networks. Today, only about 40 percent of the country's population live in rural settlements, and even many of these rural residents are long-distance and long-time commuters who work and live part time in the cities. About 58 percent of the population are urban dwellers; over 20 percent of the country's total population reside in Budapest.

Approximately 62 percent of the population is Roman Catholic; 25 percent is Protestant; 3 percent Greek-, Romanian- or Russian-Orthodox; 1 percent Jewish; and the rest is made up of smaller denominations, often new sects that have been mushrooming since the late 1980s. Despite the relatively homogeneous ethnic and nationality composition of the population since the 1920 Treaty of Trianon there are ethnic problems both within Hungary and between Hungary and its neighbors. Anti-Semitism, which is now independent from the actual and relative number of Jews in numerous societies, is an issue, but only in popular and informal spheres.

Vestiges of the Hungarian Past

Let us look briefly look at the some of the historical sources of ethnic and nationality identity and diversity. Some of the vestiges are foreign occupations, sorrows, losses, and with these, lachrymosity. In Hungary, diversity developed during centuries of spontaneous migrations, and also with purposively planned resettlement of empty villages and towns following various wars and occupations (János 1982; Huseby-Darvas 1990, 1992; Hanák 1991).

Hungarians, who call themselves Magyar (pl., Magyarok), comprise the most populous group in the Finno-Ugric subfamily of the Ural-Altaic people. If today one drives about three hours from the center of the country in any direction, one is in a different country with people speaking a very different language, eating different foods, and having a rather different historical and cultural heritages. The Hungarians arrived in the Carpathian Basin in 896. Their geographic and geopolitical position contributed to a quest for national identity that is often troubled and problematic and always in relation to the national identity of the Other, either in the neighboring countries or within Hungary itself vis-à-vis the internal or indigenous Others.

Language was and remains an important criterion of Hungarianness within the Carpathian Basin.

"We are all alone," wrote Hungary's István Széchenyi in the middle of the nineteenth century. "This motto," György Bárány (1974:11) notes, "echoing Széchenyi's anxieties about Magyardom uniquely isolated situation in Europe was not only the title of a biographical novel on Széchenyi written in 1936 by Nicholas Surányi, but also was later misappropriated for a notorious Jew-baiting organ edited by the right-wing extremist[s] . . . from 1938 to 1944."

There is still an ongoing scholarly and often politicized and heated debate as to whether the Hungarian people constitute an isolated island or a bridge between East and West, between the various groups of people and their languages in east-central Europe. Hungarian has no linguistic relative nearby: all the neighboring cultures (the eastern, northern, and southern Slavs, the Germans, and the Romanians) belong to the Indo-European family of languages, whereas Hungarian is a member of the eastern division, the Ugric group of the non-Indo European Finno-Ugric language family.

The language is written in Latin script with additional letters and diacritical marks (Abondolo 1987); it is spoken by about ten million people within the present boundaries of Hungary and an additional five million distributed around the world. Of these five million, about three and a half million live in the surrounding countries (Romania, Slovakia, the northern part of the former Yugoslavia, eastern Austria, and the western part of the former U.S.S.R.), making this group the largest European ethnic minority population living in Europe outside its homeland. This is a crucial fact sui generis and for the present discussion. The remaining one and a half million are in Canada, the United States, Australia, and elsewhere, as will be discussed later.

Today's Hungarians trace their history to the tribal Magyars, a nomadic people of Asian origin, who entered the Carpathian Basin in 896 led by their chieftain, Árpád. After several military campaigns into Western Europe and the Balkans, the Hungarian Christian state was established in 1000 by King Stephen I. The conversion to Christianity was confirmed by Pope Sylvester, who, to symbolize this act, sent King Stephen a crown, thus marking Hungary's entry into the European feudal community.[14]

In the thirteenth century Hungary was invaded by Tartars, reducing the population to one-tenth its former size. Three centuries later, in 1526, Ottoman Turks defeated the weakened country at Mohács and occupied the central plains of Hungary for 156 years. At the same time, Hungary's western and northern regions were ruled by the Austrian Hapsburg dynasty. In the late 1600s Hapsburg forces drove the Turks out of Hungary but then the Hapsburgs took control and were the occupiers until the end of World War I. They reunited the country and settled many thousands of Germans in areas that had been depopulated by the Turks.

Led by Ferenc Rákôczi, Hungarians rose against Hapsburg colonization in 1703 but were defeated, with Russian intervention, in 1711. Reform movements culminated in another attempt to obtain freedom in the revolt of 1848-49, led by Lajos Kossuth. This was ultimately crushed by the Hapsburgs who were helped by the Russian czar. War-weakened Austria signed a compromise with Hungary in 1867, thus establishing the Dual Monarchy of Austria-Hungary, making Hungary internally independent, although with common external services and military.

The period between 1867 and the outbreak of World War I brought urbanization, industrialization, and the growth of capitalist economy (János 1982; Hanák 1988, 1991), which led to more acute divisions between urban and rural populations, as well as between the Magyars and some of the nationality groups and ethnic groups. There were massive emigrations. The decades between the 1880s and 1914 was the first period in the modern history of Hungary when a very large number of people (an estimated one and one-half million) emigrated from the country for economic reasons; although some returned to Hungary, many settled permanently in the West and in the Americas, mainly in Canada and the United States.

The Trianon Treaty and Its Consequences

Defeated with the other Central Powers during World War I, Hungary was forced to sign the Treaty of Trianon at Versailles in 1920. The treaty compelled Hungary to cede 68 percent of its land and 58 percent of its population.[15] As a result of this treaty, which divided the country and its population into different political entities, so many ethnic Hungarians live outside the country today.

Largely because of the losses at Trianon and the promises of Mussolini and Hitler regarding the return of lost territories and populations, Hungary joined the Axis powers in World War II. Between 1937-1941 with the help of Italy and Germany, the country regained some of its lost territories—but at horrendous human and moral costs.

During World War II hundreds of thousands of Hungarians died and six hundred thousand Hungarian Jews were killed. After the war, many people left for the West, joining the millions of displaced persons who either settled in Western Europe or left for and settled in the United States, Canada, and Australia; the latter are the second largest and probably the most politically active Hungarian group in the West.

Tens of thousands died in the Hungarian uprising of 1956; subsequently many were persecuted and imprisoned, some were executed, and two hundred thousand fled to the West. The great majority of these refugees settled in Western Europe, Canada, the United States, Australia, and elsewhere in the Western world, thus comprising the third most populous and (at the time of their emigration) the youngest, best-educated group that was readily assimilating among Hungarians living outside their homeland (Weinstock 1969).

At the end of the next section, where I discuss "long-distance nationalism," I return briefly to the emigrant populations and their roles in the moral and financial support of a particular Hungarian ethos through the past century and particularly since the passage of the Trianon Treaty.

Echoes of the Hungarian Immigrant Communities in North America

The relationship between immigrant communities and their natal homeland was and remains intense and complicated. The significance of diaspora nationalists who are nurtured by and are nurturing what Benedict Anderson calls "long distance nationalism" in the growth and manifestation of ethnic and national conflicts in the homeland cannot be overstressed.[16]

For over two decades after the Trianon Treaty was enacted, millions of Hungarian schoolchildren recited the "Magyar Creed" twice daily. It ended with the inspirational cry: "Truncated Hungary is no country, whole Hungary is heaven" (Bárány 1969:268). There was an explicit and often-repeated emphasis on denial of the terms of the imposed treaty, the cry of "*Nem, Nem, Soha*!" (No, No, Never!) (Deák 1965). Hungarians living in the United States and Canada were also highly aroused by the Treaty of Trianon. As Beynon (1941:73-75) recalls, Hungarian colonies in and around Detroit collected and sent funds to the "bleeding motherland" in response to the plea: "Let us not permit our brethren to be lost for Magyardom." Perpetual, strong, and pained outbursts were commonplace in Hungarian church services and fraternal organizational meetings throughout North America over this issue. The primary focus was on those "Magyar brothers who lived in regions torn away from the mother country" (Beynon 1941).

Thus, the Hungarian ethos was brought across the ocean and found fertile ground in immigrant communities in the Americas. Ironically and painfully, Hungarian-Americans were living and working in, and often considered themselves loyal citizens of, a country whose leaders had dictated the conditions of the Trianon Treaty and thus had caused all the problems in their natal homeland (Kertész 1953).

At least one Hungarian immigrant was able to reduce the cognitive dissonance created by this perverse situation. In 1924 Louis Birinyi appealed to the American people from Cleveland for justice for Hungary and for world peace using the arguments he presented in his self-published book, *The Tragedy of Hungary*. Birinyi wrote that Hungary was not punished for its involvement in the Great War, for the Big Four never believed that Hungary was at fault. Nor did Trianon occur because of the nationality question since it was generally well known that Hungary was most kind to her non-Magyar nationalities. Throughout history "Hungary was the defender of Christianity, the champion of democracy and the bulwark of civilization," so there was no reason to mutilate that country, but there was a *purpose*. That purpose was, according to Birinyi, that the commerce of the world could be controlled by the Jewish financial magnates. Therefore, the author concluded, the Trianon Treaty only appears to be the horrible creation of the Allies, but in reality it is the brainchild of the ever-present Jewish world conspiracy. It is safe to assume that these rambling ideas were not those of a single and isolated individual but were representative of the classic scapegoating and blind fanaticism of many on both sides of the Atlantic Ocean and mutually reinforced by some individuals in the homeland as well as in the immigrant community.

What was then frequently called the "white, mutilated body of the motherland" surrounded with the four black "severed" pieces was displayed on posters with glaring letters of "No, No, Never!" throughout the schools, offices, homes, public buildings, and parks in Hungary and in private among immigrant Hungarians. The losses Hungary suffered from the treaty were indeed real, both from a material point of view and from a psychological perspective. The real, however, was condensed, distorted, and transposed into a gendered, decidedly sexual, and sadomasochistic image: the violation of the thousand-year-old sacred Carpathian frontier, and the mutilated white-bodied homeland with its amputated, black limbs tossed to the wild, savage neighbors to be devastated.

This image was imprinted on the minds of Hungarians for nearly a quarter of a century and it became a powerful national symbol, the key to unite, incite, and lead. It united Hungarians on both sides of the ocean. At the same time, however, it brought to the surface even more sharply the "we are all alone" syndrome, thus further dividing the world into "us" and "them" and causing increasing hostility between the Magyars and their neighbors. It incited patriotism but inhibited growth and curbed the expression of socioeconomic frustration throughout the era of the Great Depression. It led the nation out of the anomie that pervaded Hungarian society in the late nineteenth and early twentieth centuries[17] by dictating strong normative beliefs for the sake of the "cause," but it misguided the Hungarians and blinded their leaders to hasten down a road of no return: entering World War II on the side of the Axis powers. Thus, the bizarre national symbol was reified into grotesque and tragic reality.

Ethnonationalism and Pronatalism in Hungary and Abroad

There are "politicians, scholars and others who hold women responsible for what they call 'the death of the nation.'" These also explicitly evoke historical images of women as the bearers (double meaning fully intended) and guardians of the nation, while hailing mothers as the very core of national identity, perpetuators of an indigenous culture that is somehow untouched by foreign influence and thus 'incontrovertibly Hungarian.' They portray women in history as active helpers of men in nationalist struggles against the enemy, whether the enemy was Tartar, Turk, Hapsburg, Russian or other" (Huseby-Darvas 1991, 1995). Womanhood and motherhood are infused with nationalist meaning.

Since 1989 a number of nationalists have increasingly vocalized against what some of them call "nonsensical socialist phrases such as 'women's free decision power,' . . . and the fallacies of such notions as abortion being part of women's human rights."[18] It is ironic that in Hungary, where there are few feminists (around one hundred), some politicians blame the dismal birth rate on feminism and feminists. Gyula Fekete (*Hitel* 1989:9), one of the founding members of the Hungarian Democratic Forum, declared that feminism is the "murderers of mothers" because "the dissemination of feminist tenets are immediately accompanied by the [total] devaluation and abuse of motherhood" (see Huseby-Darvas 1991).

In these and similar constructs, the vigorous financial support and passionate moral support of "diaspora nationalists" is not to be underestimated. Throughout their long decades of exile in the West these people nurtured and were nurtured by long-distance nationalism (Anderson 1992). As one of these men told me, "We eagerly open our wallets and freely raise our voices to put an end to the murder of millions of unborn Hungarian children and thus help the Hungarian mother retrieve her traditionally true, naturally instinctive place in Hungarian society."

In a similar vein, diaspora nationalists are also at work in support of the Hungarian Mothers' National Party, a recent and equally small advocate group.[19] The nationalism expressed by Mr. and Mrs. Sokoray, the founders of this party, is based upon what György Csepeli (1988, 1989, 1990) calls "an old-fashioned, typically paranoid definition of the Hungarian nation which has only enemies, repressed by foreign powers,[20] [e]ndangered by an influx of "foreigners" of all kinds,[21] and weakened by internal faults or sins of the Hungarians themselves." For example, this couple views reluctance to reproduce (i.e., failure to increase the number of Hungarians) as a sin against the nation. The party's relationship with the Hungarian diaspora in the West is important in a number of ways. Both Sokorays stated in an interview conducted in August 1994[22] that they had many positive responses from immigrants: Hungarians living in Sweden, Switzerland, Canada, the United States, and elsewhere contacted them with expressions of concern along with financial support for their political formation.

The Refugee Crisis and Other Vestiges from the Hungarian Past

Amid the escalating and increasingly obvious current refugee crisis, categories of Other become magnified and more pronounced, so there is a changing perception among the population of both individual and national Hungarian identity. With growing internal socioeconomic difficulties in the transition period since the late 1980s, the responses of the Hungarian host population to the seemingly endless flood of refugees have changed considerably. By July 1992 there were serious concerns, well publicized inside and outside of the country, that the entire refugee-supporting infrastructure would soon be crumbling in Hungary.[23] The situation did not improve in 1993 (Huseby-Darvas 1993, 1995).

Most Hungarians were at first open and helpful to refugees, but eventually many became ambivalent, even hostile, toward their uninvited guests. (It is not possible to explore this immensely complex and continuing issue in the present chapter, regardless of its pertinence here.[24]) Clearly, these reactions of the host population are neither surprising nor unique to the region or to Hungary alone. Nevertheless, I find the responses of particular concern for a number of reasons. Among these are Hungary's own historical experiences of massive emigration and still ongoing migrant labor force and the current discourse about asylum seekers, often focusing less on their plight than on Hungarian national identity, Hungary's place in Europe, and what is periodically proclaimed as Hungary's "historic humanitarian mission in a singular moral universe amid the inactions of the West." I will briefly discuss the latter point only, since it has direct relevance to Hungarian ethnicity and nationalism. Although there are perhaps as many different voices responding to the refugee situation in Hungary as there are respondents, I will only outline here different levels of positive and negative reactions.

Many Hungarians take pride in accepting the refugees because it is the "humane thing to do." But there is also anger toward the "proud and wealthy and compassionless West" for turning away trainloads of refugees.[25] In reaction to the disclosure that Jacques Attali, then representative of the International Monetary Fund and the United Nations High Commission of Refugees once again promised, but did not send, enough money for the maintenance of the refugees, a prominent Hungarian intellectual wrote "the West is turning away from us and from our needs, so we are, one more time behind the back of God and the West." This particular phrase was used with great frequency. The mayor of one of the cities with a large refugee camp told me that "like so very often in Hungarian history, now, too, the West is turning its back to us while we get stuck with the trouble and troubled." Nevertheless, the same mayor said:

> Let me tell you that, after the initial mistrust, the people in our city took readily to the refugees. Not only have they helped in many ways but they also have built multiple connections between the city and the camp. For example, there are football matches between our teams and those of the camps. . . . And imagine: on Christmas day there was a joint program in the [Catholic] church where even the Bosnians were singing "*Kis Karácsony, Nagy Karácsony*" [lit., Little Christmas, Big Christmas, the title of a Hungarian Christmas song], and we all cried. . . . Of course, I have to make certain

> that the city folks know that the refugees don't take any jobs away from the natives and the refugee camp does not cost any money directly to the city. For that matter, we benefit in the long run: last year a Japanese foundation specifically wanted to help a settlement that aided in the housing and medical care of refugees and gave us 11 million forints[26] for medical equipment so we were able to replace an old x-ray machine. Otherwise, if the city would have to support the refugees the relations would not be so peaceful. . . .

A similar, yet more extreme version of the positive response highlights even further the victimization of Hungary and Hungarians. On the one hand, the goodness, helpfulness, and humanitarian ways of Hungarians who act in the spirit of Saint Stephen, the founder of the Hungarian state, are emphasized. This makes the Hungarians' actions during the escalating refugee crisis an altruistic, historical, missionlike feature of Hungarians being in the Carpathian Basin, and, by extension, of Hungarian ethnic identity. On the other hand, into this view of the national self enters the concern that is best expressed by the following news article: "[O]nce again we are being put upon: the West is, once again taking advantage of us, once again we are the protectors of European humanitarian values but we are once again pushed out on the semi-periphery between the Balkans and the European community" (Kéri 1992). Reports are published about the average, simple-hearted, hardworking man of the street, folks who take it with great aversion that "again Hungary, this little island of peace, is taken advantage of by the West and used as a *végvár*" (final fortress) of a Christian civilized Europe" (Kéri 1992). Still others believe that Hungary is in a different moral universe from the "other Europe," the Europe that prides itself as "so very sweet smelling, so affluent and civilized while it is turning away from helping the unfortunates but Hungary is still helping—in spite of the tremendous economic burden that the great flow of refugees means to the country, the country that is already struggling with unemployment and inflation, that is accompanied by political and socioeconomic hardships" (Verebes 1992).

Then there are the negative, at times overtly hostile and racist, reactions to the presence of refugees. The proponents of these construct and pass on different types of stereotypes than those discussed in the previous section. It is best illustrated by some of the voices. For example, a forty-two-year-old clerical worker in Budapest told me indignantly,

> Demszky [the major of Budapest] wanted all these foreigners to come here. Don't ask me why, I don't know. So now all the Gypsies, Romanians, Yugoslavs, and other foreigners are all over the place. To top it off, Demszky urges us to give these foreigners clothes, blankets, food. But from what? We hardly have enough for ourselves anymore. Listen, today there are people in Hungary who are starving. There are decent people on fixed incomes, on retirement and disability pensions. There are people who go to the streets and chant in processions of tens of thousands that "we are hungry, we are cold." So why should we give anything to these strangers? They

> come here, and then decent Hungarian folks are fired from their jobs so the foreigners can be hired because they are willing to work for a quarter of what the decent Hungarians were paid. Where is the justice in this? Tell me. A few days later, the same person said to me, "Even when I turn on the tap, instead of water now news about refugees pours out. Enough already! Who the hell cares?"

Many people blame the refugees not only for the economic problems but also for the explosive growth of street crime, drug use, and prostitution rings. This kind of scapegoating is strikingly similar to what others found elsewhere (Rydl and Slonkova 1992). As another informant, a commuting skilled worker in his late thirties told me, "Now here is this mob. Strangers, you know: rabble from only God knows where [*szedett-vedett, jöttment népség*]. Not that long ago they killed a decent Hungarian kid nearby. No wonder everyone is against them. Everybody curses at them in the factory [in which I work], too. The government set up a proper camp for the *Jugók* [Yugoslavs]. So I told the wife: "soon they will be eating better than we are eating." Imagine: meat every day, in these hard times. So what did this foreign mob do? They rebelled and beat up the decent, hard-working Hungarian guards. Let the barbarians in and this is what you get for thanks. . . ." Here, clearly the identities of "us," the good, decent, helpful, hard-working, humane Hungarians are juxtaposed to those of the Other, the evil, barbarian, the foreign, the rabble, whose lot by some weird quirk of fate has destined them to become privileged people at the expense of their host population.

Similar to these reactions, yet more extreme, is the reaction of the far right. Hungary's skinheads, who proudly declare themselves to be "number one in Eastern Europe," and whose leaders carefully cultivate their association with German, Austrian, and other Western skinhead organizations, focus their frequent verbal and written attacks generally on foreigners as well as on Hungary's Jewish and Roma populations. The slogans of the far right, "Hungary for the Hungarians" and "Arabs, go home" are central to their ideology (Gerlóczy 1991). "Out with all foreigners!" is the battle cry of other organizations of similar ilk, like the Hungarian neo-Fascists (Hajba 1992:1, 4), and of the most recent formation like the extreme rightist populist party, the Világnemzeti Népuralmista Párt (*HVG*, January 22, 1994). By far the most vicious of these nationalist and xenophobic attacks are lyrics of Hungarian punk groups who play the so-called *oi* music (Helsinki Watch 1993; Hockenos 1993:69). One is entitled "Immigrants' Wages":

> We'll get rid of everyone whom we don't need
> Including the garbage immigrants.
> The immigrants' wage can only be death
> We'll have to chase away all of the Blacks.
> For the Arabs machine guns await
> Above Palestine atom clouds gather.

It is crucial to note that even though these and similar xenophobic voices amid new popular expressions of prejudice have been heard clearly and increasingly in Hungary since 1989, the growing number and increasing visibility of refugees have not (as far as I am aware) elicited the kind of rampant xenophobia characterized by blind, pogromlike eruptions against refugees as they have elsewhere and as they did against some of Hungary's Roma population (Helsinki Watch 1993). However, there is clearly official concern.[27]

There is no question that in Hungary, as throughout the former Soviet bloc, these are critical times. The transition of the economy from central control to market orientation is difficult and it is likely that its ramifications were not fully thought out by the initiators. Among the various attempts to fill the ideological vacuum are efforts of still relatively small but rabidly fanatical and loudly belligerent groups. Some of these groups, using ultranationalist rhetoric and symbols from the darkest period of recent Hungarian history, incite xenophobia and spread hatred and fear among a growing number of followers. With Hungary beyond the saturation point in playing reluctant host to an increasingly needy and growing refugee population, the imbalance is becoming critical between the real, tremendous economic and social problems and the ideal self-image of Hungarians as the noble, helpful, nurturing folks who are helping the downtrodden while the West is turning its back.

Both the symbolic and actual boundaries between East and West, and between the needy refugees from the East and their reluctant hosts in the West, are being reinforced. Unlike when the Iron Curtain was erected, the curtain is now buttressed from the western side, yet kept porous enough to take advantage of a major, lucrative new market. Hungary, like other countries in the former Soviet bloc, is viewed and treated by the West as increasingly peripheral, but at the same time it is taken advantage of both as a market for goods and as a "dumping ground" for refugees and displaced people (Charlton 1993; Halpern 1993).[28]

Ritual Manifestations of Hungarianness: August 20, 1990

August 20 was traditionally Saint Stephen's Day and the Day of New Bread in Hungary, but during the forty-some years of socialism it was officially declared Constitution Day. On that day in 1990 throughout Hungary there were pomp and ceremony, celebrations, processions, public addresses, and political declarations regarding the first openly celebrated such event since the late 1940s. The high holiday mass was nationally broadcast on television. It was celebrated by Cardinal Paskai in Budapest's Saint Stephen's Cathedral with the consecration of the new great bell—a gift of gratitude from Germany. Behind the cardinal came the *Szent Jobb Körmenet*, a procession of hundreds of thousands, including leading politicians and scores of priests carrying the glass-enclosed, embalmed right hand of Saint Stephen, Hungary's first king.

At the same time, across the Danube River, in Buda's historical castle district, the Fair of Traditional Hungarian Crafts was attracting many tens of thousands. Artisans from throughout Hungary and Transylvania gathered to display their skills and to offer their products for sale. There was Hungarian folk music and singing, Hungarian folk dancing, and the reenactment of the ancient bear-feeding ritual by groups of Ostyaks and Voguls, linguistic relatives of the Hungarians. For the first time in over seventy years, these groups came from the Soviet Union to participate in the revelries. In addition to all the emphatically Hungarian festivities, the day was filled with political speeches.

As in the interwar period, not the only, but decidedly the most frequently and loudly heard self-identifiers were *nemzeti és keresztény* (national and Christian). The prime minister stressed that the nation was returning to the fold of Western Christianity to which it belonged since the reign of Saint Stephen, but from which it was torn away in the last four decades. Other politicians highlighted positive attributes of the Hungarian people. The president of the republic, in an otherwise enlightened address, emphasized the crucial importance of "unique Hungarian qualities," which "once again in this time of major transition with wisdom and never with vindictiveness make the people recognize what to do, when to do it, and how to do it."

In a rather different tone, some politicians brought up the historical concern: "Who is a Hungarian?" Unquestionably, who is or who is not Hungarian is a temporally and situationally shifting category. Exclusionary attitudes and behaviors are suggested by it, but just who are excluded from the Magyar category changes with time and place. For example, as Ferenc Fejtô notes in the new postscript of his republished volume, *What Is a Hungarian Now?* (1990:208, first published in 1937), in 1937 the answer to the question "Who is a Hungarian?" was "more or less everybody who is a permanent resident of Hungary with the exception of the Jews."

The leader of one faction of the Small Holders Party,[29] unexpectedly and with physical force with the help of sixty of his constituents, took over the main stage at the Fair of Traditional Hungarian Crafts in the middle of the Square of the Holy Trinity. He then declared, amid explicit anti-Semitic, antiurbanist, anticapitalist, and anti-Communist comments, that Hungary's future depends on the "real people of the soil," namely the members of his party. On the same day, but at a different forum (in Sopron), the same Mr. Torgyán encouraged his "people of the genuine Hungarian blood and soil" to hop on their tractors and Zetors (farm machines), drive these to Budapest, and park them on the square in front of the parliament, thus showing "those Communist strangers" in the parliament the "real laws of the land."

Clearly, the procession and the fair manifested interpretations of Hungarianness, whereas the political speeches articulated the meanings of being Hungarian in 1990. Displayed everywhere were signs, placards, posters, and graffiti carrying such centuries-old themes such as "Hungary: Between East and West"; "Hungary: The Last Bastion of Western Civilization"; "Hungary: Protector of Western Christianity and Its Traditions", as well as such sentiments as "We Are All Alone: We, the Genuine-Mély Magyar Folks," "We, People of Blood and Soil," "Alone Amid the Strangers, the Cosmopolites among Us, Versus the Potentially Dangerous Neighbors that Surround Us." With varying degrees of subtlety, Hungarian national identity was not only on display on August 20, but, as in previous times of social, economic, and political crises and tensions, it was also alternating between lachrymose certainty and triumphant chaos, i.e., vacillating from tearful remembrance of the *noble Magyar historical manifest destiny* and expressions of victorious yet chaotic bewilderment about *Magyar uniqueness*, *Magyar mission*, and *deep Magyar identity*.[30]

Closing Remarks

> *. . . [T]he people in this part of the world always seem so much more ready and eager to take in and go wild over tyrannical, demagogue, single-caused ideas than democratic liberal ones. . . . (Konrád 1989)*

But, as on August 20, 1990, in these times of critical liminality and confusion, one of the most salient issues is the discourse about who is and who is not "real, or deep, or pure" Hungarian. The concept of *mély magyar* can be translated as "deep Hungarian" or "thoroughly Hungarian." It was first coined by László Németh, and published in 1939 in an essay entitled *Kisebbségben* (Being a Minority), a particularly fraught term in the context and the time, meaning that the majority population is relegated to minority position. Németh asserted that he is in the minority, since his position is "from the very center, the very core of pure Hungarianness," although he disclosed that he borrowed Proust's concepts on French identity.

Here I look at some aspects of Hungarian nationalism, self, and other stereotypization, and expressions of national identity. The struggle of many Hungarians, at home and in immigrant communities, regarding their ethnic and national identities brings to mind one of Walter Zenner's studies. While examining the lachrymose conception of Jewish history and relating defeat, martyrdom, and suffering with increased ethnocentrism, Zenner (1977:156-166) said that "lachrymosity is an important theme in ethnic and national ideologies." Then he reminds us that "the lachrymose conception of one's own history is . . . present in the dramatic presentation of all histories, . . . lachrymose melodrama and tragedy, however, is [*sic*] more characteristic of those who are defeated and oppressed, rather than those who are dominant and victorious." In Hungary many national catastrophes are recalled with some regularity in both public and private discussions. Among the causes for "the lachrymose certainty" are the tragedy of the Battle of Mohács, when in 1526 the Turks won a decisive battle and ruled over much of partitioned Hungary for 150 years; the sorrows of the Revolutionary War of 1849; the humiliating Trianon Treaty of 1920, in which Hungary lost large territories and substantial populations; and the defeat of the 1956 uprising.[31]

Discussing the results of several studies that focused on contemporary Hungarian national identity, György Csepeli (1989:29-41) illustrates that in one study in which Hungarianness is defined on the bases of language, nationality, self-ascription, place of residence, and familiarity with cultural and historical norms and values, 82 percent of those responding said that they are proud, satisfied, and happy to be Hungarians. In the 1970s the majority of those asked expressed pride in their national identity because of major public factors (primarily because of the singular success of "Hungarian industry, agriculture, and socialist construction," and secondarily because of what they interpreted as the pertinence of Hungarian history, literature, and science).

By the middle of the 1980s, it was harder to maintain the living standards of the previous decade, so there was considerable change from relating pride in Hungarianness with major public factors to relating it to such everyday, personal matters. At the same time, people were expressing countless anxieties about their Hungarian national identity. For instance, it is clear in this and other studies that remnants of interpretations and misinterpretations of the 1791 Herderian prediction, concerning the eventual inevitable absorption of Magyars by neighbors (Germans, Romanians, and Slavs) appear to be still very much with us.

To a question in a national survey that asked "Will there be a Hungary in the year 2500?," only one-sixth of the respondents replied in the affirmative. Seventy percent of the answers contained such qualifiers such as "[P]erhaps there will be a Hungary if the international situation will be favorable for us," or the even more ominous qualifier "[It] depends on the subsequent formation of socialism" (cited in Hanák 1981:5). The rapidly decreasing size of the population; the high rates of death, suicide, alcoholism, and divorce; the various forms of "moral deprivation"; and the worry about the survival of Hungarian minorities in neighboring countries are realistic reasons for concern (Csepeli 1989:33).

Many Hungarians still view their land as "the last bastion of Christianity" and "the protector of the West, the West that left it alone to fight for itself at Mohács, that betrayed it at the Treaty of Trianon, the West that did not come to help in 1956." As a result of these and other historical adversities, there is an overly emphasized Hungarian image of self as being surrounded by hostile enemies and constantly suffering at the hands of *balsors*, or wrongful misfortune (Csepeli 1989; Lendvay 1989:37-41). Similarly, the lyrics of the Hungarian national anthem also illustrate a collective national sorrow over historical misfortune (see Hankiss 1982).

To the old mistrusts new ones are added. One such is that of not only being abandoned but being exploited and used by the West.[32] Hungarians believe they are being particularly exploited economically by what some leading political figures between 1990 and 1994 called *karvaly tôke* (vulture capital) that is descending from the West and taking advantage of the exploited and exploitable Hungarians. Relatedly, since 1989 there is a renewed sense of self-pity and the still vivid idea of "we are all alone," expressed as "to be Hungarian in Europe is to be the perpetual loser."[33]

Pondering the question of Hungarian identity in the postsocialist period also brought to mind Michael Herzfeld's (1985:xviii, 208-209, 215) discussion of disemia, or the negotiation of contrasting identities. The past five years of precarious transition finds Hungarians in the process of negotiating, or rather struggling, between contrasting identities: Hungarians between East and West; Hungary between what is perceived as backwardness, discord, and "the dangers of potential Balkanization" as against finding and following the road to pluralism, democracy, and the European community.

In this chapter I have examined particular aspects of Hungarianness and what appears as the reconstruction of national identity, along with past and present stereotypization by self and others. It seems clear, that, not unlike the Hungarian national ethos of other critical periods, in the present time traditional ideologies and old scapegoats are being dusted off, used, and buttressed with greatly magnified historical images. As a former, highly esteemed professor of mine, Roman Szporluk, likes to muse, "nationalism does not recognize a statute of limitations." Indeed, old stereotypes and anticipations, old biases, and hostilities do not merely ascend at times of great radical social and political upheavals as we have seen in east-central Europe during the past half decade, they also ferment and grow, and take on new lives of their own.

Whether or not we think of 1989 as the Year of Hungarian Revolution, we need to understand that the past is very much in the present. We must consider Ferenc Pataki's (1990:3) warning that "The most dangerous delusion during times of critical turning points is the enchanting idea of a clean sweep, the tabula rasa, the childish illusion of starting entirely anew, with the past completely obliterated.

NOTES

1. I am grateful for the generous support of IREX (The International Research and Exchanges Board), Fulbright Hays, and the Hungarian Academy of Sciences during various stages of my fieldwork. Without the help and comments of friends and colleagues—particularly Eszter Bornemisza, György Csepeli, Norma Diamond, Tamás Hofer, Ádám

Levendel, Åkos Róna-Tas, Endre Sik, Mária Székelyi, and Tibor Závecz—this essay could not have been published. Finally, I thank György Csepeli and the editors of the present volume, Lola Romanucci-Ross and George A. De Vos, for their extensive help in editing and restructuring earlier versions of the manuscript. I alone, however, am responsible for any errors in the present study.

2. The life story from which these excerpts are taken were recorded in Budapest, in three sessions between May 12, 1990, and August 24, 1990, two and a half years before the death of the man whom I call here Dr. Årpád Gyula Huszár; he was eighty-nine years old at the time of our interviews. Following customary anthropological practice, I gave all people and places pseudonyms. For example, Zala is the anonym of a southwestern Hungarian city in Zala County, Transdanubia, where secular assimilations prevailed.

Based on documented accounts (Kerecsényi 1978, 1979, 1985), the Jewish community was officially established in 1786 with just over 100 members. After bitter disputes, it was the first to join the reform movement, and in the early nineteenth century it was one of the first to introduce ten violinists and a choir in all services with the exception of the New Year and the Day of Atonement. An organ was also introduced a decade and a half later, the first one in a Hungarian Jewish temple.

In the 1920 census, when the city had of a population of 30,416, there were 3,663 Jews, of whom 800 were taxpayers. This, however, is a significant drop from the 1910 figure of 4,278; the drop in the Jewish population was due to loss of lives in World War I, to out-migration during and after the revolutions in 1918 and 1919, and to the White Terror with its officially condoned anti-Semitic excesses that followed. In May 1944 2,700 of the town's Jews were deported to Auschwitz or sent to forced labor service elsewhere. Of the 2,700 people, 300 survived and returned to the town in 1945.

3. The Piarist Gymnasium was a Roman Catholic parochial middle-school with eight forms that was run by members of the Piarist order.

4. Årpád is one of the most Hungarian of names: it was the name of the chieftain who led the Magyar tribes into the Carpathian Basin in 896 A.D.

5. Here, as at several other points during the interviews, Dr. Huszár illustrated his story with photographs from his youth. It was evident that he was very proud of the way he lived between the 1920s and 1944; the photographs buttressed his stories about being an active sportsman who hunted, rode horses, played tennis, and always wore Hungarian gentry garb.

6. There were at the time 100,000 so-called Jewish Christians (also called Christian Jews) in Hungary; they had converted, but still were considered Jewish according to the anti-Jewish laws enacted in 1941. Of these 89,640 lived in the territory of Trianon Hungary: 62,350 lived in Budapest and 27,290 in the countryside. Only 10,360 Christian Jews from the territories were returned to Hungary from Romania and Czechoslovakia for a brief period during World War II because of strong orthodoxy in the outlying northern and eastern regions (Braham 1981:453).

7. In his contribution to a binational project, entitled Life History as Cultural Construction/Performance, Tamás Hofer notes that by comparing anthropological approaches to the life trajectory concept, on the one hand, with surveys of sociological mobility, on the other, it becomes evident that with social statistics life courses appear as "tiny lines on the map of society." With an anthropological approach, however, we get a closer look not only

at historical events and social life, but also at cultural constructs on several levels. Hofer suggests that from completed life stories that are narrated at an advanced age we can reconstruct, among other things, social and cultural patterns, historical events, and turning points that influence life paths.

Among the many intriguing aspects of narrating one's life story is that it creates a suitable past useful for the present. Further, it gives the narrator an opportunity to reorganize life events and key transitions so as to give meaning and structure to the current situation and present moment. Simultaneously, inconsistencies, detours, and contradictions can be eliminated. These aspects need to be kept in mind in the life story excerpts of Dr. Huszár.

8. This is not the place to deal with some of the larger issues, like passing and its multiple and enormous costs. At the same time, it is worth taking a brief look at De Vos's (1972 [1982:26-30]) and Rotschild's (1981:141) discussions of passing. For example, Rotschild writes that

> . . . the phenomenon of passing out of one's native—generally subordinate—group into another—usually dominant—one merits some discussion. . . . Passing in effect means that ethnic affiliation is perceived as a matter of calculation and manipulation for strategic advantage—mobility advantage and/or power advantage—rather than an enduring dimension of identity. In some sense, therefore, it is the other side of the coin of the . . . mentioned reactive ethnic militancy to secure organizational leverage. Since passing is an exercise in mobility, it is most practicable in multiethnic societies . . . and in societies that are ruled by relatively cosmopolitan and ethnically latitudinarian central elites, such as old, premodern Poland and Hungary. Would-be passers who are rejected in their quest often boomerang into ethnic militancy. Those who succeed are permanently lost to their native ethnic communities.

In his work, *Stigma*, Erving Goffman (1965) writes about the three strategies of passing, covering, and disclosure and suggests that the choice of any of these strategies depends on the stigmatized identity. He defines passing as the process of trying to assimilate, to blend with the majority population completely; disclosure as clear manifestation of all the cultural and social signs of stigmatized minority status; and covering as stressing another identity, rather than the stigmatized one (for example, emphasizing occupational identity, supranationalist identity such as a born-again something, or a rubric implying world citizenry).

9. See below where I discuss the Trianon Treaty and its consequences.

10. I don't subscribe to the still popular myth that militant ethnicity and nationalism were kept dormant throughout the region for the more than four decades of Soviet rule. The contention is that the regime—with its official ideology about internationalism, friendship, and brotherhood between all socialist peoples—moved away from distinct ethnic and national identities toward a socialist merging of peoples, performing a successful restraining function. It was actually much more complex: there was official and overt suppression and denial of nationalism and ethnicity and blunt denials that there were any problems that even approximated nationalism or ethnic strife. At the same time, however, there was what Elemér Hankiss (1982, 1988) calls the "communization of nationalism" and the "nationalization of communism." For example, the use and abuse of national symbols by Communist leaders during the period is evident in every Soviet-bloc country including Hungary, where in the

early 1950s there was a Kossuth cult and a Kuruc cult. Ethnic and nationality policies between the late 1940s and 1989 show clearly that ethnic and national symbols were manipulated by unpopular Communist leaders in their attempts to legitimize an unpopular regime. Elsewhere, for example in Romania between 1965 and 1989, these processes were perhaps even more glaring.

11. Increasingly, scholars are questioning whether a revolution really occurred in 1989 in Hungary and elsewhere in east-central and Eastern Europe. What is "revolution"? Since the eighteenth century, and particularly since the French Revolution, revolution has meant fundamental, radical, and usually violent change in the values, political institutions, social structure, leadership, and policies of a society. In seventeenth-century England, however, revolution meant the return or restoration of a previous structure.

12. The elections in 1994 resulted in a majority vote for a socialist and liberal coalition to replace the right-to-center government of the four previous years, clearly manifesting to some that the majority of the population is not really buying the nationalist rhetoric of many right-wing politicians (Csepeli, personal communications; Ferge 1994). In my view, however, the elections of 1994 revealed a particular nostalgia toward an economically safer, socially more certain past, rather than a genuine move toward the left. Thus, the voters in Hungary voted more *against* the insecurities of a capitalist market economy and the confusions of an uncertain democracy, with their accompanying ideological vacuum, than *for* the return of the left.

13. See, among other literature on the topic, the *Special Issue on the War in the Former Yugoslavia, East European Anthropology Review*, edited by David Kideckel and Joel Halpern, 1991.

14. The Crown of Saint Stephen, with its distinctive bent cross, is still the most prominent symbol of Hungarian nationhood. Although the original crown was lost, a later version was endowed with the symbolic power of the original. Throughout the centuries the crown also inspired an enormous scholarly and popular literature inside and outside of Hungary. The return of the crown to Hungary by the Carter government in 1978 elicited an indignant and furious response from the Hungarian and other "Captive Nations" immigrant communities in the United States. The spokespeople argued that the crown should not be returned to the homeland while a Communist government was still there because it legitimized the government.

15. Transylvania and Bánát were given to Romania; Slovakia and Carpatho-Ruthenia to the newly assembled Czechoslovakia; Croatia and Bácska to the also newly established Yugoslavia; Port Fiume to Italy; and the Burgenland and the rest of the western part of the country were transferred to equally defeated Austria.

16. It is important to quote Benedict Anderson (1992:7ff.) here at length. He notes that the long-distance nationalist is almost always a male; thus there is a consistent use of the word "he."

> The two most significant factors generating nationalism and ethnicity are both linked closely to the rise of capitalism. They can be described summarily as mass communications and mass migrations. Up until the 19th century the vast majority of the people in even the most advanced states could neither read nor write, and for the

most part lived and died near where their ancestors had lived and died before them. But capitalism, and especially industrial capitalism, changed all this, first in Europe and in the Americas, later, and with increased speed, around the rest of the world. . . . In the 19th century appeared the mass-oriented newspapers . . . mass migration [became] . . . very huge and very rapid market-driven migration. The new migrants were . . . able to keep in touch with their old homeland in ways unimaginable in earlier centuries. . . .

Capitalism had its own way of helping them [the immigrants] imagine a more mediated identity. . . . The vast migration produced over the past 150 years by the market, as well as by war and political oppression, have profoundly disrupted a once seemingly "natural" coincidence of national sentiment with lifelong residence in fatherland or motherland. In this process "ethnicities" have been engendered which follow nationalisms in historical order, but which are today also linked to such nationalisms in historical order but which are today also linked to such nationalisms in complex and explosive ways. . . . It may well be that we are faced here with a new type of nationalist: the "long distance nationalist." . . . For while technically a citizen of the state in which he comfortable lives, but to which he may feel little attachment, he finds it tempting to play identity politics by participating (via propaganda, money, weapons, any way but voting) in the conflicts of his imagined *Heimat* [homeland]—now only a fax-time away. But this citizenshipless participation is inevitably nonresponsible—our hero will not have to answer for, or play the price of, the long-distance politics he undertakes. He is also easy prey for shrewd manipulators in his *Heimat.*

17. Goode (1978) is not alone is suggesting that, originating in the radical economic and social changes in the nineteenth century and culminating with the defeat of the Revolution of 1848, traditional structure and culture in Hungary was undermined and anomie pervaded the society.

18. Sadly, the man who said and wrote this is a law professor, teaching constitutional law at Miskolc University. Others, for example Béla Sebestyén of the Association for the Protection of Hungarian Spiritual Values, assert that "We need very drastic measures to stop legal abortions and [thus we must] return to the normal state of affairs . . . like we had during the interwar period when Hungarian folk experienced a most wholesome growth" (cited in *Magyar Nemzet* [Budapest], October 5, 1991).

19. The Hungarian Mothers' National Party was founded in December 1992 by thirty-five-year-old Mrs. Sokoray née Ágnes Tell, a hairdresser in the small Transdanubian town of Pápa. When interviewed in 1994, Mr. Sokoray was on a disability pension and Mrs. Sokoray was on maternity leave. Their social frustration, lack of social security, and inability to control their fate were clearly motivating factors in their founding of the party. This couple can be seen as political entrepreneurs experimenting with a sort of conservatism focusing on the nation, family, social policy supported by the state, and national defense. Shortly after founding the party, Mrs. Sokoray gave an interview in which she credited her husband, the then-president of the Independent Small Holders Party in Veszprém County, for giving her the idea of founding her party. She said: ". . . [although] I have a good political sense . . . like all people born under the sign of Pisces, I too have that certain seventh sense for

forecasting [processes]. . . . [Still] I can thank my husband for everything. . . . It was [his] idea that I should found the party and he was also instrumental in working out our constitution . . ." (*HVG*, January 30, 1993:98).

Even though this party, like other extremist political movements, failed to exert substantial influence on the Hungarian voters in 1994, its program and ideology should be examined as a document indicating a dangerous potential that indeed exists. How strong is its influence? Although the Hungarian Mothers' National Party is still a small and relatively unknown political organization, its goals and program and even its logo (a woman's hands holding up a heart with the national emblem of Hungary being balanced on top of the heart) illustrate both the attractions and dangers of confused and confused elements of romanticized nationalism *combined with socialism* for women in Hungary. They illustrate the highly idealized, utopian attributes of nationalist-socialist notions about women's role in society, motherhood, family, gender relations, politics, and economics, and, at the same time, they evoke historical paradigms, both actual and illusory, both indigenous and also borrowed from National Socialist Germany.

20. Yesterday's enemies such as Tatars, Turks, and Germans (Hapsburgs), and Russians are replaced today in these constructs particularly by the International Monetary Fund and the World Bank.

21. These foreigners include immigrants, refugees, transients, or any non-Magyar temporary asylum seekers.

22. I am indebted to Maria Székelyi of Budapest University (ELTE) for conducting the interview and sending me the material when, for personal reasons, I was unable to do it myself.

23. These concerns were well founded, since only 20 percent of the costs to house, clothe, feed, and care for the refugees came from the United Nations and other Western sources. The remaining 80 percent was either advanced by Hungary or simply covered by Hungarian sources without much hope of reimbursement (*Hírmondó*, July 20, 1992).

24. Sík (1992), in fifteen lucid points, discusses the problem from the perspectives of public opinion. He emphasizes a deteriorating economic situation and the formation of stereotypes that are based on half-truths amid a dire shortage of "political and other institutionalized mechanisms to moderate the collective mood of the population." He concludes that "among the population, inevitably, refugee related prejudice is on the rise." In the same vein, Závecz (1992) projects that in the future, when there will be fewer ethnic Hungarians from neighboring countries among the refugees, serious problems will result from the settlement, accommodation, and even temporary asylum of refugees.

25. For example, in a well-publicized case, on June 6, 1992, 2,000 refugees from Bosnia arrived in Hungary and on July 9, 1992, were joined by an additional 1,273 Bosnians. I was told that the latter group of Bosnians were first forced out of their homes by the Serbs, then they had to buy new passports from "Little Yugoslavia," finally they had to purchase their own train tickets to their unwanted journey. Subsequently, in the unbearable heat, they were shuffled back and forth in trains between Western and east-central Europe. Ultimately, they were "deposited" in Hungary from Vienna because Austria, along with the rest of Western Europe, refused to give them asylum.

26. In 1994 1 U.S. dollar was worth 100 forints, so the cost of this equipment was a little more than $100,000.

27. For example, in April 1992, József Antall, then Hungary's prime minister, declared that "It is undoubtedly the case that there is direct correlation between acute economic problems, unemployment and the fall in the standard of living, and growing xenophobia. However, our government tries everything in its power to curb xenophobia. . . ."

In 1993, more than a year later, Mr. Antall's successor, Péter Boross was also addressing the refugee question. He said that since the new refugee laws 1.5 million refugees had been prevented from entering Hungary. Between 2,000 and 2,500 asylum seekers were being turned away by the Hungarian border guards daily. He added that "Hungary is Europe's most endangered country: not another European country has a war so near its borders, not another country is endangered by so many refugees. . . . Our population around the borders need to be calmed constantly" (reported by MTI, cited in *Hírmondó*, 1993).

Mr. Boross neglected to say that other countries in the region are in the same or in even worse predicament. Croatia and Slovenia, particularly, are struggling with a tremendous refugee crisis and, just like Hungary, do feel the economic and social ramifications. However, the key issue is that, just as in the period after the Treaty of Trianon (although obviously for different reasons), being victimized now is, once again, part of the contemporary Hungarian ethos. As such, it permeates both popular and political culture directly effecting the formation and reformation of ethnic and national self-image.

28. Various versions of the preceding section on the refugee problem in Hungary were presented at the 92nd Annual Meeting of the American Anthropological Association in Washington, DC, in December 1993 and at the IXth International Europeanists Conference in Chicago in April 1994; they were also published (see Huseby-Darvas 1993, 1994a, 1994b).

29. The leader is Mr. József Torgyán, whose political style, acumen, and message has been compared variously to those of an garrulous antihero of an operetta (by Tamás Gáspár Miklós) and (by some members of the Hungarian media) to a strange combination of Benito Mussolini and Jean-Marie Le Pen.

30. Doing fieldwork in rural and urban Hungary between 1989 and 1994 was very different from doing so during the previous socialist era. I found most overwhelming the mixture of frustration, anger, fear, apathy, and bitterness in the population. Informants, who in earlier encounters were reasonably positive and more or less self-assured, now wanted to emigrate because they were becoming increasingly afraid of the obvious and growing unemployment and homelessness and the high rate of inflation and refugee influx. Many informants, rural and urban, young and old, appeared genuinely baffled by the plethora and confusion of national symbols, the drawn-out public contention regarding the national emblem, and the heated and contorted disputes in the media and in the parliament.

31. Perhaps this is partly why György Faludy (1990:2088-2089) observed wryly that in Hungary ". . . everything is perceived as a national tragedy; we sob from the fear of losing the country, we break down over and over again . . . with vibrating excitement and Balkan-like hysteria. . . ."

32. Being abandoned by the West is not a new but a frequently recurring theme that is decidedly not without foundation since at least the Middle Ages. The Treaties of Trianon and Yalta and, of course, the uprising of 1956 are brought up as recent examples of this

abandonment.

33. Various "self- and Other" definitions of Magyars through the past few centuries show certain recurrent characterizations. From the early 1700s we have the example of the *Völkertafle*, an illustrated character map with descriptions of the various European peoples, that were usually hung in inns, markets, and other public places on trade routes. These national character maps were created by and for Germans (southern Stajers, to be exact). They served as guides to German speakers as to how to recognize a member of a particular nationality group, what to expect from them, and how to treat these strangers.

The characterization of Magyars (or that of any other group, with the notable exception of Germans, who created the chart) was not flattering. Hungarians were described as unfaithful traitors and wolflike (i.e., cruel and bloodthirsty); their favorite activity was being revolutionaries. Magyars were said to be extremely limited intellectually but colorfully dressed. They were described as lazy and sloppy in religious worship; they were said to have plenty of fruit and gold in their land, to consider those they dislike as their masters, and to die by the sword (discussed in Vörös 1987:17). Some of these descriptions found their way into often-cited and influential studies by twentieth-century Western historians and other scholars. For instance, during the interwar period, C. A. Macartney (1934:113) summed up the "peculiar war-like character of the Magyars" as "fiery warrior people, intensely proud, impetuous and always inclining toward extremes . . . even today this psychological factor remains one of the first importance."

The self-stereotypization is considerably more positive. The typical Magyar was depicted in an interwar period publication (*Révai's Lexikon* 13:186) as a person:

> of beautiful posture, calm, with a regal walk, strong, dexterous, with noble pride and courage, honest, open, warm hearted, with limitless hospitality, and burning love for the homeland. Granted, Magyars are often hot-headed and hot-blooded, and they love and hate in extremes, never in a sneaky, sly, underhanded manner, but openly and with evident honor. Actually, a certain seriousness, sorrow, a deep national sadness are typical for real Magyars, but their emotions vacillate: *sirva vigad a magyar* (Hungarians cry while having fun).

Again, some of these descriptions can be found in recent surveys about self-stereotypization. According to Lendvay (1989), Hungarians mentioned traditional Magyar hospitality as typical most frequently. Hungarians also often described themselves as having pride in and love of homeland, being hot-headed and having a "typical Hungarian volatile temperament," being hard-working but fun-loving, and being "big spenders." In contrast to earlier self-definitions, however, by the late 1980s the very positive self-descriptions became less self-assured, more uncertain. In an earlier survey, 36 percent of the respondents said Hungarians should be ashamed of something (the focus of shame was past oriented, e.g., the Horthy regime during the interwar period, the country's role during World War II, the Arrowcross Party [the Hungarian ultra-rightist national socialist party]).

By the late 1980s, 61 percent of adults found something Hungarians should be ashamed of (the focus shifted to current national problems, such as the exorbitant amount of money borrowed from and owed to the West, alcoholism, suicide, the dire state of the national economy). However, by the late 1980s and early 1990s, György Faludy (1990:2088-2089), among others, caustically remarked that there was a growing number of those whose who said, "[C]itizenship and nationality: Magyar. Mother tongue: Magyar. Occupation: Magyar."

REFERENCES

Abondolo, Daniel. 1987. "Hungarian." In *The World's Major Languages*. Bernard Comrie, ed. Pp. 577-592. New York: Oxford University Press.

Anderson, Benedict. 1992. "The New World Disorder." *New Left Review* 193 (May-June):3-13.

Ash, Timothy Garten. 1989. "Revolution: The Springtime of Two Nations. The End of Communism in Poland and Hungary." *The New York Review of Books* 36(10):3-10.

Bárány, György. 1969. "Hungary: From Aristocratic to Proletarian Nationalism." In *Nationalism in Eastern Europe*. Peter Sugar and Ivo Lederer, eds. Pp. 259-309. Seattle: University of Washington.

Bárány, György. 1974. "'Magyar Jew or Jewish Magyar'? To the Question of Jewish Assimilation in Hungary." *Canadian-American Slavic Studies* 8(1):1-44.

Barbarits, Lajos. 1929. "Nagykanizsa." *Magyar Városok Monográfiája* (Monographs of Hungarian Cities) (Budapest). Lajos Barbarits, ed. 4:383-395.

Barth, Frederik. 1969. *Ethnic Groups and Boundaries*. Boston: Little Brown.

Beynon, Erdman. 1941. "The Eastern Outposts of the Magyars." *Geographic Review* 21 (January 1):63-78.

Bíbó, István. 1986. *Válogatott Müvek I-III* (Assorted Works, Vols. I-III). Budapest: Magvetô.

Birinyi, Louis. 1924. *The Tragedy of Hungary*. Cleveland: Published by the author.

Braham, Randolph L. 1977. *The Hungarian Labor Service System 1939-1945*. Boulder: East European Quarterly; distributed by New York: Columbia University Press.

Braham, Randolph L. 1981. *The Politics of Genocide: The Holocaust in Hungary*. New York: Columbia University Press.

Charlton, Richard. 1993. "Implementation of New Relief Policy for Eastern European Political Refugees." Unpublished manuscript.

Csepeli, György. 1988. "Negativ identitás Magyarországon" (Negative Identity in Hungary). *Társadalom Kutatás* (Budapest) 4:27-38.

Csepeli, György. 1989. *Structures and Contents of Hungarian National Identity: Results of Political Socialization and Cultivation*. Chris Tennant, trans. New York: P. Lang.

Csepeli, György. 1990. *. . . és nem is kell hozza zsidó: Az Antiszemitizmus Tarsadalmi Psychologiaja* (. . . and Jews Are Not Even Necessary for It: The Social Psychology of Anti-Semitism). Budapest: Kozmosz.

Csepeli, György. 1992. *Nemzet által homályosan* (Fuzzily through Nation). Budapest: Századvég.

Csepeli, György. 1995. Book review of Samuel Popkin's (1991) *The Reasoning Voter*. Chicago: University of Chicago Press; Budapest: JelKép.

Csepeli, György, and Antal Örkény. 1991. *Ideology and Political Belief in Hungary: The Twilight of State Socialism*. London: Pinter.

De Vos, George A. 1982. "Introduction." In *Ethnic Identity: Cultural Continuities and Change*, 2d ed. George A. De Vos and Lola Romanucci-Ross, eds. Pp. 26-30. Palo Alto: Mayfield.

Deák, István. 1965. "Hungary." In *The European Right: A Historical Perspective*. H. Rogger and E. Weber, eds. Pp. 364-407. Berkeley: University of California Press.

Dienes, István. 1972. *The Hungarians Cross the Carpathians*. Budapest: Corvina.

Eberstadt, Nicholas. 1994. "Health and Mortality in Central and Eastern Europe: Retrospect and Prospect" In *The Social Legacy of Communism*. James R. Millar and Sharon L. Wolchik. eds. Pp. 196-225. Cambridge: Cambridge University Press; Washington, DC: Woodrow Wilson Center Press.

Enyedi, György. 1976. *Hungary: an Economic Geography*. Boulder: Westview Press.

Erôs, Ferenc et al. 1987. "Jews and Hungarians: Jewishness in Hungary." *Soviet Jewish Affairs* 17(3):55-66.

Faludy, György. 1990. "A demokrácia csapdáival együtt is a létezés maga" (Democracy, Even with Its Pitfalls, Means Existence). *Tallózó* (Budapest weekly) 44(November 2):2088-2089.

Fejtô, Ferenc, ed. 1990 (orig. 1937). *Mi most a magyar*? (What Is a Hungarian Now? Studies about the Most Critical Questions of Existent Hungarian Situation) Budapest: Cserépfalvi, Gondolat, Tevan.

Fekete, Gyula. 1989. "Anyák Napi Köszöntô Tövisekkel" (Mother's Day Greeting with Thorns). *Hitel* 1 (Budapest) 2:9.

Fél, Edit, and Tamás Hofer. 1969. *Proper Peasants: Traditional Life in a Hungarian Village*. Viking Fund Publications in Anthropology. Chicago: Aldine.

Ferge, Zsuzsa. 1979. *A Society in the Making: Hungarian Social and Societal Policy*. New York: M. E. Sharpe.

Ferge, Zsuzsa. 1992. "A nép nem hagy magából csôcseléket csinálni" (The [Hungarian] People Does Not Allow Itself to Be Turned into a Mob). *Népszabadság* (Budapest daily), January 18, p. 17.

Fermi, Laura. 1968. *Illustrious Immigrants: The Intellectual Migration from Europe, 1930-1941*. Chicago: The University of Chicago Press.

Fishman, Joshua. 1966. *Hungarian Language Maintenance in the United States*. Bloomington: Indiana University Press.

Gáti, Charles. 1988/1989. "Eastern Europe on Its Own." *Foreign Affairs* 68(1):99-119.

Gellner, Ernest. 1990. "Ethnicity and Faith in Eastern Europe." *Daedalus* 119(1):279-294.

Gerlóczy, Ferenc. 1991. "Magyar Bôrfejüek" (Hungarian Skinheads). *Heti Világgazdaság* (Budapest), November 30, p. 17.

Goffman, Erving. 1965. *Stigma: Notes on the Management of Spoiled Identity*. Englewood Cliffs, NJ: Prentice-Hall.

Goode, Stephen Ray. 1978. "Cultural Pessimism and Hungarian Society: A Study inAnomie." Ph.D. diss., University Microfilms, Rutgers University.

Hajba, Ferenc. 1992. "Szabadlábon vannak az ujfasiszták" (Hungarian Neofascists Are Freed), and "A Gyanusitott Nyilatkozik" (The Suspect Gives a Statement). *Népszabadság* (Budapest daily), January 21, p. 7.

Halpern, Joel. 1993. "Refugees as 'Dirt' and 'Livestock.'" In *The Anthropology of East Europe Review. Special Issue: War Among the Yugoslavs*. David Kideckel and Joel Halpern, eds. 11(1-2):6-15.

Hanák, Péter. 1981. "Viszonylagos nemzettudat" (Relative National Consciousness). *Élet és Irodalom* (Budapest weekly), July 25, p. 5.

Hanák, Péter. 1988. "A Másokról Alkotott Kép" (The Image Created about the Others). Pp. 81-111. In *Kert és a Muhely* (Garden and the Workshop). Essays by Péter Hanák. Budapest: Gondolat.

Hanák, Péter, ed. 1984. *Zsidókérdés, Asszimiláció, Antiszemitizmus: tanulmányok a zsidókérdésrôl a huszadik századi Magyarországon* (The Jewish Question, Assimilation, Anti-Semitism: Studies about the Jewish Question in Twentieth-Century Hungary). Budapest: Gondolat.

Hanák, Péter, ed. 1991. *The Corvina History of Hungary. From Earliest Times until the Present Day*. Budapest: Corvina Press.

Hankiss, Elemér. 1982. *Diagnózisok. Társadalmi Csapdák* (Diagnoses. Social Traps). Budapest: Gondolat.

Hankiss, Elemér. 1988. "The 'Second Society': Is There an Alternative Social Model Emerging in Contemporary Hungary?" *Social Research. An International Quarterly of the Social Sciences* 55(1-2):13-42.

Hankiss, Elemér. 1989. *Kelet-európai alternatívák* (East-European Alternatives). Budapest: Közgazdasági és Jogi Könyvkiadó.

Hankiss, Elemér. 1990. "In Search of a Paradigm." *Daedalus* 119(1):183-214.

Helsinki Watch. 1993. *Struggling for Ethnic Identity: The Gypsies of Hungary*. New York, Washington, Los Angeles, London: Human Rights Watch.

Hernádi, Miklós. 1987. "Ottó—Franz—György" (Lifepaths [of] Otto [Weininger], Franz [Kafka], and György [Lukács] family backgrounds). *Világosság* (Budapest) 37(7):444-452.

Herzfeld, Michael. 1985. *The Poetics of Manhood: Contest and Identity in a Cretan Mountain Village*. Princeton: Princeton University Press.

Hírmondó. Hungarian Language Electronic Mail News from Budapest.

Hockenos, Paul. 1993. "Hungary: Black in the Land of the Magyars." In *Free to Hate: The Rise of the Right in Post-Communist Eastern Europe*. Pp. 143-164. New York and London: Routledge.

Huseby-Darvas, Éva V. 1990. "Migration and Gender: Perspectives from Rural Hungary." In *East European Quarterly, Special Issue on "Gender Contradictions/Gender transformations: Cases from Eastern Europe,"* 23(4):487-498.

Huseby-Darvas, Éva V. 1991. "'Feminism, Murderer of Mothers': Neo-Nationalist Reconstruction of Gender in Hungary." Paper presented at the 90th Annual Meeting of the American Anthropological Association, Chicago, November 23.

Huseby-Darvas, Éva V. 1992. "Hungarians." In *The Encyclopedia of World Cultures*. Pp. 142-145. New Haven: Yale University Press.

Huseby-Darvas, Éva V. 1993. "Needy Guests, Reluctant Hosts? Refugee Women from the former Yugoslavia in Hungary." *Refuge: Canada's Periodical on Refugees* 12(7):6-11.

Huseby-Darvas, Éva V. 1994a. "A Balkánról menekült nôk Magyarországon" (Women Refugees in Hungary from the Balkans). In *Jönnek? Mennek? Maradnak?* (Are They Coming? Going? Staying?). Endre Sík and Judit Tóth, eds. Pp. 130-139. Budapest: Political Science Institute of the Hungarian Academy of Sciences.

Huseby-Darvas, Éva V. 1994b. "'But Where Can We Go?': Refugee Women in Hungary from the Former Yugoslavia." In *Selected Papers on Refugee Issues, III*. Jeffery L. MacDonald and Amy Zaharlick, eds. Pp. 63-77. A Publication of the Committee on Refugee Issues, General Anthropology Division, a section of the American Anthropological Association. Arlington, VA: The American Anthropological Association.

HVG (*Heti Világgazdaság*) [Weekly World Economy]. Hungarian Language weekly, published in Budapest.

János, Andrew. 1982. *The Politics of Backwardness in Hungary, 1825-1945*. Princeton: Princeton University Press.

Karády, Viktor. 1985. "A Magyar zsidóság helyzete az antiszemita törvények idején" (The Situation of Hungarian Jewry during the Period of the Anti-Semitic Laws). *Medvetánc* (Budapest) 2-3:41-89.

Kende, Péter. 1987. "Körkérdés 'Van-e Ma zsidókérdés Magyarországon?'" (Is There a Jewish Question in Hungary Today?). *Világosság* (Budapest) 27(7):436-443.

Kerecsényi, Edit. 1978. "Adatok Nagykanizsa Településtörténetéhez a 'polgárok lajstroma' (1745-1826) alapján" (Addenda to the Settlement History of Nagykanizsa Based on the 'Citizen's Roster'). *Zalai Gyüjtemény* (Zalaegerszeg, Hungary) 8:115-134.

Kerecsényi, Edit. 1979. "A Nagykanizsai Gutmann-Család Felemelkedése a Nagyburzsoáziába" (Nagykanizsa's Gutmann-Family's Ascent to the Upper Middle Class). In *Zalai Gyüjtemény* (Zalaegerszeg, Hungary) 12:147-166.

Kerecsényi, Edit. 1985. "Nagykanizsa társadalma és egyleti élete 1900 táján" (Nagykanizsa's Society and Its Associational Life around 1900). *Zalai Gyüjtemény* (Zalaegerszeg, Hungary) 21:105-120.

Kéri, Tamás. 1992. "Menekülhetnek-e a menekülôk?" (Can the Escapees Escape?) *Népszava* (Budapest daily) July 16.

Kertész, Stephen D. 1953. *Diplomacy in a Whirlpool: Hungary between Nazi Germany and Soviet Russia.* University of Notre Dame, Committee on International Studies Series. Notre Dame, Indiana: Indiana University Press.

Király, Béla. 1960. *The Hungarian Revolution of 1956.* New York: Columbia University Press.

Konrád, György. 1989. *Kerti Mulatság* (Garden Party). Budapest: Szépirodalmi.

Kovács M. Mária. 1994. *Liberal Professions and Illiberal Politics: Hungary from the Habsburgs to the Holocaust.* Washington, DC: Woodrow Wilson Center; New York: Oxford University Press.

Magyar Statisztikai Zsebkönyv (Hungarian Statistical Handbook). 1991, 1992, 1993, 1994. Budapest: Central Statistical Institute.

Lendvay, Judit. 1989. "Magyarországgal és a magyarokkal kapcsolatos nemzeti sztereotipiák" (National Stereotypes Associated with Hungary and the Hungarians). In *Janus.* Péter Niedermüller, ed. (Published by Janus Pannonius University in Pécs, Hungary), 6(1):37-41.

Macartney, C. A. 1934. *National States and National Minorities.* Royal Institute of International Affairs Series. London: Oxford University Press.

McCagg, William. 1972. *Jewish Nobles and Geniuses in Modern Hungary.* Boulder: East European Quarterly.

N.A. 1991. "Situation demographique en Europe de l'Est." In *Population.* Vol. 46:443-768. Paris: Institut National d'études Demographique.

Németh, László. 1992 (orig. 1939). *Minôség Forradalma. Kisebbségben: politikai és irodalmi tanulmányok, beszédek, vitairatok* (The Revolution of Quality; Being in Minority: Political and Literature Studies, Lectures, Discussions). Budapest: Puski.

Nyíri, Pál. 1994. "Kínai élet és társadalom Magyarországon: Vázlat egy szociopolitikai kulturális elemzéshez" (Chinese Life and Society in Hungary: Sketch for a Cultural Socio-political Analysis). In *Jönnek? Mennek? Maradnak?* [Are They Coming? Going? Staying?) Endre Sík and Judit Tóth, eds. Pp. 50-85. Budapest: Political Science Institution of the Hungarian Academy of Sciences.

Pataki, Ferenc. 1982. *Az én és a társadalmi azonosságtudat* (The Self and the Comprehension of Social Identity). Budapest: Kossuth.

Pataki, Ferenc. 1987. *Identitás, Személyiség, Társadalom. Az identitáselmélet vitatott kérdései* (Identity, Personality, Society. Controversial Questions on the Theory of Identity). Budapest: Akadémiai Kiadó.

Pataki, Ferenc. 1990. "Társadalomlélektani tényezôk a Magyar rendszerváltásban" (Social Psychological Factors during the Transformation of the Hungarian Political Regime). *Valóság* (Budapest) 6:1-16.

Révai Lexikon (Révai Encyclopedia). 1937. Vol. 13. Budapest: Révai Kiadó.

Róheim, Géza. 1969 (orig. 1950). *Psychoanalysis and Anthropology.* New York: International University Press.

Rotschild, Joseph. 1981. *Ethnopolitics: A Conceptual Framework.* New York: Columbia University Press.

Rupnik, Jaques. 1990. "Central Europe or Mitteleuropa?" *Daedalus* 119(1):249-278.

Rydl, Jan, and Sabina Slonkova. 1992. "A Russian, Ukrainian, Uzbek and Chechen Mafia in Czechoslovakia. A Report." *Prague News* 11, May 29-June 12:3.

Schöpflin, György. 1988. "Jews and Hungarians: Introduction." *Soviet Jewish Affairs* 17(8):55-56.

Schöpflin, György. 1990. "The Political Traditions of Eastern Europe." *Daedalus* 119(1):55-90.

Sík, Endre. n.d. "Reconversion in the Course of Migration. Transylvanian Forced Migrants in Hungary." Manuscript.

Sík, Endre. 1992a. "A menekültekkel kapcsolatos elôítéletesség növekedésének elkerülhetetlensége" (The Inevitability of Growing Prejudice Against Refugees). In *Menekülôk, Vándorlók, Szerencsét Próbálók* (Refugees, Wanderers, Fortune Hunters). Endre Sík, ed. Pp. 59-64. Budapest: Political Science Institute of the Hungarian Academy of Sciences.

Sík, Endre. 1992b. "Transylvanian Refugees in Hungary and the Emergence of Policy Networks to Cope with the Crisis." In *Social Report.* R. Andorka, T. Kolosi, Gy. Vukovich, eds. Pp. 366-378. Budapest: TARKI.

Sozan, Michael. 1979. *The History of Hungarian Ethnography.* Washington, DC: University Press of America.

Sugar, Peter, and Ivo Lederer, eds. 1969. *Nationalism in Eastern Europe.* Seattle: University of Washington.

Szabó, Miklós. 1981. "Nemzetkarakter és resszentiment. Gondolatok a politikai antiszemitizmus funkcióiról" (National Character and Resentment. Thoughts about the Functions of Political Anti-Semitism]. *Világosság* (Budapest) 6:358-362.

Száraz, György. 1984. "Negyven év után" (After Forty Years). *Élet és Irodalom* (Budapest weekly), August 12, pp. 5-6.

Telkes, Simon. 1976. *How to Become a Hungarian: The Artificial Reproduction of a People.* Rome: Ediziona.

Váli, Ferenc. 1961. *Rift and Revolt in Hungary.* Cambridge: Harvard University Press.

Verdery, Katherine. 1994. "From Parent State to Family Patriarch: Gender and Nation in Contemporary Eastern Europe." In *East European Politics and Societies.* Special Issue, "Gender and Nation." József Böröcz and Katherine Verdery, eds., 8(2):225-255.

Verebes, István. 1992. "Én vagyok, mert lehetnék! (But for the Sake of God, There Go I)." *Mai Nap* (Budapest), July 18.

Vincze, István. 1988. "Zsinagógák, uj hivatásban" (Synagogues, in New Function). *Szabad Föld* (Budapest), March 25, p. 13.

Vörös, Károly. 1987. "Az Európában Található Népek Rövid Leirása" (A Brief Report on the European People). *História* (Budapest) 9(1):17.

Weinstock, Alexander S. 1969. *Acculturation and Occupation: A Study of the 1956 Refugees in the United States.* The Hague: Nijhoff.

Závecz, Tibor. 1992. "Csökkenô Rokonszenv: A Magyar társadalom itéletei, viselkedései a menekültekkel kapcsolatban" (Decreasing Empathy: The Refugee-Related Opinions and Judgments of Hungarian Society). In *Menekülôk, Vándorlók, Szerencsét Próbálók* (Refugees, Wanderers, Fortune Hunters). Endre Sík, ed. Pp. 49-58. Budapest: Political Science Institute of the Hungarian Academy of Sciences.

Závecz, Tibor. 1993. "A rokonszenvtôl az elôitelétességig" (From Empathy to Prejudice). *Napi Világgazdaság* (Budapest), June 19, 1993, P. 15.

Zenner, Walter. 1977. "Lachrymosity: A Cultural Reinforcement of Minority Status." *Ethnicity* 4:156-166.

PART IV ■

Conflicts Due to Exclusory Ethnicity in Nation-States

MARY KAY GILLILAND ■

Chapter Nine

Nationalism and Ethnogenesis in the Former Yugoslavia

Introduction

The clashes among Serbs, Croats, and Muslims, the major ethnic nationalities in the south Slav region, are portrayed outside the former Yugoslavia as ethnonationalist revivals, the consequences of deep-seated, historically constructed enmities, festering beneath the surface of forty-five years of relative political calm. It is said that only heavy-handed oppression kept the peace under Yugoslavia's charismatic socialist leader, Josip Broz, "Tito." There is also talk, especially elsewhere in Europe, of the "wild Balkans," and reminders that World War I began in Sarajevo (Bakic-Hayden and Hayden 1992), usually offered as an argument for ignoring the problem because these people are "primitive" and "could never get along." People distance themselves from the experience; it becomes a "Balkan" problem, not a human one.

Even within the former Yugoslavia members of different groups tend to focus now on the violent stereotypes of the other groups. For some Serbs (but certainly not all), *all Croats* have become Ustasha—the fascist Croats of World War II, members of the movement that allied itself with the Nazis. To Muslims and Croats, Serbs have become Chetniks, who in World War II favored the return of the Serbian monarch and Greater Serbia. Even the violence of Muslim Turks against Serbs, in the fourteenth century, is brought up in the press and in conversations.

A different argument is that the roots of the war are economic or are about power and the machinations of elites. I have argued elsewhere that the Serb-Croat war (prior to the war in Bosnia) could be better explained by political and economic variables than by repressed ethnonationalism resurfacing since Tito's death (Olsen 1993; see also Fox 1990:65).[1] I still maintain that political and economic factors play an important part in the current war, but reducing ethnonationalism and war to *either* materialist *or* ideological explanations oversimplifies complex social, cultural, and psychological phenomena. This essay addresses the connection between ethnic nationalism and the current Balkan wars. It approaches ethnicity or nationality as an identity that is always subject to change.

I will examine the discourse about nationalism and ethnicity, public and private, among residents of a midsize town, Slavonski Brod, which lies in the Slavonian region of eastern Croatia on the border with Bosnia, about halfway between the Croatian and Serbian capitals of Zagreb and Belgrade. I spent twelve months of ethnographic field research there in 1982-83, when Croatia was still one of the constituent republics of Yugoslavia. I spent a second period of research, five months in 1991, in Zagreb and in the Dalmatian region of Croatia. In that year Croatia became an independent state. This research provided additional data from Slavonia and comparative data from both Dalmatia and the cosmopolitan city of Zagreb. I returned in 1993 to work among Bosnian refugees in Croatia. On that occasion, too, I had contact with people from Dalmatia and from Slavonia.

Slavonski Brod: Changing Identities from 1981-1991

People in the former Yugoslavia perceived themselves to be both different and alike—sharing much in the way of language, culture, and history, and yet different in customs, dialects, religious beliefs, manner, dress, and local histories (Bringa

1993). My own experiences in Slavonski Brod in the 1980s suggest that identities were not always primarily associated with ethnicity or nationality.

The Sava River separates Slavonski Brod from Bosanski Brod in Bosnia. The two towns are old ferry crossings. (*Brod* means ship, and according to folk etymology, the names of the towns mean Slavonian or Bosnian Ship or Ferry; the names may also be derived from the verb *broditi*, meaning to cross a river [Petrovic and Belic 1970:15].) A bridge made it possible to cross from Croatia to Bosnia in minutes, by car, bicycle, or on foot. Many people did so every day, working in one town and republic and living in another. People crossed in both directions for social and other reasons; to go to markets, to the mosque in Bosanski Brod, to films or coffee bars, or to visit relatives or friends.

When I lived there I was aware that this was a border region. I was also aware of the ethnic or nationality mixture. The population of Brod and of Slavonia is dominated by Croats, but there has been, particularly since World War II, much ethnic mixing. In 1981, of roughly 170,000 residents in Slavonia, 125,000 were Croats, another 25,000 Serbs, and a remaining 20,000 other nationalities, including Hungarians, Czechs, Slovenes, Muslims (including those from Bosnia, who were primarily Slavic, and those from Kosovo who were Albanian Muslims), and Roma (Gypsies) (*Popis Stanovnistva* 1981).

I did not fully realize that this particular region was much more heterogeneous than other regions in Croatia or Yugoslavia, and, therefore, like Sarajevo, was a special case. The family with whom I lived in Brod and the people whose lives I came to share in 1982 and 1983 represented a striking ethnic mix. The majority were Croat, but there was a large Serb population (mostly Bosnian Serbs) as well as many people who came from mixed families. The most common mixed marriages were between Croats and Serbs, but I knew of several cases in which either a Croat or a Serb had married a Muslim. Other families included a parent who was Slovene or non-Yugoslav (Hungarian, Czech, German, or Italian).

In the early 1980s, contrary to my own expectations, people rarely spoke of ethnonationality. That is not necessarily an indication that it was unimportant. In fact, it seems that among some (those who remained concerned with ethnonationality, perhaps) there was a kind of taboo in talking about it. I felt and was sometimes told, when I raised it myself, that the topic was inappropriate. I heard similar conversations between others I knew, who stopped each other from discussing ethnonational differences. Many people, however, appeared to have redefined themselves not as Croats, Serbs, and so on, but as Yugoslavs. In Brod, they seemed attached to the town and the region as much as to ethnic nationality. Croats and Serbs alike expressed this attachment in the sentimental way they talked about the region, and in self-identification as "Slavonians" or "people from Slavonia." They participated in events and activities linked to local culture and history, such as state-sponsored folklore groups. Mixed marriages were not uncommon, though maybe not as common as it seemed to me at the time (Botev and Wagner 1993). I attended five weddings in 1983 and two of these were between a Croat and a Serb. In one case, the bride was Serb and the groom Croat. In a second case, the situation was reversed. People at that time were separated as much by socio-economic class as by ethnicity (though this was not true for all ethnic groups; I will come to that later).

On my first visit to Brod, at the invitation of a Yugoslav friend, Braco (whose father was a Serb, originally from Lika, and whose mother was half-Croat and half-Serb, originally from Bosnia), I spent a lazy afternoon eating fried fish with my friend's mother and mother's sister, and later drinking Turkish coffee in a neighbor's garden, perched on a wooden stool under the shade of young willows. I accompanied Braco and members of his established group of friends (*drustvo*) to town in the evening. We walked, making circle after circle, in the town square, the *korzo*, filled in the evenings with young people out for a good time. Friends greeted each other; made comments about clothing, companions, and soccer; gossiped about other people; and talked about plans to watch a film, listen to music, or go somewhere to drink wine.

I learned in the next few days that the groups of relatives, neighbors, and friends whose social gatherings I had shared were not all Croat; some were Serbs, others identified themselves as Bosnians (they would now also describe themselves as Serbs). Still others, though only a few, were Slovenian or Hungarian. People seemed interested in ethnicity as a part of their total identity, but not centrally so. The topic was first raised tangentially in conversation by my host's neighbor, because her name was "Slovenka" and she, in fact, came from Slovenia, to the north. I asked about the identities of others present. Everyone readily discussed their backgrounds and those of other family members not present (husbands or wives), but no one behaved as if this were particularly important.

In the early 1980s, even after Tito's death, there was a lingering cult of Tito in Slavonski Brod. His photograph hung in every place of business and in many homes. His birthday celebration, also known as National Youth Day, was one of the big events of the year. Partisan war films were a regular feature of a state-run television network. These films often reduced my landlady to tears. She was not alone; other middle-aged women in my neighborhood would often cry when they saw photos of Tito. The heroism of the partisans in World War II was sometimes mentioned while discussing a television film or a local cultural event connected with socialist history; on these occasions, too, someone would often shed some tears. A young mother of twenty-five held her two-year old daughter up to see a picture of Tito on a neighbor's wall (there was no picture at her own house). "That's Tito," she told her daughter, in a very positive and gentle voice. Each night the television broadcast in eastern Croatia ended with the chorus of a song: "Comrade Tito, we follow in your ways." This song, and others like it, were often sung by groups of young men and women in the coffee bars where they congregated after work.

For some people the interest in Tito may have been only on the surface. The photos were particularly common in the houses of Communists. In this region, at that particular time, however, it seemed there were more people with Communist sentiments than otherwise. I recall a village family who lived near Brod. On their kitchen wall a portrait of Tito hung next to a religious calendar. This was one of the few families in which some members professed to be both Communist and Catholic. One of my neighbors held similar views. She did not understand why one could not be both. "If Jesus were alive today," she said, "he would be a Communist." "Sure," replied the grandmother in my household, "but he wouldn't much approve of the church." Those who seemed truly to support communism and the state believed that their lives were better than those of their parents and grandparents. Many of them also believed that things would continue to improve. Their optimism was centered in the economy, despite growing evidence that all was not well. I will come to that topic shortly.

Anthropologists who have worked in more homogeneous regions of the former Yugoslavia claim that all efforts to foster a Yugoslav national identity were doomed to failure from the start, except among those who were products of mixed marriages (see especially Simic 1991). The educational system promoted a Yugoslav and socialist worldview, but in homogeneous regions (for example, the island of Hvar in the eastern Adriatic region of Croatia, where I worked in 1991), family, church, and community influences tended to ensure that many regarded themselves as Croats first, and Yugoslavs second, if at all.[2] This was undoubtedly true in small towns and homogeneous regions throughout the south Slav region. I remember feeling surprise at anti-Serbian sentiments expressed by two old women in a village on the northern Croatian coast. At the time I had lived in Brod for nearly eight months and had come to believe that ethnonationality was relatively unimportant.

In a town like Brod, however, many were products of mixed marriages or their families had migrated from elsewhere. There had been some state-sponsored resettlement of both Serbs and Dalmatians after World War II and further migration as a result of army service, marriage, and the search for jobs. Also, there was no obvious advantage to being Croat or Serb. In such situations, ethnicity as a dimension of personal and group identity tends to diminish. (Muslims represented only a very small minority in Brod and were regarded differently by both Croats and Serbs. I address this difference later.) Nina, who lived with her parents and was my neighbor in 1982, reminded me in a recent letter that from her perspective things had been different in the past. "We were Yugoslavs," she wrote. "My generation grew up believing that."

In short, most of the people I knew in the early 1980s were relatively unconcerned about ethnonational identity and remained so in the late 1980s. The concerns people expressed most often then were economic ones. Shortages, inflation, and lack of jobs or housing were often what people talked about when I lived there, and, later, what they wrote about in their letters.

In 1991, when I returned to Croatia, things were different. Throughout Yugoslavia (which, until June 25, 1991, remained a single nation), fear, anger, and blame featured in many conversations. Individual Serbs began to be afraid. The grandmother in the household I had lived in 1982, herself a Bosnian Catholic, had married a Bosnian Serb in the period between the two world wars. Her children and grandchildren also married across ethnic lines. As a result, some but not all were Serbs. Grandma Ana's husband had been killed at the outbreak of World War by Croatian Ustashas. Ana then was twenty-seven years old, had eight children to support, and a first-grade education. When I knew the family in the 1980s, they spoke of Yugoslavs as a united people. Ana's daughter, in whose house I lived, was a member of the Communist party. Their history was the history of socialist Yugoslavia. But the family also maintained another history: the story of Ana's husband's death at the hands of (or so they believed) Ustashas (as the word has been Anglicized) persisted as a family legend. This was despite the fact that Ana herself was Croat and lived in Croatia at that time. Killings such as this were part of the history of nearly every family. Who got the blame varied.

Eastern Croatia became a focal region for ethnonationalist unrest, along with other places where Serbian enclaves lived within majority Croat surroundings (a similar scenario existed in the region of Kosovo, in Serbia, where the majority population is Albanian; see Reineck 1993). Milosevic, president of the Serbian Republic and of what remains of Yugoslavia, and Tudjman, then president of the Croatian Republic and now president of the new Croatian State, had both come to power. Both were elected on nationalist platforms. In Croatia new symbols of Croatian nationality were evident in a new flag,[3] place names,[4] and in the language being identified as Croatian instead of Serbo-Croatian or Croato-Serbian. There was talk then that Croatia might secede from the Socialist Federal Republic (SFR) of Yugoslavia. Tensions were brewing elsewhere at the same time, particularly in Bosnia-Herzegovina, a territory shared by Muslims, Croats, and Serbs. Slovenes, to the north of Croatia, also spoke of secession from the federal government.

In 1991, I saw old friends presenting themselves differently than they had in the past. Communists had become democrats and Catholics; people once unconcerned about ethnicity or nationality now spoke about it freely, and those who were ethnically mixed or married across ethnonational and religious lines were confused and apprehensive. Families who had vested interests in socialism were fearful, and those who had secretly longed for change became hopeful. People devoured news and opinions in newspapers and magazines and followed television newscasts more closely than before. Personal, family, and ethnic histories were rewritten; loyalties shifted and past experiences were reevaluated. Both Croats and Serbs claimed to have been the leading group among the partisans. Tito's life was reexamined, and there was speculation and argument about what he really was. Some Croats said that in the end Serbs controlled him, and that although he was worthy of admiration, he had not, for many years prior to his death in 1980, been able to speak his mind. (Tito was half Croat and half Slovene.) Others (including Croats and others living in Croatia) thought less kindly of Tito and traced the current problems not only to corrupt politicians in recent years, but to Tito himself or to his followers. Serbs thought that Tito had pandered to the Croats; Croats saw him as having "sold out" to Serbs. There was talk of atrocities committed by partisan bands, mass graves uncovered in Croatia, and various scandals connected to Tito's name (see, for contrast, Denich 1994).

Croats and other ethnic nationalities in Croatia spoke of Serbian unfairness and exploitation (within the context of the former Yugoslav nation). According to Croats, there was a disproportionate number of Serbs in high-ranking government and military positions. The federal government was physically located in Belgrade, which they believed gave Serbs advantages when it came to government hiring and favors (due primarily to the importance of personal connections in obtaining jobs and other benefits). This imbalance, according to Croats, had existed for many years but had, by 1991, become intolerable.

Croatian Serbs (that is, Serbs living in Croatia) voiced different concerns. They feared what might happen to them, their families, their jobs, homes, and very lives should Croatia become an independent nation. These fears were aggravated by memories of Ustasha violence against Serbs during World War II (Croats would quickly point out that most Croats were not members of the Ustasha party), and by the resurrection of symbols, such as the checkered flag, associated with that time.

I must note here that I knew many more Croats than Serbs. I was in contact with no one who was Serb and lived within a Serbian enclave in Croatia and my contacts in the Serbian Republic are few. I did travel to Belgrade and to a village in Serbia where the grandmother in my former household had relocated (she lived there with a daughter and the daughter's family). I also knew a number of Serbs who had lived all their lives in or near Slavonski Brod. Some of these Serbs (including some who lived in Croatia) began to talk about the Croatian Fascists, who sent Serbs, along with Jews, Roma (Gypsies), and others to concentration and death camps. Serbs blamed Croats and Slovenes, but particularly the former, for their own lack of economic development; the Western portion of the former Yugoslavia, they said, had gained at Serbian expense. Croats and Slovenes turned the argument around; they had been supporting the less-developed regions with the products of their own hard work. Worse, they had also been paying for a growing military and a corrupt government bureaucracy heavily dominated by Serbs.

The dominant impression that stayed with me from that time (1991) was a lack of clarity. Everyone seemed confused and afraid. Almost no one was ready to believe that war would come, yet people *behaved* as if they expected violence to break out around them at any time. The voices in each group (Serb, Croat, or Muslim) were by no means uniform. Among each of these groups could be found pacifists, others who did not think the secession of any republics a good idea, and some who thought, sadly, that dismemberment was the only feasible solution to the tensions that had grown among the various groups through the past decades. Some continued to assert that ethnic nationality was of no importance, while in other, subtle ways, showing renewed interest in nationality issues and in religion.

Serb-Croat violence began in February 1991, not far from Slavonski Brod, in the town of Pakrac, also in Slavonia. I was sitting at my former neighbor Lita's kitchen table, eating a meal with her family—a Bosnian Serb woman, Lita, her Croatian husband, their son, and Lita's daughter (my friend Nina) from a previous marriage to a Bosnian Muslim. They all expressed fear that nothing good could come of the current political situation, or of secession, or of war. "If war does come to Croatia," said Nina, "it will be absolutely the worst in Slavonia, because here we are all mixed." Her mother said, "It will be even worse in Bosnia! Who would have thought we would even be talking about this?"

At first, each act of violence was regarded as an isolated incident. People expressed shock and dismay. They denied that this could really be happening; there must be some way to solve political problems peacefully. They suspected that what was shown in the news was not all it seemed to be (or worse, that behind it lay some larger conspiracy orchestrated by one or another elite organization). The brutalities, however, were widely publicized and contributed to a growing sense of ethnonationalism and to unrest. The media coverage was, of course, selective. Serb atrocities against Croats were broadcast on Croatian news stations in detail, complete with footage of massacred bodies. Coverage of events in the Serbian Republic was the other way around.

Today, the bridge between Slavonski Brod and Bosanski Brod is destroyed. Houses in both towns have been shelled with artillery and rocket grenades. Hundreds have fled the region, leaving behind most of their belongings. Their houses have been occupied by displaced persons or refugees from towns such as Vukovar, where most buildings have been entirely destroyed. Among those who remain in Brod, life can only be lived day to day. All that people once counted on has been shaken by war. Many have also lost their identities or have been forced to redefine themselves along ethnonationality lines. They no longer know who they are or where they belong. Nina told me when I saw her in 1993 that my friendship was more precious now than before, because for me, an American, she was not Nina the Croat or Nina the Serb, but simply Nina, my friend. Even now, when I do not answer her letters promptly, she worries that I have turned against her because of her nationality, although she knows this is not a realistic fear.

Nina is now coming to terms with a new sense of who she is. We never talked much about ethnicity before, though she was proud of her "Bosnian" grandmother, who turns out to be a Serb, not a Muslim. Nina herself claims that she never thought much about whether her friends were Croat or Serb or Muslim or Catholic; in those days few people in Brod town were religious, and none of that really "mattered." She recalled a wedding we had both attended in 1983. I had been one of the few guests who knew what to do at a Catholic mass. Nina and her friends had to follow my lead. They were all greatly amused, since it was usually I who did not know what to do in social situations. Now, of course, religion does matter, since to be a Croat is also to be Roman Catholic. Likewise, *Srpstvo* (Serbianness) is defined by membership in the Serbian Orthodox Church. Muslims are also, to some extent, defined by religious affiliation.[5]

Nina's biological father was a Bosnian Muslim. That he was from Bosnia I knew; that he was a Muslim Nina did not mention until 1993, ten years after I first met her. He abandoned Nina and her mother when Nina was an infant. She had not seen him for fourteen years when I met her in 1982. Nina was raised by a Croatian step-father. She speaks a Croatian dialect, writes in Roman (not Cyrillic) script, and dated both Croatian and Serbian men before marrying her husband, who is Croat. When their children were born, they wrote Yugoslav for the children's nationality. Nina wrote to me in August 1991, just after the Croatian declaration of independence, that she would have to change the children's nationality to Croat. Yugoslav was no longer a permissible national category in Croatia.

Economic Factors

"It's an artificial war, really, produced by television," said Milos Vasic, founding editor of *Vreme*, an independent magazine still publishing in Belgrade (quoted in *The New Yorker* 1993:4). In Sarajevo, until the war broke out there, television broadcasts could be received from both Belgrade and Zagreb. Pajic, a professor of law at the University of Sarajevo, agreed with Vasic: "On Beograd TV the Croats became Ustashas. On Zagreb TV, all Serbs were Chetniks. These are terms from the second world war that today are ethnic insults. And then both stations began to play with the notion that Muslims are unreliable, dangerous fundamentalists. You could just watch these stations and know that something really big was rolling behind." Vasic, the journalist, continued, "It's very easy. First you create fear, then distrust, then panic. Then all you have to do is come every night and distribute submachine guns in every village, and you are ready."

The media and propaganda had an important role to play, but why were they used at all to foster nationalism in these former Yugoslav republics? The production of fear was an important element, to which I return later. But how and why was the conflict begun at all?

I begin by considering economic factors. In the 1980s in Brod, there was, to borrow the novelist Andric's words, the appearance of peace and progress, an overriding optimism. But under the surface tensions were evident (Andric 1977). These tensions, however, seemed to be economic, not ethnic. One of the hallmarks of Tito's communism was decentralization of power to the republics (except for the army, foreign policy, and some other areas of national concern). In the early 1980s, there was much talk about Yugoslavia's hard currency debt. My neighbors in Brod understood that each republic had managed its internal financial matters independently from the others, with little coordination. Western nations required repayment of Yugoslavia's large debts and the lack of hard currency became a serious problem. The dinar had been repeatedly devalued. In 1981, after Tito's death, an austerity program was introduced, designed to limit imports and promote exports. A system of rationing gasoline, coffee, and laundry detergent was instituted in 1982. Restrictions were placed on foreign travel. This was intended to limit the use of hard currency abroad, and to restrict black marketeering, particularly in coffee, detergent, and denim and leather clothing.

The average salary then for a family of four was approximately $150.00 per month. Nina, who had been working for two years as a bookkeeper for a state-run hospitality firm, made only $80.00 per month. Her step-father, a clerk, had a monthly salary of $110.00. My landlady, a bookkeeper with some administrative duties, made just over $100.00 per month. A loaf of bread cost $.20, as did a cup of coffee or a beer in a cafe; rent on a state-subsidized flat was about $10.00 per month, and a pair of leather shoes about $20.00. One could travel from Brod to Zagreb by train or bus (a three-hour ride) for $2 to $3 one way.

Shortages became increasingly common. Some items, such as coffee and detergent, could only be bought periodically, with ration coupons. The purchase of gasoline, and in other regions, cooking oil and sugar, was also restricted. Other items, including chocolate, toothpaste, and nylon stockings, were available only irregularly, and sometimes disappeared from the store shelves for months on end. The random disappearance of consumer goods for unpredictable lengths of time added to the anxiety.

This enhanced an attitude toward government that had existed for a long time; people like the grandmother in my own household distrusted any government. She had seen several governments collapse, and had endured the wars that followed. Shortages encouraged people with government jobs, or access to anything in short supply, to steal, or cheat for their friends, whenever possible. People in this region had always relied on networks of relatives and friends, who provided access to goods, services, jobs, housing, and other needed or desired commodities. These attitudes, and the practice of helping relatives and friends, did not disappear during the Tito era. According to stories I was told, people continued to look out for their self-interests in these ways. Networks, however, became particularly important during difficult times. In Slavonski Brod one's connections might not necessarily be a member of the same ethnonational group.

Still, there was optimism. At the time, in a town such as Brod, which was still relatively prosperous compared even to the recent past, and in nearby villages, which were also economically stable (because agriculture provided a reliable source of income), people did not have to worry about basic survival. They did worry, however, about children who remained without housing or jobs. In the 1980s, there was a shortage of housing and of jobs (people had to wait on lists for several years after they finished school), but once an apartment or a job was acquired, it was impossible to lose. They worried as well about rising costs and the increasing scarcity of some consumer goods. Nonetheless, new houses were being built, young people went out on the town at night, new clothing was purchased, and almost everyone could afford a vacation within Yugoslavia. These were working-class and middle-class people (low-level professionals), among whom the standard of living varied little. There was very little outright poverty in the region, aside from Roma, who were marginalized. There was also little conspicuous wealth, except among local political leaders, who might have foreign cars or weekend houses or other status symbols that others could not afford. None of these individuals in Brod lived outrageously beyond the potential reach of an ordinary family. It was not unrealistic for people to hope.

The goal of the austerity program was to stabilize the national debt, ironically by 1991. Even at the end of 1983, however, the people in Brod believed the program would not succeed. By that time, a new system of rationing included electricity. The town was divided into three districts. Each day one district was without electricity from 2 until 11 p.m. This plan was tolerated at first and was even a source of hilarity. Older folks noticed that it promoted more visiting and talking in the evenings, when people couldn't watch television or went to another part of town to watch with a relative or friend. In a short time, though, electricity rationing began to be an irritation. My landlady had purchased a deep freeze with the dollars I paid her for rent. In late summer, we killed and plucked fifty chickens and ten ducks, and she froze them to see her family through the next winter. Of course, the chickens partially thawed every third day, and she feared they would spoil. This represented a large financial investment and an important source of material security. The tolerance for any system of rationing dwindled. Before the end of the year, the system had disappeared. By the time I left Yugoslavia, in November 1983, coffee and other luxury items were once again available in stores, but at much higher prices. People complained; they had not anticipated inflation.

By the time I returned in February 1991, the dinar had been devalued twice. Then a 2 dinar note (a new note) was worth the same as an older 20,000 note. Pensions and other "fixed" incomes were barely adjusted to accommodate the inflation. Many received their salaries in theory only; at my host institute in Zagreb there were several pay periods when no one received checks and several others when people got half the pay they were owed. At other organizations, they heard, workers received envelopes with IOUs inside. Discontent was rising along with prices. People who lived in Zagreb now drove to Graz, Austria (three hours by car), to buy groceries. They did this despite the high cost of gasoline, which was no longer rationed. Trips to Italy or Hungary for clothing and household goods were not uncommon. Inflation, unemployment, and increasing economic instability were evident. This became a source of friction and anxiety in everyday life.

In 1990, there was talk in Croatia of creating a confederacy, or of outright secession from Yugoslavia. My friends and colleagues in Zagreb were angered by the economic muddle. They argued that the wealth of the country was concentrated in the north and west. The Adriatic Coast generated tourist dollars and deutschmarks. They also had mineral resources, industry, and business. Some claimed that as much as 70 percent of the republic's gross income was taken in taxes by the federal government. This figure was quoted in newspapers and on television news. The money supposedly went to help the development of poorer regions in the east and south, but many believed that their taxes, their labor, and wealth were supporting an increasingly corrupt government, and a too-large army.

This suspicion was encouraged by Franjo Tudjman, then president of the Croatian Republic. Croatia, under Tudjman, reinstituted many powerful symbols of Croatian nationalism, such as the old checkered Croatian flag, which then began to appear throughout the Croatian Republic. The names of streets, squares, and other public places were changed from those of socialist heroes to Croatian ones. In 1990, for the first time since before World War II, Christmas was an official paid holiday in Croatia. There was an increasing desire for self-determination and self-government. This sentiment was not universal among Croats, nor was it uniformly resisted by Serbs and other minority nationals in Croatia. Nevertheless, members of non-Croatian nationalities, particularly in places like Brod, began to be apprehensive.

The official Serbian response, and the response of Serbs within Croatia, was not to block independence for its own sake, but to protest that Serbian enclaves in Croatia had not been guaranteed any of their rights. The Serbs demanded a clear policy of protection. (Croatian commentators pointed out that the pretext of protection of a Serbian minority was also the justification for Serb aggression against Albanians in Kosovo.) Croats, however, claimed that Serbian leaders in Belgrade were more afraid of losing their jobs than they were of potential Croatian violence against Serbs. Serbs within Croatia were regarded as extremists. While Croats accused Serbs of promoting ethnonational self-interest, they maintained that nationalism was not at the heart of their own concerns.

Why did the discontent over economic and political power turned to nationalist violence? The rape of women, violence against children and the elderly, the destruction of cultural monuments, and the killing of intellectuals reveal a hatred that goes beyond a desire for political and economic reform. There are economic, political, and social motivations for change in Croatia and Bosnia, but more than these phenomena are needed to account for the regeneration of ethnonationalism.

Nationalism

The terms "ethnicity" and "ethnic group," like "family" and "household," are variously defined. Most definitions take the following form: an ethnic group is a "self-perceived group of people who hold in common . . . traditions not shared by others with whom they are in contact" (De Vos 1975:5). These traditions include religious beliefs and practices, language or dialect, a sense of historical continuity and common ancestry. For such groups, for example, the former Yugoslavs (or southern Slavs), the term "nationality" would be appropriate.[6]

In what used to be called the Serbo-Croatian language, now separated as Serbian and Croatian, *narod* translates as "nationality," but it may also be glossed as "people" or "folk." This is the term people use to refer to Serbian, Croatian, Macedonian, or other identities that we would call "ethnic." Each of these groups has a unique historical identity, associated in most cases with former kingdoms or empires. Almost all of them have been dominated by other, more powerful entities, such as the Austrian Hapsburgs or the Ottoman Turks, for the better part of modern history, in some cases more than five hundred years. Each group has a language it considers its own, although Serbian and Croatian have been described as a single language with two alphabets and numerous dialects. Each group has a dominant religion and customs it considers distinctive. Often people define themselves in opposition to others, who do things differently (Bringa 1993:71).

The case of the Muslims is different. Many, mostly outsiders, argue that Muslims are a religious group, not an ethnic one. They do not, for example, have a separate language. In Bosnia, they share a homeland, and to some extent a history, with Croats and Serbs. Serbs and Croats believe that Muslims are fellow Slavs who "sold out" under the Turks. Some Muslims, however, claim a different origin for themselves, tracing their ancestry to an earlier religious group, the Bogomils, who were persecuted by Croats and Serbs before the invasion of the Ottoman Turks. Muslims regard themselves as a nationality as well as a religion. In the former Yugoslavia, official policy denied the category "Muslim" a religious identity. They were counted as an official nationality *(narod)*. Bringa points out that the lack of agreement about nationality status is particularly striking for Bosnian Muslims, who are regarded variously as an ethnic group, a religious community, or a nationality. She also reminds us of the significance of official definitions in socialist multiethnic states. In the former Soviet Union and in Yugoslavia, there were official nationalities and national minorities. The same is true of the People's Republic of China, (Gladney 1991; Bringa 1993:70; see also Hammel 1993).

Except where large ethnonational minorities reside, and mixed marriages are tolerated, nationality and territory tend to coincide. But in the past fifty years there has been increased physical mobility. People have moved from villages and small towns to cities, and in border regions, like Slavonia, from one republic to the next, because of jobs. For a time all men were conscripted into the army for one year, and military service was never in the conscript's own republic. This practice was partly responsible for more intermarriage than had been the case earlier. Increased mobility and intermarriage mean that there are individuals scattered throughout the southern Slav territories who do not "ethnically" belong where they live.

Moreover, the ethnonationality conflict is not clear cut. Not all Serbs in Croatia were against the independence movement. Although I have no reliable numbers, I was told by Croatian colleagues (quoting Croatian news sources, which tend to be biased) that of the Serbian ethnonationals living in Croatia (approximately 15 percent of the total population), only one-fifth fought with Serbs against Croats. The remaining four-fifths were in favor of an independent Croatian state.

Some, like my one-time neighbor Nina, were against the independence movement at first. Later, although she is Serb, she has come to feel that her current situation can largely be blamed on Serbian aggression in Croatia. Serbian bombs struck her parents' house. No one was seriously hurt, but Nina became afraid for her children's safety. Her husband had been working in Rijeka. He urged her to leave Brod, and to bring the children to live with him in a workers' camp. Nina became convinced, eventually, that the federal government (that is, the Serbs) was to blame for the war.

Braco, my former landlady's son, had once been a true believer in communism and Yugoslavia. He is Serb (another child from two generations of mixed marriages, who had until recently been a Yugoslav). His wife is Croat. He openly sided with the movement for Croatian independence. He had his son baptized Roman Catholic. He hoped there would be a future for his family in an independent Croatia. By the end of 1991, however, he became completely disillusioned, and took his family and a few possessions, abandoning their house and remaining property, and fled to Italy, where they now reside on refugee visas. His male cousins, Bosnian Serbs, are fighting against the Muslims there; his wife's family live in fear of Serbian bombs.

In the same way, not all Croats, Slovenes, or now Muslim Bosnians, were clearly for secession. Some, including a number of individuals I knew in Zagreb in 1991, would initially have preferred some political compromise to Croatian independence.

There is much confusion about the role that ethnonationalism plays and whether it has been rekindled or entirely reinvented, not only among scholars, but among citizens who have lived with the fear and horrors of the war. The work of myself and my Croatian colleagues in the more homogeneous region of the Croatian Dalmatian coast, and the work of others in homogeneous villages and towns throughout the former Yugoslavia, indicates that for some people a conscious ethnonational identity persisted throughout the Tito years, whereas for others, ethnonationalism was subconscious or unconscious. For what I now see to have been a minority, Yugoslav citizenship replaced ethnonationality. My data indicate that these were usually people who had no clear *narod*. They have recently had to choose the ethnonationality of either their mother or their father.

Plejic, a Croatian ethnologist, has collected life histories and war narratives from displaced citizens of Vukovar and Mirkovci in eastern Croatia. Vukovar and Mirkovci are also in Slavonia, and the population was a mixture of ethnonational groups in both places. The interviewees, according to Plejic, struggled in their stories to clarify events of the war. They could not believe that such violence would occur among people who had once lived together peacefully. The changes in relations between neighbors were highlighted in many narratives. Plejic writes, "The categories of neighbor, friend, relative, even fellow citizen, had dominance, in times of peace, over the category of nationality" (1992:233). This is reflected in the perplexity expressed by informants, all displaced persons as a result of war in eastern Slavonia, in Croatia. "With people who sat at your table and drank with you yesterday. . . . He wants to slaughter you . . ." said one informant, identified only as Ivan from Vukovar, referring to former Serb neighbors. Ivan is a Croat.

Another Croat, Ema from Mirkovci, tells of a Serb who came to warn them that trouble was brewing in the region. "We really had good relations, and really, we never had any bad experience with Serbs," she said. That Serbs could simultaneously be good neighbors and brutal aggressors was difficult for her to comprehend. Ema, like many others, began to distinguish between local Serbs, whose sins were only of not standing up for their Croat neighbors, from "outside" Serbs who were the real villains in the war (Plejic 1992:223). I heard similar stories from former neighbors in Slavonski Brod, as well as from displaced persons and refugees from Croatia and Bosnia, now living in refugee centers on the Croatian island of Hvar (Gilliland, Spoljar-Vrzina, and Rudan 1995). Other anthropologists report similar conversations, similar struggling among Croats, Muslims, and Serbs, to make sense of the unthinkable—neighbor turning against neighbor, people brutalizing each other in the name of nationality.

These narratives express a lack of conscious interest in ethnic nationality. At the same time, individuals were at least aware of nationality differences and commented on "the lack of trouble" with ethnic Others; if there had truly been a total lack of concern with ethnicity or nationality, a person's *narod* might not even be known to others. In just these fragments, we can also see how people begin to personalize the violence. Serbs as a group were regarded as neighbors, or friends, or at least "not a problem"; suddenly individual Serbs, people who had *taken food and drink at your own table*, turn against you. This brings the war symbolically into one's own home. For many of these interviewees, the war has been experienced and is real. Their actual homes had been destroyed, and neighbors and relatives killed. These near or actual experiences of violence change people's thinking (Bailey 1988:13-20).

No single factor can explain the resurgence of nationalism in the Balkans, or the horrible brutalities that continue there daily, but nationalism is a part of historical and individual experience, and it provided a metaphor, a discourse, for redefining group relations. Throughout human history, people construct others whom they define in opposition to culturally constructed selves. These boundaries are never firmly fixed, but subject to negotiation and redefinition. This is also true in the Balkans. In the recent past, other dimensions of personal and group identities took precedence over ethnonationality, at least in some of the south Slav regions. Ethnonationality, as one dimension of identity, did not disappear, but for some, perhaps many southern Slavs, it ceased to make sense to define oneself or others primarily in such terms. In the current war, political leaders and other elites have used ethnic nationality to gain backing for political agendas that may not have been primarily motivated by nationalism itself. This tactic, however, could not have worked, if nationality had been entirely a nonissue.

Political and economic variables have contributed to the resurgence of nationalism and the start of war. But they alone have not *caused* either the war or the brutalities against women, children, and the elderly. Another contributing factor is the discourse about the past.

Experience, Recollection, and Reinvention

Wariness of others grows out of the experience of deprivation, violence, and loss. For my oldest informants, this is the third war to be fought on their soil in their lifetime. Because life was difficult, and because others protected their own interests, not yours, families and small groups tended to look inward for mutual support and for protection against the insecurity of the world outside. Boundaries were closely drawn, to insulate and protect. But they could also be opened to admit someone who proved trustworthy or useful.

This attitude of wariness tended to be fostered in families where grandparents took an important role in child care and in passing on cultural values (Gilliland 1986; Olsen 1989, 1990; Olsen, Spoljar-Vrzina, Rudan, and Barbaric-Kersic 1991). Younger people also had a direct experience of shortages and inflation in the period following Tito's death, which perpetuated expectations that others are not to be trusted. This perception of others, as looking for opportunities to take advantage and promote their own interests, has been translated to ethnonational levels.

My research in the early 1980s focused on questions of social change and cultural reproduction in families and small communities. I was concerned not only with the behavior of household groups (Olsen et al. 1991), but with the symbolic construction of concepts of family and household and notions of belonging to family, neighborhood, or community groups (Gilliland 1986; see also Halpern 1963, 1965, 1967, 1969; Erlich 1966; Baric 1967; Hammel 1972; Simic 1972, 1982, 1983; Hammel and Yarbrough 1973; Denich 1977; Halpern and Kerewsky-Halpern 1986). In Slavonski Brod before 1990, the interests of families, households and personal networks (*drustva* and *veze*, literally "company" and "connections") took precedence over those of ethnonational affiliations, particularly among people who were of mixed nationality.

I describe elsewhere concerns that focus on family, household, and network boundaries (Olsen 1989, 1990). To be socially viable, these groups must allow the entry of new members. This raised questions, even in the early 1980s and before, of the degree to which outsiders (however defined) could be trusted. This included women marrying into families, people from different neighborhoods, new colleagues, neighbors, and friends. I argued that the drawing of very close boundaries, the emphasis on the family, household and kin group, and on the local community or immediate personal networks, were survival strategies known to the oldest members of families from earlier remembered days of hardship and war (Gilliland 1986; Olsen 1990). People depended on family and friends to see them through periods of difficulty that threatened basic physical survival.

The new construction (or reconstruction) of nationalities is accomplished through a language of belonging familiar from the recent and the more distant past. The right or the necessity to protect the interests of oneself and other members of a salient social group is expressed in part through metaphors of suffering, deprivation, and self-sacrifice (Olsen and Rudan 1992). Others have hurt one or members of one's group in some way. Often those who make such claims also claim that they have, in fact, helped those who now have turned against them. They are therefore entitled to protect themselves, to exclude or turn against those who have done them wrong. This language is used in public discourse to justify behavior on all sides of the current political crisis. It is the same language of protest, justification, and claim to privileged status used in families. Women, particularly, make claims to moral superiority based on self-sacrifice (Gilliland 1986; Olsen 1989; Breuner 1992; Olsen and Rudan 1992).

The notion of a unified Yugoslavia, a nation of southern Slavs who shared a common past and future, was predicated largely on the events of World War II, the success of Tito and his partisans, a nationally mixed group. The media, political leaders, and individuals now have begun to talk again of a history prior to that war. The times and the events they invoke depend on the claims they wish to further. Croats claim that Mostar, which had belonged to Croatia in the eleventh century, should really be a part of Croatia now. Serbs speak of Greater Serbia, which according to their view of history, included the Dalmatian coast and Bosnia. Who did what during World War II, the ratio of Croats to Serbs in the partisan army, and traditions of "democracy and hard work" as opposed to "authoritarianism and patronage," are invoked in heated discussions, television interviews, and films.

Religious holidays once again became important, primarily as markers of ethnonational identity. Weddings, baptisms, and funerals began to be associated with church services more often (Gilliland 1986). Selective histories, religion, ethnonational (rather than the federal Yugoslav) flags, and the changes of public place names—these and other very powerful symbols—are promoted, particularly by the media (heavily censored on all sides).

The first instances of nationalist violence in the early winter of 1991 were also aired on television. Each side was eager to show mutilated bodies. This was very effective in rousing anti-Serb feelings among Croats, and undoubtedly was used in a similar way in other republics. Living in Zagreb, I had access primarily to Croatian news. I had occasion, however, to travel to Belgrade and also received information about the media second-hand, from individuals living in Serbia, both Serbs and Americans.

The media continues to play a central role in the ongoing war as evidenced by a letter I received in December 1992 from my former landlady's niece, Draga. She is a young wife and mother, living near Deronje in the Backa region of Serbia. In 1982-1983, Draga lived with her aunt, my landlady, in Slavonia. She seemed at that time unconcerned about nationality or religion. Many of her friends were Croats, and her family is mixed.

Draga now has a husband in the Serbian volunteer reserve. "You cannot believe," she wrote, "what our lives are like. The news you hear is nothing compared to the reality of the situation. Ustashas and Muslims are raping four- and five-year-old girls. [She has heard this on the Serbian news.] They are not normal humans." She did not believe that Serbs committed atrocities. She considered that Serbs had been betrayed by the West and were the victims in the current war.

Draga's new or heightened sense of *Srpstvo*, and her redefinition of other ethnic nationals as enemies, appears to have come about since the war began. She has not, however, said anything against her cousin who married a Croatian woman and who fled the country rather than be caught in the war. How Draga has resolved this in her own mind I do not know.

On all sides, however, people have redefined themselves and others. "Slavonians" became Croats, Serbs, or Muslims. In 1980, I knew many "Bosnians." This term is now politically incorrect, or rather inaccurate. Bosnia is comprised of people who are Roman Catholic (Croat), Orthodox (Serb), or Muslim. Now we hear about Bosnian Serbs or Muslims or Bosnian Croats. The associations with place have become secondary.

Conclusion

I asserted earlier that in 1982 and 1983 nationality was relatively unimportant. At that time, people talked about economic difficulties. They were preoccupied with the cost and availability of certain items and with the cultivation of networks that would provide access to goods, services, or jobs. Celebrations that were traditionally specific to one ethnic nationality or another often included guests who were ethnically different. This was another indication that ethnicity did not much matter. I was many months into my research before I began to learn about my neighbors' ethnic histories.

There were some incidents in which ethnicity or religious affiliation came up. My landlady's great-aunt insisted she spoke Croatian, not Serbo-Croatian or the Yugoslav language (as it was commonly then called). The celebration of a wedding between a Bosnian Serb and a Croat was nearly ruined by hostility between the families, expressed initially as crude jokes, and later as open ethnic prejudice. These incidents and the general unwillingness of people to speak of nationality, and even the sense I had on some occasions that this was a forbidden topic, should have indicated to me that there were more tensions over ethnonationality than I realized at the time. But they were isolated incidents and there are still more people surprised that war broke out than expected it.

When I look through my notes and recall conversations, there are clear indications of a lingering ethnonationalist prejudice under the surface of good relations. There was an implicit hierarchy in which Gypsies hardly counted, and Albanians were only a little better. Muslims were regarded by some as inferior to Croats or Serbs, though Bosnian Muslims were generally more acceptable to Croats and Serbs than were Albanians (most of whom are also Muslim). My landlady's sister-in-law had married a Muslim whom the family never entirely accepted. While this man was active in the community, and treated to his face as an equal by his neighbors and near associates, comments behind his back about his lack of initiative (a trait commonly attributed to ethnic minorities) were not infrequent. A young man who brought back a bride from Kosovo (where he served in the army) was cut off by his parents (she was Albanian Muslim). Jokes were made at the expense of Bosnian Muslims, a good indication that Serbs and Croats regarded them with ambivalence at best.

Anti-Muslim sentiments may have been a source of solidarity between Serbs and Croats. Grandma Ana said that Muslims in a village near her own had provided her with food and shelter when she had to flee her own home during World War II. Because she was a Catholic, it surprised her they had done so. A neighbor explained to me early in my stay that Muslims "married four wives." This erroneous belief was enough for her to describe them as "animals," not even human, and justified her disdain, at least in her own eyes. No one contradicted her, though four other people were in the room at the time. Whether they agreed or not I do not know.

At the other end of the scale, Croats did not denigrate Slovenians or Hungarians. Sometimes Slovenians were said to be "colder" than other Slavs, "more like Germans." This explanation was given often to account for the unwillingness of one of my neighbors to participate in gossip. Jokes were made about the way in which

Hungarians spoke Serbo-Croatian (their confusion about gender was exaggerated). Slovenes and Hungarians did, however, more often differentiate themselves from others, as being superior.

Although good relations generally held between Serbs and Croats, people still sometimes made comments in private about the events of World War II. In 1982, the names Ustasha or Chetnik were not spoken publicly, as a rule, but the stories of personal losses were recounted in private, as I described earlier. By 1991, however, references to these groups were being made in public, and used by Croats and Serbs to dehumanize each other and to justify separateness, and then violence.

The experience of nationality in Slavonski Brod seems to be a special case, as it may be in other border regions, or even urban areas where there is an ethnic mix. For more than forty years, for many people, not only the children of mixed marriages but also believing Communists, ethnic nationality ceased to be a primary marker of social advantage and social distance. Yet a folklore of ethnonationality remained. There was continued discrimination, in public, against the groups who remained marginal—Muslims, Albanians, Roma, and Jews. More important, perhaps, private family histories kept ethnonationalist sentiments and fear alive. These memories were there, waiting to be called into action, if the times were right, if someone wanted to make use of them, and if the means of communication were available.

In the present situation, all three conditions were met. The economy was falling apart and people were impatient for change. The current leaders of the Croats and the Serbs emerged in this climate. They had something to gain—power—and needed ways to legitimize themselves. The Marxist idiom of deprivation by a ruling class was bankrupt, since people realized that socialist economic policies had failed. Moreover, all the would-be leaders had themselves been associated with socialism in the past.

Serbs who lived in minority enclaves within Croatia began to blame Croats for keeping them in a disadvantaged situation. Croats blamed Serbs in Belgrade, and less-developed regions of Yugoslavia in general, for the Yugoslav and Croatian economic decline. Serbs countered with further concerns for the welfare and safety of Serbs in Croatia. Stories of past oppression began to move from private discourse into the public realm. And so the situation escalated, in spite of an initial level-headedness, in spite of the mixture of ethnic nationality, and in spite of the many people on all sides who resisted secession or war. The media played a central role. Censorship and sensationalism added to the growing climate of fear.

The experience of ethnonationality in a border region such as Brod is, in some ways, unique. But it does highlight the inadequacy of explanations for the war that claim nationalism to have been "always" a part of life in the Balkans. At the same time, however, without a history of nationalism divisions along these particular lines would have been less likely to occur. Economic and political variables alone will not explain why people move from disagreements about the distribution of resources to unmitigated hatred.

NOTES

1. Fox, in discussing the rise of a Hindu national identity in India, emphasizes the roles of changing material conditions and class relations in India since independence. "Without this class analysis, I could say only that nationalist ideologies are cultural constructions–which is not very illuminating by itself" (1990:65).

2. In 1991, sentiments had also changed among people in Brod. Even strong supporters of the state in 1982, such as my landlady's son, regarded the federal government differently in 1991. The failure of economic reform contributed largely to this change, as did perceived discrimination on the basis of nationality, and associated emotions such as resentment, anger, and fear.

3. The new Croatian flag replaced the Communist red star with a "chessboard" of red and white squares at the center. This chessboard had also been at the center of the wartime flag of the Ustasha state. Croats deny that it has anything to do with fascism, but Serbs see this as a symbol of exclusion of all non-Croats in the territory and associate the symbolism with Serbian genocide (see Denich 1994:378).

4. Names with socialist associations were replaced by names associated with Croatian heroes and history. Some of the "new" Croatian names were actually old pre-1945 names, which had been resurrected. Square of the Republic in Zagreb, for example (*Trg Republika)*, had previously been Square of Ban Jelacic, and has now been named once again Square of Ban Jelacic (*Trg Ban Jelacica*).

5. In fact, in the past, religion did matter to people who wanted to practice their religion openly. Old people went to church, but most younger people felt they were not really free to make that choice. One young man, who openly attended church and professed his religious feelings, claimed this was the reason for his lack of success in advancing at his job. The issue is currently complicated by people who are reconstructing their own histories. Some who have chosen not to deny publicly that they were once supporters of socialism criticize those who pretended to be socialists for personal gain and now pretend to have been devout Catholics all along.

6. Yug, or *Jug,* means south in the Croatian, Serbian, Slovenian, and Macedonian languages; thus, Yugoslavia was a nation of southern Slavs, compared to the northern Slavs, who are Russians, Poles, Czechs, Slovaks, and others.

REFERENCES

Anderson, Benedict. 1991 (1983). *Imagined Communities.* London: Verso.

Andric, Ivo. 1977 (1945). *The Ridge on the Drina.* Chicago: University of Chicago Press.

BRIDGE

Bailey, F. G., ed. 1971. *Gifts and Poison: The Politics of Reputation.* New York: Schocken Books.

Bailey, F. G. 1988. *Humbuggery and Manipulation: The Art of Leadership.* Ithaca: Cornell University Press.

Bakic-Hayden, Milica, and Robert M. Hayden. 1992. "Orientalist Variations on the Theme 'Balkans': Symbolic Geography in Recent Yugoslav Cultural Politics Since 1987." *Slavic Review* 51:1-15.

Baric, Lorraine. 1967. "Traditional Groups and New Economic Opportunities in Rural Yugoslavia." In *Themes in Economic Anthropology.* Raymond Firth, ed. Pp. 253-281. London: Tavistock Publications.

Botev, Nikolai, and Richard Wagner. 1993. "Seeing Past the Barricades: Ethnic Intermarriage in Yugoslavia During the Last Three Decades." *Anthropology of East Europe Review. Special Issue: War Among the Yugoslavs.* David Kideckel and Joel Halpern, eds., 11(1-2):27-34.

Breuner, Nancy F. 1992. "The Cult of the Virgin Mary in Southern Italy and Spain." *Ethos* 1(20):66-95.

Bringa, Tone. 1993. "Nationality Categories, National Identification and Identity Formation in 'Multinational' Bosnia." *The Anthropology of East Europe Review. Special Issue: War Among the Yugoslavs.* David Kideckel and Joel Halpern, eds., 11(1-2):69-76.

Denich, Bette S. 1977. "Women, Work and Power in Modern Yugoslavia." In *Sexual Stratification.* Alice Schlegel, ed. Pp. 215-244. New York: Colombia University Press.

Denich, Bette S. 1993. "Unmaking Multi-Ethnicity in Yugoslavia: Metamorphosis Observed." In *The Anthropology of East Europe Review. Special Issue: War Among the Yugoslavs.* David Kideckel and Joel Halpern, eds., 11(1-2):43-53.

Denich, Bette S. 1994. "Dismembering Yugoslavia: Nationalist Ideologies and the Symbolic Revival of Genocide." *American Ethnologist* 21(2):367-390.

Devereaux, George. 1975. "Ethnic Identity: Its Logical Foundations and Its Dysfunctions." In *Ethnic Identity: Cultural Continuities and Change.* George A. De Vos and Lola Romanucci-Ross, eds. Pp. 42-70. Chicago: University of Chicago Press.

De Vos, George A. 1975. "Ethnic Pluralism: Conflict and Accommodation." In *Ethnic Identity: Cultural Continuities and Change.* George A. De Vos and Lola Romanucci-Ross, eds. Pp. 5-41. Chicago: University of Chicago Press.

De Vos, George A. 1983. "Achievement Motivation and Intra-Family Attitudes in Immigrant Koreans." *The Journal of Psychoanalytic Anthropology* 6(1):25-71.

Erlich, Vera St. 1966. *Family in Transition: A Study of 300 Yugoslav Villages.* Princeton: Princeton University Press.

Filipovic, Zlata. 1994. *Zlata's Diary: A Child's Life in Sarajevo.* New York: Viking Press.

Foster, Charles, ed. 1980. *Nations Without States.* New York: Praeger.

Fox, Richard G. 1990. "Hindu Nationalism in the Making, or the Rise of the Hindian." In *Nationalist Ideologies and the Production of National Cultures.* Richard G. Fox, ed. Pp. 63-80. American Ethnological Society Monograph Series. No. 2.

Gilliland, M. K. (see also M. K. G. Olsen). 1986. "The Maintenance of Family Values in a Yugoslav Town." Ph.D. diss., University of California, San Diego.

Gilliland, M. K. S. Spoljar, and V. Rudan. 1995. "Reclaiming Lives: Variable Effects of War on Gender and Ethnic Identities in the Narratives of Bosnian and Croatian Refugees." *The Anthropology of East Europe Review* 13(1):30-39).

Gladney, Dru. 1991. *Muslim Chinese: Ethnic Nationalism in the People's Republic.* Harvard East Asian Monographs. Cambridge: Harvard University Press.

Green, Linda. 1994. "Fear as a Way of Life." *Cultural Anthropology* 9(2):227-256.

Halpern, Joel M. 1963. "Yugoslav Peasant Society in Transition—Stability in Change." *Anthropological Quarterly* 36:156-182.

Halpern, Joel M. 1965. "Peasant Culture and Urbanization in Yugoslavia." *Human Organization* 24:162-174.

Halpern, Joel M. 1967. "Farming as a Way of Life: Yugoslav Peasant Attitudes." In *Proceedings of the Conference on Soviet and East European Agriculture.* Jerzy Karcz, ed. Pp. 356-384. Berkeley: University of California Press.

Halpern, Joel M. 1969 (1958). *A Serbian Village.* New York: Harper.

Halpern, Joel M., and Barbara Kerewsky-Halpern. 1986 (1972). *A Serbian Village in Historical Perspective.* Prospect Heights, IL: Waveland Press.

Hammel, E. A. 1972. "The Zadruga as Process." In *Household and Family in Past Time.* Peter Laslett and Richard Wall, eds. Pp. 335-374. Cambridge: Cambridge University Press.

Hammel, E. A. 1993. "The Yugoslav Labyrinth." *The Anthropology of East Europe Review. Special Issue: War Among the Yugoslavs.* David Kideckel and Joel Halpern, eds., 11(1-2):35-42.

Hammel, E. A., and C. Yarbrough. 1973. "Social Mobility and the Durability of Family Ties." *Journal of Anthropological Research* 29:145-163.

Hobsbawm, Eric, and Terence Ranger, eds. 1989 (1983). *The Invention of Tradition.* New York: Cambridge University Press.

Huseby-Darvas, Éva V. 1994. "But Where Can We Go? Refugee Women in Hungary from the Former Yugoslavia." In *Selected Papers on Refugee Issues: III.* Jeffrey L. MacDonald and Amy Zaharlick, eds. Pp. 63-77. Arlington: American Anthropological Association (a publication of the Committee on Refugee Issues, a committee of the General Anthropology Division of the American Anthropological Association).

Jelavich, Charles. 1990. *South Slav Nationalisms: Textbooks and Yugoslav Union Before 1914.* Columbus: Ohio State University Press.

Lewin, Carroll McC. 1993. "Negotiated Selves in the Holocaust." *Ethos* 21(3):295-318.

McKay, James, and Frank Lewins. 1978. "Ethnicity and the Ethnic Group: A Conceptual Analysis and Reformulation." *Ethnic and Racial Studies* 1:412-427.

New Yorker. 1993. "Comment: Quiet Voices From the Balkans." March 15, pp. 4-6.

Olsen, M. K. G. 1989. "Authority and Conflict in Slavonian Households: The Effects of Social Environment on Intra-Household Processes." In *The Household Economy: Reconsidering the Domestic Mode of Production*. R. Wilk, ed. Colorado: Westview Press.

Olsen, M. K. G. 1990. "Redefining Gender in Rural Yugoslavia: Masculine and Feminine Ideals in Ritual Context." *East European Quarterly* 23(4):431-444.

Olsen, M. K. G. 1993. "Bridge on the Sava: Ethnicity in Eastern Croatia 1981-1991." *The Anthropology of East Europe Review. Special Issue: War Among the Yugoslavs*. David Kideckel and Joel Halpern, eds., 11(1-2):54-62.

Olsen, M. K. G., S. M. Spoljar-Vrzina, V. Rudan, and A. M. Barbaric-Kersic. 1991. "Normal Families? Problems in Cultural Anthropological Research Methods and Methodology." *Collegium Antropologicum* 15(2):299-308.

Olsen, M. K. G., and Vlasta Rudan. 1992. "Childlessness and Gender: Example from the Island of Hvar." *Collegium Antropologicum* 16(1):115-124.

Patrias, Carmela. 1993. "Tales of Teleki Square." *Oral History: Ethnicity and National Identity* 21(1):22-34.

Peoples, James, and Garrick Bailey. 1991. *Humanity*, 2d ed. St. Paul: West Publishing Company.

Perks, Robert. 1993. "Ukraine's Forbidden History: Memory and Nationalism." *Oral History: Ethnicity and National Identity* 21(1):43-53.

Petrovic, K., and B. Belic. 1970. "Prehistoric Cultures in the Area of Brodsko Posavlje." *Materijali VII: Simpozijum praistorijske sekcije arheoloskog drustva Jugoslavije* (Materials VII:Symposium of the Prehistoric Group of the Archeological Society of Yugoslavia). Slavonski Brod 1970, Belgrade 1971.

Plejic, Irena. 1992. "All That We Had, All That We Were, Reduced to Memories: Personal Accounts and Letters of Displaced Persons from Eastern Slavonia." In *Fear, Death and Resistance: An Ethnography of War, Croatia 1991-1992*. Lada Feldman, Ines Prica, and Reana Senjkovic, eds. Pp. 229-239. Zagreb: Institute of Ethnology and Folklore Research, Matrix Croatica X-Press.

Popis Stanovnistva i stanova (Census records). 1981. Republicki zavod za statistiku SR Hrvatska (Census of Population and Dwellings). Zagreb: Government Printing Office.

Povrzanovic, Maja. 1992. "Culture and Fear: Everyday Life in Wartime." In *Fear, Death and Resistance: An Ethnography of War, Croatia 1991-1992*. Lada Feldman, Ines Prica, and Reana Senjkovic, eds. Pp. 119-150. Zagreb: Institute of Ethnology and Folklore Research, Matrix Croatica X-Press.

Povrzanovic, Maja. 1993. "Ethnography of War: Croatia 1991-1992." *The Anthropology of East Europe Review. Special Issue: War Among the Yugoslavs*. David Kideckel and Joel Halpern, eds., 11(1-2):117-125.

Reineck, Janet. 1993. "Seizing the Past, Forging the Present: Changing Visions of Self and Nation Among the Kosovo Albanians." *The Anthropology of East Europe Review. Special Issue: War Among the Yugoslavs*. David Kideckel and Joel Halpern, eds., 11(1-2):85-92.

Rodman, Margaret C. 1992. "Empowering Place: Multilocality and Multivocality." *American Anthropologist* 94(3)640-656.

Rubic, Ivo. 1953. *Slavonski i Bosanski Brod. Zbornik za narodni zivot i obicaje juznih slavena* (Slavonski and Bosanski Brod. Journal for Folk Life and Customs of the Southern Slavs), Vol. 36. Zagreb: Jugoslavenska akademija znanosti i umjetnosti (Yugoslav Academy of Science and Arts).

Simic, Andrei. 1972. *The Peasant Urbanites: A Study of Rural-Urban Mobility in Serbia*. New York: Seminar Press.

Simic, Andrei. 1982. "Urbanization and Modernization in Yugoslavia: Adaptive and Maladaptive Aspects of Traditional Culture." In *Urban Life in Mediterranean Europe*. M. Kenny and D. Kertzer, eds. Pp. 203-224. Urbana: University of Illinois Press.

Simic, Andrei. 1983. "Machismo and Cryptomatriarchy: Power, Affect and Authority in the Contemporary Yugoslav Family." *Ethos* 11(1-2):66-86.

Simic, Andrei. 1991. "Obstacles to the Development of a Yugoslav National Consciousness: Ethnic Identity and Folk Culture in the Balkans." *Journal of Mediterranean Studies* 1(1):18-36.

Suárez-Orozco, Marcelo M. 1990. "Speaking of the Unspeakable: Toward a Psychosocial Understanding of Responses to Terror." *Ethos* 18(3):353-383.

Suárez-Orozco, Marcelo M. 1994. "Doing Anthropology at the *Fin de Siècle*." In *The Making of Psychological Anthropology II*. Marcelo Suárez-Orozco, George and Louise Spindler, eds. Pp. 158-194. Fort Worth: Harcourt Brace College Publishers.

Verdery, Katherine. 1991. *National Ideology under Socialism: Identity and Cultural Politics in Ceausescu's Romania*. Berkeley: University of California Press.

ACKNOWLEDGMENTS

An earlier and much briefer version of this paper appeared in *The Anthropology of East Europe Review Special Issue: War Among the Yugoslavs* 11:1-2, 1993.

GANANATH OBEYESEKERE ■

Chapter Ten

On Buddhist Identity in Sri Lanka[1]

The object of this paper is to understand the nature of the Sinhala-Buddhist identity. The pervasive view that emerges from examining ethnographic and historical sources is that to be Sinhala (Sinhalese) is ipso facto to be Buddhist and that these two labels are a facets of a single identity. I suggest that up to the arrival of the European powers in the early sixteenth century, this was the dominant identity among the Sinhalas but that it was seriously undermined by the conspicuous presence of Sinhalas who were Christians, initially Catholic and later Protestant.

The earliest colonization of Sri Lanka was mainly of the coastal areas, first by the Portuguese in 1505 and later by the Dutch. However, the major blow was the conquest of the whole island by the British in 1815 and with it the fall of the last independent kingdom of Kandy. Kings were guardians of the doctrine and with the loss of kingship Buddhists lost their political, economic, and cultural dominance to Sinhala Protestants.

I document a revival of Buddhism in the mid-nineteenth century and the emergence of a leader who, in resolving his own personal identity conflicts, helped to refashion the identity of Sinhala Buddhists. If the Buddhist aspect of Sinhala identity was traditionally taken for granted for the most part, it had to be affirmed and vindicated in the nineteenth and twentieth centuries. I describe this process of "identity affirmation" and its culmination in the mid-twentieth century, when Buddhists, having obtained political power, began to claim Sri Lanka as a Sinhala-Buddhist nation.

In contemporary language use, the Sinhala term for Buddhism is *buddhāgama*, the āgama (nowadays religion, originally tradition) of the Buddha. In general, when Sinhalas want to refer to their religion they say, "*mama buddhāgamē*" (I belong to the religion of the Buddha). The term "*bauddhayek*" (Buddhist) is also used, I think, as a translation of the English term. These self-referential words are cultural labels of recent developments in Sri Lanka, though based on terms in vogue in fourteenth-century Sinhala literature.[2] They came into use after 1505, the date of the arrival of the first Portuguese colonizers. The widespread use and diffusion of these terms, however, is a phenomenon of British rule in Sri Lanka, which lasted from 1815 to 1948.

The situation is in some sense analogous to what happened in India, where an overall religious label, "Hindu," was used to include Vaishnavite, Shaivite, Lingayat, and various regional, folk, and sometimes "tribal" religious life-forms. In India, as well as in Sri Lanka, these newly introduced cultural labels have been accepted by many people in a manner that has a great deal of significance for their collective identity. I will examine the newly emergent identity of Buddhist—and relate it to its historical and social background—and the immediate sociopolitical and economic factors that led to its development. The words "Buddhist" and "Buddhism" are used in two distinct ways in this paper. One is my own reference to practitioners of the religion and the second is a self-referential and self-identification term the people use themselves.

The older Sinhala term for Buddhism was the Pali, "*buddha sāsana*" (the universal Buddhist church). Though its literal meaning was universalistic in significance, its specific relevance for the Sinhalas was entirely particularistic. The *sāsana* was inextricably linked with the country's dominant ethnic group, the Sinhalas. The great historical chronicles written in Pali known as the *Mahāvaṃsa* and composed at different times in Sinhala history, as well as literary and historical works written in the Sinhala script from about the thirteenth century onward, constantly emphasize the destiny of the *sāsana* with the destiny of the Sinhala people. The myths or histories that legitimize this ideology are also sung in collective rituals performed in villages in most parts of the Sinhala-speaking areas of the nation to this day. As such, these myths are vitally important for understanding the equivalence of the terms "Sinhala" and "Buddhism" and the whole problem of Sinhala cultural identity.

According to the popular myth exemplified in the *Mahāvaṃsa* account, the island of Sri Lanka was originally inhabited by nonhumans—*yakṣas* and *nāgas* (demons and snake-people). The first chapter of the chronicle records three visits of the Buddha to Lanka. The first visit was when "at the ninth month of his Buddhahood, at the full moon of Phussa, [he] himself set forth to the isle of Lanka, to win Lanka for the faith. For Lanka was known to the Conqueror as a place where his doctrine should [thereafter] shine in glory; and [he knew that] from Lanka, filled with *yakkhas*, the *yakkhas* must be drawn forth."[3] In his first trip he quelled the demons at Mahiyangana in eastern Sri Lanka, which today is a leading pilgrimage center where people go to worship the collarbone relic of the Buddha and propitiate the powerful deities, Saman and Kataragama, that reside there. During his second visit he quelled and converted the *nāgas* or snake beings that dwelled in the northern tip of the island known as *nāgadipa*, which was also a center of Buddhist pilgrimage until recently.[4] "When the Master, having alighted on the earth, had taken his place on a seat there, and had been refreshed with celestial food and drink by the *nāga*-kings, he, the Lord, established in the [three] refuges and in the moral precepts eighty *koṭis* [a *koṭi* is a traditional number today glossed to mean ten million] of snake spirits, dwellers in the ocean and on the mainland."[5] His third visit, eight years after his enlightenment, was to Kelaniya, near Colombo. During this visit he also "left traces of his footprints plain to see on Sumanakuta," an impressive peak, the foremost place of Buddhist pilgrimage.[6] From there he went to Digavapi on the east coast, and to various places in Anuradhapura, which later became the first capital of the Sinhala kings.

All these places consecrated by the Buddha have been, and still are, great centers of Buddhist pilgrimage. The significance of the myth is clear: the island has been consecrated by the Buddha himself and "malevolent" forces have been banished or subjugated or converted preparatory to the arrival of the founder of the Sinhala "nation," Prince Vijaya. The *Mahāvaṃsa* describes that founding thus: "The prince named Vijaya, the valiant, landed in Lanka, in the region called Tambapanni on the day the Tathagatha [i.e., the Buddha] lay down between the two twin-like sala trees to pass into *nibbāna* [nirvana]."[7] But before the Buddha died he summoned Sakka, the king of the gods and the divine protector of the universal Buddhist church or *sāsana*, and instructed him thus: "Vijaya, son of King Sinhabahu, is come to Lanka from the country of Lala, together with seven hundred followers. In Lanka, O lord of gods, will my religion be established, therefore carefully protect him with his followers and Lanka."[8] Sakka, in turn, handed the guardianship of the newly consecrated land to a god named Uppalavannassa (lotus hued), later identified with Vishnu. Vishnu himself, in the guise of an ascetic, met Vijaya as he landed in Sri

Lanka with his followers and "sprinkled water on them from his water-vessel and . . . wound a thread about their hands," in order to protect them from demons, much as contemporary monks do for lay followers in Buddhist thread-tying rituals known as *pāritta*.[9]

Vijaya's men were lured into a cave and captured by a demonness, Kuveni. Vijaya rescued them, and afterward married the demonness who begat him a son and a daughter. Later he discarded the demonness and banished her into the forest with her two children. He himself married a Tamil princess from the royal family of Madurai in south India; his followers also married Tamil women from the same area and from these unions were formed the Sinhalas. The son and daughter from Kuveni married incestuously and from them sprang the Veddas or hunters. Thus, the myth develops the first contrastive set, Sinhalas and Veddas. As for the Sinhalas themselves, they are begotten from matrimonial alliances between Sinhalas and Tamils. Because the *Mahāvaṃsa* was written about the sixth century A.D. it must be assumed that the Sinhala people of that time saw no problem with their being constituted of the "blood" of both Vijaya's people and the Tamils through marriage.

These myths, which are repeated in a variety of contexts—literary, historical, and ritual—crystallize the situation of the Sinhala cultural identity until the advent of the colonial powers. However, we must be careful in extrapolating cultural identity from those texts that deal with that identity because some texts actively help construct notions of cultural identity, whereas others reflect already constructed identities. The importance of this distinction was driven home to me through my reading of Richard Helgerson's *Forms of Nationhood.* In it he deals with a number of Elizabethan writers who, he says, helped to construct the *idea* of an English nation, sometimes in differing and even contradictory ways.[10]

Although it is virtually certain that the *Mahāvaṃsa* performs a similar task, there are others that perform both. Thus, ritual texts sung in Sinhala in village exorcistic and thanksgiving rituals repeat the myths initially depicted in the *Mahāvaṃsa*; these texts are thus *reflective* of the cultural identity; they help *maintain* and continue that identity; and they assist in *creating* that identity for groups weakly integrated into the Buddhist "nation." That weakly integrated groups existed seems clear from the contrastive identity, Sinhala and Vedda. Vedda was a class name for a variety of groups who lived by hunting and gathering and engaging in life-forms that were different from the Sinhalas, the most critical feature being that they were not Buddhist.[11]

The myths that I have mentioned equate two cultural labels, Sinhala and Buddhist, as twin facets of a single identity. These myths constitute an expression of the self-perceived historical role of the Sinhala-Buddhists as a nation. Their kings are the guardians and protectors of the *sāsana* (the Buddhist church), a historic role decreed by the Buddha himself. Myths, in this sense, are more powerful than the empiricist historiography of modern historians because so-called empirical events may not have much bearing on the lives of people unless they are given meaning, or have been mythicized, that is, repatterned in terms of, or incorporated into, the preexistent myths of a nation. Myths are present in the minds of people at any given point in history and sum up for them the meaning of their country's history and their self-perceived historical role.

The self-perceived history of the Sinhalas as depicted in their chronicles had an important pattern: with a few exceptions Sri Lanka was consistently invaded by south Indian kings who were depicted simplistically as "Tamils," even when they sometimes were not. The Tamil invaders soon adopted a role very much like the French-Catholics in Linda Colley's book *Forging the Nation*, a beautiful account of the way in which Great Britain was forged after 1707, in the two well-known senses of "forge."[12] In both Britain and in Sri Lanka the developing sense of the Other was crucially significant for the maintenance and perpetuation of the cultural identity. In Sri Lanka the major contrastive identity developed in the chronicles was Sinhala (Buddhist) versus Tamil (Shaivite unbelievers). However, this did not mean that different views of the Tamils did not exist, particularly the historically enduring idea of Tamils as affines. Links of affinity coexisted with the divisions based on cultural identity along with other links and dividing lines. After all, the invaders, as well as other kinds of immigrants, have to be incorporated into the social structure (at least in those areas where the Sinhalas were dominant) and one way of ensuring this is through affinity. In fact, the distinction between affinity and consanguinity is abolished, after the initial alliance, through the so-called Dravidian kinship that virtually all groups (and this included Muslims) shared.[13] Elsewhere I have discussed the significance of "colonization myths" and ritual dramas where other processes of assimilation are depicted.[14] Consequently, it is not likely that the virulent hatred for the Tamils that animates contemporary discourse had the kind of historical uniformity that Colley records for French-Catholic and British-Protestant relations during the period when the British nation was being fabricated.

I have said that the content of the Sinhala-Buddhist cultural identity had an important thematic content: the Sinhala kings as defenders of the *sāsana* and the invaders as opposers of the *sāsana*. This theme is not always in accordance with the facts of history. Tamil kings who ruled over Sinhala people, either through conquest or through complicated rules of succession, often took upon themselves the traditional role of Buddhist kings and many became Buddhist themselves; and Sinhala kings sometimes pillaged temples and robbed monasteries of their wealth.

Yet the myths are not entirely fictitious because the self-perceived historical role of the Sinhalas was real in their own "definition of the situation." And on occasion Sinhala people could be mobilized by their rulers to fight foreign invaders by appealing to the sentiments underlying the myths, so that the myths themselves becoming rallying points for their "nationalism." Finally, there is a phenomenon, familiar even in Western nationhood, where actual historical events begin to be interpreted as validating the themes of history or myth—themes that define the self-perceived historical role of nations.

Let me now consider one of the most powerful of the those mythicized events in the history of Sri Lanka—the myth of King Dutugamunu. Though there is little doubt of the historicity of this king and his works of Buddhist piety, I am mainly interested in his mythicization, for he is preeminently the Sinhala-Buddhist hero who saved his country from the Tamils.

In the second century B.C., the capital of the Sinhala kings fell into the hands of the Cholas of South India and the Tamil king Elara reigned there (145-101 B.C.). Resistance to Elara came from Dutugamunu, the son of the ruler of the southern principality of Sri Lanka. The *Mahāvaṃsa* and other chronicles describe how Kavantissa asked his two sons, Dutugamunu and Sadhatissa, to promise that they would not fight the Tamils. They both refused, and Dutugamunu crawled into bed. "The queen came, and caressing Gamini [Dutugamunu] spoke thus: 'Why dost thou not lie easily upon thy bed with limbs stretched out my son?' 'Over there beyond the Ganga [the Mahaveli River] are the Damilas [Tamils], here on this side is the Gotha [O]cean, how can I lie with outstretched limbs?'"[15] Subsequently, Dutugamunu defeated the Tamils and assumed the kingship of the whole country. Since I am not interested in the empirical historicity of Dutugamunu, I shall list certain mythicized events in the *Mahāvaṃsa.*

1. In the war with the Tamils, Dutugamunu marched in front of his army with his mace, within which was embedded a Buddha relic. When he had mobilized his army he said, "I will go on to the land on the further side of the river [the direction of the capital Anuradhapura where the Tamils were entrenched] to bring glory to the doctrine."[16]

2. He marched into battle with five hundred monks: never before or since have monks taken such an active part in a military campaign.

3. Dutugamunu felt guilty about the lives lost in the war. Like Arjuna of the *Mahābhāratha* he tells the eight *arahant*s (monks who have achieved nirvana) who come to console him: "How shall there be any comfort for me, O venerable sirs, since by me was caused the slaughter of a great host numbering millions?" But the *arahant*s, like Krishna of the Hindu epic, reply:

> From this deed arises no hindrance in thy way to heaven. Only one and a half human beings were slain by thee, O lord of men. The one had come unto the [three] refuges, the other had taken upon himself the five precepts. Unbelievers and men of evil life were the rest, not more to be esteemed that beasts. But as for thee, thou wilt bring glory to the doctrine of the Buddha in manifold ways; therefore cast away care from thy heart, O ruler of men.[17]

4. After his death Dutugamunu went to the heaven of Tusita where lives the next Buddha-to-be, Maitreye. The *Mahāvaṃsa* goes on to say: "The great king Dutthagamani [Dutugamunu], he who is worthy of the name of king, will be the first disciple of the sublime Metteyya [Maitreye], the king's father [will be] his father and the mother his mother. The

younger brother Sadhatissa will be his second disciple, but Salirajakumara, the king's son, will be the son of the sublime Metteyya."[18]

It is correct, as some Sri Lankan historians assert, that this is the only instance in the chronicles where there is an explicit justification for war and killing that better fit the *Bhagavad Gita* than the Buddhist *suttas*. But we are dealing with lived Buddhist history, not the *suttas*, and the mythic significance of the episode totally outweighs its statistical import. Whereas the details of the wars fought by Dutugamunu and faithfully recorded in the *Mahāvaṃsa* might easily have been forgotten, his mythic significance as the savior of the Sinhalas and of Buddhism grew through the years and developed into a series of important myths, ready to be used as a powerful instrument of Sinhala nationalism in modern times.

It goes without saying that these myths are not uniformly important in all periods of history; nor are they the only ones available. They belong to a class of myths that "eternally return" in times of invasion and other cultural crises. In several of them are embedded the powerful notion: "Sinhala kings are defenders of the *sāsana* and their opponents are the Tamils." Yet, I have already shown that Tamil invaders and immigrants were a constant phenomenon in Sri Lankan historical experience, and they had to be accommodated through marriage and other ways into the Sinhala social structure. This was quite unlike the situation in England with respect to the Spanish (and later the French), where the threat or fear of invasion was the reality.

To get back to the historical narrative: certain institutional arrangements, from very early times, provided further expression to the idea of a Sinhala-Buddhist nation. The first Buddhist missions were sent to Sri Lanka during the time of the Emperor Asoka (circa 270-230 B.C.), and an event of great symbolic significance occurred there during this time. A branch of the *bōdhi* tree under which the Buddha achieved enlightenment was planted in Anuradhapura, the capital of the Sinhala kings: the tree lasts to this day. Also enshrined were relics of the Buddha, including the right collarbone and the almsbowl, the former in the Thuparama *stūpa* (a large mound that enshrines Buddha relics) in Anuradhapura. Rahula summarizes the significance of these events:

> The planting of the *bōdhi* tree was symbolic of the establishment of Buddhism and Buddhist culture in the island. The relics of the Buddha were regarded as representing the Buddha himself and their enshrinement was as good as Buddha's residence in Lanka. The *pātradhātu*, or alms bowl, of the Buddha was kept within the king's house, and it became a national "palladium" of the Sinhalese, just as happened later in the case of the "tooth relic."[19]

The calendar itself was partially Buddhicized; thus, the full moon day of the month of Vesak celebrates the birth and nirvana day of the Buddha and Poson commemorates the introduction of Buddhism to the island.

To sum up: very early in Sri Lanka's history two key ideas were developed. First: not only was the island consecrated by the Buddha himself, but he was immanent in his relics enshrined in the great centers of pilgrimage scattered over the country. Second: two of the relics became associated with Sinhala sovereignity and the legitimacy of their kings, initially the bowl relic and later the tooth relic. These relics were carefully guarded, housed in a special building, and paraded ceremonially every year. No foreign invader or claimant to the throne felt secure without possessing the relics. They therefore not only symbolized the living presence of the Buddha, they also symbolized the idea of the Sinhala Buddhist nation and the legitimacy of its rulers. Soon a third idea emerged: that the king was a future Buddha or a Bodhisattva, a Sinhala version of the divine right of kings. Thus, the king was defender and guardian of the faith; the order of monks were its visible representatives; the laity represented the Buddhist congregation; and the major guardian deities, most of them originally Hindu, were also Buddhicized as divine defenders of the faith and converted into Bodhisattvas.

Through a long historical period culminating in the sixteenth century (the period before the arrival of the colonial powers), there have emerged other visible markers of Sinhala identity. There is the common language, Sinhala, which, in spite of minor dialectal variations, is intelligible to all who consider themselves ethnically Sinhalas. Thus, language and ethnicity are fused. Then, there is the religion, Buddhism, which involves the belief in the Three Refuges, namely, the Buddha, the Dhamma (doctrine), and the Sangha (the monk order). Sinhalas worship the Buddha who is a kind of "super-deity" heading the pantheon.

This universal worship of the Buddha is important, for though many Sinhala groups may worship other deities in the pantheon, these lower deities (particularly regional gods and demons) can vary from one area to another. Yet, while variations in beliefs occur on the lower levels of the pantheon, all Sinhala beliefs merge in the apex in the worship of the Buddha and sometimes of the guardian gods who, we have already said, are future Buddhas (Bodhisattvas). Further, Tamils and Veddas may worship some of the Sinhala guardian gods like Vishnu or Skanda, but the Buddhists alone worship the Buddha as their primary deity.

The Dhamma is also considered by all as the true teaching of the Buddha. The Sinhalas believe that the true doctrine is enshrined in Pali texts, the *sutta*s, and the true knowledge of the doctrine is the prerogative of the order of monks, the Sangha. The knowledge of doctrine by the laity is highly variable, yet I think all share a common set of ideas or concepts ultimately derived from the doctrine. These concepts are of crucial importance in giving meaning to their everyday lives and shaping their worldview. Concepts like karma, *dāna* (giving), *sila* (virtue), *bhāvanā* (meditation), *pavu-pin* (sin and merit), *karunā* (compassion), and many others in common use are all derived from Buddhist doctrinal sources or Dhamma. In addition, all Sinhalas share a common knowledge of several Pali prayers, particularly the recital of the "five precepts," that virtually defines a Buddhist as such. Thus, all Sinhalas share a common idiom—I call it a "salvation idiom"—that constitutes their shared knowledge of the Dhamma.

The Sangha (monk order) is necessary for people to maintain the knowledge of the Dhamma because the Sangha is the depository of the doctrine. The Sangha, through their sermons, are primarily, though not exclusively, responsible for the propagation and diffusion of the Dhamma. The laity, in turn, support and pay homage to the Sangha. By virtue of their saffron-colored vestments, the Sangha are a clearly identifiable feature of the social landscape and they are worshiped by the ethnic Sinhalas and by no other group in the island.

The cultural markers I have described set off the ethnic group—the Sinhalas—as a moral community, a body of people sharing common norms or values. It is obvious that an ethnic moral community is not a primary group or a face-to-face community in the strict sociological sense of the term; nor is it one with clearly defined boundaries. It is what Anderson calls an "imagined community," possessing a sense of self-consciousness and belongingness; it is also a "latent group," in the sense that the *possibility* exists for people to form themselves into unified groups on the basis of their larger cultural identity.[20] Such "translocal" imagined communities must contain within themselves the practical possibility of forming groups, however transient they may be. The *concretization* of the imagined community is a sine qua non for its very existence in the imagination of people. And this is true whether one is dealing with modern nations that concretize the sense of belongingness in such things as collective celebrations, media representations of national games or wars, and so forth, or whether one is talking of premodern polities like that of Sri Lanka.

In my thinking, the most powerful mechanism in many premodern polities that concretizes the idea of a translocal group consciousness is the "obligatory pilgrimage." I felt its power and importance when I first did fieldwork in 1958 in Rambadeniya, an isolated village in the eastern part of the central province of Sri Lanka. Here, people performed annual rituals to the chief deity of the region, and these rituals brought the village together as a moral community participating in common worship. Their's was a local deity unfamiliar to groups outside this area in the central province. However, once a year people from Rambadeniya go on pilgrimage to Mahiyangana, thirty-five miles away through forest trails, where the collarbone relic of the Buddha is enshrined. As soon as the pilgrim group leaves the village, it joins other pilgrim groups in other villages, and after a few hours of travel there is a literal expansion of the moral community such that by the time we reach the pilgrimage center, people of different castes, villages, and regions literally merge into one large mass of people. A powerful act of concretization has occurred. Further, at Mahiyangana, Rambadeniya folk will temporarily renounce the worship of their local deities and instead pay homage to the great guardian deities of the center, the gods Saman and Kataragama, and, of course, the Buddha himself, immanently present in his relics.

If the rituals of the village define the limits of the moral community at the local level and validate status differences therein, the rituals at the pilgrimage center are open to all with little concern for status distinctions. The once discrete and separate moral communities of the several villages now lose their identities in the larger translocal moral community of Sinhala Buddhists. Similar sacred pilgrim centers are scattered throughout the island, and whereas it is doubtful that individuals had the time and opportunity to do the ideal pilgrimage, it is certain that most did go to some of them, enough for them to feel a sense of community and common identity outside the limited moral and physical universe of the village.

Identity and the Vicissitudes of History

It is time now to make some tentative theoretical observations regarding the cultural identities that are associated with such things as ethnicity and nationhood. "Identity" is not something found in the lexicon of Sinhala; it is something social theorists have invented to conceptualize scattered ideas implicitly held by people. It helps us unscramble what people mean when they say they are Sinhalas. It has a cultural content the salient features of which I have sketched above. Further, it has personal psychological meaning that surfaces when that identity is under threat; it is associated with sociological mechanisms that permit the group to imagine itself as a translocal community.

The taken-for-granted or "axiomatic" character of ethnic and similar identities is nothing unusual because it is a key feature of virtually *any* social or cultural identity, such as caste and kinship. Intrinsic to the axiomatic character of cultural identities is the key idea of birth. Take an obvious example: son is a status in the conventional sociological sense of a bundle of rights and duties. As an *identity*, however, it is associated with birth, together with emotional investments of various sorts, for example, feelings of filial piety or love and all sorts of ambivalent emotions. That identity also has a cultural content, part of which is subsumed under the conventional designation "status." The axiomatic or taken-for-granted quality of the identity can get a jolt, however, if I begin to question whether my father deserves my love or whether fatherhood is a bourgeois institution that ought to be abolished.

Now carry the logic of this argument to a larger cultural identity like ethnicity or nationhood. For example, the sense of being a citizen of a modern nation (being French or English) or possessing an ethnic identity within that larger one (being Jewish or Indian) is associated with birth. The etymology of the word "nation" is birth; the popular term for caste in many South Asian languages is *jāti*, which also means birth. One must be born Jewish to be a Jew; and aliens have to be "naturalized" to become citizens of European nations. It is not surprising, therefore, if the birth of nations themselves are everywhere celebrated in large-scale communal festivities. In Sri Lanka, the birth of a Sinhala-Buddhist nation is associated with the *poson* festival that commemorates the founding of Buddhism in the island, whereas the birth of Buddhism itself is celebrated in every Buddhist nation in the preceding month of Vesak.

Birth becomes an axiomatic feature of an ethnic or national identity only after that identity is in place, not when that identity is being constructed or refashioned. And it this cultural construction of translocal identities that is most problematic and difficult to grasp, quite unlike that of such things as kinship identities whose cultural content is more easily created and recreated through socialization. Hence, the historical question: how were translocal identities created in the first place? This, it seems to me, is the kind of question that recent historical studies (such as that of Richard Helgerson's *Forms of Nationhood*, Linda Colley's *Britons: Forging a Nation*, and Eugen Weber's *Peasants into Frenchmen*) attempt to answer.

Weber, for example, convincingly shows that although the idea of French nationhood was created at the time of the French Revolution, the practical realization of the ideal was achieved only by the late nineteenth century by a process of violent "internal colonization," which stamped out internal language and cultural differences.[21] And Colley shows that Great Britain was forged, on the negative side, through forms of racial and cultural stereotyping, scapegoatism, and hatreds projected onto the Other.[22] Nowadays, these processes are reserved for nasty movements such as those labeled "fundamentalism" and "ethnonationalism," but I believe that they are also endemic to nationalism in the making.

The end product of such violent and nonviolent internal colonization of local and regional identities (sometimes destroying them, sometimes incorporating them) is clear though: *the idea of birth associated with such things like kinship identities has to be transferred to the new translocal domain and transfused into it, such that it too becomes a taken-for-granted or axiomatic identity*. I suggest that when this occurs, such identities often, though not always, seem to take on a primordial quality, and this primordialism is not the exclusive preserve of Third World nations. They are often built into translocal cultural identities to render them powerful or effective. Primordialism is the affective counterpart of the inherent birth associated nature of axiomatic identities. Yet birth and primordialism have to be culturally constructed, and the demonstration of their construction has to be through systematic historical and ethnographic investigation. Moreover, primordialism is not a unique feature of translocal identities either; what is unique to them is the difficulty of creating and maintaining such ideas and feelings.

Let me deal with a familiar and contrasted example: sonship is a nonproblematic axiomatic identity for most cultures, but the affective dimension of sonship may range from deep allegiances ("primordiality") associated with such things as filial piety to much less powerful affects, all inculcated in socialization and cultural learning. Thus, the affective dimension of birth is never culturally uniform even though one can assert that axiomatic identities, in general, are woven into the fabric of one's being and affects one's sense of self-worth.

Whereas birth is the one inescapable and invariant part of national or ethnic identity, primordiality is much more free ranging and depends on the historical processes that went into its creation. Further, primordiality is for the most part associated with modern nations such as the United States, Great Britain, and France and they, rather than, say, Switzerland, where primordiality is weak, exemplify the nationalist condition. Primordiality in national polities is not fixed either. If local (ethnic) ties still remain and are powerful they can take on a primordial emotional load and pave the way for ethnic tension and conflict, and ethnic identity might eventually become the primordial national identity—a process occurring in many parts of the world today.

I shall thus make the following unpopular argument: primordial loyalties were seen by scholars such as Edward Shils, and more recently by Clifford Geertz, as a force associated with primary groups and often disruptive of civil order.[23] Although primordial loyalties can exist in such identities such as caste or kinship, I suggest that they are also exemplified in the making and perpetuation of modern nation-states, including those in the West. Further, such feelings were *not* as powerful in traditional polities such as that of Buddhist Sri Lanka as they are in modern ones.

This affective and variable dimension of axiomatic identities, local and translocal, that can be metaphorized as primordialism, accounts for the pride associated with national glory ("patriotism," as it is sometimes called)—in wars and football games. So is the anxiety aroused by the questioning of, or violation or threat to, axiomatic identities. This is endemic to most forms of modern nationhood, and I think its presence can be demonstrated whenever there is a threat to national identity, real or imagined, whether we are dealing with wars or threats to national pride such as the Falkland wars for Britain or the threat of Saddam Hussein for the United States. Anderson's notion of nationalism as a detached and intellectualist stance is of some consolation to us intellectuals, but it is achieved by denying primordialism and by making a radical hiatus between such things as nationalism, racism, and patriotism.[24] I believe that the latter cannot be easily disaggregated from nationalism. Racism, for example, may exist independently of nationalism but sometimes it is dependent on it, as was the case in Nazi Germany. When it is dependent, nationalist primordialism gets an added "paranoid" boost.

Let me now apply some of the preceding thoughts to the specific historical situation in Sri Lanka by synoptically continuing the historical narrative from the heyday of Sinhala-Buddhist civilization of King Dutugamunu's time until the abandonment of the old capitals of the kings and the movement of the civilization to the southwest of the island and then to the coastal areas.

The wars between the Sinhalas and Tamils continued until the sixteenth century. In the tenth century the old capital of Anuradhapura had to be abandoned owing to Tamil incursions, and the capital was moved eastward to Polonnaruva. Sinhala fortunes reached a low point in the late tenth century because of much more systematic invasions from south India, and Sri Lanka itself became a principality of the Tamil Chola kings until 1070, when a Sinhala chieftain named Kirti raised the standard of revolt successfully and assumed the crown as Vijayabahu 1 (1059-1114). But the respite was temporary. In 1214 Magha of Kalinga, in what is now known as Orissa, landed with an army of south Indian mercenaries. The Pali and Sinhala chronicles graphically describe the devastation wrought by these wars. One chronicle written several centuries after the event noted that Magha "settled Tamils in every village and reigned nineteen years in the commission of deeds of violence."[25]

As a result of these invasions, the centers of the old civilization in the northern dry zone were abandoned and the Sinhala kings moved to Dambadeniya in the southwest and, in the middle of the fourteenth century, to Gampola near Kandy. In the beginning of the sixteenth century there were three virtually independent kingdoms in the island: in the central hills in Kandy, in Kotte near Colombo, and in Jaffna in the north where an independent Tamil kingdom existed. The existence of the latter implied the existence of a Tamil community that today is the focal point for the devastating ethnic conflict in the nation. There were also groups of Tamil-speaking Muslims scattered in various parts of the country and possessing a communal identity (or several such ones) distinct from that of both Sinhala-Buddhists and Tamil Hindus. Finally, as always, there were many intermediate zones, where people were neither one nor the other, an issue that I cannot get into here.

I now refer to a text that was written in the fourteenth century during the period of steep decline of Sinhala fortunes. The *Pujavaliya* has an extraordinary account of the Sinhala Buddhist identity in its thirty-second chapter, containing a synoptic history of Sri Lanka from its very founding. Here is this text in reasonable English.

> Sri Lanka in non-Buddhist times (*abaudhakālaya*) was entirely the home of demons (*yakṣas*) but during the dispensation of the Buddhas (*baudhopādakālaya*, lit., when Buddhas arise or are born) by humans. Several previous Buddhas at their very enlightenment controlled (or destroyed) the *yakṣas* and the country became home to humans; other Buddhas actually visited this country, defeated the *yakṣas*, and established the *sāsana* [the "church"]. Because during the enlightenment of countless Buddhas, the right branch of the Bodhi tree and the *dhammadhātus* ("essence-teaching") will no doubt be preserved, this island of Lanka is like a treasury of the Triple Gem [that is, the Buddha, the Dhamma, and the Sangha]. Just as the demons could not find permanence here, neither can this land become a place of residence for

> nonbelievers (*mityādrusṭi gatavungē vāsaya*). If any nonbeliever becomes a king of Sri Lanka by force at any time, that dynasty will not last owing to the special influence of the Buddha. Because this Lanka is rightfully those of kings who have right views [Buddhists], their rightful dynastic tenure (*kula praveniya*) will absolutely prevail. For these various reasons the kings of Sri Lanka are drawn by a natural love of mind to the Buddha, and will establish the *sāsana* without delay or neglect and protect the wheel of the law and the wheel of the doctrine and reign so that the rightful dynastic tenure will be preserved.[26]

The text adds that "in the time of the very first Buddha of our *kalpa*, Kakusanda, this land was called *ojadvīpa*, that is, the land that contains the creative life-force or *ojas*. At that time Anuradhapura was called Abhayapura and the king was Abhaya. . . . These visits were the repeated by the other Buddhas of the present epoch (*kalpa*), namely, Konagamana, Kasyapa and finally our own Buddha, Gautama."[27]

Here is the reassertion and refashioning of the primordial identity: the old idea of the consecration of the land by the Buddha is reaffirmed. More significantly, the notion that alien or nonbelieving kings will have no rightful tenure and, further, the land iself has been subject to the eternal return of the Buddhas. This new myth-charter leads me to consider a further feature of national identity, perhaps not as invariant as birth but also associated with the feelings of primordiality, namely, the idea of "land," which in Western culture is personified as *patria* (associated with the law of the father) and motherland (associated with maternal nurture). The myth states that the land had existed from the very first Buddha of our epoch and it contained the vital essence of all life, *ojas*. Once the land and its rightful tenure is defined in this way, the settling of aliens (a conventional ploy of invaders in South and Southeast Asia) was bound to produce considerable anxiety. Several texts in my possession depict the processes whereby alien Tamils are Sinhalized and Buddhicized without apparent resort to violent pacification. To put it differently: in these texts the Sinhalas appear willing to recognize their hybridity as a historical phenomenon as long as the outside groups were converted into Sinhala-Buddhists, thus effacing that very hybridity. But this kind of conversion could only occur if there was a relative absence of contestation by the aliens settled in their midst.

Personal Identity and Cultural Crisis: Conquest and the Aftermath

I cannot deal here with the impact of Portuguese and Dutch colonialism. It was with the British that the island lost its independence with the surrender of the last kingdom of the Sinhala kings in Kandy. Let me discuss briefly the impact of colonial rule on Sinhala identity, getting back to the problems I highlighted at the beginning of this essay.

First, there was a split in Sinhala identity as a result of the existence of Sinhalas who were not Buddhists. Second, with the deposition of the king, Buddhism ceased to be the religion of the state and Sinhala-Buddhists lost their political and economic dominance. Under British rule Protestantism became the dominant religion, and Protestant churches were built in the proximity of old Buddhist temples, acts that symbolized the supercession of the old religion by the newly dominant one. The loss of kingship was a powerfully demoralizing event expressed, for example, in the following ditty composed by a monk soon after this event.

Alas, O ants,
Even you have a king!
What can one do
Our own karma must come to pass.

If a king is given to us
That day we'll eat milk-rice
And perform a parade
Shout "sadhu" and sing for joy![28]

Some Buddhists took seriously the treaty of surrender, which stipulated that the British government would take over the functions of Kandyan kings in continuing Buddhist traditions and worship. As a result, Queen Victoria graced the entrances to some Buddhist temples. But this illusion did not last too long, and there soon developed a millenial-type myth that said a new Sinhala culture hero, Diyasena, would arise and kill all Christians and nonbelievers and restore the glory of the Buddha *sāsana*. This millenial fantasy is the product of the hopeless plight of Sinhala-Buddhists, unable to take positive action to reestablish their lost past in a situation where the majority of Buddhists were living, as they always did, in small-scale villages, while power was in the hands of colonial rulers and a small, native, Christianized, and English-educated elite.

The resistance to British rule resulted in two rebellions, which were severely crushed by the British. Resistance then took a different form: from around 1848 Buddhist monks from the low country who were already acquainted with Dutch and Portuguese colonialism, started a campaign of protest against the missions that had greater chance of success than confrontation with the imperial government. This took on rapid momentum in the later half of the century as resistance to the missions soon spread to the educated Sinhala laity trained in vernacular schools and to an influential village intelligentsia consisting of monks, Ayurvedic physicians, and village government officials created by the British bureaucracy, such as village headmen and registrars of marriages and deaths. They were joined by some

Buddhist elites in the city educated in mission schools but they were not numerically significant.

This period also saw the establishment of two great Buddhist monastic colleges: the first, Vidyodaya Pirivena in 1873, soon followed by Vidyalankara near Colombo in 1875. Most importantly, in the 1860s there were a series of public debates between monks and Christian priests. One of the most popular of these debaters was Miguttuwatte Gunananda, whose fame spread throughout Sri Lanka and beyond to the New York Theosophical Society, founded in 1875. Two of its co-presidents, Colonel Henry Steele Olcott and Madame Blavatsky, left New York to carry the theosophical message to Asia from its new Indian headquarters in Adyar, Madras. I have discussed in great detail the profound influence of these two people on Buddhist and Hindu modernity respectively.[29]

When Olcott and Blavatsky visited Sri Lanka in 1880 they took under their wing the son of a Buddhist entrepreneur who had migrated to Colombo from a village in southern Sri Lanka. Although Olcott's influence on the Buddhist revival was profound, the actual anti-imperialist and antimissionary leadership was soon taken over by this disciple, Don David Hevavitarana, who later shed his Western personal name and Sinhala family name and adopted the title Anagarika Dharmapala. The social background and psychobiography of Dharmapala reveal striking similarities to Luther and Gandhi in Erikson's studies.[30]

Briefly, Dharmapala was educated in a variety of vernacular and English mission schools—Catholic, Baptist, and Anglican. Yet, while he was studying the Bible intensively at school, he was socialized in Buddhism; not the village Buddhism of his father's village but the doctrinal, intellectual Buddhism favored by Olcott and the Buddhist monks. A few quotations will illustrate the conflict between the school and the home environment, the humiliation he experienced in school, and the eventual triumph of his Buddhist upbringing, largely because of the influence of the Buddhist revival movement.

> Every half an hour the class had to repeat a short prayer in praise of the Virgin Mary, and I got accustomed to Catholic ways, *although I was daily worshipping my Lord Buddha.*[31]
>
> The padres gave us bonbons and stroked our hair to show us that they loved us. But they would also say to us constantly: 'Look at your mud image. You are worshipping clay.' *Then the Buddhist boy would turn in shame from his native religion.*[32]

In resolving his own personal and cultural identity, Dharmapala exemplified what many native intellectuals in similar circumstances were experiencing. His lack of roots in the traditional social structure—the absence of village, caste, or regional identities—impelled him to seek his identity in Buddhism. "My family, which is Sinhalese, has been Buddhist without a break for twenty-two hundred years."[33]

Moreover, insofar as he lacked local identities, he could appeal to all sectors of the educated Sinhalas. His religious conflicts led him to be an inveterate and implacable foe of the Christian missions, and he brought into Buddhism the zeal, enthusiasm, and bigotry that characterized the missionary dialectic.

In 1902 he wrote (in English): "The sweet gentle Aryan children of an ancient historic race are sacrificed at the altar of the whiskey-drinking, beef-eating belly god of heathenism. How long, O how long will unrighteousness last in Lanka?"[34] And: "Practices that were an abomination to the ancient noble Sinhalese have today become tolerated."[35] And again: "Arise, awake, unite and join the army of Holiness and Peace and defeat the hosts of evil."[36]

He became what I have called a "Protestant Buddhist," a reformer of the Buddhist *sāsana*, infusing that institution with the puritan values of Protestantism. All these had tremendous influence on a group of people who were in a sense like Dharmapala himself, alienated from the traditional culture of the village, and from the politicoeconomic system controlled by the British and the English-educated elite of Colombo. Later, the ideology he espoused had a hegemonic impact on Sinhala Buddhists in general as they moved into modernity in the twentieth century.

Forging a New Sinhala-Buddhist Identity

Anagarika Dharmapala started a process of what I call "identity affirmation." His affirmation of his "Buddhist-ness" was a direct precipitate of his personal and cultural identity conflicts. On the personal level, identity affirmation helps to enhance an individual's self-esteem when it has been lowered by shame or humiliation. Dharmapala insisted that others affirm their identity also. Here is an instance in which the needs of the individual matched the needs of the group, so that today Sinhala Buddhists are constantly affirming their collective identity.

As a collective phenomenon, identity affirmation is a partly conscious process whereby an ethnic group is impelled to display its unity through visible symbols and overt symbolic actions, or through the reiteration of grandiose ethnic or national myths. Viewed sociologically, the process is complicated and probably always occurs as an intrinsic part of cultural identity consciousness but is accelerated under certain conditions. First, when there is an actual or perceived threat to the unity of the group or nation it will affirm its collective solidarity and maintain its self-esteem. Second, identity affirmation occurs when the cultural identity is disintegrating and new attempts are being made to reconstruct, renew, or resurrect that identity. Third, when an ethnic group attempts to define or redefine itself for political, economic, or other purposes where the self-image is not well defined, as, for example, with Amerindians and American blacks in the recent past.

I shall now document the manner in which Anagarika Dharmapala initiated the process of identity affirmation and describe the people he influenced. These people, as I said earlier, could be characterized as a village intelligentsia and a minor bureaucratic class who lived in the village but did not belong to the peasant class. They were educated in Sinhala schools, had high aspirations for themselves and for their children, but were cut off from the sources of political and economic power. It was for these people that Anagarika Dharmapala provided a new and regenerated Buddhist ideology. If the old identity, before the advent of the Europeans, was Sinhala and for the most part implied Buddhist, the new identity had to affirm being both Sinhala and Buddhist, in opposition to Sinhalas who were non-Buddhist and non-Sinhalas who were non-Buddhist.

How did Dharmapala set about this process of identity affirmation? His technique was powerful, though simple. He *shamed* people into realizing their folly and ridiculed their aping of Western ways and religious beliefs. His psychological intuition, as far as the Sinhalas were concerned, was incisive and right on target. Having reduced their self-esteem (that is, having shamed them), he provided a means for enhancing it in the cathexis of the glorious Sinhala past. In his speeches and in the newspaper he founded, the *Sinhala Bauddhayā* (the Sinhala-Buddhist), he castigated the Westernized elites and idealized the glories of the past. The following passage is typical: "My message to the young men of Ceylon is . . . believe not the alien who is giving you arrack, whisky, toddy, sausages, who makes you buy his goods at clearance sales. . . . Enter into the realms of our King Dutugamunu in spirit and *try to identify yourself with the thoughts of that great king who rescued Buddhism and our nationalism from oblivion.*"[37]

He held up the glories of the Sinhala past as an ideal worth resurrecting. "No nation in the world has had a more brilliant history than ourselves."[38] "There exists no race on earth today that has had a more triumphant record of victory than the Sinhalese." The present degradation is due to evil Western influence on the part of the missionaries and the colonial powers. The country, as he sees it, is a Sinhala Buddhist one, and there is hardly any place in it for minority Muslims and Tamils, both of whom are viewed as exploiters. The Christians are condemned as meat eaters of "low caste." "The country of the Sinhalese should be governed by the Sinhalese." Though on occasion he addresses himself to Sinhalas qua Sinhalas rather than as Buddhists, the general bias in his polemics is for a Sinhala Buddhist nation.

The immediate effect of Dharmapala's teaching was quite dramatic—it took the form of massive name changing. Names are identity badges, and name changing implies self-consciousness about one's identity. European-type personal and surnames were changed into Sinhala or Buddhist ones. Again, this name changing was not a village phenomenon; it was confined largely to the alienated intelligentsia. But it soon became the general pattern, so that by the 1930s most parents, including

Christians, gave Sinhala or Buddhist personal names to their children even if they did not change their own names.

A similar dramatic effect was almost immediately felt in the area of female fashions. Well-to-do Sinhala females in the low country—that area that had been subject to three centuries of Western contact—generally wore Western dresses. Dharmapala mercilessly ridiculed these clothes in his speeches and in cartoons in his newspaper. Again, the technique was the same —shaming, lowering self-esteem, and providing an alternative. In this case he exhorted the women to wear the Indian sari. Anagarika's mother was the first to wear this dress which soon became the standard national dress for women of the low country.

One of the most significant innovations of the time was the Buddhist flag, developed by the city supporters of Olcott and Dharmapala. Hitherto Buddhists had no flag. The Sinhala national flag was all that was necessary. With identity affirmation initiated by Dharmapala, the Buddhist flag became popular very soon. It began to be hoisted on all ceremonial occasions and incorporated both into the national life and international Buddhism.

As Erikson says, identity makes no sense except in relation to the "core of the communal culture." Traditionally, the core of the communal culture was adapted to village life. In the twentieth century, social changes had produced the growth of cities and massive economic change. Dharmapala provided a new orientation in Buddhism consonant with the new identity. This orientation was an active involvement in the world. The model for this involvement was a Protestant one. The *anagārika* model was associated with a strongly "this-worldly asceticism," if not the "inner-worldly" Protestant ethic.

Though Anagārika Dharmapala is more symbol than a person for most contemporary Buddhists, the *anagārika* role is a function of a specific sociopolitical and historical context. In the Buddhist Pali texts, the term "*anāgrika*" (homeless) was exclusively applied to monks. *Anagārika* and monk were equivalent; the resurrection of the term by Dharmapala to designate a specific intermediate status between monk and layperson was his innovation. The new *anagārika* practiced celibacy but did not live in a monastery. An *anagārika* could engage in political, economic, and social activity, traditionally shunned by village monks, permitting him to lead a homeless life while living in the world.

The life and work of Anagarika Dharmapala anticipated much of the social and political life of contemporary Buddhism. In his writing his audience is never the villager; it was the educated Sinhala-speaking or bilingual intelligentsia. He not only enhanced their sense of self-esteem but in the political changes of the mid-twentieth century, his life and work also provided a "charter" for modern Buddhism.

In his idealization of this-worldly asceticism, he castigated the laziness of the Sinhala people, emphasizing thrift, saving, and hard work. He exhorted people to reject the propitiation of the Hindu-derived gods (*devas*) of the pantheon and instead urged them to worship the Buddha daily at home and every week in the temple. He exhorted parents to get their children interested in meditational activity (generally accepted in contemporary Buddhism, but an innovation at that time because such activity was confined to old persons). He condemned again and again the consumption of meat and alcohol, but he remained singularly silent about fish.

Another critical aspect of his charter for modern Buddhism involved a code of lay ethics. Buddhist doctrine has no systematic code of lay ethics, though the rules for the conduct of the monk order were minutely formulated, great emphasis being placed on personal decorum and good manners. As far as the layperson was concerned, only broad generalizations were available but this absence of specificity facilitated the historic spread of Buddhism in farming communities with diverse and even contradictory moral codes. However, in 1898, Anagarika Dharmapala laid down a systematic code for the laity published as a pamphlet in Sinhala under the title, *The Daily Code for the Laity.*[39] When the nineteenth edition appeared in 1958, nearly fifty thousand copies were sold. Rules were formulated for public, personal, and familial morality and comportment in a variety of situations—eating and drinking, defecating, behavior in public and private situations, relations within the nuclear family, the manner of conducting Buddhist festivals and decorous behavior in temples, and so forth.

Anagarika Dharmapala devised two hundred rules guiding lay conduct. I cannot go into the details of these rules except to highlight two things: the largest number were geared to the control of women (their enbourgeoisment, as it were) and all the rules were addressed to a literate Sinhala intelligentsia. Many proscribe behavior that villagers are supposedly given to, for example, bad eating, dress, and lavatory habits; indiscriminate betel-nut chewing; and use of impolite forms of address (though Dharmapala himself used these same terms in a letter to one of his servants). This is a code for an emerging Sinhala elite.

But alongside traditional norms of conduct are many Western ones. Even the condemnation of village manners and mores is based on a Western yardstick. That is, Dharmapala attempted to formulate a code based on traditional norms as well as on the norms prevalent in the wealthy society in which he was raised. Here is an aspect of the process that I had noted earlier, namely, the assimilation or incorporation of Protestant values as pure or ideal Sinhala values. The case of Dharmapala is especially interesting because his avowed intention was to reject Western ways. Yet regulations about the correct manner of using the fork and spoon are also given. Elsewhere his admiration for the West breaks through the polemic and comes out into the open. "Europe is progressive. Her religion is kept in the background for one day in the week and for six days her people follow the dictates of modern science. Sanitation, aesthetic arts, electricity, etc., are what made the European and American people great. Asia is full of opium eaters, *ganja* smokers, degenerating sensualists, superstitious and religious fanatics. Gods and priests keep the people in ignorance."[40]

Anagarika Dharmapala was an inveterate anti-imperialist though he had often to deny this in order to avoid arrest and imprisonment. His strong anti-imperialism was viewed with suspicion not only by the British but also by the local politicians who later conducted successful negotiations with the British for independence. These conservative politicians were in power until 1956 when they were thrown out by Prime Minister S. W. R. D. Bandaranaike, who mobilized the very intelligentsia that Dharmapala had already politicized. Dharmapala provided for them a model for emulation—a national consciousness, a nativistic sense of past glory and present degeneration, and very importantly, an ascetic involvement in this-worldly activity, both of an economic and a political nature. The details of this transfer of power to the native intelligentsia are found in Howard Wriggins, *Ceylon: Dilemmas of a New Nation.*[41]

With increasing socioeconomic changes as a result of universal free education and mass literacy, massive population increase, migration into cities, and the development of a large middle class, there was a concomitant loosening, if not breakdown, of local identities based on family, kinship, caste, and region. In my view, this context was ripe for the further acceptance by Sinhala-Buddhists of Dharmapala's heritage. Why? *When one's commitment to one's other identities have weakened, one's commitment to one's larger identity (national or ethnic) will be enhanced, particularly if an ethnic or national ideology is already in place.* The power that is associated with the older identities are easily displaced onto the ethnic or national identity, thereby furthering the process of primordialization.

Identity as a Form of Life

The preceding account suggests that it is futile to reduce an identity into a purely psychological, social, or cultural substrate. Identities have meaning and significance at all these levels and the more complex (the more translocal) the identity, the more difficult to subsume it under any of the above conventional social science rubrics. Identities are human constructions and as such they constitute what one might call, following Wittgenstein, "forms of life." Consider some of the features of the Buddhist identity before the advent of the colonial powers. There was cultural content (kingship and the multiplicity of cultural markers noted earlier); a communal consciousness and a sense of translocal unity (as in the obligatory pilgrimage); and a psychological dimension to that communal consciousness manifest mostly when the identity is under threat (as in the wake of south Indian conquests).

Once we view identity as a complex life-form, then it is not difficult to imagine it being fashioned and refashioned under different time periods, though it is extremely difficult for us to reconstruct this for those periods where there is a paucity of historical and ethnographic materials. The notion of axiomatic identity sketched above does not imply stasis; to create such an identity is a task, or *work*, consciously or even unselfconsciously undertaken by leaders and groups. To put it differently, in using the term "axiomatic identity" I am not essentializing the phenomenon of identity but suggesting that such an essentialization is part of the "work of culture" that, in turn, helps to "forge" a particular form of life.

Let me demonstrate this idea with respect to Anagarika Dharmapala. There is no way that a crucial feature of the traditional identity could be recovered, namely, kingship. Dharmapala was not foolish enough to assume, as some did, that Queen Victoria, or her successor George V, could be the legitimate head of Sinhala Buddhists. He did envisage a free nation, but one governed by Sinhala-Buddhists; other Sinhalas would be tolerated but not non-Sinhalas. He could not explicitly suggest how minorities could be incorporated into such a nation; implicitly, it must surely be through forceful pacification, internal colonization, and enculturation into the larger polity. For Sinhalas, however, he did invent considerable cultural content, as for example, the rules he devised for bourgeois living. But the crux of the issue is, how did he begin to create a new identity that is not only axiomatic but has the emotional feel of primordiality? It was done by glorifying the past, in effect creating an imagined past that would be seen as real by his audience. Dharmapala himself asks the youth of Sri Lanka to *identify* themselves with their great king Dutugamunu. It is no accident that this king became the rallying point for Sinhala politicians and chauvinists in their ethnic conflict with Tamils that escalated much later.

One important mechanism whereby the new identity could be essentialized and primordialized, and at the same time appeal to Sinhalas who were *not* Buddhists, is through the invention of the term "Aryan" to characterize all Sinhalas. The "Aryanization" of Sri Lanka was directly influenced by European scholars who had discovered the common basis for Indo-European languages and then erroneously assumed (and even demonstrated through etymologies) a ur-Aryan culture. This term was picked up by native intellectuals in India to show the superiority of north Indian languages and culture to the "inferior" culture of the Dravidian south, which included the Tamils of Sri Lanka. Aryanism was also a means of hitting at the British, to show that Indians and the imperialists shared the same historical and racial heritage. I further think it permitted the colonized to "identify with the aggressor." As far as the Sinhalas were concerned, their language itself, needless to say, was an Aryan (Indo-European) language as against the Dravidian Tamils. Thus, another oppositional feature was added to the already existing binary distinction of Sinhala:Tamil.

With Aryanism there is a final and complete denial of the hybridity that was given historical recognition in the older texts. Dharmapala himself railed against hybridity: "Aryan Sinhalese have lost [*sic*] his true identity and become a hybrid."[42] From this point onward it was easy to essentialize Aryanism. Aryan then became a part of the identity consciousness of Sinhalas. Virtually every school text to this day asserts that Sri Lanka was founded by Aryans, in spite of recent research that has been critical of the earlier studies and has shown the complexity of the so-called Aryan migrations.

Unhappily, Dharmapala and others did not anticipate that in the 1920s European archaeologists were to "discover" the civilization of the Indus Valley that was indigenous, historically prior, and culturally advanced. With the entry into history and to myth of the people of the Indus Valley, the Dravidians could now claim that *they* were the ur-inhabitants of the subcontinent and that *their* culture was superior to that of the Aryans. In Sri Lanka itself, in its current ethnic conflict, this has produced a new dialectic: ur-inhabitants ought logically to have prior claim to the land and Tamils now can do so. This has forced some Sinhalas to revise their ancestral histories for the first time by abandoning the idea that Vijaya was the founder of their race. To do this, however, they have had to fall back on a pan-Indian myth of the *Rāmāyana*, which describes the island as being ruled by a five-headed king (wrongly defined as a "demon" by the *Rāmāyana*) living in an even more glorious civilization than any before.

The dialectic between Sinhalas and Tamils has now escalated into something analogous to what Bateson has called schismogenesis. That is, as one group affirms its identity through grandiose actions, the other group repeats a similar one though with added emphasis and, as this process continues, the existing divisions between the two groups get more and more sharpened (schismogenized).[43] Thus, Buddhists nowadays are everywhere erecting images of the Buddha in virtually every kind of public space, conquering that space, as it were, on behalf of Buddhism. For their part, the Tamils, in the territories over which they have control, have begun to eliminate existing signs of the earlier Buddhist presence by destroying archaeological sites and forging new place names. And so the devastating dialectic goes on as new histories get constructed in the wake of essentializing identities.

Postscript

When the earlier version of this paper was written, I had focused primarily on ethnic identity instead of national identity. That paper was written in 1975, before the devasting ethnic conflict between the Tamils and the Sinhalas had developed. I now believe that it is futile to make sharp distinctions between ethnic, national, and other kinds of translocal identities. These translocal identities not only share common features, they also share "family resemblances" with other kinds of axiomatic identities. I think the critical problem is one of scale: when identities become more and more translocal it becomes more and more difficult to effect internal unity and a sense of belonging without resort to violence and to various forms of internal colonization.

Dharmapala wanted to construct a nation on the basis of the Sinhala Buddhism as he, and others of his class, had defined it. For such a vision to become viable, one must have a homogeneous community, which simply was not the case in Sri Lanka. Or, one must have separate kingdoms, which was the situation in precolonial Sri Lanka where there were several states (including a Tamil one in the north) claiming universal sovereignity over the island. Or, the Sinhala-Buddhists must try to force the minorities into compliance through forms of internal colonization.

The last alternative was feasible in France in the eighteenth and nineteenth centuries, but there was no practical chance of it succeeding for the Sinhala in the mid-twentieth century. Because the Tamils deny the Sinhala claim for exclusive nationhood, it is inevitable that the Sinhala view of their Buddhist identity as national must inevitably shrink into a smaller ethnic identity in the long-term contestation of power between them (and with the Muslims who have begun to assert their own separate identity). On the other hand, if the Tamils and the Sinhalas decide to divide the country into two separate states, then the ethnic identity of each could revert to a national identity, thereby illustrating the manner in which translocal identities can get displaced.

One can, of course, construct a rational model of a unified nation containing multiple ethnic identities, if a general consensus can be found among warring groups, but the question still arises whether a national identity constructed from rational principles can remain viable. Nevertheless, does one have any other choice but to *forge* ahead and create new bonds and resurrect old ones that could tie that nation together in a larger communal consciousness? Then one wonders whether such bonds can be effectively *forged* or fabricated, in the nonpejorative sense of weaving a new fabric of unity, but without internal colonization or *forging*, in the sense of hammering out through force, a new unity.

NOTES

1. The original version of this paper was entitled "Sinhalese-Buddhist Identity in Ceylon" (in *Ethnic Identity: Cultural Continuities and Change*, 1975, George A. De Vos and Lola Romanucci-Ross, eds., pp. 231-258, Palo Alto: Mayfield Publishing House. Since then Ceylon has officially reverted to what it has always been to native speakers, namely, Sri Lanka. I prefer now to use the term "Sinhala" to designate the country's major ethnic group, rather than the older term "Sinhalese." The present paper has been considerably revised to include my most recent thinking on the subject of ethnic identity. See also my paper, "Buddhism, Nationhood and Cultural Identity: A Question of Fundamentals," in *Fundamentalisms Compared*, Vol. 5, of the *Fundamentalism Project* sponsored by the American Academy of Arts and Sciences, to be published by the University of Chicago Press, 1995.

2. For our purposes, the most important of these texts is the *Pūjavaliya* of Mayurapada Thera. This has not been translated into English.

3. *Māhavaṃsa*, edited and translated by Wilhelm Geiger (London: Pali Text Society, 1980), I:19-20 [chapter:lines], p. 3.

4. Nagadipa is now under the control of Tamil militants.

5. *Māhavaṃsa*, I:61-62, p. 7.

6. *Māhavaṃsa*, I:77-78, p. 8.

7. *Māhavamsa*, VI:47, p. 54.

8. *Māhavaṃsa*, V11:3-4, p. 55.

9. *Māhavaṃsa*, V11:8-9, p. 55.

10. Richard Helgerson, 1992, *Forms of Nationhood: The Elizabethan Writing of England*, Chicago: University of Chicago Press.

11. To my thinking, the Vedda were a powerful presence in precolonial Sri Lanka. The fact that they do not often appear in literary chronicles means that these texts were mostly written by Buddhist monks who were indifferent to the Vedda presence. Village ritual texts, by contrast, deal with their presence.

12. Linda Colley, 1992, *Britons: Forging the Nation 1707-1837*, New Haven and London: Yale University Press. I am not sure Colley would approve of my pun on "forge."

13. This form of kinship implies symmetrical cross-cousin marriage, where ideally (in kinship terminology) one's wife's father and mother are one's own mother's brother and father's sister. These kin terms are maintained even if one marries an outsider; thus, technically, there are no in-laws in the scheme.

14. See my *Cult of the Goddess Pattini*, 1984, Chapter 8, Chicago: University of Chicago Press on "Colonization Myths" and pp. 306-321, which discuss mechanisms for incorporating outsiders into Sinhala Buddhist culture.

15. *Māhavaṃsa*, XX11:85-86, p. 154.

16. *Mahāvaṃsa*, XXV:2-3, p. 170.

17. *Mahāvaṃsa*, XXV:108-111, p. 178.

18. *Mahāvaṃsa*, XXX11:81-83, p. 227.

19. Walpola Rahula, *The History of Buddhism in Ceylon*, 1956, p. 58, Colombo: Gunasena and Co.

20. Benedict Anderson, 1983, *Imagined Communities: Reflections on the Origin and Spread of Nationalism*, London: Verso.

21. Eugen Weber, 1976, *Peasants into Frenchmen: The Modernization of Rural France, 1870-1914*, Stanford: Stanford University Press. For his discussion of the formal origins of French nationalism, see Chapter 7, "France, One and Indivisible" (pp. 95-114), and everywhere in the book for the reality. For the important notion of "internal colonization," see pp. 490-496.

22. See Note 12.

23. Edward Shils, 1957, "Primordial, Personal, Sacred and Civil Ties," *British Journal of Sociology*, Vol. 8, pp. 130-145; Clifford Geertz, 1973, "The Integrative Revolution: Primordial Sentiments and Civil Polities in the New States" (in *The Interpretation of Cultures*, pp. 255-310, New York: Basic Books). Here is Geertz on primordial loyalties: "Congruities of blood, speech and custom, and so on, are seen to have an ineffable, and at times overpowering, coerciveness in and of themselves." Or: "[primordial loyalties exist] by virtue

of some unaccountable absolute import attributed to the very tie itself" (p. 259). I think many people can articulate the nature of these ties and specify why they are overpowering; anthropologists have just not bothered to ask.

24. Anderson, *Imagined Communities*, p. 129.

25. *Rājāvaliya*, 1900, translated by G. Gunasekera, p. 52, Colombo: Government Press.

26. Mayurapada Thera, 1986, *Pūjāvaliya*, edited by Pandit Kirialle Gnanavimala, p. 746, Colombo: Gunasena and Sons, my translation. I have translated the technical term "*dhammadhātu*" into what I think was the popular nontechnical meaning as the "essence of the doctrine" rather than as "mental objects as irreducible elements."

27. Mayurapada Thera, *Pūjāvaliya*, pp. 746-747.

28. Quoted in P. Dolapihilla, 1959, *In the Days of Sri Wickramasinha, Last King of Kandy*, p. 275, Maharagama, Sri Lanka: Saman Press, 1959; my translation.

29. Gananath Obeyesekere, 1991, "Buddhism and Conscience: An Exploratory Essay," *Daedalus*, Summer, special issue on Religion and Politics, pp. 219-239, and 1995, "The Two Faces of Colonel Olcott: Buddhism and Eurorationality in the Nineteenth Century," *European Influences on Sri Lanka in the 19th Century*, Colombo: German Cultural Institute.

30. See Richard Gombrich and Gananath Obeyesekere, 1988, *Buddhism Transformed: Religious Change in Sri Lanka*, pp. 201-240, Princeton: Princeton University Press; and 1976, "Personal Identity and Cultural Crisis: The Case of Anagarika Dharmapala of Sri Lanka" (in *The Biographical Process: Studies in the History and Psychology of Religion*, Frank E. Reynolds and Donald Capps, eds., pp. 221-252, The Hague: Mouton).

31. Anagarika Dharmapala, 1965, *Return to Righteousness. A Collection of Speeches, Essays and Letters of the Anagarika Dharmapala*, edited by Ananda Guruge, p. 698, Colombo: Government Press, 1965; my emphasis.

32. Anagarika Dharmapala, *Return to Righteousness*, p. 683; my emphasis.

33. Anagarika Dharmapala, *Return to Righteousness*, p. 682.

34. Anagarika Dharmapala, *Return to Righteousness*, p. 484.

35. Anagarika Dharmapala, *Return to Righteousness*, p. 494.

36. Anagarika Dharmapala, *Return to Righteousness*, p. 660.

37. Anagarika Dharmapala, *Return to Righteousness*, p. 510.

38. Anagarika Dharmapala, *Return to Righteousness*, p. 735.

39. This fascinating document has been reprinted in *Dharmapāla Lipi* (Dharmapala Papers), 1965, edited by Ananda Guruge, pp. 31-46, Colombo: Government Press.

40. Anagarika Dharmapala, *Return to Righteousness*, p. 717

41. 1960, Princeton: Princeton University Press.

42. Ananda Guruge, "Introduction" to Anagarika Dharmapala, *Return to Righteousness*, p. 51.

43. Gregory Bateson, 1965, 2d ed., *Naven*, pp. 175-197, Stanford: Stanford University Press.

PART V ■

Minority Inclusion/Exclusion and National Identity

CZESLAW MILOSZ ■

Chapter Eleven

Vilnius, Lithuania: An Ethnic Agglomerate

This chapter represents the experience of a man who comes from a very unusual spot in Europe: the city of Lithuania known as Wilno or Vilnius, which in its mixture of languages, religions, and traditions is rivaled only, and not quite successfully, by Transylvania, Bukovina, or Trieste. My observations were made before World War II, but, as will be seen, the present appears again and again.

Today, if I call this city which is the capital of the Lithuanian Soviet Republic "Vilnius," I give a hint as to my Lithuanian identity. If I call it "Wilno," I present myself to the Lithuanians as probably a Pole or a Russian. Behind the double names lie the complex historical events of several centuries.

Before 1939 this city belonged to Poland, and the languages spoken by its inhabitants were first, Polish, and second, Yiddish. In the schools, instruction was in Polish, Yiddish, Hebrew, Lithuanian, Byelorussian, and Russian. The question of who was sent to each of these schools has much to do with the problem of ethnicxx divisions, yet to assume that every ethnic group favored schools in which instruction was given in its own language would be far from the truth. Religious divisions cut across language divisions. Roman Catholicism, Judaism, Greek Catholicism, Orthodoxy, and Islam coexisted, and to these should be added the ethnoreligious group of Karaites, a Judaic sect.

Lithuanians and Poles

The meaning of the statement "I am a Lithuanian" was undergoing a change at the end of the nineteenth and the beginning of the twentieth centuries. Previously it was used by the members of the upper class, the nobility or the petty gentry, whose ancestors had spoken Lithuanian or old Byelorussian, but who no longer used those languages at home. The "Polonization" of the upper classes, a result of the personal union between the Kingdom of Poland and the Grand Duchy of Lithuania in 1385, and of their gradual fusion, was nearly complete by the seventeenth century. Thus, "I am a Lithuanian" was not opposed to "I am a Pole," but meant "I am from here" as opposed to "He is from there," namely, the Kingdom of Poland. The equivalent of such a feeling could perhaps be found in the British Commonwealth where there was opposition of Scottish and Irish to English, but not to British.

In Latin, which was in that area the language of liturgy, of many legal documents, and to a large extent, of literature, a "Lithuanian" was defined as a man who is *gente Lithuanus natione Polonus*, while the name of the state, embracing the Kingdom and the Duchy, was neither Poland nor Lithuania, but Respublica. As to the Lithuanian language, its fate was similar to that of Gaelic. A non-Slavic language, and therefore already handicapped at the moment when, during the Middle Ages, the Grand Duchy of Lithuania absorbed large areas inhabited by Eastern Slavs, it was not used in writing.

Paradoxically, before its union with Poland, the Grand Duchy adopted an Eastern Slavic dialect (which was to become Byelorussian in the north and Ukrainian in the south) for administrative purposes. Lithuanian, increasingly the language of the peasantry only, remained a low-status idiom. By the sixteenth century, it was used in writing only by those who wanted to descend to the people, in order to convert them to their religious domination. To that end, Protestants and Roman Catholics produced prayer-books and catechisms. A Polish-Latin-Lithuanian dictionary, published in 1629, was proof of a Jesuit's zeal. Literature in Lithuanian appeared late and was connected with a revival of national feeling, which challenged the "Lithuanianishness" of the upper classes and made the language spoken at home a distinctive mark.

The Lithuanian national movement, created by the new intelligentsia of peasant origin in the second half of the nineteenth century, regarded the formula *gente Lithuanus natione Polonus* as an unbearable reminder of defeat: the historical Lithuania had lost its upper classes through Polonization. The necessity of choosing between being a Lithuanian and being a Pole seems to be a result of the idea that nationality is defined by language. And indeed, in the twentieth century many families had to decide upon their nationality, with the not unusual consequence that one brother called himself Lithuanian, another a Pole, and the third Byelorussian. One has to go back in time in order to explain the strange myth about Lithuania that persists today in Polish cultural patterns.

Lithuania, the last country in Europe to become Christian, was converted in 1386. As a land of primeval forests, of abundant wildlife, and of pagan dieties, it fascinated Polish writers as early as the sixteenth century. This literature contributed to certain stereotypes. The Jesuit Academy of Wilno, founded in 1578, two centuries later became the best Polish university and a hotbed of romanticism. One of its pupils, Adam Mickiewicz (1798-1855) became the most important Polish poet of all time. The most cherished of Mickiewicz's work, a long tale in verse, *Pan Tadeusz*, opens with an invocation not to the Muse but to Lithuania: "Lithuania, my native land." Throughout all Mickiewicz's works, nature is Lithuanian. As a sort of emotional puzzle, consider the peasant child in Poland today who has to cope with a poet who called himself Lithuanian. Let us also add that the first history of Lithuania was written and published (nine volumes, 1835-1841) in Polish by another disciple of the University of Wilno, Teodor Narbutt.

A curious game of superiority-inferiority has been played by natives of Lithuania, speaking Polish with their half-compatriots from Poland. "Lithuanians" looked upon themselves as serious, obstinate, persistent, deep, conceding magnanimously some truth in their being in the eyes of the Poles bearish, uncouth, and miserly. It was assumed that great men of Polish letters could only come from Lithuania, and Mickiewicz's myth was a basic asset in such a contention. But there seems to have been something to the myth, since many eminent personalities come from ethnically Lithuanian families, as did, for instance, a precursor of modern Polish poetry, Cyprian Norwid (1821-1883), whose name in the Lithuanian form was once Narvidas. The question arises as to why a feeling of a separate identity did not express itself in Lithuania as it did in Ireland, where William Butler Yeats and others did not have to use Gaelic in order to be considered Irish patriots. One could go also to Finland, where the intelligentsia once had adopted Swedish, but where the use of Swedish did not exclude one from belonging to the Finnish nation.

That things evolved differently in Lithuania can be ascribed to many causes, but in all probability there is one primary cause underlying all the others. The Polish language was connected with a cultural pattern completely different from the pattern of the Lithuanian peasantry. It would be incorrect to maintain that only the nobility spoke Polish in Lithuania. It was also spoken by the petty gentry who tilled the land themselves and lived practically like peasants. The merchants and tradesmen, if they weren't Jewish, also used Polish at home, as did the non-Jewish artisans and workers in Wilno and in small towns, either because they were descended from the petty gentry or because they were former servants in the manors. All of those people were permeated, however, by the "culture of nobility" and considered their use of Polish a mark of the status that distinguished them from the Lithuanian-speaking boors.

Thus, we observe a class hostility combined with a linguistic conflict. But to make the matter more difficult for investigators, the have-nots could be found on both sides, for rich Lithuanian peasants were often better off than the artisans or the laborers of a neighboring small town. Yet the very idea of an independent Lithuania was greeted by Polonized segments of its population with scorn and hostility how could the boors pretend to become a nation and impose upon the rest of the people their boorish language? The new Lithuanian intelligentsia that appeared in the second half of the nineteenth century was, with very few exceptions, of purely peasant origin, and since, for a peasant family the only possible social advancement was to make one of their sons a Roman Catholic priest, clergymen were largely responsible for the emergence of the national movement.

In the twentieth century educated members of the higher classes, who for a long time had proclaimed their loyalty to Lithuania for sentimental reasons, realized that they had to choose between Polish and Lithuanian loyalties, that one could no longer be at the same time a Lithuanian and a Pole. In 1918, when an independent Lithuania was being created, some of them opted for the country of their ancestors and started to learn the difficult, non-Slavic language. A very few looked for an intermediate solution, an equivalent of the relationship between English and Gaelic in Ireland. The majority, however, even if they became citizens of the new state, looked upon themselves as Poles. After World War I the region around Wilno leaned towards Independent Poland, and for a short time was a separate political entity, loosely bound to Poland, leaving in history a not very important but interesting trace in the form of postage stamps, a rarity today. That entity, "Middle Lithuania," was absorbed by Poland in 1922, and remained within the Polish borders until 1939.

Relations between Polish-speaking Lithuanians and Poles displayed infinite ambiguities. On the one hand, "Lithuanians" indulged in a certain self-idealization, and on the other, owing to a myth transferred through literature, they were idealized by those outside it. Self-irony became an increasingly prominent ingredient of that peculiar "Lithuanian" ethnic identity. The difference was disguised as innocent snobbery. Yet it cannot be said that "Lithuanian" ethnic identity belongs completely to the past. "Lithuanians," whether they lived in the region of Wilno or emigrated to ethnic Poland (which occurred en masse after World War II), have been bringing to Polish arts and letters a particular perspective. One may guess that a man who grows up surrounded by people who speak various languages and who belong to various cultures acquires a different personality than does a man brought up in a homogeneous ethnic milieu. Let us add also that "Lithuanians" were much more open to Russian thought and Russian literature than were Poles. This did not make them partisans of Russia, yet did endow them with some kind of openness to the seriousness of the "Russian phenomenon."

It would be interesting to examine modifications of the "Lithuanian" myth in Polish literature of the last few decades, including the avant-garde literature of the grotesque, the macabre, and the theatre of the absurd. In literature in which the aristocratic origin of a character is equated with degeneration and idiocy, a certain mocking respect is shown toward characters from Lithuania. After World War II, Poland became a melting pot of people with different languages and regional backgrounds, as a consequence of the shift of its borders from the east to the west. In this new melting pot, "Lithuanians" and Poles have been mixing. Even today, however, among some groups it is considered more dignified to marry within one's own group of emigrants from the East. A relatively small number of the "Lithuanians" who spoke Polish remained in Lithuania. Centered for the most part around Wilno, they represented the artisans and workers who had been inhabitants of that city for many generations.

Lithuanians

Among the peoples of Baltic stock only the Lithuanians succeeded in creating a state which, in the thirteenth and fourteenth centuries, expanded south and east, mostly thanks to the weakening of the eastern Slavic principalities in the wake of Tartar invasions. The Lithuanian dukes had a strong army, since ethnic Lithuania seemed to be more densely populated than the regions of neighboring Slavs. Moreover, the Baltic Lithuanian ethnic area reached farther east and south than it does today. As a result of the conquest, the Grand Duchy of Lithuania, extending at one point as far south as the Black Sea, counted among its subjects people speaking an eastern Slavic idiom (Ruthenian) and confessing the Orthodox faith, while the ruling

Lithuanian ethnic group remained pagan. Penetration of the Duke's court by Eastern Orthodoxy, owing to marriages with Christian princesses, and the victory of the eastern Slavic vernacular as the administrative language throughout the state, prefigured, so to speak, what happened after the union with Poland in 1386.

At that point ethnic Lithuania began to convert to Roman Catholicism, the Polish language slowly (though not before the sixteenth century) supplanted the eastern Slavic idiom, and the Latin alphabet replaced the Cyrillic. Lithuanian survived as the language of folksongs of great beauty and Ulty. In some of these songs, called *dainos*, heroes are pagan planetary deities. Protestant and Catholic catechisms and hymns were the only documents of written Lithuanian until the second half of the eighteenth century, when an ethnically Lithuanian Protestant minister in a corner of East Prussia, Kristijonas Donelajtis (1714-1764), wrote his long poem Four Seasons, depicting the miseries and joys of peasant life. The national revival in the nineteenth century was indebted to partisans of Lithuania who wrote scholarly books in Polish, and to German collectors of Lithuanian folksongs, who were entranced to find in Europe a language still closely related to Sanskrit. But let us imagine the situation of a Lithuanian intellectual (usually a clergyman) in search of his ethnic identity: the glory of the country belonged to the past, for not only was his country a part of the Russian czarist empire, but Lithuania bore a strong Polish imprint; moreover, to be a Lithuanian carried the stigma of a boorish status.

It would not be an exaggeration to say that for such a man the language itself was both his fatherland and his passport. A desperate search went on for the names of illustrious men, which in their Polish spelling preserved Lithuanian vocables. There was also jealous competition with the Poles for the claim to some eminent writers. Thus, since Adam Mickiewicz invoked Lithuania as his muse, he was added to the Lithuanian pantheon. Typical of the Lithuanian language are family name endings in "as" or "ius." Thus Mickiewicz had to become Mickevicius. An eminent French poet, O. V. de L. Milosz, a relative of the author of this paper and a Lithuanian by option–in contrast to the other "Lithuanian" members of his family–had his tomb in Fontainebleau engraved with "Milasius." The extremely ambiguous state of ethnic identity among the Polish-Lithuanians often became hostility when confronted with the nationalism of the "boors." This is more understandable if we keep in mind that the word "Lithuania" designated both the Grand Duchy as a whole and the ethnic area alone.

Many Polonized families, natives of the Grand Duchy, had nothing to do with the Lithuanian stock, since their ancestors were eastern Slavs who spoke old Byelorussian. Animosity was also exacerbated, especially during World War I and immediately after, by the Wilno question. Once the capital of Lithuania, Wilno contained by the twentieth century only a small group of people who spoke Lithuanian, a fact which seemed to validate Poland's claim to it. The religious factor introduced an additional complication. Both those who spoke Lith-uanian at home and those who spoke Polish were Roman Catholics, and the traditional attachment to the idea of the Commonwealth (*Respublica*) was strengthened in the minds of the Polonized by their sensitivity to the danger menacing their religious faith first from Russian Orthodoxy and then from communism. The tiny Baltic states created in 1918 were too weak to provide protection. The question of Wilno, which was appropriated by Poland (with the support of its inhabitants) exacerbated the feud between the two groups in the period between the two world wars.

The experience of Poles and Lithuanians as American immigrants forms a marked contrast to their life in Europe. In Lithuania everything Polish enjoyed prestige, but in America Poles enjoyed little social status, ranking well below such groups as the Scandinavians or even the Irish. As a consequence of the predominantly upper-class culture in the Polish-Lithuanian *Respublica*, illiterate Poles emigrating to America were particularly helpless in that industrialized nation, since they could rely neither on the status of the "Polish culture" nor on the relatively weak tradition of their own village. In all probability the Lithuanian ethnic group in America fared a little better. One may guess that the "boor," a Lithuanian peasant, left to himself and rooted in his folkloric tradition, proved to be less vulnerable and somehow in a position closer to that of a Scandinavian, German, or an Irish plebeian. Moreover, independent Lithuania between 1918 and 1939 produced a whole new educated class, an intelligentsia with peasant backgrounds. Thus every peasant family there wanted to give their children a high school and university education. This ambition affected the Lithuanian immigrants after 1945. Examples abound of rare tenacity and self-sacrifice on the part of Lithuanian parents when they found themselves in America. A typical example is the case of some friends of mine, both with university degrees, who became manual laborers in order to provide higher education for their children.

A kind of cold war between Lithuania, which claimed Wilno as its capital, and Poland, which held it, did not make life easy for the small Lithuanian ethnic group in the years between the two wars. One high school conducted in Lithuanian, some newspapers, and a fraternity of Lithuanian students at the university who steered clear of their Polish-speaking colleagues, serve to illustrate the situation of a city where Roman Catholic churches had no Lithuanian sermons and songs—except one, St. Nicholas, where the majority of the faithful was composed of servant women, transplanted from their native villages.

Jews

The great number of Jews in the Grand Duchy of Lithuania was for centuries completely separated from the rest of the population by their religion, language (Yiddish), profession (nonagricultural) and even dress. The frozen division between

Jews and Christians was a phenomenon typical of several areas and therefore need not be discussed here. What should be mentioned, however, is the place of a non-rural group in a purely rural civilization. They monopolized many branches of handicraft and trade, acting as suppliers of goods to the manor and village, as innkeepers, and as buyers of agricultural products. Their religious communities were closely supervised by their elders, so that the contamination of Jews by the Christian milieu and vice versa was minimal. The one exception came toward the end of the sixteenth century, when a radical Protestant movement with an antitrinitarian orientation (Arianism, Polish Brethren, the Minor Church) invoked the authority of the Old Testament against that of the New Testament. This led to friendly theological disputes between the sectarians and Jewish rabbis. In the eighteenth century a messianic sect founded by Jacob Frank found many followers among the Jews of the Grand Duchy. Frank, a Jew whose teachings bore a strong Manichean imprint, embraced Catholicism after he had been anathemized by the synagogue, an act which he conceived as a necessary preparation for the advent of a new world. This movement left some marks, since many upper-class families in Lithuania trace their ancestry to "Frankists," the Jewish followers of Frank, who had been baptized. In a way, Frank was a precursor of the Jewish rush beyond the confines of the ghetto.

The Enlightenment touched the ghetto at the very end of the eighteenth century and the beginning of the nineteenth century, but here the political predicament of the area made the whole problem of Jewish assimilation a complex one. The entire area, as a consequence of the partitions of the Respublica, came under the domination of Russia. Of course, the choice of a language which would supplant Yiddish imposed itself upon the Jews. Polish had preserved throughout some three decades of the nineteenth century a half-official standing, and the *Haskalah* (Enlightenment) movement among the Wilno Jews turned at first to Polish as the instrument of written expression. The career of an interesting writer, Julian Klaczko (1825-1906) illustrates this. A native of Wilno, he started to write in Hebrew, then switched to Polish, only to change his language once again when he emigrated to Paris, where he remained a Polish patriot, though renowned as a contributor in French to the best Parisian reviews. Not many such instances, however, could be quoted in Lithuania.

After the end of a liberal policy in St. Petersburg and when the official language was increasingly imposed upon reluctant subjects of the newly acquired territories, those Jews who were emancipating themselves from the traditional ghetto felt the attraction of a huge area with its unified culture. Things went a different way in other parts of the Polish-Lithuanian *Respublica* after its partition by foreign powers. In central Poland a considerable number of Jews entered the ranks of the intelligentsia, thus becoming Poles of Jewish origin. In the Hapsburg Empire, German and Polish competed for the allegiance of the Jews. The seductive power of Vienna was strong and the story of Sigmund Freud's family is rather typical. Yet many Polish scholars and writers in Galicia had a Jewish background, especially at the time when the Polish intelligentsia was changing its character and absorbing groups which until now had been barred from access to higher education (peasants, Jews, and women); that process gathered momentum at the very end of the nineteenth century. The Russian orientation of the Lithuanian Jews produced a large group of the so-called Litvaks, namely those Jews who, instead of Yiddish or Polish, spoke Russian at home.

Antagonism existed between Litvaks and the Jews from central Poland, not to mention the Jews from Galicia, for whom Russian was a completely alien tongue. Since the policy of St. Petersburg in Lithuania consisted of a forceful Russification, especially after the uprising of 1863, the non-Jews regarded Jews as allies of the czarist government by the very fact of their switching to the Russian language and spreading the gospel of great Russian literature. A continuation of that state of affairs was also noticeable in the revolutionary movement, beginning with the 1890s. The movement split into two socialist parties, the Polish Socialist Party and the Social-Democratic Party of the Kingdom of Poland and of Lithuania, with the two parties unequally dividing sympathies of emancipated Jews. Most favored the second party, since it rejected the national aspirations of ethnic groups that had been absorbed by the Russian Empire and relied upon the All-Russian Revolution which would solve all the problems automatically. The socialist Jewish organization, *Bund*, represented a specific program close to that of the Polish Socialist Party, yet its members were not Litvaks, but Jews clinging to Yiddish.

In the period between the two wars, when Wilno belonged to Poland, the Jewish community was internally divided in a fantastic way. Russian schools in Wilno could count on Jewish pupils only because the number of Russian Christians was exceedingly small. However, Wilno was a strong center of studies in Yiddish and Hebrew. The Jewish Institute of Wilno was to be transferred during World War II to New York. Books and newspapers in Yiddish testified to the vigor of the language, but many young people were also trained in Hebrew and were subsequently instrumental in making Hebrew the official language of Israel. Polish schools did not attract many Jewish pupils, and in this respect the situation was different from that in Central Poland, where Poles whose fathers or grandfathers had used Yiddish were numerous. As to the Lithuanian and the Byelorussian languages, they attracted almost no Jews in the region of Wilno.

Politically, varieties of Zionism competed with socialism and communism; the latter was rather popular, since in this area it was a direct descendant of the Social Democratic Party of the Kingdom of Poland and Lithuania. The result was anti-Semitic slogans, since the Poles and the Lithuanians only rarely were sympathizers of Russia, in its czarist or Communist incarnation.

In the region of Wilno, anti-Semitism was not as strong as in central Poland where there existed a class of non-Jewish small shopkeepers. The right-wing anti-Semitic Polish National Democratic Party (*Narodowa Demokracja*) scored successes primarily at the university, where Jews and non-Jews had separate student unions. The composition of the student body did not, however, correspond to the ethnic composition of the city, since it admitted students from all over Poland, thus representing rather a cross-section of the whole country.

What was characteristic of Wilno was the prevalence of the type of Jew who was quite sure of his ethnic identity, whether he was Litvak or a speaker of Yiddish. If there were some Poles of Jewish extraction, they were mostly imports from Poland proper. In general, survivals of the traditional set-up were so strong until 1939 and the economic backwardness of the area so marked that it is difficult to guess what the probable course of Jewish assimilation would have been, had not the crime of genocide committed by the Nazis put an abrupt end to the centuries-old life of Jewish Wilno.

Byelorussians

To my knowledge there is practically no literature on this subject free from Polish or Lithuanian bias. It is also doubtful whether those few Byelorussians who wrote about their compatriots in the region of Wilno are any more reliable. The Byelorussian nationality was probably the last to appear in Europe.

As to the identity of those who once used old Byelorussian in writing, the idea of calling themselves Byelorussians would not have occurred to them. If they belonged to the privileged class, they considered themselves for centuries nobles of Lithuania. Like their brethren of ethnic Lithuanian stock, they abandoned their tongue for Polish. For peasants the concept of nationality was alien up until the 1930s. Upon being asked during a census about nationality they answered either Catholic or Orthodox, or simply: "I am from here."

That does not mean that the notion of an ethnic identity (of being "from here") was absent. Religious denomination served here as the dividing line. The Orthodox religion distinguished one village from a neighboring village inhabited by Roman Catholics. It also distinguished between the inhabitants of the village and those people in the neighborhood who represented a higher social status, i.e., those who spoke Polish, whether they belonged to the petty gentry, owned a manor, were foresters, or were craftsmen. Those people also confessed to Roman Catholicism. It should be mentioned here that peasants of Eastern Orthodox faith were former Greco-Catholics: the Greco-Catholic or Uniate Church, created as a consequence of the Union of Brest (1596) which had been engineered by the Polish Jesuits, was administratively destroyed by the czarist government in 1838; in other words, these peasants again became members of the Eastern Orthodox Church.

The Byelorussian peasant remained throughout all the turbulent history of the area the passive object of powers incomprehensible to him. He was gaining silent victories wherever his village neighbored on a Lithuanian village. For complex and little-elucidated reasons, the non-Slavic Baltic element had a tendency to recede territorially. Through intermarriage and gradual adaptation to Byelorussian, a Lithuanian village would melt into a Slavic and Orthodox mass. In such a fashion the area south and east of Wilno, once Lithuanian, became Byelorussian. Byelorussian villages, however, in the close neighborhood of Wilno, no longer in the twentieth century spoke Byelorussian, but rather a peculiar slang of "people from here," namely, Polish strongly influenced by Byelorussian and to some extent by Lithuanian. That idiom was somehow reminiscent of sixteenth-century documents, many of which preserved a curious mixture of Polish and old Byelorussian, as well as a mixture of two alphabets, Latin and Cyrillic. The ethnic identity on the level of high school or university education was, during the period between the two wars, more or less closely related to communism.

A young Byelorussian who harbored strong class resentment looked with hostility at the manor and at the Polish administration and looked for his sense of history to the capital of the Soviet Byelorussian Republic, Minsk, with its Byelorussian University, its press and books published in his native tongue. Stories of purges and persecutions related by escapees from the Soviet Republic contributed to the effort to create some sort of independent national movement. But the intolerance of the Polish authorities, for whom the Byelorussian nationality was a bizarre invention, strengthened the appeal of communism.

For other groups it was very difficult to understand what Byelorussianism was about. Traditionally, the language was considered a folk dialect closer to Polish than, let us say, Provençal is to French. To boost the national morale the young Byelorussian intelligentsia invoked the official language of the Grand Duchy of Lithuania, claiming it to be their own, although it differed considerably. These young enthusiasts also laid claim to literary monuments as the first printed translation of the Bible into the vernacular in the Polish-Lithuanian *Respublica*, since that vernacular was not Polish but old Byelorussian (Franciszek Skoryna's *Bible*, printed 1517- 1525). Also the speeches of lords from Lithuania in the Polish Diet were frequently given in old Byelorussian.

The past, however, was irretrievable, since the dialect had earlier been used by the nobility and some burghers in cities, classes which later switched to Polish. Thus, Byelorussian remained a language suddenly halted in its literary development and revived by nationalists only at the beginning of the twentieth century. Its rich folklore and particularly beautiful folk music have not been matched by literary works of genuine value, except by a small number of poems. Perhaps this judgment is unfair, since we should take into account the unenviable conditions of national life that still persist.

Yet this perspective reflects the attitude toward the Byelorussians of all the other groups in the region of Wilno and explains why young Byelorussians identified education with training in nationalist-leftist militancy. As I said before, there were instances when in the same family one man heeded "the call of blood" to become a Byelorussian, his brother the same call to become a Lithuanian, the third to become a Pole. Yet even though we may debate the rank in the social hierarchy of any particular group, it was generally recognized that the lowest place on this scale was for the Byelorussians. This was certainly nothing new—Byelorussian folksongs are heart-rending in their melancholy tone and their images of centuries of oppression.

Tartars

Since no native inhabitants of Lithuania would have embraced the Moslem religion, the mosques in Wilno and in some neighboring villages testify to the presence of immigrants who arrived many years ago, mostly in the fourteenth and fifteenth centuries. Lithuanian dukes had gladly used them as soldiers and recompensed them for their services with land. Because of their religion the Tartar villages preserved their separation from the surroundings. Their status was superior to that of peasant villages, because being settlers from outside, the Tartars were never just serfs of landlords. As to their native tongue, they abandoned it during the seventeenth century, preserving for quite a long time, however, the Arabic alphabet. Some extant religious books are written in a mixture of Polish and old Byelorussian, but in Arabic letters. Being quite energetic, many Tartars acquired estates and titles of nobility. In such a way the upper class in Lithuania numbered not only people of Lithuanian, eastern Slavic, immigrant-Polish, and immigrant German stock, but also Frankists and Tartars. The social peers of the Frankists and Tartars accepted them, but on different bases. The acceptance of the first was due to their being Christians, while for some strange reasons a noble of Tartar origin was accepted even if he remained a Moslem. Tartar villages, on the other hand, could be cited as a case of religious barriers that led to economic barriers. If certain professions were a distinctive mark for the Jews, something similar applies to the Tartar villages, which in certain districts monopolized the production of leather goods, such as sheepskin coats or gloves.

The ethnic identity of Moslems was well preserved, taking the form of pride in their warrior ancestry. In the 1930s two periodicals (the *Tartar Yearbook* and *Tartar Life*) appeared in Wilno, both published in Polish. They are interesting by virtue of their catering to the ideal of the "Lithuanian Tartar" (of Polish language) well rooted in his adopted country. Those publications usually traced the history of the deeds of valor performed by the Tartars in the service of the Polish-Lithuanian commonwealth. The upper-class orientation on the part of the Moslems explains their being little attracted by the Lithuanian element and the Byelorussian element, though some Tartar villages spoke Byelorussian rather than Polish. In general, however, Moslems had a tendency to melt into the Polish-speaking intelligentsia of gentry origin.

Karaites (Karaim)

A tiny ethnic and religious group which in this century numbers barely a few thousand all over the world, the local Karaites were, like the Moslems, a relic of the Grand Duchy's expansion far to the south, to the shores of the Black Sea. At one time the Kievan Rus' dealt with the Khazars, an industrious tribe that had converted to Judaism. Karaites, a Judaic sect not recognizing the Talmud and the tradition, was a part of the Khazar scene. The history of the sect in the subsequent centuries is obscure, no less obscure than the circumstances in which some Karaites settled in Wilno and the surrounding neighborhood during the reign of the Grand Duke Vytautas at the end of the fourteenth century. Karaites created an exotic island, being neither Christians nor Jews. They were distinguished by their physical type and their language, which was incomprehensible to others. They were by tradition cucumber growers. They are mentioned here because their influence in Wilno was quite out of proportion to their small number. The most closed religious-ethnic group, they possessed a temple (*Kenessa*), a head of their religious hierarchy who was their spokesman, and published one periodical in Polish (*Karaite Thought*) and one in the Karaite language.

Conclusion

Wilno, as a city marked by the social transformations of the twentieth century, reflected to a large extent the ethnic differentiation in the countryside. A rural district possessed manors where Polish was spoken; a few gentry villages inhabited by Polish-speaking farmers with titles of nobility though they labored in their fields like ordinary peasants; their little towns, Yiddish in their commercial center, Polish in their workers' and craftsmen's outskirts; and villages, either Lithuanian or Byelorussian. Since Wilno lacked villagers, Polish and Yiddish prevailed. The intelligentsia, white-collar workers, and merchants were either of noble origin or of Jewish origin. The local burgher class, although its traditions went back a couple of centuries, had become extremely weak. The core of the Wilno population lived either in the narrow, picturesque streets of the ghetto or were artisans and workers who lived in the village-like outskirts of the city. For the majority of the population in that area the modern idea of national identity that followed the lines of language and ethnic stock came as a surprise. Yet choices had to be made and for the most part they were made, thus creating a web of mutual resentments and mutual hostilities.

If one takes a detached view, the tragic fate of that corner of Europe acquires comic and macabre dimensions. Poland and Lithuania could not resolve peacefully the question of Wilno, which remained a bone of contention throughout the two decades between the two wars. The Soviet Union, in fulfilling the Molotov-Ribbentropp agreement, occupied Wilno in September 1939, only magnanimously to offer it two weeks later to Lithuania. However, already at that time the fate of all three Baltic states was sealed. They were incorporated into the Soviet Union in 1940. The Nazi offensive in the summer of 1941 reached Lithuania in a couple of days and opened three long years of terror and genocide. The whole Jewish population of Wilno was first closed within the walls of the ghetto and then massacred. After the terror and mass deportations applied by the Soviet Union between 1939 and 1941, Lithuanians and Byelorussians, much like the Ukrainians in the south, for a while attached some hope to the arrival of the Germans. They were soon disillusioned, and the Nazi policy in that part of Europe was exemplary in its folly, though consistent in one respect—scorn for the subhumans, i.e., any ethnic group other than German. It is difficult to know if the Germans were responsible for the hostilities that emerged between the ethnic groups, particularly between the Poles (or rather, "Lithuanians") and Lithuanians, before the Red Army entered Wilno again in 1944. Perhaps the massacre of Polish and Lithuanian guerrilla units by each other in the name of patriotism were the result of old hatreds. The Poles maintained that Wilno should belong to Poland, the Lithuanians that Vilnius has always been and would be a part of Lithuania. Perhaps those sardines fighting each other in the mouth of a whale are not untypical of the relations between humans when they search for self-assertion through ethnic values magnified into absolutes.

Postscript

In 1992 I returned to Wilno after fifty-two years. It is now officially Vilnius and is the capital of independent Lithuania. The three tiny Baltic states—Lithuania, Latvia, and Estonia—succeeded in separating themselves from the Soviet Union into which they had been incorporated by force in 1940. Yet they bear the scars of a long totalitarian rule.

People who have not had the opportunity of comparing a given place in two different phases of its history may be surprised by a term I use to describe the situation in Vilnius: degradation of reality, or decay of reality. Many buildings bear the scars of the war and the Jewish quarter, with its medieval narrow streets, was practically razed. Yet it is the progressive decay of houses in the beautiful old town, not renovated for decades, that is responsible for the grayness typical of the Communist system, and the smell of poverty to which Orwell was so sensitive in his *1984*. Yet the Baltic counties fared much better under that system than did Russia, and for the Russians they were the epitome of the West. Vilnius has grown, and the Lithuanian architects have succeeded in limiting the impact of the barrack-style Soviet prescriptions when designing new buildings.

Perhaps the tensions between national groups, the subject of my article, fill the air with an undefinable malaise, or there are just too many taboos in talking about the past to move in that city with ease. There are no Jews, and the shadows of the assassinated have not been exorcised by bringing to light the role of Lithuanian death squads. The goal of Lithuanian nationalism, recovering the city as a historical capital of Lithuania, has been achieved but as a result of the pact between Hitler and Stalin that partitioned prewar Poland and deprived Lithuania of its independence for fifty years.

The Polish-speaking population of the city, threatened by mass deportations to Siberia, left in a mass exodus for Poland in 1945. Vilnius, however, is far from being homogeneously Lithuanian. The Polish-speaking inhabitants of the republic, around 8 percent, are concentrated in Vilnius, as are the groups of new arrivals, Russians and Byelorussians. Around 40 percent of the people in Vilnius speak minority languages, which creates a problem somewhat similar to that in Latvia and Estonia, countries with a large Russian minority. Poland makes no claim to the city, and in its conciliatory attitude goes so far that local Poles accuse it of forgetting to defend their interests. Some rightist elements in Poland are inclined to raise the issue of the Polish minority in Lithuania, but they have only a small following. There is no doubt, though, that Vilnius is a part of Polish cultural history and as such it attracts many tourists from Poland who visit it as a kind of shrine.

Vilnius, in my opinion, has a tremendous potential as a tourist city. Its location, on the banks of two rivers, between pine forests on the hills, enhances the charm of its baroque architecture. It is adorned by some forty churches, mostly from the seventeenth and eighteenth centuries. They have been preserved, as is the university campus, a vestige of the Jesuit Academy founded in 1578. One of the most beautiful cities of northern Europe, Vilnius at the time of this writing is struggling with the erratic course of a post-Communist economy.

GEORGE A. DE VOS ■
HIROSHI WAGATSUMA

Chapter Twelve

Cultural Identity and Minority Status in Japan

Japan was the first non-Western, non-Caucasoid country to become an industrialized nation. This occurred in a surprisingly short period of time, after 1868, following three hundred years of feudalism and isolation. Since the end of World War II in 1945, Japan has accomplished a miraculous industrial recovery, again within a brief time. Today Japan is the third largest industrial complex in the world. As a major industrial state it has lost any isolation that once insulated it from other areas of Asia, and it is reluctantly interchanging residential population with other areas of the globe. In this process, at least, Japan is the polar opposite of the United States. As the chapter by Margaret Mead indicates, it is still problematic about who is to be included or excluded in an American identity.

Definitions of American citizenship begin with awareness of diverse origins comprising its citizenry. Determination of who is a Japanese citizen starts from completely different traditional premises—that Japanese are of a totally homogeneous origin. Given the effects of its recent colonial past, contemporary worldwide labor mobility, and international industrial interpenetration, three important questions arise about present-day Japanese ethnic identity.

First, there is the question of a shared continuing national purpose in the homeland as related to its past historical cultural identity, individual and collective. Is Japanese ethnic identity to remain coterminus with the nation-state and its traditional population? Does being Japanese remain a racial question? The second unresolved issue is how Japanese at home view themselves physically, intellectually, and culturally vis-à-vis their Asian neighbors and the European-American Caucasoid Westerners who opened up Japan to foreign commerce and industry in the nineteenth century. Third is the modern dilemma of all modern nation-states—namely the relationship of citizenship to an exclusively defined ethnic identity. How does the state recognize, socially and legally, and without discrimination, the increasingly diverse origins of many newer, permanent residents in Japan within a nonethnic definition of full citizenship? The latter is particularly difficult for Japanese, given their still abiding belief in a mythological assertion that Japanese are of a unique, homogeneous racial and cultural origin. For most Japanese, citizenship or social acceptance cannot as yet be well distinguished from a racially defined ethnicity.

What Is It to Be Japanese?[1]

Commodore Perry first came to Japan with his black warships in 1853. His visit helped instigate the overthrow of the Tokugawa Shogunate. In the years after the symbolic restoration of the emperor in 1868, Japan transformed itself from a feudal country into an industrialized nation by learning from the West. A second vigorous wave of Westernization occurred from the mid-1920s to the mid-1930s. During that time not only Western technology, but also liberal democratic ideas and even American music, movies, and fashions had an impact on urban Japanese. Then came the war in 1941. Following defeat in 1945, Japan found itself once again learning "lessons of democracy" from its American teachers during the Occupation.

As a result of mass media, the impact of American culture was unprecedented. Things American flooded Japanese society. When the Occupation ended the flood began to subside. Recent political, diplomatic, and economic developments indicate a new increase of exclusionary nationalistic feelings. Intellectual and political leaders seem to be grappling continuously with the problem of relating a uniquely conceived national purpose and cultural pride to present economic affluence.

Identity problems were first recognized by Japanese intellectuals soon after Japan had begun its vigorous efforts to "Westernize itself in order to resist the West" (Passin 1962). Japanese intellectuals struggled to escape from their "historical predicament" (Pyle 1969), the conflict involved national pride and the desire for cultural borrowing; in short, the need to be both modern and Japanese. The "cultural colonization" (Passin 1962) during the postwar Occupation shattered once and for all not only the militarism and ultranationalism, but everything that appeared to be associated with it, namely, Japanese tradition itself. Amid economic affluence the hundred-year-old question seems to remain largely unanswered and the dilemma unresolved. How can Japanese become modernized yet remain Japanese? What makes the Japanese uniquely Japanese, and something that they can be proud of? Japanese intellectuals are still trying to find some meaningful way of relating their isolate past to an interactive present and future, but apparently without much success.

Influences on the Purity of Language

Certain sectors of contemporary Japanese life and the language describing them are Westernized. Although not limited to Japan, fads and fashions in dress, music, and the arts come directly from U.S. and European cities, arriving in Japanese cities perhaps more quickly than they reach corners of rural America and Europe. Well-known books by Western intellectuals, particularly Americans such as Herbert Marcuse or Peter Drucker, are quickly translated (or mistranslated) into Japanese and avidly read by white-collar workers in overcrowded commuter trains. In television commercials two-thirds or more of the words used for brand names and descriptions of products are English or French, although such words are systematically mispronounced so that they fit into the Japanese phonological system, a process that renders them quite incomprehensible to actual speakers of English or French. Some linguists estimate that a Japanese needs to know about 2,200 foreign words for ordinary daily conversation, and about 3,000 additional words to engage in sophisticated discourse. The number of words of foreign origin (*gairai-go*) included in Japanese dictionaries published at different times in Japan's modern history indicates a definite increase in words that first came into Japanese as foreign words (*gaikoku-go*) and were eventually adopted (Yazaki 1964).

One can also point out the "conceptual Westernization" of Japanese academic theory. For example, Japanese social psychologists omit the variable "Japan" in most of their recent writings. They do not pay enough attention to the social psychological reality that is uniquely Japanese, but tend to be satisfied with Western theories that are based upon Western psychological reality and not necessarily directly applicable to Japan (Wagatsuma 1969).

Racial Aesthetics

Westernization is also found in what one might call the "racial" sexual aesthetics of the Japanese. As analyzed elsewhere in detail (Wagatsuma 1967, 1969, 1972), prior to any sustained contact with the Caucasoid Europeans the Japanese valued white skin as beautiful and depreciated "black" (that is, suntanned) skin as ugly.

With the introduction of Western technology and values in 1868, the Japanese perception of feminine beauty also began to change. Although they admired the white skin of the Westerners, they considered Caucasian hair color and hairiness as distasteful. Wavy hair was not attractive to the Japanese until the mid-1920s, for curly hair was considered characteristic of animals.

During the second peak of Westernization in the 1920s and 1930s, the Japanese, especially those in cities, adopted Western customs and fashions, including singing American popular songs and dancing in dance halls. They watched motion pictures with delight, and made great favorites of Clara Bow, Gloria Swanson, and Greta Garbo. Motion pictures seem to have had a strong effect in finally changing hair styles and notions of beauty. During this period, many Japanese women had their hair cut, and, in spite of the exhortations of proud samurai, had it waved and curled. They took to wearing long skirts with large hats and emulated the clothes worn by Greta Garbo. Anything Western was considered modern, and therefore superior.

This trend lasted until the mid-1930s when, under the pressure of the ultranationalist militarist regime, ties with Western fads and fashions were systematically broken. On the other hand, the subtle, almost unconscious trend toward an idealization of Western physical features apparently became of increasing importance in the 1920s. It remained, it seems, a hidden undercurrent even throughout the last war, when Japan, as the "champion" of the Asian nations, fought against the whites.

Plastic surgery, especially to alter eye folds and to build up the bridge of the nose, has become standard practice among Japanese movie actors and actresses and among many ordinary people. Japanese women also attempt to increase the actual or apparent size of their breasts by surgery or by wearing padded brassieres. These various attempts by younger Japanese, women in particular, to alter their physical appearance suggest that the Caucasian standards of beauty and sexual attractiveness became the standards for the Japanese.

Attitudes toward the skin of Caucasians fall into opposites of likes and dislikes, which may coexist within an individual, either appearing alternately or being expressed simultaneously. White skin may be considered inferior to that of the Japanese because it is rough in texture, with many wrinkles, blemishes, and furrows, whereas Japanese skin is smooth, tight, and resilient, with far fewer spots and speckles. Most Japanese, however, admit that Caucasian facial and body structures are more attractive than the "flat face" and "less shapely body" of the Japanese.

Japanese men, especially those over forty years of age, tend to be concerned more with the skin texture of a Japanese woman than with the measurement of her bust and hips, whereas Western men will first think of the shape of a woman rather than her skin texture. One might say that the Japanese man's taste with respect to sexual aesthetics has traditionally been "surface oriented," whereas the Western man's is "structure oriented." Among younger Japanese, however, structure orientation is quickly replacing surface orientation, as the popularity of plastic surgery shows. Japanese in the United States admire the beauty of white skin in Caucasian women, but also point out their inaccessibility.

Finally, Westerners smell different. They have stronger body odors than do Japanese. The ambivalence about Western physical attributes leads to mixed feelings of admiration, envy, fear, or disgust, and the sense of being overwhelmed or threatened that are evoked in the Japanese mind by the image of a hairy giant whose great vigor and strong sexuality can easily satisfy an equally energetic and glamorous Caucasian female.

Spiritual-Racial Values Versus Material Intrusion

Such trends have certainly invited criticism from intellectuals. Particularly among the older generation one observes dissatisfaction and irritation with "too much Westernization." For example, Takeo Kuwabara, a professor of French literature at the University of Kyoto and a prolific writer, used bitter words in criticizing the Japanese preoccupation with things Western: "I want the Japanese to be more proud of themselves as modern people (*kindai-jin*) with human dignity and individual rights. The Japanese should have 'guts' (*konjo*) as a nation. They should stop worshipping foreign countries and stop regretting that Japan never had the same history as the West" (1963).

But in spite of plastic surgery, Japanese know very well, perhaps too well, who they are and especially who they are not. For the Japanese, group identity is an assured given. They tend to believe that there is a greater degree of physical homogeneity among themselves than actually exists. And they tend to believe that they look uniquely alike and always look different from other Asians. In the Japanese mind only those born of Japanese parents are genetically Japanese—nobody can *become* a Japanese.

By 1867, toward the end of the Tokugawa feudal era, the sense of crisis was expressed in two contrasting ways. The first was based on recognition of the material superiority of Western civilization and of the necessity to learn from it in order to maintain Japan's political independence. The second one was based upon the recognition of fundamental differences between Japanese and Western civilizations and of the necessity to reject Western influences so as to maintain Japan's cultural autonomy. The followers of the first line of thought emphasized that Japan should open itself up to the West they were called *kaikoku-ha* (the open country wing). Those who followed the second line of thought insisted that Japan drive the Westerners away; they were called *joi-ha* (the expulsionist wing). Both groups, despite fierce and often bloody battling between them, shared the same goal—Japan's survival in the face of the Western threat.

Following the visit of Perry's ships to Uraga in 1853, the Tokugawa government changed its policy from "expulsion of the barbarians" to "opening up the country."

After complicated changes of alliances among the lords and among the antigovernment forces, and after battles and bloodshed, the Tokugawa regime was overthrown in 1867. The Meiji emperor was restored to the throne, and the building of a new modern nation was begun under those who were anti-Tokugawa, some of whom had favored expulsion of the outsiders and others of whom had advocated opening up the country. All these young leaders agreed on the goal of making their country as rich and powerful as Western ones so that Japan would not become a foreign colony of the West. Most were former samurai and they were sensitive to the grave threats that the Western powers posed to Japan's independence and autonomy. They focused their efforts on building a rich nation and a strong army (*fukoku kyohei*).

Some intellectual leaders even advocated the "physical" Westernization of the nation. Twenty-four-year-old Arinori Mori, later the first minister of education, was in the United States in 1871 as Japan's first ambassador. He declared that Japanese students in the United States should marry American women and bring them home so as to produce physically and mentally stronger children (Nagai 1965). In 1883 a book proposed that the Japanese import women from the West and marry them, in order to produce "racially superior offsprings" (Takahashi 1937:38-39). Incredible as it may sound today, the prime minister, Prince Hirobumi Ito, took this proposition seriously enough to write to Herbert Spencer,[2] asking for his opinion. At about the same time, a newspaper article advised the Japanese to eat more meat and drink more milk. "Japanese are intellectually smart by nature, but, unlike the Westerners, they lack persistence and tenacity," said an article. "Japanese lack persistence and tenacity because they do not eat beef and drink milk. . . . Cows are stupid animals but they are persistent and tenacious. Those who eat their meat and drink their milk become persistent and tenacious like cows" (Kosaka 1938). As a matter of fact, Emperor Meiji, setting up a model for the nation, had begun drinking milk twice a day in 1871, and in 1872 the imperial family had started eating meat regularly (Sabata 1971).

In 1885 *Youth of the New Japan* was published. Urging youth to seek total Westernization of Japan, the book soon became very popular among young people (Tokutomi 1885 [1931]). Its author, Soho Tokutomi, organized young intellectuals into a group called the *Min'yusha* (Friends of Nation). Writing for the group's periodical, *Kokumin no Tomo* (subtitled in English "The Nation's Friends"), he became the leading spokesman of the new generation. Following Herbert Spencer, Tokutomi believed that a universal process of social evolution, impelled by historical forces, was molding all nations, including Japan, along similar lines. When the government made it an official policy (particularly with the promulgation of the Imperial Rescript on Education in 1890) to adopt the past-oriented Confucian ethics as the moral backbone of national education, Tokutomi severely attacked the policy as proceeding with industrialization while maintaining identification with the East.

An alternative to the *Min'yusha*'s Westernism was proposed by a second group of intellectuals, the *Seikyosha* (Society for Political Education), founded in 1888. Their emphasis on the preservation of Japan's cultural autonomy gained increasing popularity. Although its members had been strongly influenced by Western values and were committed to the adoption of many Western institutions, they believed that only by maintaining a distinct identity could the Japanese feel equal to the Westerners and recover their own national pride.

In 1894 and 1904 Japan won its wars with C'hing Dynasty China and czarist Russia. Japan was able to make the Western nations agree to relinquish their extraterritorial privileges only after winning these two wars, and not after the *Rokumeikan* masquerade of 1887, when high Meiji government officials and their families dressed in Western clothes and invited foreign diplomats to balls to persuade the foreigners that the Japanese were civilized enough to deserve equal treatment. The improvement in their international status made the third answer to the problem of cultural identity increasingly convincing.

The Meiji government formulated and propagated a national ideology that justified its power and called for great loyalty on the part of the people to achieve the nation's industrial and military goals. In the newly established universal education and military training the government reasserted the old values of loyalty, filial piety, solidarity, and duty to superiors, and promoted ethnic-racial myths about the sacredness of the emperor. The pressure to conform to this national orthodoxy came not so much from the government as from "forces within Japanese society" (Jansen 1965). The receptivity to a national ideology was a natural revivalist[3] reaction to the sense of uprootedness and the emotional stress and dislocation produced by the rapid changes during the first two decades of the Meiji period. This national ideology of the past helped the Japanese compensate for their new lost sense of security.

During the 1920s, following its industrial expansion and economic depression, Marxism also became popular among urban intellectuals, as did certain political and labor movements. As mentioned before, things Western (this time, mainly American)—jazz, dress, dance, and movies—also attracted the urban Japanese. The countries of the West continued to be regarded as advanced nations (*senshin koku*), and Japan as backward (*koshin koku*). Ishida describes the period after World War I as "an extension of the previous age of inferiority feelings among the Japanese toward the West."[4]

Then came the war, first in Manchuria in 1931, then spreading to north China, then to the whole of China, and finally to the Pacific and Pearl Harbor. Ultranationalism, with its mythical glorification of the "descendants of the Sun Goddess," drowned all liberal thought. The problems of cultural-racial identity were answered by a clear definition of the national goal of the "sacred war," in which Japan's role was to become the leader and protector of the Asian nations and to drive out the Western imperialists. During this disastrous war, the importance of "Japanese soul and spirit" was greatly stressed. The chauvinistic emphasis on the superiority of the traditional warrior-Confucian-Shinto value system over the "corrupt Western civilization" became almost hysterical, for the "corrupt" West proved to be much more powerful, and there was no sign of the "divine wind" (kamikaze) blowing to protect the "land of gods."

When the war ended, the Japanese began to receive a "democratic education" from their American teachers, toward whom they felt rivalry mixed with admiration. Japanese society and traditions were all put on trial, not by Americans, but by Japanese intellectuals. Historians separated Japanese history from the myth of the origins of the imperial line. The mechanisms of Japanese fascism were analyzed for the first time in scientific terms (Maruyama 1963). Sociologists pointed out the predominance of small communities in Japan, and particularly the institution of the patriarchal family (Kawishima 1948). Psychologists analyzed the "irrational," "premodern," or "feudal" characteristics of the Japanese (Minami 1949; Miyagi 1950, 1956; Takagi 1955) and emphasized the necessity to overcome such characteristics as so to accomplish the democratization of the Japanese people.

All this demonstrated a "wide-spread realization of Japan's backwardness" (Kato 1965). Anything associated with defeated Japan—whether the emperor cult, calligraphy, judo, "a father who tells his daughter to come home before supper," or "a mother who wants her son to marry her best friend's daughter"—was condemned as feudal (*hoken-teki*), and therefore to be rejected. Intellectuals, through lectures and writings, urged the Japanese to become modern (*kinadai-teki*), rational (*gori-teki*), and democratic (*minshu-teki*), and not infrequently, the implication was "like the Americans." To those intellectuals, as to Min'yusha members of the 1880s, there seemed once again to be an assumption that Japan should move along the ladder of unilineal social evolution, from the feudal or premodern stage to the modern and democratic stage. Moreover, many of them, pointing out what the Japanese should no longer be, seemed too busy to think what the Japanese would eventually become when they were fully democratized and modernized.

The Occupation ended and the flood of things American subsided. In terms of economy and in the sphere of material life the Japanese rebuilt everything they had lost and more, "except for a sense of values and national purpose to replace those shattered by the war" (Rosenthal 1963). Bad as the old system might have been, "it had given meaning and purpose to life, a way of viewing the world, and an opportunity for service and sacrifice to a larger cause" (Passin 1962). "The thought that the Japanese were not passively accepting Western civilization, but were holding themselves as the last fortress in Asia against the Western powers, gave the nation pride and a sense of mission" (Kosaka 1968). This was all lost, and the rapid changes, the confusion, the "transvaluation of values," and the discrediting of the old authority without replacement by a new one created what the Japanese themselves refer to as "a spiritual void."

The drive toward Westernization has slowed down somewhat since the middle of the 1950s, especially with the recent economic prosperity of the country. Japanese intellectuals now seem again increasingly concerned with the century-old question of cultural identity. An anthropologist, Mitsusada Fukasaku (1972), contends that with these basic "unchanging" characteristics the Japanese have adopted various foreign cultural elements "without ever really understanding their essential nature." He asserts that the Japanese adoption of foreign cultures has been no more than "monkey's imitation" (*saru-mane*, a superficial imitation), and that the Japanese have remained essentially the same in the relative isolation afforded by a self-sufficient rice agriculture. But Japan is no longer geographically isolated from the international community, agriculture is no longer the basis for the Japanese economy, and Japan's once beautiful natural, traditional settings have been destroyed by pollution, urbanization, and commercialization.[5]

The issues raised above by Wagatsuma in his original chapter written in 1970, summarized here, remain. Intellectuals of the 1990s do not insist on Japanese uniqueness, but they recognize a continuing Japanese isolation within the international community. A Japanese brand of exclusory racism persists in the general public. There is aversion to extending citizenship toward those of non-Japanese origin and toward a segment of its population that bears the stigma of past premodern outcaste status, still attributed by many to some supposed non-Japanese ancestors. In international business ventures, the Japanese have difficulties in creating organizations at home or abroad that include foreign personnel on an equal basis. These are issues to which we now turn in the context of ethnic identity and minority status in Japan.

Minorities within the Japanese State

By most serious estimates, Japan has various minorities that probably total about 4.5 percent of its population (De Vos and Wetherall 1983). Some are technically citizens, some are not. The issues of social self-identity in some instances, strictly speaking, are not of an "ethnic" nature. Nevertheless, from the standpoint of the majority Japanese all of these individuals, regardless of the category into which they are placed, are not "true" Japanese. They, therefore, at least occasionally, face some form of social discrimination.

The largest minority group are the former outcastes of Japan, Burakumin, comprising close to three million individuals, including many who are secretly "passing."[6] They are the premodern descendants of hereditary pariahs who were a debased caste beneath the four classes of ordinary Japanese.

The three next largest groups result from Japanese expansion into Okinawa and Taiwan as a result of its war with China in 1894 and its official takeover of Korea in 1910. There are over a million Okinawans, whose languages were similar to but distinct from that of the majority Japanese. These languages are rapidly disappearing, but Okinawans, seen as smaller and hairier, still face various degrees of nonacceptance when they move to the four main islands of Japan. There are close to a million people of Korean descent, most of whom remain technically noncitizens and live in large ghettos in many urban areas. Some have taken citizenship, many with fabricated Japanese names practicing various degrees of hiding ancestry. Those of Taiwanese background are fewer in number and less conspicuous, but occasionally suffer slights when they venture into ordinary business relationships. Children of Japanese and Korean or Taiwanese parents are considered *konketsuji*, or racially of "mixed blood."

There remain relatively small remnants of Ainu, indigenous people who were driven to their remaining villages in the northern island of Hokkaido over a period of eight hundred years in the Japanese early occupation of the northeastern territories. They are treated in much the same way as is the native population of North America. That is, they are often considered quaint or primitive. Now much intermixed with ordinary Japanese, they nevertheless maintain, in many instances, a sense of separate identity.

Of more immediate moment are residential minorities created by more recent events. There are the *hibakusha*, survivors of the atomic bombs dropped on Japan at the close of World War II. Considered irrevocably contaminated, they have been shunned by other Japanese.

There have been a number of intermarriages and other liaisons during and after the postwar American occupation of Japan. Children resulting from these relationships have been subjected to various forms of continuing discrimination by members of their extended family as well as by unrelated neighbors and others coming in contact with them in various circumstances. More than any other minority group in Japan, offspring of Japanese and non-Asian foreigners are maliciously stereotyped in mass media, including popular literature, films, and comic books. Unlike white Japanese *konketsuji*, who may have physical features that many Japanese find exotically attractive, black Japanese tend to have the kinds of features that some Japanese openly despise (Wagatsuma 1967:427-434).

Increasingly, Japan hosts many foreign residents of long-term duration, both as skilled professionals and, now more recently, as unskilled labor. Given the complex legal difficulties, only a very few are able to obtain Japanese citizenship. A recent notable group are South Americans of Japanese ancestry, mainly from Brazil, who come to Japan to do unskilled work, receiving a much higher rate of payment than is possible to gain for professional, let alone skilled, work in their homeland. Despite their Japanese ancestry they do not gain social acceptance among ordinary

Japanese given their problems with language, and, more offending, their "un-Japanese" bodily comportment and more openly expressive social habits.

We shall examine in some detail identity issues raised by two of these groups that we have researched in some detail, namely the Burakumin and the Koreans. The first group is fully Japanese and are legally so. However, the majority population questions their origins since they are considered innately inferior people. The second group, the Koreans, have for the most part maintained a separate identity as Koreans and wish to have this ethnicity respected without losing the opportunity of being able to receive Japanese citizenship or equal treatment in professional and commercial careers. They, too, are considered unrefined and inferior. Polls rating relative acceptability, place them just above Africans or African-Americans on so-called social distance scales.

Citizenship Is Not Enough: The Outcaste Tradition in Modern Japan[7]

Discussed only briefly, if mentioned at all in general histories, are two subgroups of the traditional, premodern society. They are the *hinin* (nonpeople)—a heterogeneous melange of beggars, prostitutes, itinerant entertainers, mediums, and religious wanders—and felons or former felons who had fallen out of the four-tier class system. These were not inherently polluted and could be rehabilitated by proper purification ceremonies.

Beneath these outcasts were the true hereditary outcastes, officially called Eta, a defiling word written with characters meaning "full of filth." They traditionally performed tasks considered ritually polluting, including animal slaughter and disposal of the dead. By extension, they worked on armor and musical instruments (which contained animal products such as leather). Some other professions, such as basket weaving, for now unknown reasons, were also consigned to Eta. During the modernization period the Eta were declared "new citizens," but their status did not change much, they were still people of special villages, *Tokushu Buraku*. Burakumin, village people, became a generally used neutral, nonpejorative term of reference. This word is beginning to be rejected by some in favor of more euphemistic terms such as "yet unliberated people."

There are striking functional parallels between the social problems and the resultant sense of social alienation resulting from the discrimination encountered by the Japanese Burakumin and the problems faced by African-Americans in the United States. However, these striking parallels may be obscured by a number of seeming dissimilarities. First, the Burakumin are not *not physically distinct* or visibly discernible in any way. Second, a major collectively exercised "coping" technique of contemporary Japanese society with respect to members of this group is avoidance or *direct denial that any such group continues to exist*, or indeed that there is any problem. Consciously or not, a Burakumin must choose between four limited alternatives in social self-identity and group belonging, available also in other cultural settings, to many disparaged minorities who are not visibly distinct.

1. Maintain an overt and *direct identity* with one's past and a present minority status, whatever that implies with respect to social degradation. By so doing, one may be *passively receptive and resigned* to the stigmata of past definitions of the society.
2. Gain increased social advantages or changes in status through *concerted cooperative action* with others sharing a demeaned status.
3. Go into a *selective disguise*, in which one maintains expressive family affiliations and group membership within the Buraku community, but for occupational and other instrumental purposes one may lead a life of semidisguise among members of the majority population.
4. Attempt to *pass* completely; move from the home community and cut off overt contacts with family, forging an entirely new identity, and in some cases fabricate a new past.

Many complex societies have parallel situations in which the difficult process of social assimilation to full status within a majority culture is likely to face similar problems. Utilizing a psychocultural framework,[8] let us illustratively explore some Burakumin minority status problems and their psychological consequences. Erik Erikson (1959), discussing the nature of identity formation, provides excellent theoretical background for this discussion.

Relative Social Status and Occupation

In Buraku communities, caste separation from the majority Japanese does not preclude the appearance of internal class distinctions in social participation. This is also true of American colored communities, though these have the further complication of complex attitudes about shades of skin color and kinds of hair. Such distinctions do not function among the Burakumin, but differences in occupation do (Cayton and Drake 1964).

In our work in Japan starting in the early 1950s, we did not find it difficult to apply an index of class-status characteristics to the 2,400 majority Japanese interviewed in both city and village that distinguished them into upper-, middle-, and lower-class patterns. Our indices[9] were slightly modified from those developed by Lloyd Warner and his colleagues in his intensive urban anthropological study of Newburyport, Massachusetts, in the 1930s (Warner et al. 1963). Occupation, education, internal conditions of the home, the area lived in, and source of income generally held up as significant variables.

Specifically within an outcaste community, area lived in, in *most* instances, was a known ghetto, but we also interviewed some who were passing by living in majority areas. With regard to other class variant characteristics, Burakumin differed among themselves in line with internally considered class distinctions that regulated their relationships.[10] Also, a number of high-status families lived outside these enclaves in good housing. They passed in public situations but maintained socially stratified class contacts within close-by Buraku communities. The Buraku community had a great deal of social stability. A few families within each community owned land and rented out houses; their status was that of families whose wealth continued through several generations.

Most inhabitants were unskilled day laborers in construction or similar work—"lower lower" in Warner et al.'s system. A number worked for the city, often on a daily or temporary basis, doing street cleaning, garbage collecting, or (at the time we studied them) night-soil collecting. Some members of the community achieved Warner's "upper-lower class," i.e., blue-collar status within the community. Workers under the direction of a local *oyabun*, or boss, worked with leather for the shoemaking industry, a stigmatic sign that marked a traditionally degraded occupation in the community. This *oyabun* occupied a status somewhat below that of others generally acting as supervisors of ordinary daily laborers.

General stores within these communities sold fried tripe, a favorite Buraku snack, the taste of which is considered repugnant by other Japanese. Butcher shops within a Buraku community also sold raw tripe, hence their slang name, *iremon-ya* (literally, a "container"—i.e., "stomach"—shop). The owners of these shops were also upper-lower class, perhaps because the scorn of lowly merchants typical of Tokugawa Japan has persisted longer in Buraku society. The proprietors of other establishments—barber shop, a public bathhouse, and a drycleaning store—were accorded somewhat higher prestige. There were a good number of women among those employed in small stores and in some cases as factory workers. If the husband worked in a store or factory, generally the social status of the family seems to be classifiable as upper-lower class. If, however, the father worked as a day laborer or casual construction worker and his wife or daughter worked as a factory hand, the family was considered by our informants to be in the lowest class position. This also was the case if the father or the household head was dead or an invalid.

Almost every member of some communities, including those who have moved out and were then more or less successfully passing, maintained strong religious affiliation with one or another Buddhist temple. Middle- and upper-status families sent their children to kindergartens outside the community.

Markers of Identity: Distinct Customs within the Urban Buraku

Food

Eating meat was once exclusively a Buraku habit, disapproved of by other Japanese in accordance with Buddhism. Only since the end of the nineteenth century has it become general. Most butchers are still thought outcastes, and, except for increased consumption of liver and kidney among the young postwar generations, eating internal animal organs continues to be an abhorred Buraku characteristic.

Dress

Within the Buraku community itself, dress is extremely informal and can be described as careless, however well off the family. At the time of our study, one specific article of dress in one Kyoto Buraku was a special sandal, *setta zori*. This was a somewhat self-conscious tradition, and there are indications that the continued use of this form of *zori* evokes some feeling of belonging and self-enhancement.

Speech and Comportment

Those familiar with the intricacies of local dialects agree that the Buraku have speech patterns of a more "informal" and "less refined" nature than the general society. There are distinctive definable characteristics in vocabulary and pronunciation. Patterns of speech, dress, and comportment shared by all individuals help maintain a strong sense of in-group social solidarity, though individuals of the wealthier families may also learn to behave in a style acceptable to the outer society.

Within the Buraku, given its small perimeter, it was very difficult for individuals with higher incomes to isolate their children from the rest of the community. Although children were sometimes sent to schools outside their community, the speech patterns and modes of behavior are generally shared, whatever the economic means of the family. Emotional alienation occurs in individuals deciding to pass. But if they desire, they can easily reassume language patterns and other gestures of communication spontaneously, since they have had ample first-hand experience growing up with peers in the community. They can "code switch" when necessary.

In-Group Solidarity

In order to live in the face of strong social discrimination and prejudice, the ordinary Burakumin has to rely heavily upon the group. With the exception of government service, a man cannot easily take a job in the majority society unless he has the capacity to successfully pass, and few succeed in getting into the big firms. A considerable number of individuals living in Buraku communities are on some form of public relief, having little opportunity for self-support.

Those who work within the community depend upon their employer. Usually the relationship with the employer has been a very paternalistic one, the traditional pattern of mutual obligation involving financial protection and income security. Occupations within the communities studied in Kobe and Kyoto were mainly in the leather industry, shoemaking, animal slaughtering, metal or rag picking, and the handling of corpses and burial of the dead. As long as an employee remains passively loyal and hard working, he can enjoy a modicum of emotional and financial security. If, for instance, he or his family members get ill, the boss will protect him and help defray medical expenses.

Endogamy is still the rule. Only occasionally will an individual make a "love" marriage with a person of non-outcaste background in the face of the difficulties engendered. As with relations between blacks and whites in the United States, differences in caste position prevent marriage, but not love affairs. A sense of family solidarity is coupled with a high rate of endogamy; everyone knows everyone else. Parents do not worry when the child does not show up at home for two or three days, as long as they are sure the child is within their community. There is usually a very well-built large Buddhist temple in the middle of many Buraku communities, in impressive contrast to the shabby-looking houses in the vicinity. There is some indication that Burakumin, as a mark of solidarity, tend to maintain adherence to their Buddhist religion with a greater tenacity than is now noted generally in Japan.

Problems of Passing

Not physically different, only one's place of residence might identify outcastes with any degree of certainty. Many outcaste individuals succeed in passing as far as external conditions are concerned. Nevertheless, the intrapsychic tensions and difficulties over self-identity make it impossible for most to continue their passing role.

Successful passing, therefore, requires moving and changing both one's place of registry and family register. Although now an illegal requirement, a copy of one's registry is still expected to be provided when applying for a job. The procedure to change is very complicated. Even when a change of residence is recorded, the previous address is recorded. Therefore, to be secure in not revealing Buraku residence, the family must make at least two changes of residence. But, by and large, they remain bound to bosses within the community by both psychological and economic ties, and since they have little direct social contact with outsiders, they are not continuously exposed to feelings of rejection that they are likely to face if they move in among majority Japanese. For some upper-class Buraku families, motivation for passing has not been compelling for other reasons. First, their sources of income and prestige lie within the community itself. Second, if they are particularly wealthy, they can afford to visit hot-spring resorts and be treated as ordinary guests in good hotels. In effect, they can pass when they wish in recreational activities. The pressure to pass is felt most strongly among the middle-class families who are sufficiently well-off to provide the education and financial support for their children necessary for them to become established as white-collar workers. The Japanese emphasize family interdependence. They are not socialized for independent individualism. Passers are therefore particularly prone to an alienation and marginality.

It is especially on the issue of intermarriage that caste feelings toward the Burakumin remain strong. Neighbors may be friendly and sociable, although suspicious of the Buraku origin of a family, until the family seeks to establish marital liaisons in their new neighborhood. Then latent suspicions will come to the fore and deliberate investigations might be made. A frequent solution is for a boy of a passing family to marry an eligible girl of another passing family. In the period before World War II, a good number of matches between American-born nisei were broken off when one family's register was found to record an old Buraku address in Japan. Even in the 1950s, a Japanese woman student at the University of Chicago was astonished to find that several nisei who took her out volunteered at the start of their acquaintance that they were not of Eta origin. I met a group of Japanese artists in Paris in the 1970s. One revealed to me that many of the older members were minority outcastes and that some others were Korean with Japanese names.

Socialization, Social Identity, and Burakumin Status

Differential Socialization within the Community

Interviews both within and outside the communities revealed that Burakumin are considered somewhat more impulsive and volatile than other Japanese and, related to that, hostile and aggressive to individuals from the outside society.[11] There is some evidence that in socialization practices the Burakumin tend to be less restrained than other Japanese in expressing aggression toward their children. According to some informants, parents, especially fathers, do not hesitate to resort to physical punishment in handling children. Not only shouting loudly or wildly but also slapping and hitting on the head or cheeks are common expressions of disfavor when provoked. There is less hiding of sexual relationships in Burakumin households. Many Burakumin children have a shorter latency period than those in more restrained Japanese households; some do not have any latency period. In general, there seems to be less stringent impulse control demanded of either sexuality or aggression of the Buraku child. The adult relationships witnessed in childhood also illustrate that role-modeling adults do act impulsively and can give vent to their feelings when they are under the influence of strong emotions.

Differential Role Expectations in Sex, Property, and Aggression

In certain Buraku communities, at least among their lower strata, there is considerable casualness about marriage ties and sexual fidelity. A husband who goes to a distant place to work for a year or two is likely to find another partner where he lives and works, and his wife may take another man if the opportunity occurs. In the majority society, such a situation would provide a good subject for gossip and criticism. The Burakumin consider it necessary for a Burakumin woman to have someone to rely on for income and training of children, as well as for her own pleasure, which is an acknowledged part of the relationship of the sexes.

According to the opinion survey by a Japanese sociologist quoted by Cornell (1956), Burakumin think they have "inferior" sexual morals compared with people of the majority society. The stringent double standard of majority society did not apply in the Buraku. However, relative sexual freedom does not seem to imply general equality of status between man and wife. Women among the Burakumin, as in the traditional society, are required to be subservient and docile and to appear nonaggressive, at least toward their husbands. Husbands beat their wives, but wives are not supposed to hit back. Mothers are also less violent with their children than fathers, but probably more violent than mothers of the majority society. Physical attacks between women are known to occur.

Self-Image as Part of Social Identity[12]

Informants shared memories of shame about self-discovery. One boy, as an art assignment at school, was asked to draw his father at work. He drew a picture of his father as a shoe cobbler. When he brought the picture home, his parents were very upset. They forbade him from ever again revealing his father's occupation to outsiders, but the boy was not told why. Living away from the Buraku, his parents had hoped the child would pass at school. From the serious reaction and the tone of his parent's voice, he could sense that he had done something seriously wrong, that there was something secret about his family that should be hidden from the eyes of others. This was his painful initiation into understanding that he was marked as a Burakumin. Once, when this same informant delivered shoes to a customer, the money was given him tied to the end of a bamboo pole—an ancient way of avoiding the "unclean" by those needing the services of outcastes in Kyoto. This cruel reminder of his unclean status made him feel somehow very lonely and helpless.

Another painful memory included discovering his mother's deep capacity for violence. On a fearful occasion she, normally a calm, gentle woman, wildly hit out at the wife of another shoemaker family, who were also partially passing. Angered by something he had done, this woman had shouted "Eta!" and "*Yotsu*!" (four-legged beast) at her son. The incident reminded the boy of fights he had seen between other women in the Buraku who pulled each other down into the street, rolling in the dirt. It forever destroyed his idealized picture of his mother and simultaneously undermined the self-identity he had tried to create of himself as a non-Buraku person. He then felt consciously that he could never escape his debased group.

Conservative, Passive, and Intrapunitive Elements of Self-Images

A very difficult aspect of minority status is a continual need to cope with a negative self-image, automatically internalized as a child becomes socialized within an enclave surrounded by a disparaging outer society. In *Japan's Invisible Race* (De

Vos and Wagatsuma 1966) our most poignant case material was about the conscious as well as unconscious negative self-images that various informants showed to us. There are severe inner problems with developing a conscious negative self-image; but a developing negative self-image is not always conscious.

Some revealing materials have been gathered by a few Japanese social scientists concerning the Burakumin's group identity. For example, Koyama (1953) illustrated the mixture of active resentment against the majority society and a passive sense of personal inferiority in Burakumin attitudes. These attitudes reflect, though not completely passive helplessness, a great deal of intrapunitive thinking, such as "we should behave better; we should give up our slovenly behavior and keep our houses and clothes clean; we should seek more education; we should cooperate with one another; we should move out of this dirty area; we should change our occupations to more decent and respectable ones," and the like.

Deviant Attitudes toward Authority in Educational, Legal, Medical, and Welfare Matters

The social role expectations of adult Burakumin do not induce as strong a conformist identification with prevailing authority as is found in middle-class Japanese. They are loathe to internalize the forms of *responsibility* more readily assumed by the majority. A basic means of expressing discontent with discrimination is through *cooperative* political action. Some of this behavior is expressively quite hostile; some is persistently instrumental. The more educated Burakumin find outlets for discontent through leftist political organizations that seek to change social attitudes through changing their society's pattern of political-legal sanctions. A basic defensive maneuver is to find methods of trickery to outwit authorities. By so doing, the minority-group member salvages some self-esteem and "gets back" at an authority structure that is perceived as operating to maintain degradation or to hinder freedom rather than to benefit the individual in any way. One may refuse to conform to expected patterns. Deviant attitudes become emblematic of a minority identity.

Selective Permeability and the Educational Experiences of the Burakumin

One striking parallel between the value systems of American and Japanese culture is the emphasis of both on occupational and educational achievement. Although minority members, whether they are African-American or Burakumin, are well aware that they should seek personal training and education, they also know they will be faced with a highly problematical situation when applying for a job in the profession or skill for which they have received training (Ogbu 1974, 1978). Our study in Kobe reported the truancy rate among Buraku children as high as that reported for African-American and Mexican-American children in California.[13]

Dependency, Deviousness, and Apathy in Relation to Health and Welfare Authorities

Members of a minority group who have experienced a long tradition of discrimination commonly exhibit a combination of defensive hostility toward the dominant group and attitudes of economic dependency. This is evident in response to U.S. welfare policies to "help" Native Americans or in the welfare policies set up to aid single parent families, a large proportion of which are black.

Deviousness is a balm to the ego and allows the individual to maintain a shred of self-respect by not having one s dependent needs make one feel completely helpless. Individuals in the majority culture sometimes are angered when they discover some form of "relief cheating." It confirms their prejudice concerning the worthless nature of the individuals who are being helped through the efforts of the more humane elements within their community.

Burakumin have developed certain expectations that they are "due" economic assistance from the majority society. They deem it a right that goes with their minority status. We have cited graphic evidence of the prevalence of such attitudes among Burakumin, as compared to their relative absence among ordinary Japanese (De Vos and Wagatsuma 1966; Wagatsuma 1984).

Relative Indices of Delinquency and Crime

Members of the Kobe family court, when interviewed, indicated that although the Burakumin are a small minority in Kobe City, they comprise a disproportionate number of cases of both family problems and delinquency coming before the court. There is also court evidence from Kobe, as well as in Kyoto, that Burakumin inspire fear in the rest of the population. A criminal career is one available for passing. *Yakuza*, the generic name now used for the organized underworld, draw into their ranks youth who can contribute talent to their organizations.[14] If a Buraku youth is successful in becoming a member of a criminal gang or *Yakuza* group, his outcaste background is discreetly forgotten.[15] Therefore, the Buraku youth may feel more readily accepted in this career activity than in attempting to face the more overt discrimination that occurs in other occupational pursuits. In the same manner, Buraku women who become entertainers, bar girls, or prostitutes find it an easy way to pass and to remove themselves from the Buraku community.

Overt Recognition of Psychocultural Problems and Their Possible Amelioration

Personal individuation and maturation among the Burakumin is a more difficult challenge than among ordinary Japanese, for to become a mature adult, one must overcome any need to obtain ready acceptance from members of the majority culture. One must avoid a regressive acquiescence to a debased self-image, while noting that others of one's group have incorporated such images of themselves, yet they, too, must be accepted, loved, and share a feeling of belonging.

Today, the Japanese government, in its official policies at least, is eager not to discriminate among its citizens; it seeks to be more "universalistic" rather than "particularistic" in the field of human rights. It is now seeking to alleviate the position of the Burakumin by general welfare programs, providing relief for the unemployed and the destitute in the manner of other modern states.

The situations described in our 1966 volume (De Vos and Wagatsuma 1966) have not been much altered by educational programs and the improvements in public housing now put into the areas with the worst slums. Like numerous African-Americans, many former Burakumin outcastes have been able, with great difficulties, to make noted contributions to their society and live felicitous lives. Nevertheless, a disproportionately large number of the Buraku minority do suffer psychologically, as do members of discriminated minority groups in other cultures.

Law enforcement officers seem to be, generally speaking, attempting to be more nondiscriminatory than in the past. But tensions and animosities persist. In the United States, African-Americans today are still trying to overcome a general fear inspired by a continuing potential for violence on the part of the police toward them. The majority American public, aware of the greater amount of violence in the black community, fear that the internally inflicted black violence will spread beyond city ghettos into the more protected urban suburbs. To some degree, the situation in Japan is similar in that now the general public is more in fear of the Burakumin than are the Burakumin in fear of the majority. Generally, the contemporary Burakumin themselves fear being demeaned, rather than being physically attacked.

Modern Japanese society no longer supports either the economic base or the rationale underlying the caste system that prevailed during Tokugawa times. The rigid hereditary hierarchy has given place to a fluid industrial class and underclass structure in which occupational adaptation is subject to the marketplace and social standing depends largely on occupational function. Lineage is less emphasized. There are no hereditary prescribed behavior patterns, deviation from which can make one an outcaste, and there are in principle, no unclean occupations.

Yet, as with African-Americans, where caste status developed out of the feudal plantation system of the South, remnants of former attitudes continue into the present. The question arises, therefore, as to what the functions are of a continuing caste attitude in Japan. The persistence of these attitudes could be ascribed to conservative beliefs concerning hierarchy and biological continuity in talent. But there are other functions of the outcastes that, once established, become a continuing part of the society, and one has to explore these as well. Elsewhere, I have discussed at length the expressive forms of social exploitation that are still in evidence.[16]

Implications for a Theory of Social Exploitation[17]

There are functional similarities in the treatment of Japanese outcastes and of African-Americans, despite the fact that in Japan it is not phenotypic visibility that leads to racism. There is no physiological difference that singles out the Burakumin, or the Koreans to be discussed below. For me, the bases for cross-cultural generalization about caste or racism are the psychocultural mechanisms involved.

Various visibly different physical characteristics may be suggested as necessary criteria for differentiation, but nonvisible features can be used with the same force to segregate a portion of the population of a society as essentially inferior, or in religious terms, "impure." Particular language forms and modes of physical comportment or eating practices, just as much as physical differences, can come to be interpreted as genetically transmitted forms of "ugliness," if they differ from the standards aimed at by the majority. Equally among American minorities or Japanese Burakumin and Koreans, prejudice categorizes. Such attitudes overlook individual differences within any outcaste group and categorizes the group as genetically inferior. Most Japanese still believe that Burakumin are of an alien origin. In this sense, they remain an ethnic minority, despite their offical citizenship. The caste concept is not consciously used either in the United States or Japan. We use race, Japanese use ethnicity in a pejorative sense. For me, it is generically an example of caste endogamy based on a concept of special hereditary inferiority.

It is obvious that purely economic explanations of caste are comparable to those of class in the Marxist system of thought. Such lack of distinction among the structural forms of minority status is inadequate. Human behavior has expressive as well as instrumental aspects, and every culture defines certain forms of expressive behavior as highly valued, whereas others are reprehensible and disavowed.

For caste differences, the disavowal is accompanied by abhorrence—the abhorrent activities having to do with oral, anal, and genital functions, all initiated as well as responded to with the human autonomic nervous system. It is these aspects, examined anthropologically and psychologically, that ensure the endogamy of caste groups and their hereditary perpetuation. These considerations find no explanation in Marxist theory. Just as the economic exploitation of blacks within a plantation economy is no full explanation of the attitudes toward them in modern America, so, too, we must look for deeper psychological feelings that maintain the untouchable status of the Burakumin. The outcaste, whether black, Burakumin, or witch, is in one sense, a scapegoat. The kind of scapegoat he or she is depends on the particular kind of behavior that the culture is most concerned to disavow and attribute to others who are less virtuous, in short, what is "projected" out. Thus, as Dollard (1957) has shown in his now classic work, a predominant element in the southern white's stereotype of the "Negro" was his *potent and primitive sexuality. Dirtiness* and *aggressiveness* were also components.

Japanese stereotypes directed toward both Burakumin and Koreans contain the same basic components. In the case of the Burakumin, the relative emphasis on unacceptable sexuality and aggression found directed toward African-Americans is reversed. Concern with the aggressiveness and crudeness of the Burakumin or Korean is more intense than worry about their sexuality. Although there is ample evidence that the sexual behavior of the Burakumin is "looser" than allowed in the majority society, it is their "unclean" habits with reference to language and manners, as well as supposed tendencies to be inordinately violent and aggressive, that are emphasized. Within Japanese society sexual experience is more tolerated if exercised at the right time and place, but there is a great need to disavow the appearance of direct aggression in everyday relations and to emphasize specific rules of propriety. In both cases, however, "purity" remains the prime cultural concern.[18]

There is no doubt that caste prejudice may involve feelings of economic competition. Nevertheless, the main psychological factors maintaining prejudice with any force in society are these deeply expressive intrapsychic conflicts over internalized social values[19] and expectations that are also projected outward. A thorough understanding of these psychological forces, as well as the society's cultural history and the economic functions of discrimination, are necessary if we are ever to understand the nature of continuing prejudice in modern society. What has been considered about the Burakumin situation also applies directly to the Koreans, a more recently acquired, overtly ethnic minority.

Japan's Colonial Heritage: The Case of the Koreans

The central political and social issues facing minority Koreans in Japan today are strongly influenced by the deeply subjective ethnic feelings developed between Japanese and Koreans long before the defeat of Japan in 1945. The political and legal difficulties resulting from the subsequent reestablishment of an independent Korean state cannot be settled without some necessary modernization of the concept of citizenship, as distinct from that of ethnic identity.

Both Japanese and Koreans have great difficulty at arriving at such a distinction due to certain cultural-historical continuities in both countries. Ethnicity is a complex combination of both expressive and instrumental motivations that operate within any conflict-ridden, changing social structure. Former colonial people who live in the territory of the former colonizer face similar difficulties that are often compounded by persistent racist attitudes. They are prevented from merging into the general population. But many, as in the case of the Koreans, have strong motives for maintaining their ethnicity, even when they are tempted to pass.

Space will only allow a partial illustration of the categories of interpersonal interaction involved in maintaining a defensively protective separate ethnic identity that I have used in my research. Following are some attitudes about affiliation and belonging—and the personal sensitivities to social degradation that can occur in many of these situations—as they relate to Koreans in Japan. These issues are discussed more fully in Lee and De Vos (1981).

Affiliation Versus Isolation

A sense of belonging can be expressed through one's identity with a group. It is a means of finding one's harmonious place in a spiritual entity larger than oneself. The need for affiliation, however, can also be directed more toward the satisfaction to be gained from intimacy and close contact between specific individuals, either in bonds of friendship or in heterosexual attachments. Being alone, isolated, or alienated is intolerable for most human beings. Marginality and apartness are sources of inner agony and tension. General ethnic group membership may supply the forms of contact and affiliation necessary for day-to-day living. But some individuals may feel such a strong need for personal autonomy and independence that they find themselves capable of doing without sustained social contact.

For Koreans in Japan, as for Burakumin, resolving the need for affiliation is related to whether or not an individual chooses to pass, leaving one's own family and childhood friendships behind in seeking an individual route of social mobility in Japanese society. Individuals who seek to leave a group are subject to various forms of sanctioning. The principal threat, of course, is that of ostracism and rejection. A group that, in turn, feels rejected by a former member can even become physically destructive toward a perceived deserter or traitor. For some, the threat of isolation or of aggressive rejection can be a very heavy sanction that keeps them within the group.

For Koreans a sense of intimacy is first fostered within a primary family strongly influenced by a Confucian tradition. I have noted elsewhere (De Vos 1992, 1993a) that Korean and Japanese families may provide a deep sense of psychological security without necessarily supplying intimate companionship to any of its members. Regardless of the priority given to direct companionate types of intimacy and contact, the majority Japanese family continues to afford other forms of warmth and a sense of dependent belonging for the individual.

With Koreans in Japan, however, the psychological test material we collected thus far emphasizes a very strong sense of alienation in many youth (De Vos and Kim 1993). In contrast with the more positive family concerns found in majority Japanese records, one may infer that many Korean families in Japan have suffered internal breakdown generationally, due to the chronic unemployment and degradation of family heads. In many instances, mothers have been forced to become the economic support of the family. This has undermined the dignity of the traditional male family role. Working mothers do not devote as much time at home as do traditional ones. As a consequence, children experience less expressive gratification, not only in intimacy but in harmony, self-respect, and affection.

Many Korean children seem to do relatively poorly in school for reasons similar to those found to operate in some American minorities, such as among African-Americans or Mexican-Americans (De Vos 1992). Individuals do not identify or internalize standards and expectations set for them by members of the external majority (De Vos 1993a). Instead, for some a deviant peer group becomes the main source of affiliative gratification, discouraging acquiescence and conformity to the school as an institution. Such a peer group can also become the arena for demonstration of prowess and competence, the source of appreciative judgment from other youth (De Vos 1993a:ch. 7). Attitudes of protective association and antagonism toward the outside are sometimes perpetuated into adulthood.

Korean-Japanese seem to seek out individual affiliations in marriage. Although their Confucian tradition emphasizes family role patterns rather than intimate companionship, today they seem less prone to concern themselves with family considerations. Among younger Koreans, just as among younger Japanese, there is a greater desire for closeness and intimacy in the marital bond. Indeed, romantic love today in some few instances transcends the social barriers set up between Koreans and Japanese. In some, but not all instances, such marriages can compound problems of identity on the part of the Korean partner. He or she is faced with the necessity to affirm or deny Korean affiliations outside of marriage and at the same time to maintain solidarity with his or her mate. There are numerous instances of difficulties arising in mixed marriages owing to external pressures of family or internal problems of divided loyalty. In turn, mixed marriages produce children with their own identity problems as *konketsuji* (mixed-blood children); they, too, must make decisions as to their principal allegiances and the principal groups from which they will seek out companions.

Appreciation Versus Disparagement

Ultimately, perhaps, the issue of social acceptance and dignity is the main concern of any ethnic minority. The Japanese, themselves sensitive to appreciation or depreciation from outsiders, generally have been deprecatory and derogatory toward Koreans. They cannot accept different Korean customs; they cannot even accept Korean eating habits. The poverty to which Koreans have been historically subjected is used to classify them as inherently uncouth and uncivilized.

The Japanese cannot accept some aspects of the freer interpersonal expressions, both positive and aggressive, that Koreans manifest. Freer, less restrained behavior goes against the greater degree of self-constraint exercised by Japanese generally.[20] More rigid forms of self-constraint have been particularly apparent in Japanese society from the time of the annexation of Korea through the prewar militaristic period, and it has been maintained by many into the postwar era. It is difficult for any majority group to accord equal value to the behavioral patterns of others who may stimulate tension in themselves. Only a very open, self-possessed individual who arrives at his or her own behavior out of choice rather than out of severely internalized constraints can accept others who behave differently than they do.

As we shall presently discuss, the Japanese have great difficulty feeling comfortable in cultural settings other than their own. This discomfort is not limited to those with Koreans alone but includes contacts with other peoples throughout eastern and southeastern Asia. The Japanese have been quick to disparage and derogate what is different from their own expectations. Their sense of uniqueness, their susceptibility to criticism, and their need for approval are the opposite sides of their readiness to disparage and disapprove of others. In short, Koreans have been vulnerable to scapegoating because their behavior is not thoroughly Japanese.

Their anomalous status within Japanese society continues. The deviant behavior of some is used by many Japanese as supportive evidence to maintain a massive deprecatory attitude toward all. One need not belabor the point that Koreans are deprecated not because they eat garlic or have a higher delinquency and crime rate, but because they are vulnerable objects for psychological projection and displacement. This brings up again the crucial problem that some members of a disparaged ethnic minority may be subject to self-hatred and self-disparagement (De Vos and Wagatsuma 1966). Lee and I garnered poignant evidence, similar to that given us by the Burakumin, from Koreans in several urban settlements (1981). No theoretical statements can better express these processes at work than the actual writings and comments Wagatsuma and I gathered from those who must deal with their own damaged self-esteem (1966).

Because of their Confucian traditions, Koreans and Japanese continue to revere their family lineages. A particular point at issue is that Japanese expect equally Confucian Koreans to give up their family names in order to gain better social acceptance in Japan. This expectation implies that being of Korean ancestry has less value than being of a Japanese family lineage. To change one's name is, to some degree, to accept this implication. There is, at present, no consensus among Korean parents in Japan as to whether a child should use his or her Korean name in public.

Intermarriage occurs in any multiethnic state, raising questions of identity for the children of parents of different ethnic backgrounds. In a racist society where certain ethnic groups are considered inferior, marriages between members of dominant and the inferior groups are deemed contaminated, and the children of such liaisons are identified with their less acceptable minority heritage (De Vos 1967).

In situations of conflict, children faced with the need to choose between parental heritages will sometimes opt for the minority identity, seeking to protect the heritage of the demeaned parent out of a sense of honor and personal integrity. But in situations imputing nothing pejorative to either ancestry, a child will happily identify with a more complex heritage. When the school teaches the cultural history and language of both, the child acknowledges both ancestral backgrounds without conflict over the expediency of the integrity of being one or the other.

A relatively democratic Japanese state cannot long sustain the illusion of separate origin. Scientific archaeological inquiry in Japan is presently not being repressed. New findings increasingly reveal how their cultural heritage has been interwoven with that of Korea. Prehistorically, there is good evidence to suggest that the mythological imperial lineage might have been from the Korean peninsula. Later in the sixth century, it was Sinicized refugees from elite Paekche families, with their artisans and priests, not Chinese, who brought literacy, medicine, and architecture as well as the Buddhist and Confucian religious heritages to Japan. This elite intermarried with the local Japanese rulers. The later invasion of Korea by Japan in the sixteenth century brought in new neo-Confucian learning and ceramic traditions. The latter are still the pride of Japan, but current historians in Japan recognize their Korean origins.

Education, Legislation, and Ethnic Maintenance

By and large, Korean children growing up in Japan, even those being sent to special Korean schools, are becoming culturally, if not socially, Japanese.[21] Korean language schools in Japan are steadily declining, despite the interest in ethnic education on the part of some Japanese as well as many ethnically Korean educators who want to bring about a more open cultural pluralism in Japanese society. Koreans in Japan are culturally Japanese.

However, *social* assimilation, without a denial or a problematic sense about one's ethnic background, can only take place when there is genuine respect accorded by the majority toward those of a different background. The present legally anomalous status of remaining "Korean" in Japan makes any assuagement of social disparagement a particularily difficult task (De Vos and Kim 1993). Some ameliorative measures are being attempted. In Osaka, for example, which contains a large Korean population, there is a public school program of after-school classes in Korean cultural traditions. A program of this sort stimulates some self-consciousness about being *ethnically* Korean, but, does not keep the children *culturally* Korean.

As is apparent in Japan as well as in the United States it is often the peer group rather than the family that carries on a contrastive, defensive ethnic identity (De Vos 1992). Especially for the socially disparaged minority child, if home influence is relatively tenuous due to a lack of intrafamilial closeness, it is the peer group rather than a formal school program that has the strongest influence on how ethnic separateness is maintained. Some form of contrastive peer group ethnic maintenance occurs regardless of any complete loss of separate language and other cultural content supposedly integral to that identity. In fact, a separate idiom or intonation pattern may develop rather than any genuine language difference.

Thus, to the degree the peer group becomes the predominant reference group (De Vos and Wagatsuma 1966:25ff.; De Vos 1978), a social identity is produced more through peer group interaction both in and out of school than through effects of programs instituted by officials or by families. Given these limitations of school influence on the social attitudes of students, I contend that it is the more important role of the school to see to the education of the majority in regard to ethnic diversity. There is a yet-to-be-completed task of the demythologizing of Japanese youth about their own supposed racial uniqueness.

If the past American experience of Japanese-Americans teaches us anything it is that family patterns and food habits may persist, but language and other specific features of a separate culture cannot be maintained in an enveloping dynamic society. The immigrant Japanese made notable efforts to preserve their separate cultural heritage in the United States. Some children, the so-called Kibei, were sent back to Japan. Special language and culture schools were set up. The nisei children who were sent to these schools, by and large, refused to learn Japanese. They identified themselves as Americans culturally, but continued to associate with one another socially as Japanese-Americans. The peer group had decided. For most, there remains some prideful identity with the Japanese past, but most live in the American present. The Japanese family survived despite prejudice and rejection by a racist majority.

Although the Japanese schools have instituted instructional programs to gain social acceptance for Korean students within their public schools, the problems inherent in defensively maintaining a minority identity cannot be so easily resolved by well-intentioned efforts on the part of some Japanese educators. For some Korean students, emphasis on immediate, practical, instrumental adaptation may sacrifice pride, the validity of being Korean, and one's sense of self-worth. Conversely, a too rigid insistence that being Korean resides in objective criteria, such as language proficiency or dress, may be impractical for Koreans who plan to continue to live in Japan. Furthermore, it represents acceptance of the adversary view of those Japanese who equate Japanese ethnicity with Japanese citizenship.

If Korean identity in Japan can be maintained only through attending a Korean language school, which handicaps the individual in the formal Japanese school system, then the individual becomes subject to continuous conflict, both external and internal. Conversely, if the Japanese school system derogates the assumption that it is legitimate and dignified to be Korean in ancestry, then the child perhaps has no alternative but to resist education at a cost to his or her sense of personal worth. The fact is that most children of Korean ancestry growing up in Japan will not speak Korean as their native tongue. They will speak Japanese.

Both Japan and the United States have a dynamic nature that absorbs youth, sometimes in ways not appreciated by older generations. To me one fact is obvious;

both Japanese and Koreans have to come to terms with the fact that most Korean residents will remain in Japan. They cannot remain as a marginal group without proper citizenship in a Japanese state that both legally and socially continues to confuse nationalism with ethnicity. Although most Koreans are physically indistinguishable from Japanese, they nevertheless continue to be considered racially distinct by Japanese. Whether they avow it openly, many Japanese still consider Koreans their biological inferiors.

Ethnic Identity and Continuing Difficulties in External Relationships

As a final consideration of Japanese ethnicity, I wish to point out that there are features of Japan's cultural heritage that cause them continuing difficulty in establishing emotional bonding with outside others in reaching common goals. Japanese internally can develop their unique forms of economic and social organizational abilities. At the same time, a sense of belonging as Japanese inhibits or prevents any greater contribution to international social, economic, and political organizations.

But the future is always partially present in the past. Cultural beliefs in their own uniqueness persist despite conscious attempts of a people to alter its own institutions. This is true for all societies, Japan is no exception. There are features of Japanese cultural psychology and social organization that are maintained despite the modernized institutions that give them new content and new challenges for adaptation. Japanese continue to be socialized toward behavioral conformity both in the intimate confines of the family and in the no less intimate groups that characterize schools and business concerns. Many of these learned patterns of group thought, emotional expression, and social perception are highly adaptive to situations of change in Japan. At the same time, in many these patterns are sources of personal tension and of difficulty in external relations. The Japanese sense of social belonging, especially in an international context, remains exclusionary.

Japan's industrial community is based on forms of hierarchy. Age-progressive social organizations demand a great deal of personal closeness in mentorship. These patterns have been well described elsewhere by James Abegglen (1958) Ronald Dore (1967), Masao Maruyama (1963), Chie Nakane (1970), Ezra Vogel (1975), and others. There are obvious competitive advantages to the resultant high per capita productivity and relatively high morale of Japanese commercial and industrial workers. The cultural heritage of a strong work ethic is far removed from the problems of animosity and low morale found in Great Britain, for example.

Japanese social organizations are often very close and intimate, depending heavily on informal implicit patterns. Contractual, impersonal understandings do not carry the same set of expectancies. In dealing with one another, Japanese organizations also depend heavily on personal obligations. In dealing with outsiders Japanese feel less at ease with the formal contractual structures and impersonal attitudes developed in Western settings, both internally in dealings between labor and management and externally in dealing with one another. Individual outsiders coming into a Japanese setting, whatever their special talents may be, or however much they are needed for the benefit of the organization, find it difficult to overcome this sense of remaining alien beings.[22]

As discussed above, there is still the social dilemma of Japan-born Koreans who technically remain foreigners although for four generations they have been born in Japan, go to Japanese schools, and know no language other than Japanese. They cannot easily belong to a society that discriminates against them legally and in the more subtle forms of discrimination they face day by day. In common with many discriminated groups in other countries, many become bitter and antisocial in conduct, a social liability, not only because they lack productive potential, but because social inequality experiences from early youth breeds bitterness and malaise.

In a curious way, one might say Japan needs more expatriates—independent intellectuals and scholars who can make it more necessary for the European intellectual community to study contemporary Japanese art, technology, and social thought and to take into account the considerable Japanese contribution to the arts and sciences of the twentieth century. Realistically, the Japanese have to take on the task of conversing in other languages in international communication, but if the Japanese government were so inclined, it could provide the monetary means of enticing more Europeans to Japan to take on the task of learning Japanese and learning about Japanese culture and society first-hand. Japanese living abroad permanently can form social liaisons. They can be a means of opening up and broadening channels of communication. Here, one sees the dilemma of Japanese ethnicity.

Few Japanese feel they can remain comfortably Japanese when they are not surrounded and immersed within their own society. Cultural marginality is discomforting. Japanese, by cultural tradition, find a cosmopolitan career difficult and uncomfortable. There is often a vague sense of disloyalty and loss of responsibility if one lives abroad for too long.

One does note in the younger generation under thirty in Europe, the United States, and Japan a communality of outlook and experience that brings them more easily together. For Japanese students, though, internationalism may come at the expense of a loss of interest in the contribution of Japanese cultural traditions that take considerable discipline to continue with any sense of high standards. Be that as it may—the price of communication, ironically, may be at times at the expense of having something unique to communicate. It is not at the student level that difficulties in communication is most noticeable, but on the part of those already established. Today's students, however, are tomorrow's leaders.

It is difficult for any successful assertive nation to develop a cultural perspective that accepts and embraces its own heritage without depreciating others in so doing. It is the first lesson, nevertheless, for those making international contacts. A lesson, alas, no better learned by many Americans than by many Japanese.

NOTES

1. Space limitations do not allow more than a summary of the late Hiroshi Wagastuma's original contentions from the previous edition about the cultural and physical identity of Japanese vis-à-vis Caucasoid Westerners. Here we are focusing on the continuing reluctance of the Japanese to deal with minority status problems. The unresolved issue to be examined is a continuing Japanese confusion of citizenship and ethnicity (De Vos and Mizushima 1967). This is unresolved to some degree in most modern states. When the word "I" is used in this chapter, it refers to De Vos.

2. At the turn of the century Spencer was perhaps the sociologist best known internationally. Strongly influenced by Darwin, he advocated an evolutionary approach to human society.

3. See Schwartz's discussion in Chapter 2 with respect to revivalist religious reactions.

4. In 1918 Japan sent its army to Siberia, in 1921 the liberal premier Hara was attacked by an assassin, in 1923 members of the Japanese Communist party were arrested in great numbers, in 1925 the notorious Law for Maintenance of the Public Peace (*chian iji ho*) was enacted, in 1928 the Special Secret Police (*tokubetsu koto keisatsiu*) was instituted, in 1931 Japan sent its army to Manchuria, and in 1933 it seceded from the League of Nations.

5. Such charateristics as cited by Fukasaku have become anachronistic. By the 1990s less than 7 percent of the Japanese were engaged in agriculture, and, despite bitter opposition and desperate subidies, a good percentage of rice is now imported, as are other agricultural products.

6. See the discussion of passing in Chapter 1.

7. Excerpts were taken principally from De Vos and Wagatsuma 1966, Chapter 9, pp. 373-405. Other materials were taken from Chapters 11, 13, 16, and 17.

8. I shall draw on the concept of ethnic identity and other related concepts defined in some detail in De Vos and Suárez-Orozco 1990, Chapter 1.

9. These indicies are discussed in detail in Wagatsuma and De Vos 1984, Chapter 10.

10. In this respect the class distinctions operative in urban African-American communities have parallels in the urban Buraku.

11. People too readily assume that the problems caused by social discrimination can be soon resolved if the majority society changes its attitudes and becomes more accepting of the discriminated individual. This overlooks the fact that there are often strong inducements in the socialization pattern of discriminated individuals that makes the maintenance of their minority status important to them in their psychological integration, regardless of amelioration of outside attitudes toward them. Some of the reputation of the Burakumin for being

aggressive seems to have a basis in fact. There is a relationship between aggressive behavior, out-group enmity, and patterns of socialization in the Buraku. Hatred of the outer society and hostility toward the majority society become part of the individual's total personality structure; they are not simply immediate angry reactions to prejudice and discrimination.

12. See a much fuller discussion of this material in De Vos and Wagatsuma 1966, passim.

13. The subsequent work of Ogbu (1974, 1978, especially 1978) has reaffirmed these contentions. See also De Vos (1992, Chapter 7).

14. See an extensive discussion of the history of Japanese organized crime in De Vos and Mizushima 1967, pp. 289-325.

15. Some police we interviewed claimed that close to 70 percent of the underworld is of Buraku or Korean origin.

16. See especially Chapter 17 in De Vos and Wagatsuma 1966 and Chapter 5 in De Vos and Suárez-Orozco 1990.

17. These issues are discussed at length in Chapters 4 and 5 of De Vos and Suárez-Orozco 1990.

18. See the detailed discussion of this in De Vos and Suárez-Orozco 1990, Chapter 5.

19. I discuss the particular culturally prevalent concerns of Japanese with purity and pollution in De Vos and Wagatsuma 1966, Chapter 17. See also my more general discussion of pollution in respect to caste and race (De Vos 1967).

20. In an analagous manner, as indicated above, Japanese-Brazilians are considered too loose in their comportment to be socially acceptable. They make ordinary Japanese uncomfortable (Takeyuki Tsuda, personal communication).

21. Specialists in ethnic relations (e. g., Gordon 1978) recognize this difference between cultural and social assimilation of ethnic minorities.

22. Japanese academic organizations find it difficult to meet the challenges of intellectual leadership. They remain internally oriented toward group inclusion rather than being competitively oriented as are American universities. Europe as a whole is slowly struggling toward greater exchange and mobility in its universities. There is, in effect, however, more worker mobility and business mobility than the movement on intellectuals between nations. European universities are only beginning to realize the potential development of a true exchange of intellectuals by faculty appointments across national boundaries.

REFERENCES

Abegglen, J. G. 1958. *The Japanese Factory: Aspects of Its Social Organization*. Glencoe IL: Free Press.

Cayton, Horace, and Sinclaire Drake. 1962. *Black Metropolis*. New York: Harper and Row.

Cornell, John. 1956. "Matsunagi—A Japanese Mountain Community." *Occasional Papers*, No. 5. University of Michigan: Center for Japanese Studies.

De Vos, George A. 1967. "Psychology of Purity and Pollution as Related to Social Self-Identity and Caste." In *Caste and Race: Comparative Approaches*. A. V. S. de Reuck and

Julie Knight, eds. Pp. 292-315. Ciba Foundation Symposium. London: J. and A. Churchhill.

De Vos, George A. 1978. "Selective Permeability and Reference Groups Sanctioning: Psychocultural Continuities in Role Degradation." In *Major Social Issues—A Multi-Community View*. Milton Yinger, ed. Pp. 9-24. New York: Free Press.

De Vos, George A. 1986. "Japanese Citizenship and Korean Ethnic Identity: Can They Be Reconciled? A Psychocultural Dilemma." *Seoul Law Journal* 27(1):75-100.

De Vos, George A. 1992. *Social Cohesion and Alienation: Minorities in the United States and Japan*. Boulder, CO: Westview Press.

De Vos, George A. 1993a. "A Cross Cultural Perspective: The Japanese Family as a Unit in Moral Socialization." In *Family, Self, and Society: Towards a New Agenda for Family Research*. P. Cowan, J. Field, D. Hansen, M. Scolnick, G. Swanson, eds. Pp. 115-142. Hillsdale NJ: Erlbaum Associates.

De Vos, George A. 1993b. "Problems with Achievement, Alienation, and Authority in Korean Minorities in The United States and Japan." In *Studies of Koreans Abroad*. K. K. Lee, ed. Pp. 137-194. Seoul: Society for the Study of Overseas Koreans.

De Vos, George A. and Eun-Young Kim. 1993. "Koreans in Japan: Problems with Achievement, Alienation Authority." In *California Immigrants in World Perspective*. Ivan Light and Parminder Bhachu, eds. Pp. 145-180. New Brunswick, NJ: Transaction Books.

De Vos, George A., and Keiichi Mizushima. 1967. "Organization and Social Function of Japanese Gangs." In *Aspects of Social Change in Modern Japan*. R. P. Dore, ed. Pp. 289-325. Princeton University Press.

De Vos, George A., and Marcelo Suárez-Orozco. 1990. *Status Inequality: The Self in Culture*. Newberry Park, CA: Sage Publications.

De Vos, George A., and Hiroshi Wagatsuma. 1966. *Japan's Invisible Race*. Berkeley: University of California Press.

De Vos, George A., and William O. Wetherall. 1983. "Japan's Minorities: Burakumin, Koreans, Ainus and Okinawans," updated by Kate Stearman. *Minority Rights Group*, Report No. 3. London: Minority Rights Group.

Dollard, John. 1957. *Caste and Class in a Southern Town*. New York: Doubleday.

Dore, R. P. ed. 1967. *Aspects of Social Change in Modern Japan*. Princeton: Princeton University Press.

Erikson, Erik. 1959. "Identity and the Life Cycle: Selected Papers." *Psychological Issues* 1:1-171.

Fukasaku, Mitsusada. 1972. *Nippon Bunka oyobi Nipponjin Ron* (A Study in Japanese Culture and People). Tokyo and Kyoto: San'itsu Shobo.

Gordon, M. 1978. *Human Nature, Class and Ethnicity*. New York: Oxford University Press.

Jansen, Marius. 1965. "Changing Japanese Attitudes toward Modernization." In *Changing Japanese Attitudes toward Modernization*. Marius Jansen, ed. Pp. 43-89. Princeton: Princeton University Press.

Kato, Shuichi. 1965. "Japanese Writers and Modernization." In *Changing Japanese Attitudes toward Modernization*. Marius Jansen, ed. Pp. 245-445. Princeton: Princeton University Press.

Kawashima, Takeyoshi. 1948. *Nihon Shakai no hazoku-teki Kosei* (The Familial Structure of Japanese Society). Tokyo: Yuhikaku.

Kosaka, Masaaki et al. 1938. "Meiji Bunka Shi" (Meiji Cultural History). In *Shiso Genron Hen* (A Volume on Thoughts and Speech). Tokyo: Yuzankaku.

Kosaka, Masataka. 1968. *Sekai Chizu no Naka de Kangaeru* (Thinking in the World Map). Tokyo: Shincho Sha.

Koyama, Takashi. 1953. "Buraku ni okeru shakai kincho no seikaku" (The Nature of Social Tension in Outcaste Communities). *Shakaiteki Kincho no Kenkyu* (Studies on Social Tensions). Pp. 395-410. Nihon Jinbun Kagakkai, Tokyo: Yuhikaku.

Kuwabara, Takeo. 1963. *Nippon Bunka no Kangae Kata* (The Way to Think about the Japanese Culture). Tokyo: Hakusui Sha.

Lee, Changsoo, and George A. De Vos. 1981. *Koreans in Japan: Ethnic Conflict and Accommodation*. Berkeley: University of California Press.

Maruyama, Masao. 1963. *Gendai Seiji no Shiso to Kodo* (Thoughts and Behavior in Contemporary Politics). Tokyo: Hakusuisha.

Minami, Hiroshi. 1949. *Nippon no Shinri* (Psychology of the Japanese). Tokyo: Iwanami Shoten.

Miyagi, Otoya. 1950. *Kindaiteki Ningen* (Man of the Modern Age). Tokyo: Kaneko Shobo.

Miyagi, Otoya. 1956. *Atarashii Kankaku* (New Tastes). Tokyo: Kawade Shobo.

Nagai, Michio. 1965. *Nihon no Daigaku Sangyo Shakai ni Hatasu Yakuwari* (Japanese Universities—Their Roles in an Industrial Society). Tokyo: Chuo Koron Sha.

Nakane, Chie. 1970. *Japanese Society*. London: Weidenfeld and Nicolson.

Ogbu, John. 1974. *The Next Generation*. New York: Academic Press.

Ogbu, John. 1978. *Minority Education and Caste: The American System in Cross-Cultural Perspective*. New York: Academic Press.

Passin, Herbert. 1962. "The Source of Protest in Japan." *The American Political Science Review* 54(2):91-403.

Pyle, Kenneth. 1969. *The New Generation in Meiji Japan—Problems of Cultural Identity 1885-1889*. Stanford: Stanford University Press.

Rosenthal, A. M. "New Japan—Future Beckons to Timorous Giant in Search of an Identity." *New York Times*, Western edition, June.

Sabata, Toyoyuki. 1971. *Sekai no Naka no Nippon—Kokusaika Jidai no Kadai* (Japan in the World—Her Task in the Era of Internationalization). Tokyo: Kenkyusha.

Takagi, Masataka. 1955. *Nihonjin—Sono Seikatsu to Bunka no Shinri* (The Japanese Psychology of Their Life and Culture). Tokyo: Kawade Shobo.

Takahashi, Yoshio. 1883. *Nippon Jinshu Kaizyo Ron* (Proposal for Physical Improvement of the Japanese Race). Quoted in Ishii Ryoichi, *Population Pressure and Economic Life in Japan*, Chicago: University of Chicago Press, 1937.

Tokutomi, Soho. 1885; repr. 1931. "Shin Nihon no Seinen" (Youth of New Japan). *Gendai Nippon Bungaku Zenshu* (Contemporary Japanese Literature), Vol. 5. Tokyo: Kaizosha.

Tsuda, Takeyuki, personal communication.

Umezao, Tadao. 1959. "Bunmei no Seitai Shi Kan Josetsu" (An Introduction to the Ecological History of Civilizations). *Chuo Koron* (Tokyo, monthly journal), February.

Vogel, Ezra, ed. 1975. *Modern Japanese Organization and Decision Making*. Berkeley: University of California Press.

Wagatsuma, Hiroshi. 1967. "The Social Perception of Skin Color in Japan." *Daedalus* Spring:407-443.

Wagatsuma, Hiroshi. 1969. "Recent Trends in Social Psychology in Japan." *American Behavioral Scientists* 12(3):36-45.

Wagatsuma, Hiroshi. 1972. "Mixed-Blood Children in Japan: An Exploratory Study." Paper prepared for the Conference on Ethnic Relations in Asian Countries, State University of New York, Buffalo, NY, October 20-21.

Wagatsuma, Hiroshi, and George A. De Vos. 1967. "The Outcaste Tradition in Modern Japan: A Problem in Social Self-Identity." In *Aspects of Social Change in Modern Japan*. R. P. Dore, ed. Pp. 373-407. Princeton: Princeton University Press.

Wagatsuma, Hiroshi, and George A. De Vos. 1984. *Heritage of Endurance: Family Patterns and Delinquency Formation in Urban Japan*. Berkeley: University of California Press.

Warner, W. Lloyd et al. 1963. *Yankee City*. Chicago: University of Chicago Press.

Yazaki, Genkuro. 1964. *Nihon no Gairai Go* (Words of Foreign Origin in the Japanese Language). Tokyo: Iwanami Shoten.

Chapter Thirteen

Ethnicity and Anthropology in America

Anthropology has depended—whenever it was a field science and not an armchair version of social philosophy—on human beings, as members of their own cultures, to serve as instruments for assessing and understanding other cultures. Inevitably, therefore, the forms of cultural or social anthropology developed in different countries each carry the stamp of cultural particularity. Since comparison is the basic method of anthropological work, I shall discuss here some of the parallels between American cultural attitudes towards ethnicity and American cultural anthropological practice.

Our early attitudes towards the American Indian, the African brought here as a slave and the European immigrant who spoke different languages or adhered to different religions have all been reflected in anthropological practice and theory. Whether he was Morgan meditating on the kinship behavior of his neighbors the Iroquois, or Franz Boas fresh from the university world of nineteenth-century

Germany, the anthropologist brought to his work the emotional and intellectual marks of his own place in the American ethnic mosaic and the perceptions shaped by that place.

Robert Lowie, born an Austrian, whose parents were products of the scholarly and humane traditions of Vienna, called on me the last time he was in New York. There was a formal air of farewell to that visit. I spoke of my intention to try to persuade him to go to Israel, where his combination of talents and experience would make him a strong advocate of fieldwork and a formidable opponent of scholasticism. But the Sinai war had set in, and he said he had too little time left. As we parted he referred to Israel as "a last outpost of European civilization"; then he paused and added, "not that the Arabs aren't a very fine people!" Again a pause, and a confidential smile of recognition of the profession to which we had both given our lives, saying, "But you know that Sinai campaign did remind me of a Crow War party."

So in outlining the growth of American attitudes toward ethnicity, we can develop in parallel the expression of American perceptions of the people who were found here, the people who were brought here against their will, the people who chose to come—and the part of the science of anthropology that American anthropologists forged. I shall treat American consciousness and American anthropology together, without distinguishing in detail one from the other. For while the discipline of anthropology is international, this stamp of our own character forged out of our own experiences remains to further shape the cognitive emphases of Durkheim, Levy-Bruhl, and Lévi-Strauss, the narrowly defined emphasis on social behavior of contemporary British anthropology, Malinowski's search for cultural integration (as dreamt of by Poles), and [the] universality of a Ratzel and a Graebner.

Stocking has documented the necessity for anthropology to accept the psychic unity of humankind. He shows how Tyler, for example, had not yet arrived at the comprehensive idea of "cultures" rather than "culture," a concept vital to modern anthropology. Cultural pluralism and expressions of the validity of different cultures have flourished, been repudiated, reaccepted and redefined in the American scene. When the early settlers from Europe reached American shores, they had two urgent problems to deal with: the definition of themselves, branded at home as foolhardy adventurers, renegade family members or treasonable subjects of majesties, poorly equipped and unlikely to succeed in their new venture; and the early demand that they succeed despite every hardship and setback, and show the doubters at home that they had done so. Thus they laid the groundwork for those persistent characteristics of Americans, the exhibitionistic display of victories by the young, the weak, and the small before the eyes of their elders and betters. The need to succeed at any cost, the need to elevate not only each act but each person above the actuality, is well portrayed in the descriptions of the land speculators described in

Martin Chuzzlewit, and in Dickens's contemptuous description of the Americans who spoke of "that lady across the way that takes in washing."

The vicissitudes of the early colonists in the north and south of the United States also paved the way for the various styles of treatment of the Indians. The early explorers in the south painted the portraits of the Southeast Indians as royalty and nobles, placing upon their impressive physiognomy the mark of European aristocracy and dressing them in the clothing of the courts. Faced with a need to come to terms with those who possessed the land and knew how to live on it, the settlers elevated them to petty princes before whom it was no shame to ask for help or to admit failure, in the disease-ridden, inexpertly managed colonies of the Southeast.

The colonies of the Northeast faced the problems of cold and hunger rather than malaria, but they too admitted dependence upon the Indian to supplement their slender supplies and lack of the necessary skills. The Dutch in New Amsterdam, on the other hand, found it easy to wrest huge tracts of lands from Indians in return for small payments, because the Indians lacked an understanding of how land could be alienated. It was not long before Indian camps were burned and housewives kicked the heads of hapless Indians down the streets of New Amsterdam.

Slowly there emerged that curious image, which has lasted throughout our history, of the Indian as the noble savage with barbaric customs, speaking languages so strange that they became appropriate religious jargon for spiritualists; a people brave, proud, treacherous and cruel; impressive figures on their own lands and in their birchbark canoes—magnificent to contemplate but very inconvenient neighbors. From the Indian who took offense at the white man's ways, to the Indian who drives a broken-down Ford on the highway, dangerously drunk and disorderly on the white man's liquor, or who becomes a charge of public welfare, the double image has held and been periodically incorporated in our relationships to Europe and in European understandings of America.

Jefferson, angrily defending himself and all his kin against the denigrations of Buffon, had to include the American Indian among all those living creatures who grew taller and better on American soil. The Karl May stories for German readers, the young Czechs' symbolism after World War II, the Russian Communist image of the American Indian as the victim of capitalism, the heroic Indians of children's stories, the Indian as a fit symbol on a coin and as a proper distant ancestor for a vice-president of the United States, the symbol of the match between equals which distinguishes American conflicts, whether cowboys and Indians or cops and robbers —in all of these the Indian has remained a symbol of our ambivalence toward technologically inferior people. No longer possessed of the true and exclusivist faith that guided the early settlers, we find the Indian emerging repeatedly as the symbol of the man of the land, the man who had held these plains as a trust—and it is in this sense that he has become a symbol of the new attitudes toward the earth's resources demanded by the present ecological crisis.

The early settlers (like all colonizing people who bring in a more developed technology and a religion with more universalistic claims) had to struggle with the contrast between the cultural style they found here and the subsequent breakdown and deterioration of that style. They watched as a proud tribal people, sure in their own traditions, were subjected to peonage, serfdom, proletarianization, exile into more and more remote reservations, or simple extinction.

Anthropologists, alert to the beauty and style of Indian culture, recognizing the intricate grammar of their unwritten languages, attentive to the precision of their technology, became the students of the Indian and the defenders of his right to remain an Indian, living as his forefathers had lived, and if possible on the same or similar territory. They developed a strong sense of the particularity of each of the Indian tribes, of their Indian informants as persons, as colleagues, in an atmosphere of collegiality which set the style of modern fieldwork. Traits which the anthropologists found distasteful for moral or aesthetic reasons were systematically treated as the result of European conquest, and the Indians were fed back the mixture of ethnographic and folk images to which they themselves had contributed.

Thus, in the 1930s the Indians of Oklahoma who were oil rich used to go to New York and buy theatrical Indian costumes for the poorer members of other tribes to wear in local rodeos. In Florida the remnants of different tribes gathered into an artificial synthesis, costumed in European materials, and set themselves up in tourist-oriented Seminole villages. Throughout our history we have vacillated between treating the Indian as people to be eliminated or to be assimilated. Those who espoused the Indians' cause, romanticists and ethnographers alike, have concentrated on them more as carriers of a unique native culture, rather than as human beings. The Indians responded by insisting that boarding schools for Indians were bad because they did not prepare them for life on the reservation, and sending Indians to the local schools was bad because they could not learn English on a par with children of European origin!

So we, Americans and ethnographers, have come to half-terms with the men originally in possession of the soil, just as the United Kingdom settlers of New Zealand romanticized the Maori on the one hand and scorned him on the other. Away on their reservations Maori were considered bearers of a poetic cosmology equaled only by the Greeks. But once in town they sank to the position of a colored proletariat, carrying all the stigmata that Europeans accord people who have lost their relationship to their previous tribal status and differ in physique from the European colonizers.

Thus the ethnologists of New Zealand played the role of glorifiers of the Maori myth as did the American ethnologists of the ancient Hawaiian Polynesian and, to a lesser extent, the American Indian. But on the other side of the coin bearing the visage of the proud, aristocratic savage was the view, shared by Australians, of natives as "varmints." The British settlers of Australia, however, often made no such distinction in their treatment of the Australian aborigine, who was considered a deteriorated kind of man, a wooly marauder to be hunted like a rabbit.

Our experience with the Indian has had many repercussions on our treatment of the whole question of ethnicity in the United States. Those who wish to attack our notion of citizenship—which was originally a matter of choice, and a privilege that could be withdrawn—made copious use of the suggestion, "If you don't like this country, go back where you came from." This was said to an Indian Christian pacifist in World War I, and repeated in the demand that the Iroquois Indians, who had elected not to become American citizens, register as aliens in World War II. When, in the early 1940s, Arthur Raper was assigned the difficult task of treating Georgia sharecroppers, white and black, within the same economic framework, he found that by also including the Indians, the earliest inhabitants of Georgia, he could maintain a balance and even publish his discussions of all these groups in the local newspaper.

Whenever the political climate of the world or of this country becomes infused with a question of "rights to land," Indian claims to great built-up cities come up to parallel the demands of European minorities (Basques, Scots, Irish, Welsh, etc.) for autonomy. The recent theatrical gesture by American Indians taking the island of Alcatraz parallels the actions of Caribbean revolutionaries in either revolting against foreign rule and freeing their land[s] or, in small bands, freeing other countries.

In the United States the demands of the increasingly self-conscious and powerful black minority are countered by requests that they think about other people also, and the Indians are sporadically included. Meanwhile, the lives of Indians on reservations, existing on miserably insufficient welfare payments, cut off from the larger world, cold, hungry, without adequate medical care, are perhaps equaled only by the misery of those Indians who have been, in their phrase, "turned loose too soon," who migrate to cities already overcrowded by other poorly educated and unskilled peoples.

Yet it is the conception of their differences, their uniqueness—the white settlers' insistence on a racial difference and the insistence of the Indians themselves, aided by anthropology, on each tribe's cultural distinctiveness—that has resulted in the Indians' present situation. On and off reservations they form a generally unhappy and unorganized minority. The right to a distinctive culture and language, to a distinctive adaptation to the environment, and the obligation of those in power somehow to preserve these rights [have] conflicted and conflict today with the egalitarian, individualistic doctrines of the Protestant founders of the United States, who stemmed from a tradition where "every he in England is as good as every other he." It is illuminating to inquire what effect it might have had on the American attitude toward other peoples and other races as they arrived here, if the approach of the early missionaries to the Indians, like the enterprises set up at Carlisle and Hampton Institutes, had prevailed. Individual American Indians were welcomed in the homes of English-speaking farmers and taught the style of life, of speech and of farming of the dominant culture in their day. The confusion between the rights of individuals to share fully in the duties, responsibilities, privileges and rewards of the dominant culture, and the demand that former suzerainty and traditional and archaic cultures be respected is now bedeviling not only the United States, but almost the entire world.

In the early days, when the first colonists, driven to succeed or at least appear to be succeeding in their first encounters with the wilderness, were shaping our attitudes towards ethnicity, the African slave presented as sharp a contrast to the American Indian as one could find. Where the Indian was on his own ground, secure in a superior knowledge of the natural environment, the African slave was far from home, separated from his fellow tribesmen, and without communication except through his slowly developing grasp of the language of his white owner. His social organization totally disrupted, he was left to build a new culture, under the most adverse conditions, from the scattered remnants of many different groups.

Early anthropological interest in the Negro centered primarily around discussions about which of his customs, his way of singing, his scraps of magic, his oratorical style, were or were not of African origin. The anthropologist and the folklorist reached back through the current generation of Negroes to reinvoke a primitive past, as the Indian buffalo-hunting ancestors had been reinvoked through the words of their reservation descendants. But where the Indians were independent equals vis-à-vis the early settlers and the anthropologist, the American Negro was simply abandoned, treated partly as any other ethnic group, partly as a group set aside not exactly by race or color, but definitely by origin.

Anthropologists shared the liberal traditions of the North and only very slowly, in the work of Powdermaker, and the group in Lloyd Warner's studies, came to understand something of the caste tradition of the old Southeast. Here were two peoples, deeply interrelated biologically, tied together by every kind of intimacy, yet preserving rigid caste distinctions, the violation of which upset the educated white man and robbed the uneducated, poverty-stricken sharecropper and mountain dweller of his single claim to distinction—his whiteness. The extent to which the color bar was a bar particularly against Negro Americans, those who shared part of the same white ancestry as their white neighbors, and not a bar against the darker or different peoples of the rest of the world was shown in the preoccupation in some Southern white circles with the fate of the Japanese in World War II, and in the fairly cordial treatment accorded old Jewish families. The desperate attempt to keep the black cousins in their place, and at the same time to emphasize kinship ties as all important, preoccupied the old South, blended as it was with the bitterness of conquest and Northern attempts to alter the caste system. Frank Tannenbaum has suggested that if there had been more immigration to the South from Europe and Asia, this obsessive preoccupation might have been broken, but recent experiences in introducing Negro Americans into parts of America where there are many different ethnic groups does not bear this out.

Mexican-Americans shared a fate about halfway between that of Negro Americans and American Indians. Their general proletarian status, the fact that they were thought of as indigenous rather than as immigrants—a fact strengthened by our annexations of the Southwest and our conquest of the country where Spanish speakers had lived so long—contributed to their treatment as natives. At the same time, their European language, associations with Latin America and the Catholic religion distinguished them from North American Indians. Refusals of service in restaurants, signs forbidding Mexicans to remain overnight in a town, smack of the kind of restrictions that were applied on sight to people identified by dress, language, physique and lower-class status. Efforts to improve the condition of Mexicans have been inextricably interwoven with questions of migrant farm labor, the farm workers' strikes of the 1960s and 1970s, the administration of welfare in the Southwest, and demands for the teaching of Spanish in the schools. Mexican-Americans may be contrasted to Puerto Ricans, who are often associated with Negroes, but who claim the status of American citizens, while Mexicans, even the Spanish speakers of the Southwest, are thought of as semi-indigenous foreigners.

In anthropological studies of the Southwest characteristic clusters appear, including Navajo, Mormons and Spanish-Americans, each distinct from the dominant culture of the United States. In contrast to attitudes towards Negro-Americans, Mexican-Americans outside the Southwest are typically looked upon as temporary residents whose homes are in Mexico, the country to which they periodically or eventually will return. Similar status has been extended to West Indian Negroes, people who come to the United States to work for money, who are accorded the restricted privileges of other low-status colored peoples, and who will be expected to return to their own islands after a period of money making in the United States. Members of each West Indian island community maintain active contact among themselves and with their home islands. If they become citizens, by birth or naturalization, they become indistinguishable in status from American Negroes.

The core definition of American identity, as white, Caucasian and blonder rather than darker, pervaded the American response to the appearance of Chinese coolies, and to Japanese immigrant families. They were treated as people apart, against which the country needed protection. The notion of the Yellow Peril as an Asian population of overwhelming proportions quickly blended with fear of their obtaining control of the land and with tales of tong warfare within their own communities. The success with which the Chinese maintained a closed community added to the sense of separation. The Chinese showed little interest in education and birth control, whereas the Japanese not only competed vigorously and successfully in school, but their birthrate in the second generation fell below that of native-born Americans.

Until World War II, the Japanese were seldom considered objects for study. Anthropology in Japan had hardly begun, and in the usual American studies of growth or intelligence the Japanese were treated as an Asian population with a different environmental history than Caucasians, and their ancient culture, complex and exotic, was taken for granted. As a class they fitted into the later pattern of European immigration, industrious and enterprising members of the peasantry who came to the United States to earn money, rather than to live here permanently. Those who did not want to settle permanently, or were believed not to want to, although not necessarily treated better, presented less of a problem to Americans, except in instances like World War II when, typically, the Japanese whom federal security agents could trust as informants were Japanese Communists whose style was familiar; all other Japanese were felt to share Oriental inscrutability. Both Japanese and Chinese were temporary problems, felt to be "other," members of other societies.

For Americans the problem consisted of those who wanted to stay here, of those who had no other home—Indians who were here when the Europeans arrived, Africans who had no other home to return to and no language except English, and the children of non-American parents who became citizens by birth. While the focal point of black-white contact was sex relations and marriage, the focal point of Japanese, Chinese, and at one time Armenian relationships was the ownership of land, particularly in California. There was a fear that such groups would remain a people, and would, as a people, become troublesome, as had some of the religious colonies like the Amish and the Mennonites. World War II, with the straight choice presented to American-born Japanese, sharpened the issue, as most of the Japanese, sure that man must have some absolute loyalty, transferred their allegiance to the United States.

Immigrants from Europe were subjected to the extreme racial ethnocentrism characteristic of the English-speaking settlers, who held Eastern and Southern European immigrants in low esteem. Such attitudes were primarily determined by the degree to which the foreigners stuck together, formed communities which ultimately exerted considerable political pressure, and became sufficiently assimilated to enter the economic structure at higher levels than the characteristic early positions of unskilled laborer, miner, and local boss and manipulator within their own ethnic group. When these groups also had a religious and communelike character, when they stood out against the ongoing culture by refusing schooling or military service, they strained the tolerance and hospitality of the core-culture Americans. To enter the mainstream of American culture it was on the whole necessary to change one's name, move away from an ethnic neighborhood and slowly adopt "protective coloration."

There were tremendous contrasts between the attitudes of the more established groups in any American community, and each group of newcomers, varying with the previous economic status of the immigrants, the sequence in which they arrived, their occupations, their religious allegiances, and the extent to which they contrasted in physique with the older groups. Frontier societies threw into prominence differential abilities to survive in the new environment, branding the newcomer a greenhorn, or a tenderfoot, but according considerable respect to the individual who adapted quickly. Thus the settler on the frontier was judged as an individual, on whether he established economic self-sufficiency and kept his fences mended. Small self-contained New England colonies maintained their early distinctions in which the most desirable locations in the new town went to those with the most economic resources, while the poor lived on the periphery of society and, later, in the deteriorating homes of former owners of high status. This became a persistent pattern in American towns and cities, a pattern which, in combination with the echoes of European residential restriction of various subordinated groups (Jews, gypsies, peasants), produced the pervasive American pattern that has culminated today in the ghettolike concentrations of the poor. Most recent rural immigrants, the black and Puerto Rican populations, live in the deteriorated centers where the prosperous once lived, while prosperity and high status is accompanied by flight to the countryside and the higher prestige of the more distant suburbs.

Even in suburbs, however, the former patterns are repeated. In the suburbs there is an effort to exclude others of different ethnic identity, which often masks attempts to exclude those of a lower-class position. Zoning to assure house lots and exclusive country club membership discourages those who differ in religion or style of living. Thus, today we have clusters of suburban communities that are predominantly Jewish, or Irish Catholic, or Italian-American in origin, comparable to the traditional ethnic quarters of cities.

The response of any particular American-born or American-acculturated person to each of the other ethnicities of Americans he knows or hears about is also very much determined by his experience in his own locality. Germans may have been experienced as the high-principled and prosperous burghers who fled Germany in 1848 to establish the orchestras and beer gardens of middle western cities; as the members of small, peculiar, specially garbed Protestant religious sects (Amish, Mennonites, Hutterites); as German Jews, patrons of music; or as isolated German immigrants who learned English quickly and resembled their English neighbors, in contrast to Southern Europeans who were darker in complexion, poorer and less skilled.

Italians may have been experienced as Southern Italians, Sicilians or Northern Italians, with their contrasting styles of behavior and complexion; as groups of peasants tilling the land in southern New Jersey; as unskilled workers on roads and tunnels, as highly skilled craftsmen who came to shape their imported marble; as individuals of high culture; as our allies in World War I; as our prisoners of war in World War II.

Black Americans may have been experienced as a single colored family descended from runaway slaves in some Pennsylvania or New York State community; as the members of another caste in the plantation South; as the other half of the life of the aristocratic white man, a life from which poor white men, whose ancestors owned no slaves, were excluded; as urban dwellers pouring into Northern cities to become factory workers in World War I; as rural migrants fleeing into cities for work or for welfare, after World War II; as a group whose arrival broke the fragile fiction that there was no race prejudice in Hawaii and sent each ethnic group, precariously proclaiming their solidarity in different styles and racial origin, back into their enclaves. Today's small children in Northern urban communities are experiencing blacks as magnificently and exotically attired, with flaring Afro-headdresses. Their parents had learned to think of bright colors as distinctive, and therefore degrading, signs of the inalienable and genetic inferiority of American Negroes or of all colored peoples, negative stereotypes, widely but never completely shared, within larger categories of persons: "immigrants," "foreigners," "refugees," "colored people," "Orientals," "Indians," "Catholics," "hillbillies," "damn Yankees," "kikes," "shouters," "the poor," "people on welfare," "grape pickers," "factory hands," "the Mafia," "goyim." Each of these categories of persons, regarded invidiously, has been shaped by particular and differing circumstances, and the membership of each changed in different historical periods and in different parts of the country. Political partisanship—the activities of the Ku Klux Klan and the selection of political candidates because of their ethnically identifiable names—reflects the spectrum of differential valuation and rejection which in the United States is loosely known as "prejudice," an attitude that places some other group in a lower position than one's own. Thus, an American who takes for granted his own old American stock may excoriate any prejudice against Jewish Americans, but take it for granted that "Irish Catholics" have certain well-known undesirable characteristics.

Where different ethnic groups with contrasting styles of life or physique live close to each other, it is almost routine for children to be socialized by such perjorative comments on undesired behavior as "behaving like those *x's*," whom the children have also seen denigrated in other ways. Jewish children are accused of having a "*goyisher kop*," Irish children told not to behave like "dagoes," English-speaking children not to act like "dumb Swedes," or the ethnic element may be masked in admonitions not to be "common" or "behave like people in the slums."

The frequent use of such terms in the privacy of the middle class home, or in the open street fights of the new slum, form a basis for embarrassment when it is necessary to refer to the groups who have been denigrated in public or in their presence. Then transformations into the "great Polish people" from "Polacks," become the stock in trade of politicians, while individuals struggle for the contemporary acceptable phrase and may end up saying "colored," "Negro," "black," or

"Afro-American," with the same kind of fumbling hope of being understood as the English speaker who, in traveling around the world, says, "turn on the spigot, faucet . . . er. . . tap." The contrast between public deference become expedient, either morally or politically, and private denigration, is a pervasive element in the experience of children who find their elders hypocritical. Significantly, during World War II, when members of every kind of group were packed together in trains, ethnic jokes disappeared and reappeared as "moron" jokes, while in the 1960s a type of joke originally called "Polish jokes" spread from locality to locality with different ethnic negative heroes, even appearing as "Arab jokes" in New York City.

In wartime these differences are sharply accentuated, as the country of origin of a particular ethnic group becomes either ally or enemy, often necessitating a sharp reversal of previously expressed attitudes. Thus, before World War I gramaphone records were made with the *Marseillaise* on one side, and *Die Wacht am Rhein* on the other, and children learned during the war that the record couldn't be broken because France was our ally, whose aid to us in the American Revolutionary War we were now reciprocating. After the war, when Germany was again becoming a valued friend and the French were being returned to the lesser popularity engendered among our troops abroad, the record again could not be broken because it contained *Die Wacht am Rhein*. Such shifting attitudes, compounded of distant political allegiance and foreign experience, curiously reinforced attitudes toward German neighbors ("German measles" were called "Liberty measles" in World War I), contributing to the sense of superficiality and shifting prejudices which are as much a part of American interethnic attitudes as are the much deeper, extra-American prejudices of whites, black and Asians against each other.

The dilemma of most Americans has been that they experience, especially as children, a great number of these shifts. The dilemma of the black Americans is that they do not—in spite of the extreme contrasts between the caste attitudes of the South, which approve physical and emotional closeness as long as social distance is maintained, and those of the North which will concede some political and economic equality as long as spatial distance is maintained. Their experience remains the same, independent of economic class, personal success, or the behavior of their "country" of origin. True, the rise of the new African states has begun to necessitate a certain amount of diplomatic courtesy, just as the rise of black voting power has necessitated some degree of political courtesy to black political leaders. However, the Negro-Americans of yesterday and the black Americans of today are seldom treated as if their skin color or, if the skin color is nondefinitive, their alleged possession of African ancestry were not of indelible significance. When we encounter a university professor who is Japanese in racial origin but completely "Americanized," this is a matter of mere curiosity. It carries with it, in most parts of the United States, no further stigma. It is the lack of alternative roots for the American of African, Indian, Hawaiian, Mexican, and often Puerto Rican descent, that carries a different degree of desperation and forms a basis for the periodic search for a separate identity with its own claims for racial exclusiveness, a glorious past, and the right to be underwritten economically by those who have, by conquest, exploitation and imperialism, robbed one's ancestors of their rights.

In considering deep-seated American attitudes towards social relationships, including marriage, residence and admission to an occupation, it is clear it is never possible to assert equality in one field without asserting it in the others. True, Myrdal found that equality of economic opportunity was placed highest by Negroes in desirability and by whites lowest in undesirability, but the three "rights" are really inextricably joined: the right to choose one's own spouse as an individual independent of parental, legal or social interference; the right to build one's house wherever one likes in total disregard of one's neighbors and without any recognition that one's house is part of one's neighbor's "view"; and the right to be employed at any job for which one is potentially qualified.

Counterpointed to these rights is the reflection of the way in which the country was founded—partly in fact, and wholly in myth—by those who, in choosing to risk exile and hardship and a trip across the dangerous seas for lofty religious and political reasons, earned the right to form a self-selected community and keep others out. Thus, the long history of religious, ethnic and racial discrimination in the United States has been a series of battles against one-sidedness in the exercise of these rights—either each group must have the right to form segregated communities of equally high value in pride, desirability and economic level, or the right must be denied to all.

So we have the uniquely American dilemma: the ethic of cultural pluralism, of ethnic separatism, pitted against the ethic of ethnic assimilation, the doctrine of the melting pot which states that the kind of product desired from the melting process may change through time, but the goal is always production of a standard product. Changes in the standard may be seen in the fact that Americans are no longer conspicuous in Italy. American children no longer reject pictures of fathers as brunettes, as they did [twenty-five] years ago, and the image of the fashion model or the airplane hostess as a beautiful black girl is gaining ground.

Changes in stance, in clothes, in kinesics, in speech have always been the criteria of the success of the melting pot—external, most easily acquired, waiting perhaps for two or three generations for corresponding "Americanization" in attitude. Skin color and hair have been the most intractable features to blend in, but slowly permanent waves, hair straighteners, bleaching creams and ultra-violet ray machines, cosmetic surgery and hairdos borrowed from another ethnic group are making it possible to simulate physical similarities also. Nevertheless, those for whom any of these simulations are difficult, those who are conspicuously non-European in looks, those who have difficulty in speaking or writing English, those who are both poor and ethnically identified, will continue to feel that the American view of

Americanization is one-sided, that it demands higher prices from some than from others.

Rejection of this kind of unilateral Americanization—which demands change of name, if the name is foreign or hard to pronounce, change of hair and features if they are too far removed from American style, change of speech if one speaks a dialect instead of standard English, and set standards of hygiene, clothing and manners—has been called "cultural pluralism" in the past, and today is called "cultural separatism." In contemporary America separatism is symbolized by hippies, who resist Americanization by violating all of its canons. The hippies make an effort to look and act like the poor, the downtrodden, the outcast, the blacks, and the American Indian, combining dirt, bare feet, exaggerated hairdos, and Indian headbands with clothing made of dissected and disassociated bits of old uniforms and older styles, very much as newly exposed primitive people use the cast-off clothes of the civilized peoples with whom they come in contact.

Analogously, black Americans went through a long period of working very hard at acquiring the externals of membership in the American community: the men cut their hair short and the women straightened theirs, accents were modified, stance and gesture disciplined to white standards, and personal hygiene excessively insisted upon. The new move toward flamboyant difference in dress, speech and manners illustrates the other possibility. Both types of behavior point up the continuing importance of the issue: if the melting pot style is to win, the central product must be available equally to everyone, or there will be continuing inequality, resentment, and loss of dignity on the one hand, and guilt, unease and compensatory hostility on the other. If cultural pluralism is to win out, then there will be continuing demands to equalize the position of those in each segment of the mosaic, so that their part may be comparable to that of the others.

The progression from integration as a principle to black power has marked a shift from the demand, on the part of both black and white, that individual black people be admitted as pupils, physicians, lawyers, etc., into the larger society, to the demand that black people as a group and black people as residents of particular contiguous sections of large cities or rural counties be accorded recognition as a separate people which can itself confer dignity on each of its members. Integration expressed the melting pot idea: if you will make an effort to look, act, dress, speak as much like the standard white, then though not blond like the ideal American, we will act as if you were really entirely one of us. Black power expresses the rejection of this unilateral invitation, and the demand instead for equal recognition and value based on difference.

Class plays a complex role in the American sense of identity. There is no national society and no national class structure such as exists in England. High status in one city or one part of the country does not carry the same status elsewhere and although there are general nationwide criteria of class membership, there are no absolutes of income or education that can be invoked. But there is a tremendous amount of ranking within communities, and individuals whose education, wealth or achievement makes a radical amount of mobility possible usually have to leave the town or city where they have grown up and establish new ties appropriate to their newly attained status. There are also class hierarchies within each ethnic group, although the occupations followed by the different classes may vary widely from one ethnic group to another. Within many ethnic groups there are sharp breaks, as among pre-World War II Hungarian immigrants who divided themselves into gentry and peasantry; or as among Mexicans, who exhibit a high degree of cohesiveness when they are poor, but break sharply from other members of their ethnic group when they reach a certain level of affluence; or Italians who maintain family ties despite often tremendous difference in education and class level. Within the Jewish community the hierarchy that is partly derivative of Europe is complicated by the presence of "Spanish Jews" and "Syrian Jews," so that class and national origin interweave in the expression of social inclusiveness or exclusiveness.

The core class position in the United States may be said to be the lower middle class. This group is undistinguished in any way by dress or accent from the completely assimilated foreigner, whose clothes and behavior carry the suggestion that they perform no sort of manual labor and who will be treated respectfully by the police, hotel clerks, railway conductors, airline personnel and school authorities. This cherishing of a treasured inconspicuous respectability makes group members very sensitive to loss of status; they spend differentially on symbols of status, they are intensely conforming, and they are openly hostile to the invasion of their neighborhood by any of those who are conspicuously different—racially, religiously, or in dress or deportment. In many ways they resemble the lower middle class as described by Gorer for England, or by Fromm for Germany—extraordinarily clean, neat, careful, postponing satisfactions, fearful of loss of status by invasion. These similarities may be attributed to their common origins in the working class. At the same time this picture is complicated in the United States because their origins are not only working class but also very often distinctively foreign, and the attempt to mask the signs of past immigration is included in their behavior. They also include, in the United States, a large component of those who have newly made money and are attempting to buy a way for their children if not for themselves into upper-middle-class society.

The lower middle class may be said to represent the general American values to which members of the lower class may aspire and by which the upper middle class are repelled: pride based on present position, occupation, residence and respectability; absence or even repudiation of ancestral ties; and fear of loss rather than hope for mobility. They represent a kind of immobile block in the middle of the ladder of American aspirations and American beliefs in upward mobility. They are people who are too busy keeping what they have to have much energy for impractical aspirations; if high school is necessary for their children, they send them to high school, and when college becomes necessary they send them to college. They also represent the traditional ideals of hard work, jealous egalitarianism, and puritanical self-denial of the inappropriate pleasures of the dissolute and spendthrift poor and the dissolute and spendthrift rich.

The upper classes in the United States present the anomaly of lack of any secure position, and while the upper uppers—Lloyd Warner's categories—are preoccupied with a lack of definite role, the lower uppers are preoccupied with a fear of falling, somewhat analogous to the fears of the lower middle class.

The upper middle class, college educated, engaged in professional and managerial activities characterized by style of life, is perhaps the freest from class competition but is the most acutely involved in narrow rivalries within occupational and residential settings.

In most parts of the United States we have a distinctive six class system; there are no middle lowers, middle middles or middle uppers. The classes alternate in their fears; the lower lowers have no place further to fall, the upper lowers may become lower middles, the lower middles are afraid of falling; the upper middles are relatively secure, the lower uppers, mainly the descendants of wealthier people, are afraid of falling, and the upper uppers have no place to go. But all of these more general classifications are so overlaid by regional, ethnic and racial classifications that it is primarily within the narrow arena of a particular town or an industrial establishment that they come into play. As there are very few ways in which Americans of different local class orientation can associate socially, contacts tend to be very narrow.

Like members of other societies, Americans' sense of themselves as Americans is enhanced by any international context, war, travel or the presence of foreigners. But this sense of solidarity may also be fractured by internal dissension over a war, or some widespread social issue like the integration of the schools, and then the sense of being American becomes instead a sense of being Italian-American or Irish-American, and the sense of class and race and national origin all become highly confused, as in a recently described housing development inherited by working-class Jews and [black] professionals, where each found the position of the other unexpected and inexplicable.

Within the context of American history, it may be said that the sense of being an American is seldom invoked positively. It almost always accompanies confrontation with foreigners or repudiation of some other group whose behavior is regarded as un-American. Reversion to European-derived values, upper-class accents, "culture," socialism and the display of "taste" may all be regarded as un-American. In a sense this may be seen as the attempt on the part of the assimilated American to prevent any further differentiation from his recently attained status. This is perhaps why there is such a close correspondence between the idea of

Americanization, core culture, and lower middle class status. They are all states only recently attained; the difference in the paths by which individuals reach them are so vastly different that conformity and similarity of present orientation are the only ways in which such a group can be held together. Freedom to criticize the domestic and foreign policies of the nation is, for example, almost completely an upper-middle- and upper-class privilege. Whatever their status differences in national origin, social background or race, assimilated Americans all have in common this sense of precarious attainment.

American identity stands in strong contrast to that which Geoffrey Gorer has outlined for the English, where the presence of other English of their own and other classes, real or fantasied, is essential. Without the presence of those who are thought of as non-American—immigrants, foreigners, other races, the poor and disreputable, the radical and the bohemian—Americans define themselves much more narrowly as Jones or Livingstones, as people who attended a given college, belong to a particular local church, as men who served in the Marines or belong to the Oddfellows, as Democrats or Republicans. Scots and Poles are notable examples of peoples who invest many activities and character traits with positive national identity, and learn to study, or bear pain, or face adversity, as Poles or as Scots. But young Americans hear only negatively valued behavior invoked when they are told not to behave like those foreigners down the street. In the end, being American is a matter of abstention from foreign ways, foreign food, foreign ideas, foreign accents, foreign vices. So whiskey drinking becomes identified with the Irish and, by coincidence, with Catholics, beer drinking with Germans, and marijuana with black musicians and zoot suits with minority group adolescents.

Ethnicity has been a factor in the older battles against economic and political exploitation and in the newer battles against patronizing and unilateral benevolence. The slave, the mine worker, the agricultural migrant laborer has usually been characterized by ethnic difference from the master, the mine owner, the big fruit farmer. The perhaps unavoidable American emphasis on ethnicity has made possible the exploitation of disadvantaged groups by their own members who have obtained wealth and power. In such battles ethnic prejudice and unfairness have played an important role, intensifying the fight for justice and softening the hearts of those who cannot in good conscience defend their behavior.

Today there is a different kind of revolt, the revolt of those to whom "good" has been done by those who were their superiors, in age, knowledge, wealth, or expertise. So children, students, prisoners, patients and welfare clients are all rebelling against the unilaterality of institutions hitherto regarded as benevolent and dedicated by both practitioners and supporters. Similarly, ethnic groups who have been considered weaker or inferior and have experienced the same kind of benevolent, protective treatment are rebelling. It is black students, black patients, black parishioners and black welfare mothers who are most vociferous in their demands that this unilateral patronage cease and that they be given a voice in how they are to be taught, cured, rehabilitated, saved or given welfare.

The parallel in the behavior of professional anthropologists is fascinating. We have, it is true, treated our informants as colleagues, and we have refused to let them be demeaned in any way by white bureaucracy or by methods that would turn them into guinea pigs. We have clothed them in our professional identity within an atmosphere of collegiality of the highest order. (This in effect is what Talcott Parsons, in a paper on the use of human subjects in experimentation, has suggested. In a paper for the same conference, I suggested that medical experimenters might well use the anthropological field model of the trusted and respected informant.) We have, in fact, benevolently and quite sincerely offered to share our highly valued status as scientists, just as the majority members of a society—in working for integration—have offered minority individuals a share in their status.

This has been an admittedly unilateral, although benevolent, activity. And today's American Indians who are in search of a separate, economically viable ethnic identity, or today's African nationals intent on constructing workable historical views of their own pasts do not want a share in the anthropological enterprise, which values all cultures equally regardless of where they are placed in the ongoing socioeconomic political marketplace of the wider world. So Vine Deloria complains about the very kind of behavior which accorded Ella Deloria, a Dakota Indian and professional anthropologist, such high status. He does not want a share in the particular kinds of culture-respecting activities that have been the hallmark of the traditional anthropologist. This was one of the points of extreme difference in the early arguments about action anthropology as compared to applied anthropology: the applied anthropologist maintained respect for a system, while the action anthropologist became an active partisan, even to the point of ignoring the historical records in favor of present socioeconomic needs. So, within these narrower battles, parochial and limited and essentially irrelevant to the importance of the concept of culture itself, one sees the reflection of national culture and contemporary social issues.

It seems important to recognize here the work of Erik Erikson, who has contributed so much to our understanding of identity. From his early work, notably his study of the Sioux Indians' loss of historical identity as hunters and warriors, he has continuously enriched the whole concept of the way in which the growing child, the young adult and the mature person may incorporate within his psychic structure the historical and contemporary elements of the wider culture as well as his specific place within the ethnic pattern. In his study of Gandhi, Gandhi's own caste position, the position of his friend and adversary Sarabhai, the experience of Indians in South Africa, Gandhi's own ambivalence towards the British culture in which he had once sought to participate, and the position of the untouchables within India are all given weight, and Gandhi emerges as a man shaped and informed by the ethnic complexities of his time.

In his earlier study of the Yurok Indians of California, Erikson recognized the significance of a cultural character which incorporates in detail the features of the landscape and the specifics of the major economic way of life. His own cross-cultural experience included a childhood in Germany, son of a Scandinavian father he had never known; migration to the United States as a young man; adaptation first to Massachusetts and then to California, working closely with Kroeber and Mekeel among the American Indians; a return to the study of German character in his research on the young Luther and finally, in response to time spent in India, a study of Gandhi's search for truth. His life as a whole illustrates the incorporation into illuminating theory of his own cultural experience.

In comparison, Kurt Lewin, after service in the German army (an atypical experience for a German Jew), and later participation in the Weimar Republic, was exposed to the particular style of the American YMCA, designed to induce some comradeship into the isolated lives of young white men of the lower middle class. At the same time, Lewin developed great respect for American democratic styles of behavior as opposed to the laissez-faire and authoritarian styles. His study of German social behavior as manifested in America by German and Austrian exiles also emphasized this. Brunswik, Adorno and Fromm discovered strains in American character which they identified with similar reprehensible traits in German character, and their work in America became the basis for restatements about Germans. Fromm also developed in interaction with American social scientists, and emphasized those elements in American culture which, with his respect for Jewish culture, for Marx, and for socialist aspiration, seemed to him most similar to the German lower middle class he hated and which were therefore most in need of repudiation. Lewin, on the other hand, utilized the contrasts between German and American democratic styles as the basis for his innovative experiments in group dynamics. These psychologists, all reacting within the American scene on the basis of their cross-cultural and ideological backgrounds, present a counterpoint to the earlier contributions of German and Jewish scholarship and the earlier and later contributions of English anthropologists to American anthropological theory, and to American multidisciplinary studies.

Interaction between anthropologists and the American scene also produced new insights. Lévi-Strauss was in New York in the mid-1940s as a cultural attaché to the French Mission, and had an opportunity for extended discussions with American anthropologists. And British anthropologists Geoffrey Gorer and Gregory Bateson both responded to their initial contact with American culture with provocative analyses.

In the 1970s furor broke out over the community studies that American anthropologists were carrying out in Thailand. It was argued that they might be endangering the mountain people whom they were studying. This issue intensified contemporary concern over the relationship between anthropologists and the people whom they study, necessitating attention to new ethical problems. Meanwhile, the politicizing of American Indian protests, combined with the symbolic resort to American Indian cultures by radical ecologists, has raised public consciousness of the relationship between American Indians and ethnologists. Finally, the television and magazine presentations of the Tasaday have given the general public a new sense of the dangers inherent in abrupt and unmodulated culture contact. At present, the invocation of primitive peoples as symbolic of deep ethical conflicts in the world is perhaps the most conspicuous development, a development that is often distorted by today's students into a belief that ethnologists are the ones who destroyed the old cultures, when in fact they attempted to chronicle them and cushion the contact.

BIBLIOGRAPHY

Adorno, T. W. et al. 1950. *Authoritarian Personality*. New York: Harper.

Antin, Mary. 1963 (orig. 1912). *The Promised Land*. Boston: Houghton Mifflin.

Ausubel, David P. 1965. *The Fern and the Tiki*. New York: Holt, Rinehart and Winston.

Bennett, John W. 1967. *Hutterian Brethren*. Stanford: Stanford University Press.

Berndt, Ronald M., and Catherine Berndt. 1952. *The First Australians*. Sydney: Smith.

Bridges, Roy. 1950. *The League of the Lord*. Sydney-London: Australasian Publishing.

Brown, Dee. 1971. *Bury My Heart at Wounded Knee*. New York: Holt, Rinehart & Winston.

Cartwright, Dorwin, ed. 1964. *Field Theory in Social Science*. New York: Harper and Row.

Dark, Eleanor. 1950. *The Timeless Land*. London: Collins.

Davis, Allison, and John Dollard. 1964. *Children of Bondage*. New York: Harper and Row.

Davis, Allison, Burleigh B. Gardner, and Mary R. Gardner. 1963 (orig. 1941). *Deep South*. Chicago: University of Chicago Press.

Day, Beth. 1972. *Sexual Life Between Blacks & Whites*. New York: World Publishing.

Deloria, Vine, Jr. 1969. *Custer Died for Your Sins*. New York: Macmillan.

Dickens, Charles. 1923 (orig. 1884). *Martin Chuzzlewit*. New York: Dutton; Leipzig: Tauchnitz.

Dickens, Charles. 1961 (orig. 1842). *American Notes*. New York: Peter Smith; New York: Wilson.

Dollard, John. 1957 (orig. 1937). *Caste and Class in a Southern Town*. Garden City, NY: Doubleday; New Haven: Yale University Press.

Durkheim, Emile. 1926 (orig. 1915). *The Elementary Forms of the Religious Life: A Study in Religious Sociology*. New York: Macmillan; London: Allen and Unwin.

Durkheim, Emile. 1964 (orig. 1933). *The Division of Labour in Society*. New York: Free Press; London and New York: Macmillan.

Elkin, A. P. 1958. *Aborigines and Citizenship*. Sydney: Association for the Protection of Native Races.

Ella, S. 1893. "Samoa." Report of the Fourth Meeting of the Australasian Association for the Advancement of Science 4:620-645.

Erikson, Erik H. 1963, rev. ed. *Childhood Society*. New York: Norton.

Erikson, Erik H. 1958, repr. 1962. *Young Man Luther*. New York: Norton.

Erikson, Erik H. 1968. *Identity Youth and Crisis*. New York: Norton.

Erikson, Erik H. 1969. *Gandhi's Truth*. New York: Norton.

Franklin, John H., ed. 1968. *Color and Race*. Boston: Houghton Mifflin.

Frobenius, Leo. 1925-1929. *Erlebte Erdteile*, 7 vols. Frankfurt: Frankfurter Societats Druckerei.

Fromm, Erich. 1966 (orig. 1941) *Escape from Freedom*. New York: Avon; New York: Farrar and Rinehardt.

Gorer, Geoffrey. 1955. *Exploring English Character*. New York: Criterion Books.

Gorer, Geoffrey. 1964, rev. ed. *The American People*. New York Norton.

Gorer, Geoffrey. 1966. *The Danger of Equality: Selected Essays*. London: Cresset.

Graebner, F. 1911. *Methode der Ethnologie*. Heidelberg: Winter.

Graham, Edward K. In press. *History of Hampton Institute*.

Green, Gerald, producer, and Jack Reynolds, reporter. 1972. "The Cave People Of The Philippines," NBC, October.

Handlin, Oscar. 1959. *Immigration as a Factor in American History*. Englewood Cliffs, NJ: Prentice-Hall.

Handlin, Oscar. 1961 (orig. 1951). *The Uprooted*. New York: Grosset and Dunlap; Boston: Little, Brown.

Handlin, Oscar. 1966, rev. ed. *The American People in the 20th Century*. Cambridge: Harvard University Press.

Hicks, Granville. 1946. *Small Town*. Toronto: Macmillan.

Hostetler, John A. 1968, rev. ed. *Amish Society*. Baltimore: Johns Hopkins.

Jefferson, Thomas. 1960. "On the Character and Capacities of the North American Indians." In *The Golden Age of American Anthropology*. M. Mead and R. Bunzel, eds. Pp. 75-81. New York: Braziller.

Kallen, Horace M. 1956. *Cultural Pluralism and the American Ideal*. Philadelphia: University of Pennsylvania Press.

Kardiner, Abram, and L. Ovsey. 1963 (orig. 1951). *The Mark of Oppression*. New York: Peter Smith; New York Norton.

Kimball, Solon T., and Marion Pearsall. 1954. *Talladega Story*. Drawer: University of Alabama Press.

Kluckhohn, Clyde. 1952. "Universal Values and Anthropological Relativism." In *Modern Education and Human Values*, vol. 4. Arthur T. Vanderbilt et al., eds. Pittsburgh: University of Pittsburgh Press.

Kluckhohn, Florence R. et al. 1961. *Variations in Value Orientations*. Evanston: Row, Peterson.

Lantz, H. 1958. *Coaltown*. New York: Columbia University Press.

Leighton, Alexander H. 1964 (orig. 1945). *The Governing of Men*. New York: Octagon Books; Princeton: Princeton University Press.

Lévi-Strauss, Claude. 1963. *Structural Anthropology*. New York: Basic Books.

Levy-Bruhl, Lucien. 1923. *Primitive Mentality*. New York: Macmillan.

Lewis, Oscar. 1961. *The Children of Sanchez*. New York: Random House.

Lewis, Oscar, 1965 (orig. 1959). *Five Families: Mexican Case Studies in the Culture of Poverty*. New York: American Library; New York: Bask Books.

Lewis, Oscar. 1966. "The Culture of Poverty." *Scientific American* 215:19-25.

Lewis, Oscar. 1966. *La Vida*. New York: Random House.

Lewis, Oscar. 1968. *Study in Slum Culture*. New York: Random House.

Lowie, Robert H. 1954. *Indians of the Plains*. New York: McGraw-Hill.

MacLeish, Kenneth, and John L. Aunois. 1972. "Stone Age Men of the Philippines."*National Geographic* 142:219-250.

McLuhan, T. C. 1971. *Touch The Earth: A Self-Portrait of Indian Existence*. New York: Outerbridge & Lazard (Dutton).

McWilliams, Carey. 1945. *Prejudice Japanese Americans, Symbol of Racial Intolerance*. Boston: Little, Brown.

Malcolm X and A. Haley. 1967. *Autobiography of Malcolm X*. New York: Grove Press.

May, Karl. 1969 (orig. 1893). *Winnetou*, 3 vols. Englewood Cliffs, NJ: Prentice Hall; Freiburg: Fehsenfeld.

Mead, Margaret. 1927. "Group Intelligence Tests and Linguistic Disability among Italian Children." *School and Society* 25:465-468.

Mead, Margaret. 1946. "Trends in Personal Life." *New Republic* 115:346-348.

Mead, Margaret. 1951. *The School in American Culture*. Cambridge: Harvard University Press.

Mead, Margaret, 1955. "Implications of Insight—II." In *Childhood in Contemporary Cultures*. Margaret Mead and Martha Wolfenstein, eds. Pp. 449-461. Chicago: University of Chicago Press.

Mead, Margaret. 1960. "Introduction." In *The Golden Age of American Anthropology*. M. Mead and R. Bunzel, eds. New York: Braziller.

Mead, Margaret. 1965 (orig. 1942). *And Keep Your Powder Dry*. New York: Morrow.

Mead, Margaret. 1966, repr. with new intro. (orig. 1932). *The Changing Culture of an Indian Tribe*. New York: Capricorn Books; New York: Columbia University Press.

Mead, Margaret. 1967 (orig. 1949). *Male and Female*. New York: Morrow.

Mead, Margaret. 1969. "Research with Human Beings: A Model Derived from Anthropological Field Practice." *Daedalus* Spring:361-386.

Mead, Margaret. 1970. "Bio-Social Components of Political Processes." *Journal of International Affairs* 24(1):18-28.

Mead, Margaret. 1972. "Field Work In High Cultures." In *Crossing Cultural Boundaries.* Solon T. Kimball and James B. Watson, eds. Pp. 120-132. San Francisco: Chandler.

Mead, Margaret, and James Baldwin. 1971. *A Rap On Race*. Philadelphia & New York: Lippincott.

Mead, Margaret, and Muriel Brown. 1967; 1966. *The Wagon and the Star*. Chicago: Rand McNally; St. Paul: Curriculum Resources.

Mead, Margaret, and Rhoda Metraux. 1965. "Town & Gown: A General Statement." In *The Universities in Regional Affairs. Urban Research and Education in the New York Region: A Report to the Regional Plan Association*, vol. 3. Harvey S. Perloff and Henry Cohen, eds. Pp. 142. New York: Regional Plan Association.

Morgan, Lewis H. 1901. *Ho-De-No-Sau-Nee, or Iroquois*, New York: Franklin.

Muir, Margaret Rosten. 1970. "Indian Education at Hampton Institute and Federal Indian Policy: Solutions to the Indian Problem." Master's Thesis, Brown University.

Myrdal, Gunnar. 1962 (orig. 1944). *An American Dilemma*. New York: Harper.

New York Times. "Philippine Tribe Said To Live in Caves." March 27.

Parkinson, Richard H. 1907. *Dreissig Jahre in der Sudsee*. Stuttgart: Strecker and Schroder.

Parsons, Talcott. 1969. "Research with Human Subjects and the 'Professional Complex.'" *Daedalus* Spring:325-360.

Pettigrew, Thomas F. 1964. *A Profile of the Negro American*. New York: Van Nostrand.

Powdermaker, Hortense. 1968 (orig. 1939). *After Freedom*. New York: Atheneum; New York: Viking Press.

Raper, Arthur F. 1943. *Tenants of the Almighty*. New York: Macmillan.

Ratzel, Friedrich. 1896-1898. *The History of Mankind*, 8 vols. London, New York: Macmillan.

Reichard, Gladys. 1950. *Navajo Religion: A Study of Symbolism*, 2 vols. New York: Pantheon.

Ruesch, Jurgen, and Gregory Bateson. 1951. *Communication: The Social Matrix-of Psychiatry*. New York: Norton.

Smith, S. Percy. 1904, 2d ed. *Hawaiki*. London: Whitcombe and Tombs.

Soddy, Kenneth, ed. 1961. *Identity—Mental Health and Value Systems* Philadelphia: Lippincott.

Spier, Leslie. 1921. "The Sun Dance of the Plains Indians: Its Development and Diffusion." *Anthropological Papers of The American Museum of Natural History*, Vol. 16, Part 7.

Spier, Leslie. 1925. "An Analysis of Plains Indians Parfleche Decorations." *Washington University Publications in Anthropology*, 1(3).

Spier, Robert F. G. 1967. "Work Habits, Postures, and Fixtures." In *American Historical Anthropology: Essays in Honor of Leslie Spies*. C. L. Riley and W. W. Taylor, eds. Pp. 197-220. Carbondale: Southern Illinois University Press.

Spitz, R. A. 1935. "Fruhkindliches Erleben und Erwachsenenkultur bei den Primitiven." *Imago* 21:367-387.

Steward, Julian H. 1956. *The People of Puerto Rico*. Urbana: University of Illinois Press.

Stocking, George W. 1968. *Race, Culture and Evolution*. New York: Free Press.

Tannenbaum, Frank. 1963. *Slave and Citizen: The Negro in the Americas*. Toronto: Random House, 1963.

Tax, Sol. 1952. "Action Anthropology." *America Indígena* (Mexico) 12:103-109.

Thomas, Dorothy S., and Richard S. Nishimoto. 1946. *The Spoilage: Japanese American Evacuation and Resettlement*. Berkeley: University of California Press.

Valentine, Charles A. 1968. *Culture and Poverty*. Chicago: University of Chicago Press.

Vidich, Arthur J., and Joseph Bensman. 1958. *Small Town in Mass Society*. Princeton: Princeton University Press.

Warner, W. Lloyd. 1963, abridged ed. *Yankee City*. New Haven: Yale University Press.

Warner, W. Lloyd, R. J. Havighurst, and M. B. Loeb. 1944. *Who Shall Be Educated?* New York: Harper.

Warner, W. Lloyd, B. H. Junker, and Walter A. Adams. 1941. *Color and Human Nature*. Washington, DC: American Council on Education.

Warner, W. Lloyd, and J. O. Low. 1947. *The Social System of the Modern Factory*. Yankee City Series, Vol. 4. New Haven: Yale University Press.

Warner, W. Lloyd, and Paul S. Lunt. 1941. *The Social Life of a Modern Community*. Yankee City Series, Vol. 1. New Haven: Yale University Press.

Warner, W. Lloyd, and Leo Srole. 1945. *The Social Systems of American Ethnic Groups*. Yankee City Series, Vol. 3. New Haven: Yale University Press.

West, James. 1961 (orig. 1945). *Plainville, U.S.A.* New York: Columbia University Press.

Worth, Sol, and John Adair. 1972. *Through Navajo Eyes*. Bloomington: Indiana University Press.

Zborowski, Mark. 1969. *People in Pain*. San Francisco: Jossey-Bass.

CAROLA SUÁREZ-OROZCO ■
MARCELO SUÁREZ-OROZCO

Chapter Fourteen

Migration: Generational Discontinuities and the Making of Latino Identities

In virtually all advanced postindustrial societies–including Belgium, France, Germany, and the United States–immigration has become a most unsettling topic of concern (see Cornelius, Martin, and Hollifield 1994; Suárez-Orozco and Suárez-Orozco 1995). Some studies suggest that a majority of Americans now think immigration–legal and undocumented–is harmful to the country (see Suárez-Orozco and Suárez-Orozco 1995).

In the current ethos of anxiety over immigration, there have been a number of claims regarding immigration and crime and the alleged consequences of the new immigration on the economy (Suárez-Orozco and Suárez-Orozco 1995). Lost in this heated round of debate are the new arrivals themselves. Who are they? What do they want? Why are they here? How do they experience their uncertain journey north?

In this chapter we examine some defining features of Latinos, the largest group of immigrants in the United States today.[1] We explore various aspects of the Latino experience considering first- and second-generation individual, family, and group dynamics. We look at some of the most important findings in the research on Mexican immigrants, and U.S.-born Mexican- Americans, as well as some research findings among immigrants and refugees recently arriving from war-torn Central America. We also point out some relevant findings of researchers working with Cuban-Americans and mainland Puerto Ricans. And we consider how certain enduring psychocultural features in the immigrant experience are central to understanding the condition of the various Latino subgroups.

Threads in the Latino Tapestry

Latino identity is not a monolithic phenomenon. Mexican immigrants, Mexican-Americans, Cuban-Americans, mainland Puerto Ricans, and immigrants and refugees from Central and South America are distinct populations although they have unifying characteristics. They share various degrees of familiarity with the Spanish language and such cultural traits as the importance of the extended family (familism), an emphasis on spiritual and interpersonal relationships, respect for authority, and an emphasis on the here-and-now rather than on the future-time orientation valued by the dominant American culture. Yet it is important to emphasize that Latinos in the United States are diverse demographic and sociocultural populations. They come from many different countries and different socioeconomic, educational, and professional backgrounds. Cuban-Americans (one million in 1990), for example, tend to have higher educational levels than all other Latino groups and to have higher incomes as well (Portes and Bach 1985).

On average, Cubans are older than other Latinos (according to 1990 Bureau of the Census figures their median age was 39.1). They have lower unemployment rates (5.8 percent in 1990), a lower percentage of out-of-wedlock births (16.1 percent), and a lower percentage of families living in poverty (12.5 percent). More recent Cuban refugees, including the so-called *balseros* arriving into Florida during the 1994 crisis, have included persons of lower socioeconomic status and poorer education. Likewise in 1980 some 129,000 lower-status Cuban refugees, the so-called Marielitos, came to the United States en masse. On the other hand, many earlier refugees from Cuba were of upper-status professional background. They were motivated to leave Cuba for political reasons following Fidel Castro's ascent to power in 1959. Cuban-American identities have been woven, in large measure, by the condition of exile. Some have argued that their professional and refugee background have given the upper-status Cubans in the United States "a sense of specialness which may have facilitated their adaptation to new environments and may be connected to their relative success [in the United States]" (Bernal 1982:197). Also, during the cold war, refugee policy in Washington was largely dominated by anti-Communist priorities, so the new arrivals escaping Castroist Cuba were much more likely to gain official refugee status than those escaping genocidal anti-Communist regimes in Guatemala, El Salvador, and elsewhere (Suárez-Orozco 1989).

Conversely, Puerto Ricans experience the highest degree of social dysfunction of any Hispanic group and exceed that of blacks on some indicators (about 2.5 million Puerto Ricans are living on the U.S. mainland according to 1990 figures). Thirty-nine percent of all Puerto Rican families are headed by single women. They have the highest percentage of out-of-wedlock births (53.0 percent versus 23.9 percent in the non-Hispanic population) (1991). Puerto Ricans often have the lowest levels of education and the poorest economic condition of all Latino groups (Rodríguez 1991). In 1990, the median age for Puerto Ricans living in the mainland was twenty-seven. They tend to have higher unemployment rates than other Latinos (8.6 percent) and the highest percentage of families living in poverty (30.4 percent). Puerto Ricans have the highest welfare participation rate of any group in New York, where nearly half of all Puerto Ricans in the United States live (Chavez 1991:140).

A special issue facing mainland Puerto Ricans is the relationship between the United States and the island of Puerto Rico, a condition that provides American citizenship to them. Furthermore, the quasi-colonial nature of the relationship between the United States and Puerto Rico, in addition to the stresses of migration and minority status, have created some enduring problems in the mainland Puerto Rican community (Ogbu 1978). Chavez speculates that welfare dependency was in part encouraged by certain cultural continuities in marriage patterns: the rates of formal civic or religious marriage are lower among Puerto Ricans than among other Latinos. Chavez argues that the large percentage of Puerto Rican female-headed households not only encouraged welfare dependency but obviously also subverted the socioeconomic mobility characteristic of other immigrant groups (1991:139-159).

Latinos of Mexican origin (some 13.3 million "Mexican-origin" persons were counted in the 1990 census) and the immigrants and refugees from Central and South America (2.8 million persons of "South/Central American" origin were counted in 1990) tend to fall somewhere in between the Cubans and mainland Puerto Ricans in terms of educational attainment and income levels. According to the most recent data, Mexican-origin persons (the census includes under Mexican origin both U.S.-born Mexican-Americans and foreign-born Mexican immigrants) are the youngest of all Latino subgroups: their median age in 1990 was 24.1 (versus 33.5 for the non-Hispanic population). Mexican-origin Latinos have the highest unemployment rate of all subgroups (9.0 percent) and the second lowest (second to Cubans) percentage of out-of-wedlock births (28.9 percent). In 1990 reports showed that some 25.7 percent of all Mexican-origin families lived in poverty. Mexican-origin Latinos are themselves a highly heterogeneous population, which includes new arrivals from various regions of Mexico as well as the descendants of those who were in the Southwest *prior* to the U.S. takeover of these formerly Mexican territories (see Madsen 1964; Grebler et al. 1970; Wagner and Haug 1971; Stoddard 1973; Alvarez Jr. 1987; Meier and Rivera 1993).

According to 1990 census figures, Latinos of Central and South American origin had a median age of twenty-eight. Their percentage of unemployed was 6.6, and their percentage of out-of-wedlock births was 37.1. Some 16.8 percent of their families lived in poverty. Latinos of Central and South American origin are extremely diverse: they include recently arrived asylum seekers from rural Central America as well as earlier waves of "brain-drain" professionals from Argentina, Brazil, Chile, and elsewhere. Newer arrivals from Mexico and Central and South America face special issues relating to whether they entered the United States as documented or undocumented migrants (see Chavez 1992); whether they came voluntarily or due to political persecution; whether they are seasonal migrants planning to return home, or plan to stay in the United States more or less permanently; and whether they came to the United States as a family unit or as individuals.

Although we advocate differentiating the issues facing the migrants from those facing the U.S.-born second generation, many individuals may fall between these two categories. For example, some are born on the U.S. side of the border but over the years they spend significant amounts of time back in Mexico or Central America and then return to permanently settle in the United States. Other individuals are born in the United States but maintain a cultural identity as Mexicans or Salvadorans and not as Mexican-Americans or even Latinos. They may be called the "intergenerational" Latinos. In our model, in considering such cases, we are less interested in where a person was actually born, and more concerned with their own subjective identification (e.g., as Mexican, Chicano, Latino, Salvadoreño, etc.).

Asylum seekers arrived in large numbers from Central America in the 1980s (Suárez-Orozco 1989). In addition to the problems associated with asylum (see below), the great majority of them had to deal with their undocumented status.

Migrant Landscapes

Migration is an open-ended process that differentially affects the experiences of various generations (e.g., the migrant generation, the U.S.-born second generation, the third generation, etc.). Hence, we are critical of theories of immigrant assimilation and acculturation that tend to offer premature closure (e.g., "by the second generation group X was fully assimilated") to what is, in our estimation, an intergenerational dynamic process.

Among the children and even grandchildren of migrants, past generations, family origin, "the escape," and accounts of hardship in the new land are topics that are part of everyday conversations. For many second- and third-generation Latinos, the immigrant past may also *be* the present because of the ongoing nature of immigration from Latin America. Among Latinos the past is not only kept alive in privileged family narratives, but unfolds in front of their eyes as recent arrivals endure anew the cycle of deprivation, hardship, and discrimination that is characteristic of first-generation immigrant life.

The immigrant generation often arrives in a new land as pioneers with a dream of making a better life for themselves as well as for their children. The objectives of the first generation are relatively clear: get a job, earn money, learn a new language, if possible provide education to the children, and in general improve their lot in life. Family reunification is another powerful motive driving many new arrivals. Some new immigrants, perhaps more than the current anti-immigrant public may realize, often wish to eventually return back home to settle there once financial considerations allow.

The obvious difficulties that most migrants face include language inadequacies, a general unfamiliarity with the customs and expectations of the new country,[2] limited economic opportunities, poor housing conditions, discrimination, and what psychologists term the "stresses of acculturation" (Rogler, Cortes, and Malgady 1991: 585-597; for other studies of the stresses of immigration, see Kantor 1969; Malzberg 1969; Sluzki 1979; Padilla, Alvarez, and Lindholm 1986; Arevalo 1987; Cervantes et al. 1989; Rodriguez 1989; Rogler, Malgady and Rodriguez 1989; Salgado de Snyder 1990; Padilla 1993).

Despite these obstacles, many migrants often consider their lot as having improved from what it was in their country of origin. Because of a perception of relative improvement, many migrants may fail to internalize the negative attitudes of the host country toward them, maintaining their country of origin as a point of reference (Roosens 1989:132-134). Additionally, migrants commonly view and experience their current lot not in terms of the ideals and expectations of the majority society but rather in terms of the ideals and expectations of the "old culture" (De Vos 1973). This is part of an interesting orientation that we have termed "the immigrant's dual frame of reference" (Suárez-Orozco and Suárez-Orozco 1995; see also Leman 1987). In the earliest phases of immigration, the new arrivals may idealize the new country as a land of unlimited opportunities.

During this stage, many new arrivals may concentrate on the negative aspects of life in the land left behind. As a new arrival from El Salvador told us: "Life in my country is very backward. There we live in a humble way. You are remote from everything. The people are ignorant. You can't do anything there, you can't travel, you can't learn another language. Here people are open and there is freedom, here there are people from all over the world. This is a liberal country. This is the most modern country in the world. There kids grow up in the shadows of their mother's skirts. They train you to be obedient. Here I don't see that. . . . Here you have the freedom to do whatever pleases you. Here there are opportunities we do not have [in El Salvador]."

This pattern is also found among other Latino immigrants, including many coming from Mexico. Rogler, Cortes, and Malgady (1991) explore the psychosocial consequences of an important generational discontinuity between Mexico-born parents and their California-born children that relates to the immigrants' dual frame of reference. They write, "The selectivity of the migration stream from Mexico to California tends to create a psychologically robust first-generation immigrant population who feels less deprived because migration has increased their standard of living; in contrast, the Mexican Americans born in the United States feel more deprivation because of their much higher but unrealized aspirations" (1991:589).

The children of migrants indeed evaluate their experiences in the new country differently than the immigrant generation. This is based, in part, on the fact that children of migrants —the second generation—did not experience the limitations and hardships of life in the "old country." In fact, among the children of migrants, the old country may be romanticized as a somewhat Edenic place of mythical origin (hence the complex of searching for one's roots in the old country among the children of migrants) and not thought of as what it actually was.

First-generation migrants may not only improve their own standard of living but also (and perhaps more importantly) that of the family members still in the home country. Latino migrants almost universally help out their relatives left behind with regular and substantial remittances from the United States. Every year, they send billions of dollars to Mexico and Central and South America.[3]

During the first quarter of this century, Manuel Gamio estimated that a Mexican migrant worker in the United States earned, on average, six times more than what a worker in Mexico could earn for the same type of work (1971:38). Indeed, Gamio concluded "The emigration of Mexican laborers is directly caused by the low wages and unemployment in the various parts of Mexico from which they come, indirectly by the political instability, and secondarily through the desire for progress and the spirit of adventure" (1971:171). In 1995, after the recent devaluation of the Mexican peso by 50 percent, the U.S./Mexico wage differential is 12 to 1. We add only that family reunification has also become a factor in emigration from Mexico to the United States.

A single migrant is often responsible for ameliorating the standard of living of many left behind. A sad Latino migrant paradox is that enduring psychological and cultural loss best enables one to help those back home. Hence, many migrants in a new land experience losses, marginality, and deprivation but know that they are making a tremendous difference in the lives of those left behind.

The children of migrants typically do not share their parents' dual frame of reference. They cannot frame their current experiences in terms of the old country ideals, standards, and expectations. The second generation is less likely to continue to send remittances back to the relatives in the old country. Rather than seeing themselves as better off vis-à-vis the old country (as their parents did), from the perspective of the second generation, the situation may be one of deprivation and marginality vis-à-vis the majority culture (Horowitz 1983). Thus, the second generation often faces the same discriminations and economic difficulties as their parents *without* the perceived benefits.

Ongoing discrimination and ethnic tension have an erosive effect, particularly in the more vulnerable children of migrants. Insightfully describing the phenomenon of ethnic prejudice in his classic novel, Villareal's (1959:150-151) protagonist learns about the predicament of *pachucos* (second-generation Mexican-Americans): ". . . their bitterness and hostile attitude towards 'whites' was not merely a lark. They had learned hate through actual experience with everything the word implied. They had not been as lucky as he and had the scars to prove it. . . ." Villareal's description is timeless. It was written in 1959 but it could have as easily been written in 1969, 1979, 1989, or 1995.

Several anthropologists have argued that the specific identity problems facing the children of migrants and other minority groups must be seen in the context of the distinct psychosocial experiences of each group as they enter a dominant society.[4] Ogbu (1991a) describes the special problems facing those minority groups that have been initially incorporated into a dominant society against their will—such as African-Americans through slavery or Native Americans and the original Mexican-Americans through conquest.

In addition to "instrumental exploitation" for economic purposes—for example to maintain a pool of low-paid workers to work at the most undesirable but needed jobs—minorities must often contend with various forms of "psychological exploitation" or disparagement (see also De Vos and M. Suárez-Orozco 1990). That is, they may also be the target of psychological abuse such as stereotyping them as "innately inferior," "lazy," "prone to crime," a "drain on society," and therefore less deserving of sharing in the dominant society's dream. Economic exploitation and psychological exploitation are, in a sense, two sides of the same coin: psychological exploitation and disparagement rationalize the dominant society's economic treatment of these groups.[5]

Psychological and instrumental exploitation deeply affect the children of migrants. How do they respond to such assaults on their identity? We have developed a tripartite heuristic model to examine the range in adaptations among second-generation youths. In the first heuristic category we find some second-generation youths who—although raised in a context of ethnic disparagement—may struggle to synthesize aspects of the two traditions. Among those who are successful and "make it," in the idioms of the dominant society, issues of guilt and reparation often become important. In such cases, one's success in the context of the deprivation and suffering of loved ones may create intense feelings of guilt. Guilt is often assuaged by helping less fortunate members of one's own group. Others avoid such responsibilities, but at an inner price.

In our second heuristic type we find youths who may identify with the oppressing dominant group and attempt to join them leaving their own ethnic group behind ("passing"). Those who choose this route often have unresolved issues of shame and doubt, which they may struggle to overcompensate (see Richard Rodriguez's case below).

Third, other youths may resolutely reject the society that rejects them and turn to those sharing their predicament—their peers. From this third situation typically emerge countercultural groups or gangs rejecting aspects of the dominant society—including schools—and affirming their own ethnic identity. Rageful violence in gang life can be justified by some as a reaction to the ethnic injuries and assaults endured by the members, families, and friends.

Closing the Golden Gate: Latinos in Schools

Among Latinos, poor achievement in school continues to be a serious problem (Suárez-Orozco 1989). According to 1993 Bureau of the Census data only 51.3 percent of all Hispanics aged twenty-five and older completed high school (compared with 79.9 percent of all whites), and only 9.7 percent of all Hispanics aged twenty-five and older completed four years of college or more (compared to 22.0 percent of all whites).

There are complex reasons for the overall poor performance of Latinos in schools. Vigil (1988a) attributes it to the fact that many Latino migrant parents do not have much education themselves. Thus, some may be sending the message to their children, "We made it without formal schooling, so can you." A problem with this line of argument is that Latino parents typically *want* their children to have the formal education they themselves could not have (Suárez-Orozco 1989; Reese, Gallimore, Balzano, and Goldenberg 1991; Goldenberg, Reese, and Gallimore 1992). Others have observed that Latino families encourage youths to early employment, marriage and child bearing, actions that may divert some from investing in formal education (see Navarette, Jr. 1993).

A number of theoretical models have attempted to explain poor Latino school performance. During the 1960s proponents of the "culture of poverty" (also called the "cultural deprivation" model) argued that the problem of minority—including Latino—school failure was not due to any alleged biological differences in innate intelligence as had been proposed earlier (see Suárez-Orozco 1989). Theoreticians of the cultural deprivation model argued that certain cultural backgrounds failed to inculcate children with the basic tools required for successful school functioning. In some of these writings it was proposed that among certain minorities, including

Latinos, school failure was due to cultural tradition. For example, Bloom, Davis, and Hess wrote that the roots of cultural deprivation "can be traced to . . . experiences in the home which do not transmit the cultural patterns necessary for the types of learning characteristics of the schools and the larger society" (1965:4).

In discussing the specific problems facing Latino children in American schools, Heller wrote, "The kind of socialization Mexican American children receive is not conducive to the development of capacities needed for advancement in a dynamic society. This type of upbringing creates stumbling blocks to future advancement by stressing values that hinder mobility–family ties, honor, masculinity, and living in the present–and by neglecting the values that are conductive to it, achievement, independence, and deferred gratification" (1966:34-35).

By the 1970s, leading researchers began to turn away from such explanatory models (see Ogbu 1978; Trueba 1987). These scholars noted that there were a number of serious problems in the main tenets of the cultural deprivation model. First, the assortment of a more or less arbitrary list of traits hardly constitutes a culture in the standard anthropological use of the term. Second, as Trueba (1987) and others perceptively pointed out, the cultural deprivation "rationale coheres beautifully to the American brand of ethnocentrism: minority problems are caused by *their* peculiar form of culture" (Carter and Segura 1979:77; their emphasis). Other researchers suggested that far from being the causes of school failure and poverty, such traits were the consequences of powerlessness and discrimination over generations.

Additionally, more recent studies (see, for example, Suárez-Orozco and Suárez-Orozco 1995) strongly suggest that Mexican youngsters in Mexico are highly achievement and family oriented. Hence, our data cast doubts over the generalization that Mexican socialization "is not conducive to the development of the capacities needed for advancement in a dynamic society" (Heller 1966:34). In our view, the problems facing Latinos in schools in the United States have less to do with their cultural background per se than with the process of migration and minority status. By the 1970s and 1980s researchers began to carefully examine the processes by which failure is achieved within school settings. Henry Trueba (1989a, 1989b) and his colleagues (Delgado-Gaitan and Trueba 1991; Trueba, Rodríguez, Zou, and Cintrón 1993) and others approached the problems facing Latino youths in U.S. schools by exploring majority-minority "cultural discontinuities" (in language, cognition, value orientations, and the like). According to these writers the roots of the problem is that schools fail to provide culturally appropriate educational experiences to their minority students.

Much of this important work was influenced by the theoretical breakthroughs in sociolinguistics by John Gumperz (1981; Gumperz and Hymes 1972) and his associates (see, for example, Mehan 1978). A series of careful ethnographic studies documented the language and other discontinuities between Latino students and the

English-speaking middle-class school system (see, for example, Carter and Segura 1979; Suárez-Orozco 1986, 1987; Trueba 1989a, 1989b, 1993).

In Gumperz's model (1981) communication is a complex phenomenon that includes verbal utterances (words), "situated meanings" (speaker's intentions), "context" (speaker's perceptions of the social situations), and so forth (see Gumperz 1981:3-23). For understanding to be achieved, persons must also share common metacommunication cues such as intonation, code switching, stress, syntax, and loudness. These are culturally constructed cues. Face-to-face interactions in small-scale settings such as schools often capture and re-create the class and ethnic inequalities that permeate the larger sociocultural environment.

Ogbu summarizes the strengths—and weaknesses—of this approach:

> The significance of these and other theories based on classroom studies is their elucidation of the processes or mechanisms by which school failure and school success are achieved. This knowledge is very useful in developing programs (e.g., for preparation of teachers) and in encouraging cautious interpretations of quantitative studies of children's academic performance. However, these theories cannot claim to provide general explanations of minority children's school failure or failure to learn to read. This is partly because the theories are based on research on one type of minorities *caste-like minorities* [or involuntary minorities]. They have yet to be applied to other minorities (e.g., immigrants) who are more successful in schools, although they have cultural and communicative backgrounds different from those of their public school teachers'. [1982:280]

We concur with Ogbu's caveat as to the overall usefulness of concentrating on the communicative basis of school failure. Even though cultural discontinuities are significant, and must be taken into account, they cannot by themselves account for the variability minority school failure and success. How is it that Punjabi Sikh students, for example, have done so well in California public schools (Gibson 1988)? Are their communicative skills closer to the dominant American culture than that of U.S.-born Latinos? That could hardly be the case. Ogbu (1974) has approached the problem of poor Latino performance in school from a different but related perspective. He states that educational achievement is not rewarded for them as it is for the majority population. Hence, according to Ogbu, many Latino youths do not invest in school as they do not see that they will get equivalent rewards relative to the majority population in the posteducational job market.

The latest Bureau of the Census data on educational attainment and income seem to support Ogbu's contentions. For Latinos, years of schooling completed translate into significantly less income earned than for the majority population. In the 1990s, the income inequality between Latinos and whites with the same years of schooling remains striking. The mean 1990 annual income by educational attainment for white male high school graduates was $22,521, whereas for Hispanics it was $14,644.

And what does a college education do to the white/Latino gap? How do Latinos who completed four years of college compare with their white classmates in terms of income? The mean 1990 income for white males who completed four years of college was $40,636, and for Hispanics it was $25,911.[6]

Our own research suggests that in addition to these socioeconomic factors, school personnel are typically indifferent or even hostile to the linguistic and other cultural needs as well as the special circumstances of Latino families (Suárez-Orozco 1989; Suárez-Orozco and Suárez-Orozco 1995). Latino students also reported to us that they are the targets of the racial prejudice of their white classmates, teachers, and other school personnel. Even highly motivated newly arrived migrant students are affected by such hostilities and pressures. Sensitive teachers who relished the positive attitude toward schooling and learning among newly arrived migrant students from Mexico were puzzled to see the more ambivalent attitudes toward schooling among more acculturated Latino students. A teacher noted that after only a few years in the United States, Latino students become increasingly ambivalent toward school and school authorities. As a perplexed teacher said, "The more Americanized they become, the worse their attitude in school."

In short, sociolinguistic and socioeconomic factors such as identified in the research of Gumperz, Ogbu, Trueba, and their associates, coupled with the economic pressures of providing for a large family, may lead many Latino students to eventually develop ambivalent attitudes toward school and the route of education. In addition, we argue, ongoing discrimination and disparagement are particularly destructive when learning and success in an institution of the dominant culture–i.e., the school–comes to be experienced as an act of ethnic betrayal, signifying a wish to "be white." A high drop-out rate from school continues to be a severe problem in the Latino community (Horowitz 1983; Vigil 1988a; Suárez-Orozco 1989).

Between Worlds

Stonequist (1937) described the experiences of social dislocation of "the individual who through migration, education, marriage, or some other influence leaves one social group or culture without making a satisfactory adjustment to another find[ing] himself on the margin of each but a member of neither" (p. 4). Stonequist maintained that "wherever there are cultural transitions and cultural conflicts there are marginal personalities" (p. 4). These cultural differences, we emphasize, create more difficulty in circumstances where there are sharp ethnic contrasts and hostile social attitudes. This may result in "acute personal difficulties and mental tension" for those individuals identified with aspects of both groups (Stonequist 1937:4) Stonequist ascertained that the common traits of what he termed the "marginal man" evolved from the *conflict* of two cultures rather than "from the specific content of any culture" (p. 9). We agree.

This brings us to the psychological toll paid for migrating to another country. Although migration may bring about an improvement in economic conditions, it also ruptures the "immigrant's supportive interpersonal bonds" (Rogler, Malgady, and Rodriguez 1989: 25), well recognized to be crucial for psychological well-being. In addition, migration may psychologically represent a cumulative trauma. It often results in multiple losses, the effects of which are not always immediately apparent (Garza-Guerrero 1974; Grinberg and Grinberg 1990). Rogler, Cortes, and Malgady summarize their recent overview of the literature on acculturation and mental health status among Cuban-Americans, mainland Puerto Ricans, and Mexican-Americans: "Migration is likely to disrupt attachments to supportive networks in the society of origin and to impose on the migrant the difficult task of incorporation into the primary groups of the host society. The migrant is also faced with problems of economic survival and social mobility in an unfamiliar socioeconomic system. These uprooting experiences are accompanied by problems of acculturation into a new cultural system, of acquiring the language, the behavioral norms and values characteristic of the host society" (1991:585).

For individuals who possess sufficient psychological resources to withstand the trauma and who have adequate available social support, the migration experience can result in personal enrichment and psychological growth. For many, however, the losses result in an exacerbation of psychological traits and problems (Garza-Guerrero 1974). A study of mainland Puerto Ricans reports that (not surprisingly) those "with fewest psychological resources for coping with the new environment reported the worst stress outcomes" (Rogler, Cortes, and Malgady 1991:593). Grinberg and Grinberg (1990) outline three typical patterns of psychological problems that may occur after migration. These include problems with "persecutory anxiety" (whereby the host environment that once was overidealized is now experienced as hostile and persecutory in nature), "depressive anxiety" (when the individual is preoccupied with his or her losses due to the migration), and "disorienting anxiety" (which results from disorientation about the old and the new ways of being, including issues of time, space, customs, and so forth).

Migrants may also feel "let down," a feeling of disappointment after they realize that their initial idealization of life in the new land was erroneous. This may occur with an insight that life will indeed be difficult in the new country. It is at this point that many disappointed Latino migrants may choose to go back home (Ross 1993). A man returning to his native Mexico noted, "The American dream is not true. It didn't happen. I have no more dreams, no way to pay the rent" (Ross 1993:22). As Grinberg and Grinberg (1990) describe it, a sense of depressive anxiety is characterized by the migrant's preoccupation with psychological loses. Mexican

Nobel Poet Octavio Paz describes his own feelings when he migrated for a while to Los Angeles: "Yes, we withdraw into ourselves, we deepen and aggravate our awareness of everything that separates or isolates or differentiates us. And we increase our solitude by refusing to seek out our compatriots, perhaps because we fear we will see ourselves in them, perhaps because of a painful, defensive unwillingness to share our intimate feelings. . . . We live closed within ourselves. . . (1961:19).

A young Latino migrant told us of the tremendous sense of solitude many feel in the new land: "Here I have no family, I have no home. If I had my family and a home here I would be more optimistic. Now I feel tired. I am sure that if I had a home here, my mother would be waiting for me with my food ready. Now I come back home, and I have to make my own food. I get up in the morning to go to school, and I am all by myself. I make my own coffee, iron my clothes, do everything alone. I come back from work at night and I am all alone. I feel very low. I sit in bed all alone, and I lose morale. I think about my future and about being all alone. This depresses me a lot; I feel desperate."

Note the poignant longing for maternal nurturing suggested in the wish that his mother would be there waiting for him with his food. Mother's food, that is the food of the motherland, is typically laden with symbolic and expressive significance in the lives of immigrants (see Gamio 1971:140-147). It is as if by eating their own ethnic foods, migrants symbolically attempt to reestablish a link with the lost homeland. The sense of anxious "disorientation" described by Grinberg and Grinberg (1990) among new migrants is related to what anthropologists have termed the "culture shock" one typically experiences entering a substantially different way of life. As a new arrival from Mexico stated, "Immigration was like being born again—I had to learn to speak, I had to learn to eat and I had to learn to dress."

Children of Latino migrants become the repositories of their parents' anxieties, ambitions, dreams, and conflicts. They are often vested with responsibilities (such as translating and sibling care) beyond what is culturally normative for their stage of psychosocial development. Due to a lack of linguistic skills, many Latino migrant parents are unable to help their children in school-related tasks. This may bring about further anxieties and feelings of inadequacy and shame. At the same time, and perhaps related to the last point, Latino migrant parents typically overrestrict the activities of the children and attempt to minimize the host country's influence.

Latino migrant youths, particularly young women residing in crime-ridden inner cities, told us that they had much less freedom in the United States than they did "back home." Some Latino migrant parents eventually decide to return home to avoid the Americanization of their children. Others return after sensing that the elusive American dream had escaped them. Yet others return to avoid inner-city crime.

The children of migrants may suffer shame and doubt that compromises and undermines their self-confidence and development (see Paz [1961:9-28] on the question of shame in migrants). Feelings of inadequacy and inferiority may lead to a loss in faith in the child's abilities to "make it" in the new setting (Grinberg and Grinberg 1990). A range of choices seem to emerge: at one end of this psychological spectrum some youths choose dropping-out from school and giving up on education as the key route for status mobility. At the other end, some choose overcompensation in the form of school overachieving.

Ethnic Identities

Grinberg and Grinberg (1990) and Vigil (1988a, 1988b) maintain that perhaps the most critical task facing the children of immigrants is that of developing a positive sense of identity. According to Erikson (1963), forging a sense of identity is the key issue in development during adolescence. To develop a healthy sense of who one is, there must occur a certain amount of complementarity between the individual's sense of self and the social milieu. If there is too much cultural dissonance and role confusion, there may be difficulties in developing a strong self-identity. Children of Latino migrants may suffer from what Vigil (1988a) terms "multiple marginalities," which in some cases compromise the development of a positive self-identity. Vigil and others have noted that such children are likely to experience intense culture conflict on both individual and group levels.

In some cases, second-generation youths attempt to resolve identity issues by embracing total assimilation and a wholesale identification with dominant American values. Such youths may actively reject the use of Spanish. In other cases, a new ethnic identity, incorporating selected aspects of both Latino and dominant American culture, is forged (in which cases bilingual fluency may often be achieved). In yet other cases, the adaptation is not as smooth and a "subculture of cultural transitionals" (Vigil 1988a:39) emerges. Vigil calls these transitional youths *cholos.* Within the same family each child may adapt his or her own way individually, resulting in various siblings occupying very different sectors of the spectrum—from *cholo* to Anglicized, and from bilingual to "Spanglish" speaking, to English-only speaking (Vigil 1988a).

Villareal poignantly articulates the effects of cultural marginality and discrimination on the children of Mexican migrant workers (1959:149-150). Forced to "oscillate between two irreducible worlds—the North American and the Mexican" (Paz 1961:18), many second-generation Latino youths reject some of the institutions—including schools—of the society that violently rejects them and seek refuge in their peers. It is precisely such identity issues that propel many second-generation Latino youths to a defensive identity or to join gangs. We agree with Alejandro Portes's observation, "As second-generation youth find their aspirations for wealth and social status blocked . . . they may join native minorities in the inner-city, adopting an adversarial stance toward middle-class white society, and adding to the present urban pathologies" (1993:2).

Vigil (1988a) contends that gangs are largely a second-generation immigrant phenomenon. In his studies, Vigil traces the historical pattern of Latino gang formation in urban areas since the beginning of large-scale Mexican immigration to the United States at the turn of the century. He accounts for several key factors in the development of Latino gangs. These include low socioeconomic status, urban poverty, and limited economic mobility; ethnic minority status and discrimination; lack of training, education, and constructive opportunities; and a breakdown in the social institutions of school and family. Vigil also points out major causal factors in "a first- and second-generation conflict within each ethnic group, which creates loyalty discord and identity confusion; and a noted predisposition among youths to gravitate toward street peers for sources of social associations and personal fulfillment" (1988a:4). These factors hold particularly true for many second-generation Latino youths. "*Cholo* gangs" have been a long-lasting rather than a transitory phenomenon, due to the continuous migration from Latin America that reproduces new cycles of marginality on an ongoing basis (see Vigil 1988a).

We concur with Vigil's observations. Latino youths join gangs in search of refuge and belonging. Gangs are most attractive to youths who are receiving the least parental and familial attention. A perceptive teacher told us, "The gangs are in their community, in their own barrios. They see the gangs all around them. Their parents are often gone all day at work. So these kids are alone with no supervision. The parents are not there. The gangs offer company, it gives them protection. It is kind of a family. It is cool and exciting for them to belong to a gang."

Another southern California teacher said, "These Latino kids are in a desert. The gangs offer them company and protection. There is a pressure to join. Many kids, that is all they have, their gangs. If they don't join they are left without friends. They are alone, social outcasts. These kids are alone a lot of the time. Their parents are away during the day. So they get into gangs." When parents and other adults are not "there"—due to their own work and other demands—youths who are going through adolescence in the context of the upheavals of migration and resettlement in a hostile environment are most likely to turn to their peers and join gangs.

On the positive side, gangs provide a "mechanism of adaptation for many youths who need a source of identification and human support" (Vigil 1988a:6). The gang provides a "reforging of Mexican and American patterns . . . creating a culture [and language] of mixed and blended elements" (Vigil 1998a:7). Vigil maintains that "although *cholos* are Americanized, either by accident or design, they refuse or are unable to be totally assimilated" (Vigil 1988:7).

As Paz noted, the *pachuco* (a term that is a historical predecessor but the structural equivalent, in this context, to Vigil's *cholo*), "does not want to become a

Mexican again; at the same time he does not want to blend into the life of North America" (1961:14). *Cholos/pachucos* retain certain Mexican customs, sometimes in caricature form (Paz 1961:9-28), such as a strong sense of peer group as family, daring/bravado male patterns of machismo, and an ambivalent attitude toward authority (Horowitz 1983; Vigil 1988a, 1988b).

At the same time, second-generation youths in gangs may not feel Mexican and in some cases may actually experience considerable antipathy toward Mexican migrants (Dayley 1991) and disparage wetbacks (first-generation undocumented immigrants) (see Vigil 1988a). There may be a perception of "limited good" and competition over scarce resources (such as jobs, education, housing, and so forth) with the newer arrivals. Psychologically, the second generation may view the new arrivals as embodying aspects of themselves that the second generation may wish to disclaim.

Gamio has written, "The attitude of Mexicans who are American citizens [second generation] toward the immigrants is a curious one. Sometimes they speak slightingly of the immigrants (possibly because the immigrants are their competitors in wages and jobs), and say that the immigrants should stay in Mexico. . . . The immigrant, on his part, considers the American of Mexican origin as a man without a country. He reminds him frequently of the inferior position to which he is relegated by the white American" (1971:129).

Both Vigil (1988a) and Horowitz (1983) have found that the individuals who are most heavily involved in gangs come from the most troubled families: with absent parents, a history of alcohol or drug addiction, and child neglect and/or abuse. Vigil (1988a) estimates that 70 to 80 percent of the heavily involved Latino gang members in southern California come from such family situations. For such youths, in the absence of role models to identify with, gang membership becomes incorporated into their sense of identity. Gangs offer their members a sense of belonging, solidarity, support, discipline, and warmth. Gangs also structure the rage *cholos* feel toward the society that violently rejected their parents and themselves. Although many second-generation youths may look toward gangs for cues about dress, language, and attitude, most remain on the periphery and eventually outgrow the gang mystique after working through the issues of adolescence. The gang ethos provides a sense of identity and cohesion for marginal youths during a turbulent stage of development.

Cultural dissonance, then, may lead to what we term "defensive identity" (see also De Vos and Suárez-Orozco 1990). Joining a gang or developing a *cholo persona* is but one of the forms that this defensive identity may take. In a much more sublimated manner, achievement-oriented Ruben Navarette, Jr. (1993) describes his own process of moving from Central Valley, California, where 70 percent of the residents were Latino, to the Harvard University campus. Navarette describes his feelings during his initial days of transition: "It begins appropriately, as it does with students of all color, with a distinct element of self-doubt. . . . For Latinos, and other minority students who may see themselves—indeed, have been encouraged by hometown insults to see themselves—as the winners of the dubious affirmative action lottery, the question of unworthiness endures like a stale odor. You begin to believe old critics, assuming that you have come to this bizarre place not by your own merit but by the grace of a government handout" (1993:60).

This very light-skinned young man who never felt like a minority member until he went to Harvard is now caught by—and must defend against—feelings of shame and doubt. Navarette describes in detail how at Harvard he becomes alternately alienated from nonminority students, nonethnically aware Latino students, hometown peers, and, in time, members of the Raza campus organization. In the end, who is really like him?

Labyrinths of Solitude: Instrumental Mobility Versus Expressive Affiliation

By joining gangs or developing a defensive identity, many second-generation youths reject the society that rejects them and seek refuge in others sharing their own predicament. On the other hand, second-generation Latinos who have the opportunity and choose to join the dominant American culture come to face very different day-to-day experiences, but may continue to suffer from a marginal status. According to Horowitz: "Individuals who choose to measure their competency in terms of the wider society rather than in terms of local identity risk a loss of emotional support from peers and kin. Trusting and close relationships must be developed with new people and on different terms. The movement away from the traditional sources of support and the traditional basis of social relationships can create feelings of acute loneliness. Little within the Chicano community prepares them for the competitive, individualistic Anglo world of social relationships in which they must face lack of acceptance and some degree of discrimination. They become caught between two worlds." (1983:200-201).

Those who chose to move "away from the traditional sources of support" become migrants of another sort. Richard Rodriguez's (1982) autobiographical account of his experiences growing up in Sacramento, California, provides a rich illustration of an individual who attempts to integrate himself into the dominant society, actively rejecting his native tongue, familial networks, and culture. It also poignantly captures how issues of shame and doubt are woven into situations of ethnic mobility.

Rodriguez is certainly very successful, viewed from the standards of the dominant society. As a Stanford, Columbia, and Berkeley graduate and fellow of the prestigious Warbug Institute in London, he has come a long way from the humble Sacramento of his youth. However, a close reading of his controversial autobiography shows that Rodriguez suffers from a sense of shame, marginality, and alienation.

Stymied in her own attempts to get ahead, Rodriguez's mother "willed her ambition to her children. 'Get all the education you can. With an education you can do anything'" (Rodriguez 1982:54-55). His mother is told by the local nuns to stop using the "private" language (the language of intimacy—Spanish) and start using the more instrumental "public" language (English) at home.

Rodriguez admits to being "angry at them [his parents] for having encouraged me towards classroom English" (p. 52). He found himself retaliating by intentionally hurting his parents, by correcting them when they made mistakes in English. "But gradually this anger was exhausted, replaced by guilt as school grew more and more attractive to me" (p. 50).

The more Rodriguez was propelled to the public world of school and the dominant culture, the more alienated he became from his private world: family, ethnicity, and culture. This, in part, was fueled by his sense of shame of his parents' accent and their inability to help him even with his second-grade homework. "Your parents must be proud of you. . . . Shyly I would smile, never betraying my sense of irony: I was not proud of my mother and father" (1982:52).

Unable to identify with his humble, silent Mexican father, Rodriguez turns to his powerful teachers. "I wanted to be like my teachers, to possess their knowledge, to assume their authority, their confidence, even to assume a teacher's persona" (p. 55). In carefully reading Rodriguez's account of his life, one senses that the only identification he is able to make with the father is with his silence.

With the acquisition of English and an education, Rodriguez faced gains as well as losses. He gained the capacity to enter the public arena he so much valued as well as the ability to communicate and command the attention of powerful members of the dominant culture. However, he lost emotionally on several levels. He lost his feeling of belonging to his family. With the transition to English, his family was "no longer so close; no longer bound tight by the pleasing and troubling knowledge of our public separateness" (1982:23). He lost the easy intimacy and open communication between family members: "The family's quiet was partly due to the fact that, as we children learned more and more English, we shared fewer and fewer words" (p. 23). He also lost interest in the affective nuances of language and became more concerned with content; "Conversation became content-full. Transparent. Hearing someone's tone of voice—angry or questioning or sarcastic or happy—I didn't distinguish it from the words it expressed" (p. 22).

Rodriguez developed a sense of anomic withdrawal from his family. A numbness engulfs Rodriguez, separating him from his now-distant parents. He is deeply depressed. The child of Mexican migrants, he himself becomes a migrant leaving his family behind in his journey to "success." He made a choice, then, between instrumental mobility ("making it" in the world of the dominant society) and expressive affiliation. Rodriguez is profoundly alone—alienated from his family and alienated from his peers, finding few who are able or willing to take his path. He must rationalize his choice with the consequent gains as well as losses. In doing so, he becomes a vocal opponent of both bilingual education and affirmative action: he invokes the archaic assimilationist argument, he "made it" by renouncing his ethnicity, so should others.[7]

In reading Rodriguez, one feels pity for both him and his parents. He is so alone that the only sense of intimacy he has is with his readers: "encouraged by physical isolation to reveal what is most personal; determined at the same time to have my words seen by strangers" (1982:187). His parents lost what is clearly a favorite son. The mother's attempts at intimacy and involvement are consistently rebuffed. The gulf between them seems interminable and irreparable.

Rodriguez's controversial condemnation of bilingual education deserve further comment. It is true that by using "nonmainstream" English (such as Spanglish, black English, lower-class English) one is at a disadvantage as evaluations are constantly being made based on language usage. However, we question whether it is necessary to give up one's native language, one's affective language (along with all the resulting losses) in order to "make it." In ideal circumstances, it should not be an either/or situation. An analogy here is that one does not have to forget how to play the piano before learning to play the violin. Rodriguez's devastating account goes directly to the symbolic and affective aspects of language. To see language as a mere instrumental tool for communication is to miss its deep affective roots. Giving up Spanish to acquire English is a symbolic act of ethnic renunciation: it is giving up the language of one's birth for the instrumental tongue of the dominant group.

Guilt and Repair

If Rodriguez's autobiography illustrates how issues of shame and doubt may be related to achievement orientation and ethnic status mobility, the recently released autobiography of Ruben Navarette, Jr. (1993), a "Harvard Chicano," beautifully illustrates how guilt and reparation are intimately related to Latino patterns of achievement motivation. Navarette's complex journey (migration, really) from his dusty immigrant town in the San Joaquin Valley to Harvard Square is a study of the pardoxes, contradictions, and chagrins of a society struggling to deal with its multicultural pretensions. A hard-working, A+ overachiever, Navarette, a third-generation Mexican-American, is enraged when he senses that as far as his white peers and teachers are concerned, he got into Harvard only because of some quota system.

This is particularly injurious to him because he is a light-skinned, middle-class, and self-described "fully acculturated" hyphenated American. Navarette is so acculturated that, as he himself is fully aware, his attempts at Harvard to pass as "a real Mexican" by speaking Spanish are hilarious—and even in his published book a number of the Spanish words and phrases are misspelled or misused. Navarette responds to the assaults by his white peers and teachers with a bravado that betrays his Latino origins. His journey through Harvard can be read as an exercise in showing them, and himself, that he can conquer that most exclusive institution of the WASP establishment. Yet reading his autobiography one cannot escape the feeling that his chutzpah and narcissistic arrogance is a deep cover for unsettling feelings of shame and guilt about the nature of his success.

As he deals with his own wounds, the insults reactivate the indignities and abuses endured by previous generations, including his proud Mexican grandparents, parents, uncles, and their friends. He recalls receiving a call from a woman one day: "'You don't understand,' she said. 'What you have done [going to Harvard] . . . you don't know what it means, what it means to all of us, here in this town.' Suddenly there is a sniffle. 'You don't know'—by the time she finishes her sentence, she is in tears—'how they treated us back then'" (Navarette, Jr. 1993:xv). He journeys to Cambridge, carrying not only his own fresh wounds and hopes but the ancestral wounds and expectations of generations of immigrants who came before him. Navarette's autobiography climaxes with a deep revelation. After graduating from Harvard he enrolls in UCLA's Graduate School of Education. It is worth quoting his revelation at length:

> Memory takes me back to Madison Elementary School, an inconspicuous assortment of gray buildings in my brown and white hometown. The place, where during recess, I first played with my Mexican American friends. The place where, in the classroom, I was first set apart from them. . . .
>
> One fateful day, in the second grade, my teacher decided to teach her class more efficiently by dividing it into six groups of five students each. Each group was assigned a geometric symbol to differentiate it from the others. There were the Circles. There were the Squares. There were the Triangles and Rectangles. I remember being a Hexagon. . . . The Hexagons were the smartest kids in the class. These distinctions are not lost on a child of seven. . . .
>
> I do not notice the others, the Circles and Squares and Triangles daydreaming in their boredom. I do not notice something else—a curious observation that will ultimately define the character of my life. I am an oddity. I am a Hexagon. I am also the only Mexican American Hexagon. In a classroom, in a school, and in a town were all over half Mexican American, I was the only one. The lucky one. [1993:255-259]

Overwhelmed by a sense of guilt, Navarette quit his position of privilege in graduate school to devote a great deal of energy to reaching out to the Circles, Squares, and Triangles left behind in dusty rural schools. He now not only visits these rural schools to convince Latino youths that they, too, can make it, but he became an aggressive recruiter of Latino students for his beloved Harvard. The nature of Navarette's guilt is laced with cultural meanings that are shared by other highly motivated Latino students (Suárez-Orozco 1989). Navarette is devastated when he comes to experience his success as having been possible only because others, his Latino friends in the second grade, suffered and failed.

In examining the less glamorous achievement patterns of recent arrivals from Central America, we identified a related concern with achievement motivation, "trying to become a somebody," coupled with a wish to turn toward family and loved ones, to help them and to alleviate their ongoing hardships. In this case, guilt also emerged as a powerful factor in the motivational dynamics of Latino students (Suárez-Orozco 1989).

Regardless of the current push for immigration restrictions the Latino population in the United States will continue to be a major force reshaping the American social landscape. Indeed, by the year 2025 the United States will have the second largest number of Spanish speakers in the world. Ethnic identities are often constructed around feelings of common belonging and shared past (see De Vos, this volume). Though Latinos share a number of sociocultural and historical characteristics they are, nevertheless, a diverse population. While searching for the common ground, we must not overlook differences. In the case of Latino identities some of the important ingredients of ethnic feeling are immigration status (such as documented or undocumented), country-of-origin, number of generations in the United States (immigrants, first generation, second generation, etc.), socioeconomic status, and educational attainment.

As in its past, the future of the United States will surely be shaped by the tensions and opportunities generated by immigration and ethnicity. Ethnicities will clearly shape and reshape the American future. Latinos are a growing part of that future.

NOTES

1. Throughout this essay we shall use the term "immigration" in its widest possible sense. "Migrants" refers to those coming to a new country in order to settle there. Refugees and asylum seekers are subtypes of migrants but they differ from migrants in a variety of ways. First, their departure from the country of origin is typically involuntary, often due to a well-founded fear of persecution. Second, refugees and asylum seekers may plan to return home as soon as the political climate allows. Third, refugees and asylum seekers may be more prone to develop special psychosocial problems, such as "survivor guilt" (see Suárez-Orozco 1989), with regard to the condition of those they were forced to leave behind in a context of political repression, war, and scarcity.

2. This is what anthropologists refer to as "cultural discontinuities."

3. The worldwide economic implications of immigration are extremely complex (see Suárez-Orozco and Suárez-Orozco 1995).

4. De Vos (1973, 1980, 1983; and Suárez-Orozco 1990); Ogbu (1974, 1978, 1981, 1982, 1983, 1991a, 1991b; Fordham and Ogbu 1986; Ogbu and Matute-Bianchi 1986; Gibson and Ogbu 1991; see also Jacob and Jordan 1987, 1993; for a critique of Ogbu, see Pieke 1991).

5. We have become less concerned with whether a group technically enters a situation of minority status voluntarily (i.e., new arrivals from Mexico or Central and South America) or involuntarily (i.e., African-Americans, Native Americans, the original Mexican-Americans of the southwest). Economic exploitation and social disparagement is not reserved exclusively to involuntary minorities. For us, the subsequent economic and psychological treatment of a group is just as important as the initial mode of incorporation. For example, many migrants arrive voluntarily, such as the new immigrants in Europe and the United States, but are nevertheless treated in an exploitative and disparaging manner.

6. The 1990 census data on the relationships between educational attainment and income among Latinos and whites make it clear that Linda Chavez's upbeat report that "Hispanics are 'making it' on their own—following the pattern of other ethnic groups and achieving the American dream. . . . Their education and earnings are approaching those of the mainstream" (1991:2) is largely wishful thinking in the name of a dubious neoconservative political agenda. According to 1991 census data, over a quarter of all Hispanics (28.7 percent) were living in poverty (compared to 9.2 percent in the non-Hispanic population). The income gap between Hispanics and the mainstream population, according to 1991 census figures, was likewise extraordinary: the median earnings of Hispanic males with year-round, full-time employment was $19,769 compared to $31,046 for the non-Hispanic whites. Though we do not mean to minimize the important and hard-earned progress of the Latino population, it is simply not empirically true that Latinos, as a group, have now joined the mainstream. Chavez's book, *Out of the Barrio*, might have been better titled *It Is Morning in the Barrio*.

7. Rodriguez's relationship with his ethnicity can be best characterized as a style of approach-avoidance. A detractor of bilingual education, Rodriguez now makes a living as a commentator on public television on immigrant and multicultural affairs in California. Yet Rodriguez seems uncomfortable with his ethnicity. He reveals a deep anxiety about his Mexicanness when he writes about his terror of drinking dirty Mexican water during a visit to Tijuana. A dark man, scarred by bleach from his relatives' attempts when he was little to make his skin "whiter" so he wouldn't "look so Indian," Rodriguez is understandably preoccupied by issues of dirt. After all, he grew up in a racist society saturated with references to "dirty Mexicans." In a sense, Rodriguez's education symbolically achieved what the more archaic bleach episode failed to produce: it gave him some mastery over his anxieties about what he came to experience as his "dark" and "dirty" background.

REFERENCES

Alvarez, Jr., Robert. 1987. *Familia: Migration and Adaptation in Baja and Alta California, 1800-1975*. Berkeley: University of California Press.

Arevalo, L. E. 1987. "Psychological Distress and Its Relationship to Acculturation Among Mexican-Americans." Ph.D. diss., California School of Professional Psychology, San Diego.

Bernal, G. 1982. "Cuban Families." In *Ethnicity and Family Therapy*. M. McGoldrick and J. Giordano, eds. Pp. 187-207. New York: Guilford Press.

Bettleheim, B. 1980. *Surviving and Other Essays*. New York: Vintage Books.

Bloom, B. S., A. Davis, and R. Hess. 1965. *Compensatory Education for Cultural Deprivation*. New York: Holt, Rinehart and Winston.

Carter, T. P., and R. D. Segura. 1979. *Mexican-Americans in School: A Decade of Change*. New York: College Entrance Examination.

Cervantes, R. C., V. N. Salgado de Snyder, and A. M. Padilla. 1989. "Posttraumatic Stress in Immigrants from Central America and Mexico." *Hospital and Community Psychiatry* 40(6):615-619.

Chavez, Leo R. 1992. *Shadowed Lives: Undocumented Immigrants in American Society*. Fort Worth: Harcourt Brace College Publishers.

Chavez, Linda. 1991. *Out of the Barrio: Toward a New Politics of Hispanic Assimilation*. New York: Basic Books.

Conover, Ted. 1987. *Coyotes: A Journey Through the Secret World of America's Illegal Aliens*. New York: Vintage Books.

Cornelius, Wayne A., Philip L. Martin, and James F. Hollifield, eds. 1994. *Controlling Immigration: A Global Perspective*. Stanford: Stanford University Press.

Dayley, J. 1991. "One Big Happy Family." *Reader* 20(17):5-8.

Delgado-Gaitan, Concha, and Henry T. Trueba. 1991. *Crossing Cultural Borders: Education for Immigrant Families in America*. London: The Falmer Press.

De Vos, George A. 1973. *Socialization for Achievement: Essays on the Cultural Psychology of the Japanese*. Berkeley: University of California Press.

De Vos, George A. 1980. "Ethnic Adaptation and Minority Status." *Journal of Cross-Cultural Psychology* 11(1):101-125.

De Vos, George A. 1983. "Achievement Motivation and Intra-Family Attitudes in Immigrant Koreans." *Journal of Psychoanalytic Anthropology* 6:25-71.

De Vos, George A., and Eun Young Kim. 1994. "Problems in Achievement, Alienation and Authority in Korean Minorities in the United States. and Japan." In *Overseas Koreans in the Global Context*. Kwang Kyu Lee and Walter H. Slote, eds. Pp. 1-33. Seoul: ASKA.

De Vos, George A., and M. Suárez-Orozco. 1990. *Status Inequality: The Self in Culture*. Newbury Park, CA: Sage Publications.

Erikson, Erik. 1963. *Childhood and Society*. New York: W. W. Norton.

Fordham, Signithia, and J. U. Ogbu. 1986. "Black Students' School Success: Coping with the Burden of 'Acting White.'" *Urban Review* 18(3):176-206.

Foster, George. 1979. *Tzintzuntan: Mexican Peasants in a Changing World*. New York: Elsevier.

Gamio, Manuel. 1971. *Mexican Immigration to the United States: A Study of Human Migration and Adjustment*. New York: Dover.

Garza-Guerrero, A. 1974. "Culture Shock: Its Mourning and Vicissitudes of Identity." *Journal of the Psychoanalytic Association* 22:408-429.

Gibson, Margaret A. 1988. *Accommodation without Assimilation: Sikh Immigrants in an American High School*. Ithaca and London: Cornell University Press.

Gibson, Margaret, and J. U. Ogbu, eds. 1991. *Minority Status and Schooling: A Comparative Study of Immigrant and Involuntary Minorities*. New York: Garland Publishing.

Goldenberg, Claude, Leslie Reese, and Ronald Gallimore. 1992. "Effects of Literacy Materials from School on Latino Children's Home Experiences and Early Reading Achievement." *The American Journal of Education* 100(4):497-536.

Gonzalez, David. 1992. "What's the Problem with 'Hispanic'? Just Ask a Latino." *The New York Times*, November 15, p. E2.

Grebler, Leo, Joan Moore, and Ralph Guzman. 1970. *The Mexican American People: The Nation's Second Largest Minority*. New York: The Free Press.

Grinberg, León, and Rebecca Grinberg. 1990. *Psychoanalytic Perspectives on Migration and Exile*. New Haven: Yale University Press.

Gumperz, John. 1981. "Conversational Inferences and Classroom Learning. In *Ethnography and Language in Educational Settings*. J. L. Green and C. Wallet, eds. Pp. 3-23. Norwood, NJ: Ablex.

Gumperz, John, and Dell Hymes. 1972. *Directions in Socio-Linguistics: The Ethnography of Communication*. New York: Holt, Rinehart and Winston.

Heller, C. 1966. *Mexican American Youth: The Forgotten Youth at the Crossroads*. New York: Random House.

Hollifield, James. 1992. *Immigrants, Markets, and States: The Political Economy of Postwar Europe*. Cambridge, MA: Harvard University Press.

Horowitz, R. 1983. *Honor and the American Dream: Culture and Identity in a Chicano Community*. New Brunswick, NJ: Rutgers University Press.

Jacob, E., and Cathy Jordan, eds. 1987. "Explaining the School Performance of Minority Students. *Anthropology and Education Quarterly* 18(4), Special Issue.

Jacob E., and Cathy Jordan, eds. 1993. *Minority Education: Anthropological Perspectives*. Norwood, NJ: Ablex.

Kantor, M. B. 1969. "Internal Migration and Mental Illness." In Changing Perspectives in Mental Illness. Stanley Plog and Robert Edgerton, eds. Pp. 364-394. New York: Holt, Rinehart and Winston.

Leman, Johan. 1987. "The Education of Immigrant Children in Belgium." In *Migration, Minority Status and Education: European Dilemmas and Responses in the 1990s*. Marcelo

M. Suárez-Orozco, ed. Theme Issue. *Anthropology and Education Quarterly* 22(2):140-154.

Madsen, William. 1964. *The Mexican-Americans of South Texas*. New York: Holt, Rinehart and Winston.

Malzberg, B. 1969. "Are Immigrants Psychologically Disturbed?" In *Changing Perspectives in Mental Illness*. Stanley Plog and Robert Edgerton, eds. Pp. 395-422. New York: Holt, Rinehart and Winston.

Meier, Matt, and Feliciano Rivera. 1993. *Mexican-Americans/American Mexicans: From Conquistadors to Chicanos*. New York: Farrar, Straus and Giroux.

Mehan, Hugh. 1978. "Structuring School Structure." *Harvard Educational Review* 45(1):31-338.

Mehan, Hugh, and Irene Villanueava. 1994. "Tracking Untracking: The Consequences of Placing Low-Achievement Students in High Track Classes." *The University of California Linguistic Minority Institute* 3(3):1.

Navarette, Jr., Ruben. 1993. *A Darker Shade of Crimson: Odyssey of a Harvard Chicano*. New York: Bantam.

Ogbu, John U. 1974. *The Next Generation: An Ethnography of Education in an Urban Neighborhood*. New York: Academic Press.

Ogbu, John U. 1978. *Minority Education and Caste: The American System in Cross-Cultural Perspective*. New York: Academic Press.

Ogbu, John U. 1981. "Origins of Human Competence: A Cultural Ecological Perspective." *Child Development* 52:413-429.

Ogbu, John U. 1982. "Anthropology and Education." In *International Encyclopedia of Education: Research and Studies*. Torsten Husén and T. Neville Postlethwaite, eds. Pp. 276-298. Oxford: Oxford University Press.

Ogbu, John U. 1983. "Indigenous and Immigrant Minority Education: A Comparative Perspective." Paper read at the 82nd Annual Meeting of the American Anthropological Association, Chicago, November 16-20.

Ogbu, John U. 1991a. "Minority Coping Responses and School Experience." In *Belonging and Alienation: Essays in Honor of George A. De Vos*. Marcelo M. Suárez-Orozco, ed. Special Issue. *The Journal of Psychohistory* 18(4):433-456.

Ogbu, John U. 1991b. "Immigrant and Involuntary Minorities in Comparative Perspective." In *Minority Status and Schooling: A Comparative Study of Immigrant and Involuntary Minorities*. Margaret Gibson and J. U. Ogbu, eds. Pp. 3-33. New York: Garland Publishing.

Ogbu, John U., and Maria Eugenia Matute-Bianchi. 1986. "Understanding Sociocultural Factors: Knowledge, Identity, and School Adjustment." In *Beyond Language: Social and Cultural Factors in Schooling Language Minority Students*. Pp. 73-142. Sacramento, CA: Bilingual Education Office, California State Department of Education.

Padilla, Amando. 1993. "The Psychological Dimensions in Understanding Immigrant Students: The Missing Link." Paper presented at the conference on Immigrant Students in California Schools: Theory, Research, and Implications for Educational Policy. Center for U.S.-Mexican Studies, University of California, San Diego, January 22-23.

Padilla, A. M., M. Alvarez, and K. J. Lindholm. 1986. "Generational Status and Personality Factors as Predictors of Stress in Students." *Hispanic Journal of Behavioral Sciences* 8(3):275-288.

Paz, Octavio. 1961. *The Labyrinth of Solitude*. New York: Grove.

Piaget, Jean. 1930. *The Child's Conception of Causality*. London: Keagan Paul.

Pieke, Frank. 1991. "Educational Achievement and "Folk Theories of Success.". In *Migration, Minority Status and Education: European Dilemmas and Responses in the 1990s*. Marcelo M. Suárez-Orozco, ed. Theme Issue. *Anthropology and Education Quarterly* 22(2):162-180.

Portes, Alejandro. 1993. "The 'New' Second Generation." News release. Department of Sociology, Johns Hopkins University, June.

Portes, Alejandro, and R. L. Bach. 1985. *Latin Journey: Cuban and Mexican Immigrants in the United States*. Berkeley and Los Angeles: University of California Press.

Ready, Thomas. 1991. *Latino Immigrant Youth: Passages from Adolescence to Adulthood*. New York: Garland Publishing.

Reese, L., R. Gallimore, S. Balzano, and C. Goldenberg. 1991. "The Concept of *Educación*: Latino Family Values and American Schooling." Paper presented at the Annual Meeting of the American Anthropological Association. November.

Rodríguez, Clara E. 1991. *Puerto Ricans: Born in the U.S.A.* Boulder, CO: Westview Press.

Rodriguez, Richard. 1982. *Hunger of Memory: The Education of Richard Rodriguez*. New York: Bantam Books.

Rodriguez, R. E. 1989. "Psychological Distress Among Mexican American Women as a Reaction to the New Immigration Law." Ph.D. diss., Loyola University.

Rogler, L. H., R. G. Malgady, and O. Rodriguez. 1989. *Hispanics and Mental Health: A Framework for Research*. Malabar, FL: Robert E. Krieger Publishing Co.

Rogler, L., D. Cortes, and R. Malgady. 1991. "Acculturation and Mental Health Status Among Hispanics." *American Psychologist* 46(6):585-597.

Roosens, Eugeen. 1989. *Creating Ethnicity: The Process of Ethnogenesis*. Newbury Park, CA: Sage Publications.

Ross, John. 1993. "Back to the Rancho: Fear and Anti-Immigrant Hostility Driving Some Mexicans Home." *The Bay Guardian*, August 25, pp. 22-25.

Salgado de Snyder, V. N. 1990. "Gender and Ethnic Differences in Psychosocial Stress and Generalized Distress Among Hispanics." *Sex Roles* 22(7/8); 44:111-453.

Sluzki, Carlos. 1979. "Migration and Family Conflict." *Family Process* 18(4):379-390.

Stoddard, Ellwyn. 1973. *Mexican-Americans*. New York: Random House.

Stonequist, E. V. 1937. *The Marginal Man*. New York: Scribner and Sons.

Suárez-Orozco, Marcelo. 1986. "Spaanse Amerikanen: Vergelijkende Beschouwingen en Onderwijsproblemen. Tweede Generatie Immigratenjongeren." *Cultuur en Migratie* (Brussels) 2:1-49.

Suárez-Orozco, Marcelo. 1987. "Towards a Psychosocial Understanding of Hispanic Adaption to American Schooling." In *Success or Failure? Learning and the Language Minority Student*. Henry T. Trueba, ed. Pp. 156-168. Cambridge, MA: Newbury House.

Suárez-Orozco, Marcelo. 1989. *Central American Refugees and U.S. High Schools: A Psychosocial Study of Motivation and Achievement*. Stanford: Stanford University Press.

Suárez-Orozco, Marcelo, and Carola Suárez-Orozco. 1995. *Transformations: Immigration, Family Life and Achievement Motivation among Latino Adolescents*. Stanford: Stanford University Press.

Trueba, Henry T. 1987. ed. *Success or Failure? Learning & the Language Minority Student*. Cambridge, MA: Newbury House.

Trueba, Henry T. 1989a. *Raising Silent Voices: Educating the Linguistic Minorities for the 21st Century*. Cambridge, MA: Newbury House.

Trueba, Henry T. 1989b. Rethinking Dropouts: Culture and Literacy for Minority Empowerment. In *What Do Anthropologists Have to Say about Dropouts?* Henry T. Trueba, G. Spindler, and Louise Spindler, eds. Pp. 27-42. New York: The Falmer Press.

Trueba, Henry T. 1993. "Race and Ethnicity: The Role of Universities in Healing Multicultural America." *Educational Theory* 43(1):41-54.

Trueba, Henry T., Cirenio Rodríguez, Yali Zou, and José Cintrón. 1993. *Healing Multicultural America: Mexican Immigrants Rise to Power in Rural California*. London: The Falmer Press.

Vigil, James D. 1988a. *Barrio Gangs: Street Life and Identity in Southern California*. Austin: University of Texas Press.

Vigil, James D. 1988b. "Group Processes and Street Identity: Adolescent Chicano Gang Members." *Ethos* 16(4):421-445.

Villareal, José A. 1959. *Pocho*. New York: Anchor Books.

Wagner, Nathaniel, and Marsha Haug. 1971. *Chicanos: Social and Psychological Perspectives*. St. Louis: C. V. Mosby Co.

PART VI ■

Conclusion

GEORGE A. DE VOS ■
LOLA ROMANUCCI-ROSS

Chapter Fifteen

Ethnic Identity: A Psychocultural Perspective

In conclusion we recapitulate and integrate a number of themes and theoretical arguments presented in the foregoing chapters.

Part I: Concepts of Ethnic Identity

In Part I we included three conceptually oriented chapters. Here and throughout, our authors concerned themselves with themes of origins, real and mythological, and the various contrastive definitions that comprise a specific ethnic identity. Although contrastive attributions of ethnic characteristics from outside the group help shape the inner experience of ethnic belonging during one's life, it is the internally motivated *instrumental and expressive uses* of ethnicity that are the final determinants of who we say we are. In the final analysis, ethnicity is social loyalty and existential meaning derived from a human need for continuity in belonging. It is complementary to the use of ethnicity in situations emphasizing contrast from others.

The introductory chapter by George A. De Vos provides a general psychocultural definition of ethnicity, originating from a sense of group belonging based on parentage. Scholars have often defined ethnicity *objectively*, with respect to attributes of membership set off from the outside, as well as from within, by racial, territorial, economic, religious, cultural, aesthetic, or linguistic separateness. However, like any other form of social identity, ethnicity remains essentially *subjective*, a collective sense of social belonging and ultimate loyalty related to parentage and a belief in common origins. Ethnicity is a *past* sense of allegiance, to be distinguished from forms of social identity based on any salient *present* or *future* orientation. These are not static, immutable definitions, but change with time and political or social urgencies. On its deepest level, ethnicity provides a quasi-religious sense of group belonging affording continuity and purpose.

As Schwartz shows, there is a human cognitive necessity to categorize. We invent conceptual order to comprehend the world around us. Classifications are useful in categorizing humans and objects. Schwartz relates ethnicity to the basic psychological processes of separation found in totemic thought and creation of Otherness. Among Melanesians, a totemic form of categorization can be found in an emblematic separation of groups into ethnic divisions. Schwartz shows that pluralistic cultures are not solely the results of the modern national state: throughout the stateless Melanesian macrocultural area ethnic groups interpenetrated and lived in juxtaposition with one another long before Western contact. His chapter offers elegant evidence that the conceptual limits of ethnic identity have been as problematic for Melanesians, past and present, as they are for people living in other cultures today.

Romanucci-Ross's chapter illustrates the fusion and fission processes in cultural change or cultural persistence. Continuing processes of social definition throughout a milennia created and maintained group and personal identity in an ancient region of Italy. An array of elements can be found in a cultural space out of which a lesser class of determinants of configuration characterize and distinguish it from other related *ethnes*.

In Italy, invasions came as ocean tides disturbing the "set" or array of these elements. Time-space relations, Romanucci-Ross contends, are crucial in the genesis and maintenance of the identity of an ethnic group. For the Piceni, space is very limited and historical time is very long; it loses itself in prehistory. In such a situation, determinants of cultural configuration are markedly different from those cultures in which Western historical time is brief but space is vast, e.g., the United States, Canada, or Australia. Factors to be considered are: the structure of the family and the place of romantic love among various familial constellations; the uses of formal language and dialect; models of behavior; conflict resolution strategies; work, play, exchange of goods and services; the ethics and aesthetics in the creation of "the ethnic personality"; and the culture of an ethnic enclave.

Part II: The Fabrication of New Ethnic Enclaves

Stevan Harrell, in his chapter, examines the complex patterned ethnicity of this region of Asia. First, there are processes involved in defining ethnicity by scholars using cultural-linguistic criteria. They trace the geographic and temporal story of the movement of separate groups. This process of identification, however, is not congruent with that of state recognition. Outside approaches can differ considerably from the ways local people come to perceive themselves, consider their history, and communicate to each other who they are. The "languages" of local discourse include what Harrell refers to as "ethnic markers"—present forms of dress, food, marriage patterns, rituals, and customs as well as special speech patterns. Although official categorization attempts to be consistent in its definitions, internally different groups still vary in their use of far different criteria in defining in-group membership—different signs of identity or separation, different degrees of clarity or fuzziness, and different forms of discreteness or overlap. The various definitions now in use can be quite recent or remote in time. The reasons for selective self-definition can manifest clear instrumental purposes or can be obscure as to possible motives including expressive needs. Outside observers or officials have had notable recent influence modifying group self-definitions, because they distribute resources and privileges according to official ethnic category membership.

Rapid changes in ethnic formation can occur in what might be considered an isolated region with a very low degree of technological development. Eugeen Roosens describes how a recently self-defined African group can legitimize itself by mythologizing a more distant past origin. He examines ethnic descent as a symbolic construction in the current urbanization patterns occurring in Zaire. The Bayaka (so-called by colonials and missionaries) were really three groups: the Luunda, the Yaka, and the Suku, among possibly other "peoples." Considerable confusion, Roosens asserts, has been due to the European manner of viewing "the problem."

Part III: The Emergence of National States

Victor Uchendu examines African ethnic formation in a more overall dimension. He touches on the complexity of ethnic problems in a rapidly changing Africa where postcolonial political changes, urbanization, and other forces have been influencing social and political consciousness. Uchendu sees the search for identity in black Africa as comprised of four sometimes conflicting alternatives. First, there is an identity with the entire continent, based on newly achieved postcolonial political independence. Second, one finds a uniting black racial identity. Third, there are new, somewhat synthetically achieved African national identities. Fourth is the continuing force of separate local ethnic identities. Many Africans are situation oriented and can easily become tribal or urban, depending on context. Uchendu views ethnic groups as social categories providing a basis of status ascription, a basis that can fluctuate with rapid political and economic change.

Charles Keyes looks at how the Tai state, to define itself defensively as an independent political entity, deliberately built up a Tai national ethnic identity amalgamating people of different origins in Southeast Asia. Recognition of kinship among some Tai-speaking peoples is a product not of objective linguistic or ethnolinguistic characteristics, but of processes of nationalization. These processes have been set in motion first, by the creation of modern nation-states in Southeast Asia, and then by the recent intensified flows of people, goods, and information across the boundaries of these newly constructed nation-states. Keyes affirms that premodern Tai-speaking communities were not self-defined in linguistic, ethnic, or national terms but with reference to their "genealogies" that had very different premises one from the other. The modern Tai, Keyes concludes, have been invented by others, as well as by themselves. He is most interested in these processes of invention, not in the presumed essential qualities that supposedly make Tai different from others.

Éva Huseby-Darvas cites as a paradigm a particular case of a search for a sense of self by a Jew, born in Hungary, who sought desperately to belong. In the individually illustrated case of Árpád Gyula Huszár, an unbridgeable abyss grew between the self he ascribed to himself as a Hungarian and how he was seen by others. His story reflects a general mood in Hungary in the present era that is filled with economic and political difficulties. In Eastern Europe anti-Semitism continues to be manipulated to reflect processes of scapegoating of vulnerable minorities and the availability of ethnic prejudice for politicians seeking ways to gain easy popularity. Jews and Gypsies have been used historically throughout Eastern Europe for such purposes. These traditions intertwine with the continuing ethnic antagonisms among the Christian groups of this area divided into Roman and Orthodox churches and a patchwork of linguistic heterogeneity. The truncated nation-state entity of Hungary is, after Albania and Poland, the most ethnically homogeneous country in the area. But the question of who is really Hungarian still bedevils social sentiments, especially with a new influx of refugees from other locales. People are concerned with the treatment of minority Hungarians in neighboring states. There is, therefore, a continual perturbation related to trying to redraw the geographical and psychological boundaries of Hungarianness in Eastern Europe.

Part IV: Conflicts Due to Exclusory Ethnicity in Nation-States

Mary Kay Gilliland writes of "Nationalism and Ethnogenesis in the Former Yugoslavia." Drawing on her intimate experience over the past fifteen years in what is now a "bordertown" between Croatia and Serbia, she suggests strongly that the social identities of residents were not always primarily associated with ethnicity or nationality. This view contradicts the usual perception of the long-standing nature of ethnic-nationalist attitudes among the majority of the inhabitants of this region.

As in the previous chapter by Harrell, Gilliland discusses the differences between self-definitions and the previous official government position about the Muslims, arbitrarily defining them as a separate nationality, or *narod.* And, as with Italy, discussed by Romanucci-Ross, place was also an important part of personal and group identity, in many instances taking precedence over nationality. With the war, however, many of these priorities of allegiance have been quickly realtered by the policies of those who have seized power in the various splinters of the previously united state. Gilliland contends that although ethnic nationalism has now become widespread, the war did not simply begin because of nationalism. She emphasizes how politically driven economic policies were the motor. Historically available nationalist feelings were available, though, and quickly provided a metaphor for antagonisms redefining group relations. Gilliland claims that in the current war, political leaders and other elites have deliberately used ethnicity to gain backing for political agendas that were, in their inception, not primarily ethnically motivated.

Gananath Obeyesekere, considering Buddhist identity in Sri Lanka, forcefully brings out some major points that contribute to our general conclusions both on a psychological and a societal level. On a psychological level, crises in identity tend to occur at certain times of life for various individuals or groups; therefore, ethnic identity must be assessed in the context of a total life trajectory. This perspective takes on added significance when viewed in light of Erik Erikson's psychoanalytic frame of analysis for the life history of the individual.[1] Erikson's analysis relates crises in identity, especially during adolescence, to the ways in which resolved and unresolved past vicissitudes continue to influence new experiences. Here again, it is the mythic meaning of past events, not their behavioral details, that determines how new situations will precipitate crises in the individual's concept of self.

The personal and the societal intertwine: Obeyesekere shows how "identity affirmation" can bolster self-esteem with political consequences. The British colonization of Ceylon had profound effects on Sinhalese preservative self-identity. In crises involving a perceived threat to the unity of an ethnic group, identity affirmation resolves internal stresses resulting from political and social degradation of the group. What can take place, in other words, is a collective "revivalist" response to a political defeat or dissolution. Ethnic revivalist movements commonly are manifestations of defense against threatened extinction when an externally imposed ruling polity seeks to secure the ultimate loyalty of all those it governs by its policies. Some form of identity affirmation can counter the effects of a period of dispersion and degradation by evoking old images and emblems around which members can rally to shed shame, renew ethnic pride, and gain a sense of self-acceptance.

In highlighting the life of Amagarika Dharmapala, Obeyesekere illustrates the difficulties of individual identity management in Sri Lanka in the latter period of colonial rule as the country moved toward political independence. Amagarika Dharmapala experienced a fierce intrapsychic struggle in growing up as a Sinhalese in that society—i.e., as a member of a politically and economically submerged people. He conceptualized his own struggle as an irreconcilable conflict between two bodies of religious teaching. In his case, a sustaining identification with Christian mentors failed to take hold and ultimately, through an enduring and ascendant attachment to maternal models, he reaffirmed his familial allegiance to Buddhism and successfully transmitted his conviction to thousands of his countrymen.

Lastly, on a level of social consequences, Obeyesekere demonstrates how past events have meaning for the individual only insofar as they are turned into easily communicated legends symbolizing continuity between past and present. Present identity thus is influenced more by myths of the past than by actual occurrences. In Sri Lanka, Sinhalese identity is inextricably interwoven with a Buddhist mythology. Today, to be Sinhalese is to be Buddhist; pluralism is denied as a possibility. The Sinhalese majority has attempted to resolve its problems of ethnic identity by forming a religious state. Like modern Israel, however, Sri Lanka may have created problems for itself in its religious definition of nationhood. It is still unclear how the Christian, Muslim, and Hindu minorities that together comprise a goodly percentage of Sri Lanka's population will be included in the concept of Sinhalese citizenship.

Part V: Minority Inclusion/Exclusion and National Identity

Most observers of ethnicity today are not only interested in how ethnicity still totally defines citizenship in national states, but rather in how it remains a question of *relative* acceptance or derogation among those of separate origins who have technically become "citizens" in a multiethnic modern state. Historically, the question is sometimes who is actually included in the majority and which groups are constrained to be minorities in a composite national entity.

Ethnic minorities buffeted between shifting political boundaries are a principal feature of Eastern Europe's ever-changing unhappy history. In addition to chapters on Hungary and the former Yugoslavia, we include a chapter on ethnic complexity in a Lithuanian city. Poet Czeslaw Milosz writes about his city, "Vilnius, an Ethnic Agglomerate." It is now again officially located in a newly independent Lithuania. Made up of people from many origins, religious faiths, and linguistic preferences, this city reflects, in a microcosm, the vagaries of political and social history in the Baltic area. Symbolically, the name given a city by its inhabitants can change temporally with the group that comes to power. In Lithuania class hostility combined with ethnic conflict. In addition to ethnic concerns, status aspirations also had an impact on the identities favored by its inhabitants. Patterns of loyalty reflected reference-group allegiances influenced by pretensions of nobility or higher bourgeoisie life-styles. These class concerns cut across other patterns of possible ethnic loyalty. Milosz speculates about how a person who grows up surrounded by people who speak various languages and belong to various cultural backgrounds acquires a different personality than does one brought up in a homogeneous ethnic milieu.

George A. De Vos, in a chapter partially co-written with Hiroshi Wagatsuma, examines the Japanese sense of self, both as an Asian national minority in a modernizing Western world and as a society having difficulties acknowledging its own minorities, holding firmly to its mythologically based ideology of ethnic homogeneity and uniqueness of origin. Japanese do not yet readily like to distinguish between citizenship and ethnicity. Broadly, the Japanese have been able to modernize without any radical social dislocation or political upheaval. Nevertheless, individual Japanese have manifested some vertiginous alienation due to Western contact. Some intellectuals have communicated in their intimate writings the internal tensions experienced as a result of sustained contact with an ascendant Western alien culture.

De Vos further considers the identity issues faced by two of Japan's four principal minorities. One, the Burakumin, was an officially designated pariah group in the premodern state. Today, these nearly three million people, whose segregated existence is not officially acknowledged, still suffer the daily indignities of an unresolved minority caste problem. The other minority, of close to a million Korean-Japanese, are an acknowledged ethnic constituency whose economic plight has been even more problematical. Both groups have been treated as genetically inferior people. De facto, the results of social disparagement are similar for both groups. In many respects, whatever their differences in origin, one notes the deleterious psychological and social effects of social derogation on minority adaptation within the supposedly ethnically homogeneous Japanese state.

Turning to our composite American society, the late Margaret Mead asked, "Who is American?" The formation of American national identity, as sketched by Mead, begins with colonial ambivalence about the dispossessed Native American. This ambivalence extends through subsequent U.S. history as an ethical dilemma of separation versus inclusion and ethnic pluralism versus integration. U.S. inhabitants, Mead contended, are continually changing as they change their appraisals of subsequent waves of immigrants. Ethnic separation becomes a "self-selected mutually rejecting superiority, pitted against the ethic of ethnic assimilation." Mead also drew attention to the second central dilemma to be found in the American identity—the factual barriers to mobility lodged in a class system that belies an ideological commitment to an ideal of social mobility devoid of class considerations. The American identity is a conflictful one in which inclusiveness of citizenship versus exclusiveness continues from past into present, creating the dynamic tension that shapes the course of change in American history.

The chapter on new immigrants in the United States can be viewed as a sequel to what Mead described. In a society now host to new immigrants from Latin America and Asia, the tension between inclusion and exclusion continues. These forces, operative among those already here, influence processes of identity formation among new arrivals. Carola and Marcelo Suárez-Orozco examine processes now shaping identity formation from one generation to the next among youth from Latin America. Their chapter also addresses the centrality of ethnic migration as a social and political issue in every modern industrial state. Official or majority group definitions in the United States more or less vaguely put "Latinos" or "Hispanics" into a single category that ignores complex differences among immigrants sharing the Spanish or Portuguese language. The shadow world of undocumented immigration is a particular cause for further social anxiety and more conscious arousal of interethnic tension that effects even legal immigrants. Special problems of identity formation are found in the children of immigrants, rather than in the adult immigrant generation itself. A minority identity sometimes demands resolution of internally conflictful patterns of self-acceptance or group rejection. Peer group and family dynamics play roles in forging new identities during formative childhood years.

Origins, Rules, and Contrasts in Ethnic Identity

Where Are We from? Causality and Continuity

As discussed in Chapter 1, ethnic identity is in essence a *past-oriented* form of identity, embedded in the presumed cultural heritage of the individual or group. This form of social self-identity contrasts with a sense of belonging linked with citizenship within a political state, or *present-oriented* affiliations to specific groups demanding professional, occupational, or class loyalties. It also contrasts with those identities that reject both past and present in favor of a *future-oriented* ideological commitment to a realizable future social goal.

Our first section emphasizes that to know one's *origin* is to have not only a sense of provenience, but perhaps more importantly, a sense of *continuity* in which one finds the personal and social *meaning* of human existence to some degree. It is to know *why* one behaves and acts in accordance with custom. To be without a sense of continuity is to be faced with one's own death. Extinction of a group occurs when, as a California Indian once remarked to anthropologist Alfred Kroeber, "the bowl of custom is broken and we can no longer drink of life." Ethnicity can most readily be *symbolically represented contrastively*. It may involve self-consciously perceived variations in *language* and *customs* from others. It may be symbolized in affirmative *ritual practices* such as dramatic symbolic representations recalling past collective ordeals or days of heroic triumph. Ethnicity is explained by *religious myth*, since religious beliefs or myths are, in effect, very often attempts to explain group origin and group continuity.

Two alternate forms of myth occur as widespread explanations of origin among peoples of the world. These are autochthonous myths of human origin from a given sacred place and, alternatively, religious myths that dramatize "the journey"—an event buried in the distant past. Myths explaining origin buttress a conviction that one's group arrived "here" from elsewhere. Origin, in this sense, has a spatial, territorial dimension. One's idea of social meaning is also temporal. A feeling of social belonging also obtains from moving through time or territory, both as an individual and as a member of a group and a culture. Traditions characteristically present a script for group continuity from the past into the future, carefully perpetuating factual fictions or fictional facts as links that bind generations. Concern with origins is a concern with *parentage*. To know who they are, individuals and groups look back genealogically to their progenitors and possibly eponymous ancestors. Some mythologies explain how men and women descended from a primordial mating event; others explain group diversity as totemic, as suggested in Chapter 2. Human subgroups are descended from different animals or plants. In Judeo-Christian mythology, the Tower of Babel marks the origin of linguistic diversification by punitively dividing groups from each other for their presumption to wish to reach up to the heavenly creator. Mythological explanations of origin help explain present differences between groups as well as providing the rationale for such differences.

Curiously, a number of mythological traditions indirectly reveal the converse. They are attempts by a cultural group, for the sake of present cohesion, to deny previous diversity of origin by disguising evidence of past amalgams that occurred through conquest. Greek myths excel in disguising past conflicts, including changes from matrilineal to patrilineal descent as a result of conquest, into an organized Olympic Pantheon. The book of Genesis in the Hebrew Bible, according to Freud, disguises the several separate tribal origins of Jews with different gods who were united in monotheistic allegiance. Genesis gives internal evidence suggesting that there occurred a blending of two or more deities (Elohim) into one Yaveh. Similarly, the ancient Japanese mythology preserved in the Kojiki and Nihongi gives internal evidence that prior political conflicts were resolved religiously by producing a more unified, accommodatively organized pantheon of deities. Religion is regulation. It is purpose. It is destiny. It maintains order and prevents an entropic reversion to primal chaos. An ethnic identity exists in a moral universe.

What Must We Do? Moral Control and Ethnic Belonging

Origin myths establish who one is, and, because of one's progenitors, with which group one has rights and obligations. Such knowledge helps individuals resolve priorities of loyalty and allegiance in terms of a *past* frame of reference. It helps to integrate and regulate one's behavior. It defines the classes of persons to whom one can express affection or vent aggression. It indicates those who deserve respect and those who are to be derogated. The sense of history is celebrated in collective ritual. Ritual acts are also expressions of commitment, be it to a religion, to a nation of loyal citizens, or to an ethnic group. Such acts are a collective experience that teaches those who participate who they are. The redundancy of ritual goes beyond verbal expression, reinforcing emotional response, and allowing participants to identify with one another in sharing an explicit sense of purpose. Rituals of belonging are reaffirmations of origin, dramatizations of ancestral suffering ("lachrimosity," as Huseby-Darvas refers to it among Hungarians) and triumph, out of which future purpose is born and sustained. For example, for the Jews the sacred holidays commemorate historical occurrences that reaffirm reasons for continuity. The communion ritual for Christians (ingesting the body of Christ from a common vessel) represents both the historical fact of the beginning of Christianity and the sense of belonging to a group that moves forward with a purpose to the Last Judgment.

In modern societies, as in folk cultures, the reasons for *present* rules can be explained by *past* mythology. Taboos of food and other constraints on behavior are explained in terms of past occurrences, usually a specific mythologized event. It seems that humans always have to know *why* something is or is not done, and mythology provides the explanations that justify required behavior. Many of the historical occurrences that are ritualized or become legend tend to be symbolic victories of survival or attempts at revival. In Native American history, the Ghost Dance was the revivalist ritual of a defeated people. Today the massacre at Wounded Knee and the long bloody forced marches of Native American families from their eastern homes into western reservations are tales of ordeal that stimulate a need for survival by the maintenance of group consciousness.

Revivalist movements and legends of ordeal are affirmations of the state of affairs that existed before a traumatic defeat that has marked a people, symbolizing a temporal extension backward to a time of group strength that existed before defeat. As we indicated in the introduction, the contemporary militant black movement among African-Americans in the United States contains an explicit and an implicit affirmation of a dignified and respected African identity as a point of origin.

In rituals of affirmation that reinforce ethnic identity, there is often reference to a mythical golden age before the fall. Fascist Italy returned to Roman military insignias and titles in an attempt to reestablish continuity with the past Roman Empire. Thus, some Italians sought symbolically to wipe out millennia of fragmentation, foreign conquest, and subjugation. For authentic Fascists (and there were some), this was an affirmation of pan-Italianism, as was their attempt to purge the Italian language of foreign idioms. Such uses of historical glory to assert cultural integrity are also discussed in the chapters on Hungary, Croatia, Sri Lanka, and Japan. In their zeal to eradicate borrowed impurities, some Japanese even became anti-Buddhist, since it was a "foreign" religion that had invaded Japan thirteen centuries earlier. Some French groups, alarmed by the threat of "franglais," are attempting to keep the French language "pure."

Ethnic identity can be a positive affirmation containing a negative potential for exhibiting a hysterical or paranoid defense. As in all forms of belonging, it can be used to express one's humanness, or to deny the humanness of others; its use depends on collective and individual mental health. It also depends on an agreed-upon reality of external pressure and oppression. In addition to creating a sense of common origin, ethnic identity also defines the rules of comportment. The essential correctness of one's own behavior and the behavior of one's group may or may not be contrasted with the behavior of outsiders. Groups differ greatly in the degree to which contrastive criteria are used. Social behavior in conformity to group expectation cannot be completely regulated through socialization, therefore no culture can afford the absence of "reinforcers" of desired behavior. These are understood by all group members as having an inviolability even stronger than formal law. Punishment is meted out to those who break the covenant of belonging through incorrect behavior, thereby destroying group cohesion and threatening group survival. Belonging to a group, then, means being aware of group expectations and group regulations—we know who we are through learning what we are expected to do and what not to do. Embodiment of group identity may be found in periodic ritual religious acts, as discussed by Durkheim in *The Elementary Forms of Religious Life* (1947). It may also be embodied in a written tradition that is, at the same time, a body of laws, such as the Christian and Jewish Bible or the Islamic Koran.

The need to follow unique rules may permit a given people to maintain their identity despite their *present* proximity to others. Indeed, as Schwartz pointed out in Chapter 2, such awareness of proximity and difference may cause the differences to be amplified and to become emblematic. Jews are a well-known case in point. They have kept their integrity by following their tribal regulations throughout their history. The Batak in Sumatra, by maintaining their *adat* (law), create an illusion of cultural continuity that enables them to move easily into culturally heterogeneous modern cities (Bruner 1976). Objectively (i.e., as seen by the outsider), their law changes, but those who identify themselves as Batak perceive no change in their law. Belief in the continuity of law keeps them identified as Batak.

In some ethnic groups recruitment is possible; candidates with no "birthright" may be asked to experience a rebirth ritual signifying that they will henceforth recognize and obey the laws joyfully. Such emphasis on *law* is characteristic of the boundary area between ethnic identity and citizenship. As more emphasis is placed on the political dimension of belonging, a *present* orientation begins to supplant the *past* in the sense of social identity. There is a variety of differences of emphasis between a *present* commitment to a state and to an ethnic group. In a pluralistic society, a major sanctioning force of an ethnic group is ostracism. But in commitment to the state one accedes to submission to law and, by force if necessary, to the political authority that is rationalized by all as necessary to survival.

It is possible to be simultaneously a loyal *citizen* of the state, a part of the superordinate political unit, and a member of an ethnic minority. Problems arise only if the rules are mutually antagonistic. When Jesus was asked about the coin of the Roman realm, he resolved what was supposed to be a conflict over Caesar's and God's possessions by giving each his own. Many Christians were later persecuted because they insisted on mixing logical levels (to paraphrase Bertrand Russell and Gregory Bateson) and created a dialectic that the Romans took up in a gleeful collusion to send them on their journey to Paradise. Actually, the Romans expected and accepted ethnic and religious diversity, but they would not brook the lack of respect implicit in repudiating the necessary symbolic acts of allegiance to the then-current Roman hegemony.

Like other forms of loyalty, ethnic identity is experienced as a moral commitment, making rejection of conflicting moral and legal commitments mandatory. When commitment becomes *future* oriented and therefore ideological or politicized, there is less necessity for maintaining an ethnic *past* concern with parentage and origin. The initiation ritual seems to suffice, a ritual in which the rebirth usually symbolizes rejection of actual ancestry and a pledge of allegiance to shared future goals of the new group. Allegiance shifted from past-oriented Roman gentes (origin of the word gentiles in the New Testament) to a future-oriented Christian church. Later, Marx and Trotsky repudiated Judaism in envisioning a new Communist future.

How Are We Different?

One's primary reference group is the audience observing one's behavior, and indeed some groups do not pay too much attention to outsiders in trying to define who they are. Other groups create their image at the expense of outsiders. Depending on the individual, as well as on group traditions, inclusiveness or exclusiveness may be important. Most often, a person's expected behavior tells one who one is, that is, it defines the reference group of primary belonging. Others who behave differently are not part of our group, and we come to know who we are by knowing who we are not. Of course, contrastive representations mark sex, age, and class differences.

The use of contrast is not so much dictated by geographic proximity as by the nature of the contact with another group. In identity maintenance, one has to assess the nature of the possible threat that close contact with an alien group implies. In a modern pluralistic society, where contact is intense and unavoidable, certain minor symbolic emblematic measures remain vital to maintain psychological distance from those outside one's group. In constructing any theory of ethnic identity it is necessary to consider how external or social distance factors are related to internal or psychological distance factors in identity boundary maintenance. Any or all cultural features can be used emblematically for contrastive purposes, including the prescribed and the tabooed, special foods, social rituals, ideals of physical beauty, and phonemic styles.

Many cultural effects become self-consciously contrastive only when contact with strangers suggests alternatives. Foods have seemed naturally edible or inedible; phonemic sequences natural and logical, standards of beauty divinely decreed. The manner and degree of reaction to newly discovered differences depends on the social or physiological threat posed by the contrastively perceived behavior. There are tolerable and intolerable differences within what is recognized as behavioral contrast. Others doing what is rigidly tabooed by one's own group will be most disturbing.

Romanucci-Ross was told by Sori islanders of an event that took place between themselves and Harenggan islanders (an Admiralty Island of the Bismarck Archipelago) a long time before culture contact with the West. The Sori were received with all due hospitality and given women, which the Sori thought was very nice indeed. But how horrendously crude of the Harenggan men to expect the Sori to lend Sori women when the Harenggan paid them a reciprocal visit! The Sori were so offended they broke off all diplomatic and trade relations with the Harenggan up to at least 1967 (Romanucci-Ross 1985). Projection of negative traits on an alien group is widespread. What is socially disavowed within one's own group is projected as prevalent among outsiders. In the Admiralties one group will often refer to the customs of other New Guinea groups by saying "as in the manner of pigs and dogs" (Romanucci-Ross 1985).

Contrasts may be viewed on a vertical or a horizontal dimension. Some contrasts neither elevate or degrade outsiders. In other circumstances, a particular pattern of behavior may be seem within a vertical framework of superiority/inferiority. For example, in noting racial differences, Europeans respond differently depending on whether the subject is African or Chinese.

Before the nineteenth century, Europeans were quite impressed by the achievements of the Chinese. They made invidious comparisons between the Chinese and Africans, whom they found primitive, since they understood nothing of the unperceivable (to them) complexities of some African cultures. Europeans have only recently begun to learn to appreciate the aesthetics of African art as a highly developed alternative to the naturalist traditions that persisted until the end of the nineteenth century in Europe.

In maintaining ethnic boundaries, some groups are more insistent on contrastive exclusiveness. Others are more open and inclusive, i.e., apt to bring in individuals to become part of the group rather than continue to emphasize differences. Polynesians, for example, exhibit an easy sense of inclusiveness, and Melanesians are acutely sensitive to differences. Melanesian cultures amplify all possible differences in continually creating new ethnic distinctions.

Similarly, white American attitudes have dictated that anyone with a black ancestor, no matter how remote, could not be considered white. Margaret Mead's chapter discussed the attempt to maintain contrastive racial distinctions that has been an obvious part of the dilemma of American identity. One factor determining criteria for exclusion or inclusion is reckoning of descent, whether lineage is traced bilaterally or unilaterally. Among Jews, for example, group belonging hinges on whether the mother is a group member, since, according to some scholars, the mother is considered the major disciplinary socializing influence assuring that the child recognizes and adheres to the law through his or her formative years. One might easily reason, however, that matrilineal societies, though patronymic, appear to care very much about the bloodline of the mother. In certain primitive societies, ownership of material and nonmaterial cultural elements demand certainty as to who the *real* bloodline progenetor is. Motherhood is resistant to impeachment on this issue.

At times a contrastive sense of ethnic identity actually came about through conflict. In Melanesia the cargo cult phenomenon, according to Schwartz, depended on the believers *and* on the nonbelievers, who provided the dynamic-contrastive tensions necessary for the movement to sustain itself. The sense of one's existence in such a culture depends upon a continual rivalry and confrontation within the system.

The internal or external sense of contrast in a culture may, as noted above, be emphasized in either a vertical or horizontal direction. Contrastive ethnic feelings can be directed toward individuals considered equal antagonists, or the sense of ethnic separateness may be based on viewing another group as inferior. In time such a disparaged group may indeed come to view themselves as inferior. They exhibit, in Kardiner's terms (Lee and De Vos 1981), some internalized "mark of oppression" in their self-concepts.

It is psychologically difficult for groups whose self-esteem has been based on physical prowess to avoid interpreting military and political defeat as proof of personal worthlessness. An unhappy history of ethnic identity is exemplified by some Native Americans. Some groups, as a defeated warrior people forced to live with their conquerors, have not as yet devised a satisfactory collective means of escaping the psychological effects of the destruction of their own cultural identity in the course of the past century. Jews, on the other hand, defeated and dispersed, nevertheless sustained pride in the relative invulnerability of their intellectual-religious attainments that buffered the effects of political annihilation. Scots, ambivalent as they have remained over their forced political union with the English, have found compensatory ethnic pride in commercial enterprise, with the added advantage of permitted regional self-sustenance.

Finally, the study of contrast in ethnic identity leads us back to the discussions in Chapter 1 of stratification in systems of ethnic pluralism. It also relates further to a topic not considered in this volume, namely, the entire question of regional-national *ethnic ascendancy* as it influences the political interaction of supposedly independent national states. For example, viewing European history in ethnically interactive terms as patterns of emulation, one notes the gradual cultural ascendancy of the French in Europe from the reign of Louis XIV continuing into the twentieth century. The ascendant French in Europe developed nonreciprocal relations with others, as the French language became dominant internationally. Throughout Europe, it became the language of the nobility. Intermarrying nobility (and royalty) transcended specific ethnic loyalties. The language of the Polish and Russian courts, for example, became French. Today, American commercial ascendancy is met with ambivalence with respect to its effects on ethnic identity. The language of international trade, commerce, and transportation has become English. The French are resisting, as best they can, the commercial success of the American film industry and popular music in an attempt to maintain French "culture" as still psychologically equal if not ascendant.

Ethnic Leadership

Leadership in shaping ethnic history is a topic merely broached in this book in the chapter by Obeyesekere and referred to negatively as part of the problem of political expediency by Gilliland. We need further exploration of the psychocultural characteristics of legendary heroes as well as the actual leaders of ethnic movements. How does their behavior, real or mythical, actual or imputed, correspond to the central social issues of highly desirable group traits? When examined carefully, we would probably find that minority group leaders personify some of the complexities of divided ethnic loyalties or contrastive heroic assertions against another group's possible ascendancy. "Stagalie," a folk legend of black Americans, is a heroic figure capable of exercising exaggerated violence with bravado and dominance. Such prowess is deemed necessary for survival in the harsh underworld of black counterculture, a culture developed partially as a result of the denial to blacks of access to the majority society. Clever, cunning and cruel, rogue and outlaw, Stagalie is the symmetrical inversion of the traditional, acceptable "Black Sambo," who symbolized to whites the subordinate status of blacks.

Native Americans have a store of heroes ranging from the elusive Apache, Geronimo, to the religious leader Handsome Lake. All are symbols of resistance or some form of religious revival that might allow one to avoid acknowledging final defeat. In modern times, Charles de Gaulle, represented a final attempt at ethnic ascendancy by France, the final resistance to becoming a coequal rather than a dominant partner in forming a European multiethnic community. For Turks, Kamal Ataturk has been a symbol of modern rebirth, a figure of transition through which to be Turkish could also mean to be modern.

Curiously, in numerous instances the leader who personifies an ethnic group is an outsider. Such a leader often vehemently affirms his allegiance as the means of overcoming his questionable legitimacy of belonging. Ataturk was of Anatolian ancestry, a minority group within the old Turkish empire. Hitler was an Austrian, perhaps of Jewish descent. Napoleon was a Corsican of possible Italian origin. De Gaulle's ancestors were Flemings from what became northwest France from the time of Louis XIV, who had taken on a new, more French-sounding name to emphasize their loyalty to France. Malcolm X, a leader of the black movement in the United States, was all the more motivated toward a black identity by the previous excruciating ambivalence he experienced when he once attempted to identify strongly with the majority whites (Haley 1966). The reaffirmation of his black identity was a positive resolution of a deep psychological stress—internal tensions were transmuted by a strong need to affirm the black man's right to dignity. The autobiography of Valiers (1968), a French-Canadian ethnic leader, is a highly poignant parallel to that of Malcolm X. It demonstrates the functional similarity between racially or culturally mixed inheritances in producing a divided self, a problem that for some people can be resolved only by an exemplary affirmation that may result in the appearance of a group hero.

A potential sense of alienation in many members of a minority group can be overcome by witnessing how the hero behaves in order to become a "true" person. Such a person can bend events to a realization of common purpose. Ethnic identity movements, therefore, are usually led by individuals who, at given points in their careers, manifest some resolution of previously disturbing internal states, which are also experienced by many other members of the group at large. Such movements are also collective alternatives to isolated individual attempts at passing or guarding one's ethnic feelings in silence.

If we describe leaders, we must also have an idea of characteristics of followers. Many cultures prepare the individual for loneliness, alienation, or isolation. In some simpler societies, it is in solitude that one encounters the sacred. Among the Plains

Indians, death and rebirth occurred during the Sun Dance, in which the flesh is punctured deeply beyond the muscle layer (pain is sustained alone), or during the (lonely) Vision Quest. For Amerindian missionaries, as well as those from Tibet and Siberia, only solitude in the wilderness could open doors in the human mind; doors that could, for example, make of one a healer or a great leader. "To learn and to see," said a Mexican Huichol Shaman, "one must go many times to the mountain alone."

But individuals in complex societies, where value is placed on highly narrow intentional fields, seek meaning in a leader— even in cyberspace, if necessary. (No one wants to be outside the information highway, regardless of how trivial or banal the information.) If one's fundamental belief is in science, technology, and progress, then solitude as a subjective state is to be feared and shunned. One seeks the reassurance of the leader and the comfort of an approving surrounding mass of others just like oneself.

Ethnicity and Healing: A Medical Dimension

The relevance of ethnic belonging has come to be recognized by researchers in medical anthropology. Romanucci-Ross found a hierarchy of resort within curative practices. Specific "native diseases" required specific native remedies, whereas one went to the white man's hospital for white man's diseases. Furthermore, native diseases also had points of origin in other native ethnic groups, and one had to go to *their* healers, and one had to practice preventive medicine against such foreign witchcraft. If cures appeared elusive, a local group would declare loyalty to their own diseases (Romanucci-Ross 1977). Crandon-Malamud found diversity in ethnicity and class as determining choices in a medically pluralistic society in Bolivia. She noted that groups negotiated the meanings of their ethnic affiliations through "medical dialogue," with resulting political and economic (and ethnic) implications in diagnosis and cure (1991).

The breakdown of the Soviet Union has provided fertile ground for the reemergence of shamanism, which had been targeted for extinction by the former Soviet central government (Balzer 1991). Official government vehicles brought modern Western medicine to rural villages (as local shamans were derided or even incarcerated as drunks and charlatans (Balzer 1993a). But now shamanic curing and healing are dramatically on the rise in such places and even in some urban areas (Balzer 1993b).

The shaman, in his role as technician of ecstasy and healing, traditionally created a culturally shared "inner space" in which the healing of the body and the body politic occurred. Healer and poet, a shaman was the keeper and interpreter of symbols that were cultural instruments to perceive and arrange reality. A shaman wielded and maintained for the group the generators and stylizers of forces that compelled mind and experience. One could return to a shaman for identity surrounded by a world in disarray or in ruins (Romanucci-Ross 1989).

Contextual Changes in the Individual Expression of Ethnic Identity

Society in general expects the individual to maintain some behavioral consistency. One must remain recognizable or social interaction is impossible. In moral terms, an individual is supposed to maintain "integrity." Ethnic identity, like any form of identity, is not only a question of knowing who one is subjectively, but of how one is seen from the outside. Ethnic identity requires the maintenance of sufficiently consistent behavior so that others can place an individual or a group in some given social category, thus permitting appropriate interactive behavior.

Extremes of mobility—social, geographic, or ethnic—are socially disruptive. Society needs consistency in attribution for interpersonal functioning. In other words, identity involves some internally socialized consistency with respect to behavioral norms so that the individual and those with whom one is in contact know what to expect in interpersonal relationships. It is uncomfortable to be part of a social scene or watch a dramatic presentation in which the players change their designated parts in an inconsistent fashion. To some degree, people must be able to relate in terms of approximations or stereotypic expectations. Complete unpredictability in another's behavior makes social communication impossible. Internally, an individual also has to maintain a sense of self by certain patterns of consistency. The work of George Herbert Mead describes how a "generalized other" is internalized in the composition of a consistent sense of self.

Self-consistency within given cultures is related to the periodic use of altered states of consciousness that allow a person to overcome limitations imposed by conscious control of a consistent self. Individuals in trance, for example, can act out roles that are too inconsistent with the usual self to be tolerated in an ordinary state of consciousness. A striking example of this is found in the documentary film by Jean Rouch, "Les Maitres Fous." On their weekends, natives of Ghana who are working in modern industrialized factories participate in a new religion, which consists of a communal feast. A live dog is dismembered. The individuals in trance eat and share this "communion." In their trance state they become white colonial officials, exemplifying social power and prestige. Such behavior was impossible for these people to assume in their ordinary state of consciousness. In trance, however, they could emulate the members of the then dominant Western white culture, strutting and assuming other postures of self-importance. The internal structure of these assumed roles, of course, remained a foreign mystery to the participants of the feast.

Edward Sapir (1968) talked about cultures as "genuine" or "spurious," stating that a person is only "natural" in one language. A second acquired language never takes on the internal natural emotional richness of one's language of nativity or childhood. Changes of ethnic identity, therefore, may seem somewhat artificial and external if the changes are assumed after personality structure has rigidified into the consistent pattern of an adult. To be subjectively genuine, changes in identity must start sufficiently early to make the assumption of a particular behavior feel internally natural to the individual. A sense of identity is, by definition and by implication, a conscious part of the self rather than the operation of unperceived automatic mechanisms. It is a conscious awareness of what and who one is in relation to a social group. An ethnic identity is developed through time and takes on various meanings in the course of one's life experience, as one contrasts one's social group in some measure against the dominant culture and against other groups within it.

In her chapter, Romanucci-Ross discussed briefly the continuing internal and external feedback in identity affirmation that is received and acted upon. Primary family and face-to-face identity are influenced in modern society by the multitudinous recordings of experience received through print and other message media. There is a continual onslaught of socially perceived information and continual editorializing about it, keeping a person in touch with the past history of one's group and its present circumstances. The reverberations of such experiences may not be immediate but become particularly significant at crisis periods in the trajectory of a lifetime. The social feedback mechanisms that establish, develop, and maintain an ethnic identity have immediate and delayed effects that may only become manifest much later in the life cycle.

For some, crises in consistency occur at points of challenge or choice; for others, choice or commitment is gradual or cumulative. These points of choice may be imperceptible or highly dramatic. Individuals can identify by gradually taking on a certain way of behaving, but by doing so they eliminate the possibility of alternate ways of behaving. The process need not be painful, though it often is when one cannot consciously resolve inconsistent and conflictual modes of behavior. Identity theory, therefore, must be related to some concepts of a continuing need for closure, for self-consistency, that embodies both the cognitive and the affective. Some individuals learn to live with ambiguity and dissonance (and, as a matter of fact, it is not unknown for this to eventually become a survival tactic or a means of manipulating others). These internal inconsistencies may find expression in collective social movements and in complex forms of individual adjustment or maladjustment.

Choice points are not only related to alternatives between two models of behavior, they are also related to the levels of inclusiveness to which the individuals refers his or her behavior. The individual may learn to identify with expanding circles of inclusiveness. One's first level of inclusiveness is with self alone, the next perhaps with family and other face-to-face relationships in the community. One may transcend a community by identifying with a professional world. The psychological investment in each of these widening or segmenting circles will vary in strength.

Our focus in this volume is on the level of belonging related to ethnicity as we have defined it—levels and modes of cultural separateness in one's sense of self. We cannot, therefore, consider the other realms of identity except insofar as they reflect our particular concern. For black Africans, as Uchendu has indicated, there are several alternative levels of belonging in modern societies. One goes from the community or so-called tribal group into a broader identity with a nation-state, or a group of similar nations (all of black Africa, for example), or even with an entire continent (the African continent as a whole in contrast with Europe, Asia, or the Americas). Usually, an individual can move from one such realm of identity to another without conflict, for one of these identities can be contained within the other. In the case of mutually exclusive ethnic identities, however, there can be crises in which the behavior demanded on one level is inconsistent with the behavior expected on another. It may be that the individual can find no stable position from which to resolve the resulting tensions.

In some societies, there are tragic representations of conflict related to priority of parental loyalty. Ancient Greek culture produced tragic myths concerning dilemmas of loyalty. For example, the tragedy of Orestes as presented in the Greek play grows out of the conflict produced by the competing claims of his mother and father for his loyalty. This tragedy embodies a residual problem of Greek cultural history in which patrilineal invaders overran ethnic groups with matrilineal descent. In killing his mother to avenge his father, Orestes is affirming his ultimate ethnic membership in the newly established patrilineal system. Symbolically, in the modern age we find tragic dilemmas of belonging related to social, racial, or ethnic marginality, such as the dilemma of the Eurasian in *Love Is a Many Splendored Thing*. There are many heartbreaking instances of various Eastern European family members deciding to be loyal to one or another of the political divisions into which subordinate ethnic groups were arbitrarily divided. The chapters of Milosz and Huseby-Darvas offer brief glimpses into this aspect of highly complex histories of ethnic conflict.

The mestizo in Mexico is often seen as an individual who is caught between an Indian and Spanish sense of belonging. In Mexico the condition of being a mestizo in culture and in personality is complex. Physical appearance is important but not conclusive. Mexicans rank themselves according to skin color and physical types: at the pinnacle are the most Caucasian, the most Spanish looking; at the bottom are the most Indian looking. In between there are various degrees of Indianness in skin color and comportment (Romanucci-Ross 1983). These racial and behavioral-cultural traits are almost always correlated with socioeconomic status. In Mexico, as elsewhere, there is a positive correlation between being darker and being poorer. In this context in Mexico, a sufficient amount of money or power can compensate for skin color. Questions arise as to how external social ascriptions fit or do not fit the inner identity of the person who is accorded or denied status by the ascribing group, for the social power of ascription in Mexico is quite evident (Romanucci-Ross 1983).

The present situation in the United States is more confused. There are so many standards and so much flux with regard to ethnic pluralism that individuals can transmit and receive many false signals. Passing is widespread. Names are changed. Modern plastic surgery even allows one to pick out a new physiognomy in an attempt to change one's social acceptability.

In studying the subjective sense of ethnic identity cross culturally, as touched on in the chapter by Carola and Marcelo Suárez-Orozco, the contrasting examples of Mexico and the United States raise an interesting issue. Where there are two or more rigidly defined life-styles, as in the Indian and the Spanish-Mexican, the force of group ascription may make almost irrelevant the subjective experience of the individual who is being defined. In situations where external standards are themselves in transition or lack universality, a sense of inner conflict arises out of the greater measure of choice placed upon the individual self. One is constrained to define as best one can where he or she fits in, or who one is. Thus, there are probably differences from one culture to another in the degree to which subjective conflict will have as much force in determining behavior or attempted behavior as will the external force of ascription exercised by the society.

In some circumstances, a dual or combined identity is not denied but encouraged. In Hawaii, for example, individuals of mixed Hawaiian and Chinese ancestry make a point of affirming themselves as a group, differing from either the pure Chinese or Hawaiian, just as mestizos in Mexico are a recognized ethnic group even though members are graded according to the degree of racial mixture and to the degree of Spanish or Indian cultural behavior. In a strong resurgence of ethnic specificity among the students at the University of California, a group of Eurasian students who had never united with others on the basis of their mixed ancestry found it expedient to come together as a small group to self-consciously discuss whether they identified more strongly with the heritage of their Caucasian parent or with that of their Asian parent. This type of identity decision concerns the issues raised about a contemporary democratic sense of integrity reflected in a felt necessity to affirm rather than deny the less prestigious segment of one's ancestry. This sense of integrity runs counter to previous patterns that emphasized identification with one's more socially elevated ancestors—a common mode of tracing genealogies practiced in aristocratically oriented societies.

Instrumental and Expressive Uses of Ethnicity[2]

Lastly, the social meaning of ethnicity is both rational-instrumental and deeply emotional and expressive. Instrumental interpersonal behavior is principally goal oriented—what one does or what one is concerned with is seen as a means to an end. It is behavior guided by some form of rationality. Expressive behavior, by contrast, is an end in itself, a result of a prior affective arousal or emotional need. Causal or rational concerns are secondary to feeling states.

Instrumental Behavior and Ethnic Identity

Achievement

Social definitions of success or achievement are found in every society. In a pluralistic society, personal success in one's endeavors may require one to emphasize ethnic belonging or to disguise it. In Chapter 1 we discussed passing at some length—including situations in which a person changes behavior or appearance to attain what is socially defined as success. We have also mentioned how minority status can, in some instances, stimulate compensatory striving. Many Japanese-Americans were so motivated by their immigrant parents (De Vos 1973c). In other instances, as in the situation that Ogbu (1978) discusses in understanding the poor school performance of many American black children, a defensive minority identity can prevent an individual from trying to succeed.

Crises in identity maintenance occur when one must choose between conflicting group loyalties, such as between the demands of ethnic group membership and professional integrity. In the United States as elsewhere there are continuing dilemmas over taking care of members of one's own ethnic group versus a priority of responsibility to inculcated professional standards. In Nigeria the Ibos did so well professionally and economically that the other major ethnic groups finally responded by driving them out of non-Ibo regions of Nigeria. Many other examples of the forceful suppression of too-successful ethnic minorities can be easily recalled.

The ethnic composition of various professions and trades in the United States has changed over the years. Some, however, continue to manifest ethnic differences due to earlier patterns of exclusion. The exclusion-inclusion process in trades and professions begins with admittance or nonadmittance to training programs. Patterns of ethnic prejudice, though, may readily shift to more subtle forms of recognition or nonrecognition through appointments.

Advancement related to "quality in professional performance" can be and often is ethnically controlled. The pure notion of professional integrity is somehow lost in a labyrinth of multiple causal loops, and the achievement process over time will display many of the characteristics of a self-fulfilling prophecy. Opportunities will be better used by those whose personality have been cultivated to understand and exploit ethnically biased opportunities to maximal advantage.

Competence

Ethnic identity may determine one's confidence in one's capacities to take on socially acceptable goal-oriented activities. Expectations of self are shaped by capacities or incapacities attributed by others to one's ethnic group. As part of one's ethnic identity one may face many situations that demonstrate personal inadequacy rather than increasing confidence. In other instances, an inherited high social status is, at the same time, an avowal of one's potential capacity. It is thus psychologically easier for members of certain groups to move up to expectations of group competence if there is a collective confidence shared by the group. In such a group, the social self is developed around supportive attitudes. It is more difficult for an individual to assert his or her competence when one is a member of a group with no such supportive tradition. That individual has to depend more upon independent capacities for status than do members inheriting such psychological support.

Responsibility

As we have indicated, being a member of a group is partially defined by feeling compelled to obey the group's moral codes. Individuals who identify ethnically with a group also identify ethically with it. They may feel guilt or remorse for acts of omission or commission that are related to the well-being of their group. Not only the responsibilities, but what is irresponsible and reprehensible is defined in group terms. As in the case of the Italians already cited, some groups have as part of their traditions both positive definitions of expectations and fears of how individuals, characteristically for the group, fail in meeting responsibilities. The dilemma of identity within many groups is this awareness of traditional avoidance of duty, as well as the heroic representations of what one should do to be truly moral.

Defined in ethnic terms, responsibility in all groups has an internalized moral dimension. Some who seek to escape ethnicity do so because they judge that the negative social and personal features of their inheritance far outweigh the positive. In times of crisis, however, they find themselves vulnerable to falling into a negative destiny—they may come to define their own moral failings as culturally inherited traits. In other instances, the positive expectations of what it is to be a member of a group are considered a burden to be avoided. One seeks to identify with a less demanding subgroup as a way out of the constraints of one's own tradition. But George Santayana, in his brilliant novel, *The Last Puritan* (1936), suggests that a conscious disavowal of a tradition does not erase deeper layers of socialization. De Vos (1973a), describing "psychological lag" in Japanese arranged marriages, points out how conscious avowals of a right to "free marriage" do not result in any great decrease in arranged marriages in Japan. Many Japanese do not *feel* morally right about a free marriage for themselves, although they consider it acceptable intellectually for other Japanese.

In an ethnically pluralistic society an individual may wish to take on a minority identity to take advantage of the seemingly freer pattern enjoyed by members of another group. Such individuals may attempt to take part in minority group activities but they are usually not accepted and remain outsiders. They are not considered to have the necessary "soul" to be included. In short, one's sense of ethnic identity invariably implies some assumption or avoidance of responsibility and guilt. A minority group member, by introjecting a negative ethnic self-image, may take on an internal conflict about ethical standards. Some, therefore, seek to avoid an ethnic identity as morally distasteful, or burdensome, and use it as an external explanation for personal failings.

Control or Social Dominance

We have indicated how ethnicity is related to concepts of social and political power. One tends to assess oneself, as well as one's group, as being placed by society in a superordinate or in a subordinate position with respect to other groups. If placed in a superordinate status, an individual can view as legitimate the authority wielded in assuming dominance over members of other groups. Such individuals may experience some social insecurities related to an inculcated need to maintain control over others. A sense of emphasis on group ascendancy can be used to hide individual impotence. When the dominant group feels its authority threatened, the subordinate but feared group may be pressured to show symbolic signals of its continuing subordination. The more insecure, the more the need to manifest symbolically one's dominance and the more the need to receive symbolic gestures of submission from members of subordinate groups. The emphasis on German superiority in nazism, for example, followed past defeats, including the social and economic impotence of the lower-middle-class Germans during the economic chaos of the last Weimar Republic. These groups found some psychological and social assuagement in the ideology advocated by Hitler: German ethnicity imparted a right to feel powerful and dominant—it relieved the individual of his or her own sense of weakness. Belonging to a "superior" group help resolve questions of individual assertion.

To espouse an ethnic identity a person of subordinate status may have to assume a moral imperative to seek liberation and autonomy, to reassert a necessary independence of oneself and one's group from the oppressor. Negatively, there may be ambivalence over rebellion. One may feel impelled to rebel; at the same time one senses the rebellion to be an illegitimate act of infantile origin. The psychodynamics of submission, rebellion, or autonomy are complex. The same social acts may spring from different levels of maturity—submission, for example, may be an instrumental, mature decision to survive, or it may be an infantile form of dependency uncalled for and not easily reducible to a simple psychological explanation. An individual, as part of a tradition, may inherit modes of social trickery used by subordinates in somehow maintaining themselves vis-à-vis individuals of superior status (e.g., the "laughing barrel" of American blacks). There may also be ambivalence about social submission and compliance that an individual may project outward as a problem of group identity. The relation of ethnic identity to power and exploitation is a large topic that needs no further illustration to indicate its relevance.

Mutuality

Ethnic or subcultural traditions define modes of competition as well as modes of cooperation expected of the individual by one's group. Competitive activity may be deemphasized within the group at the same time that competition with individuals outside the group is encouraged. For example, among the Burakumin, minority outcastes of Japan, competitive activities or expressions of aggression among children were discouraged within the group but were implicitly and explicitly encouraged toward the majority children.

Standards of ethical competition within a group are often quite different from those permitted when the individual is dealing with people outside the group. Very often within-group activities of an instrumental nature emphasize the need for concerted behavior and mutual trust in acting together toward the realization of goals. At the same time, some groups realize that they may be betrayed from within. This makes it difficult for the group to unite to attain political or social goals. Mexican-Americans, for example, have shown continual distrust of their leaders.

With respect to each of these dimensions of instrumental activity, the individual may be faced with a dilemma of identity, since maintaining oneself within one's own group may be a disadvantage when one is seeking to realize personal goals. One must then decide whether it is worthwhile to give up group identity or to maintain it and seek to realize goals despite the inconveniences of one's ethnic status. In some cases, conversely, allegiance to a group is reinforced because group membership affords support in the cooperative or competitive realization of goals.

Expressive Behavior and Ethnic Identity

Maintenance of one's ethnic loyalty always involves expressive, emotional needs. The psychological rewards of remaining a minority outweigh the instrumental advantages of leaving or changing behavior to gain occupational or social advantage. Such decisions are very complex. In each instance one must assess the relative strength of a variety of expressive vectors in understanding behavior related to group affiliation. The following are some fragments of topics that deserve more than the cursory comments we summarize. A fuller exposition of a psychocultural theory of ethnic identity would explore these motivational features in greater depth (Lee and De Vos 1981).

Harmony

A universal need of group living is some kind of peacefulness or harmony within one's group relationships. Feelings of conflict and contention are muted within the group; whenever possible, hostilities are displaced onto individuals not belonging to the group. Many groups, however, unfortunately also embody in their traditions of membership forms of discord, hostility, and resentment that are directed more internally than externally.

Social movements arising from within minority groups are often attempts to unite the group to achieve a new sense of harmony. The most expedient mechanism for effecting internal harmony is to find a way of deflecting socially disruptive behavior onto outside individuals. Thus, considerable emotional benefits can be gained by certain church memberships, such as the Black Muslims. Membership permits a new conceptualization of one's ethnic self in such a way that internal kinship is reinforced while at the same time the individual is given a means of deflecting one's aggressive needs onto legitimately hated outsiders. Most groups use mechanisms of this type in one way or another to maintain their continuance. By so doing, one reaches for a greater sense of peacefulness and ease within the group. Consequently, there is an increase in uneasiness, wariness, and suspicion regarding given outsiders who are cast in the role of enemy. Scapegoating is a well-established mechanism central to any social psychological study of prejudice and ethnocentrism. It is a characteristic both of majority and minority groups in plural societies.

Affiliation

The sense of affiliative belonging involved in ethnicity has been discussed throughout this volume. Social isolation is an intolerable state for most humans. The threat of separation from the group is one of the most stringent of human sanctions. An ethnic group can provide for a mutual sense of contact possible only in some areas of communication to those sharing common past experiences. In this regard, a generalized ethnic identity may in some instances supplant more direct personally intimate one-to-one relationships.

There can arise a generation gap in ethnic identity. An individual may find satisfying if not intimate companionship more readily with peers of similar ethnic origin than in contacts with primary family members of a different generation. For many Mexican-American youths, as discussed by Carola and Marcelo Suárez-Orozco, an ethnic peer group quickly replaces the primary family as the primary reference group.

Problems of ethnic identity can arise if self-affirmation signals that one is leaving one's group. This, in turn, can lead to rejection by, and enforced isolation from, others of one's group. A choice to go it alone involves severe psychological strain. In *Japan's Invisible Race* (1969) De Vos and Wagatsuma cite examples of Japanese outcastes who tried to pass for some time, but finally returned to their own group, giving up promising professional careers bought at the cost of social estrangement. The whole topic of individualism and alienation related to problems over a sense of group belonging deserves more exposition than can be given here. De Vos has covered some of these features with Hiroshi Wagatsuma in exploring alienation and suicide among Japanese (De Vos 1973b).

Nurturance

Nurturance is the transmission of care from the older to the younger generations. The sense of nurturance may not extend beyond ethnic boundaries. The parental attitude, if genuine, assumes the younger individual needs *temporary* assistance, not that he or she is permanently incapable of taking care of oneself. This attitude between groups may slip over into one of a permanent paternalism that is psychologically damaging to the recipients. The dependent role of wards that the government forced upon Native Americans has helped perpetuate chronic identity problems that have been socially debilitating for the groups that they were supposedly designed to aid.

Ethnic relationships are often expected to supply care, help, and comfort in times of need. For some, ethnic membership provides a field for expressing benevolence. Many find within themselves a need to care for others—to care for the more helpless of one's own kind. Conversely, members of an ethnic group not only expect sociability or alliance, they expect to be able to express dependency needs to other members.

Whereas individuals expect nurturance and care from their group and often feel responsible for caring for others in their own group, they may find themselves relatively deprived personally, socially, or economically within the larger society, because of their minority or ethnic group status. Many ethnic groups in plural societies set up special benevolent societies to take care of distressed members. American Jews have been pioneers in professional welfare agencies in the United States.

A major problem of public welfare programs has been the incapacity of professionally trained workers to reach people across ethnic barriers. Similar problems arise in public health programs. The recent interest in medical anthropology arises from recognition that ethnic identity and differences in cultural traditions are important social factors in reaching and aiding the disadvantaged.

Members of one's own ethnic group, when professionally trained, have the advantage of reaching people who need help. Both psychiatry and medicine require mutual trust and mutual belief; it is psychologically difficult to become dependent on an outsider. Finally, in some groups one might find that there is the unhappy perception that members are mutually depriving one another. This may not be overtly stated to outsiders but a felt experience that adds to ambivalence about maintaining group membership.

Appreciation

Ethnic identity is related basically to pride in a positive way, or to shame and degradation in a negative one. Each group seeks to create for itself a sense of humanity, dignity, self-respect, and proper status. Any human being resents the possibility of being neglected, ignored, unappreciated—or worse, actively degraded, disparaged, debased, and depreciated.

Ethnic identity often involves vulnerable feelings about self-respect or a potential sense of worthlessness. Some groups are particularly sensitive to the opinions of others, to their public image. Other groups are more self-sufficient. Perhaps the English and the Japanese are extremes of this continuum. English self-sufficiency is related to a need for appreciation limited to those within their class system. In both the English and Japanese a deep sense of shame may be aroused by improper behavior on the part of a member of one's own group. A readiness to take on external values often crucially curtails the self-sufficiency of Japanese. As a nation they are particularly vulnerable to external criticism or inadvertent disparagement.

Expressive feelings concerned with appreciation are central to understanding many difficulties that arise in intragroup and intergroup relationships. Culture traits cannot help but be evaluated. What is seen in highly positive terms within a group may, with alien contact, lose its value as soon as it is perceived by others in a devalued way.

Theodore Schwartz has discussed the origin and development of cargo cults, not as a reaction to an external dominance of Western culture, but much more directly related to the devaluation of what was of value in Melanesia in their economic interaction. That is, the Melanesians could no longer believe in their symbols of economic worth when they were faced with the knowledge of a much superior technology producing goods of greater worth than they could possibly imagine within their traditional culture.

Resultant crises in the sense of self felt acutely by Melanesians led to the development of the cargo cult preoccupation, in which they hoped for the arrival of superior cargo from some supernatural source. Without extreme self-devaluation, they could not countenance the idea that these superior material artifacts were simply the products of people like themselves.

One of the great problems of culture contact is such crises of self-assessment. These occur when a group is forced to recognize the relative merits and sometimes the superior technology of an alien group. Within pluralistic societies there is constant mutual evaluation. Such collective evaluative comparisons can add to or detract from the individual's appraisal of personal worth as a member of a group.

Pleasure and Suffering

Ethnic identity is ultimately related to questions about the satisfaction afforded by social life and to the problem of arriving at a mature capacity to tolerate the suffering and death that is the destiny of all. As in the metaphor of the California Indian sadly commenting on the death of his culture, ethnic identity is found in the "cup of custom" passed on by one's parents, from which one drinks the meaning of existence. Once the cup is broken, one can no longer taste of life. It is a light-scattering prism through which one views life with a sense of curiosity and creativity. It is both a means and an end, insofar as one develops a capacity to enjoy.

An ethnic identity gives savor, the taste of one's past. The tastelessness of instant artifice is what the younger generation today describes as "plastic"; it is the opposite of the sense of past accumulations, of meanings husbanded and passed on to a new generation. Stripped of these, individuals face indifference, boredom, and a sense of normlessness or anomie. This is the result not only of a lack of regulation governing life but of the lack of savor and seasoning that occurs with the heedless casting out of past custom. Ultimately, ethnic identity is the unexpressed meaning of anthropology. Anthropologists intellectualize about human culture, yet try to preserve in their own modes of pursuing knowledge the value of the human past; to assert that without consciousness of the past, the present becomes devoid of meaning.

In ethnic identity there is a commitment to endure suffering. In the Christian context, to change the Indian metaphor, one's culture is also the common chalice in which suffering blood becomes redemptive wine. To some few, identity can be a commitment to masochism, but to most it is simply a necessary stigmatic emblem one must learn to carry without disguise. Each group perhaps thinks that in maintaining itself it has to undergo certain forms of unique suffering not experienced by others. It may be reassuring to some and perhaps deflating to others to recognize that consciousness of suffering is not unique to any one group, but is the destiny of our common humanity, whatever our separate cultural origins.

NOTES

1. See Erik Erikson, *Identity, Youth and Crisis* (1968).

2. A scheme of instrumental-expressive social interactional concerns has been used by George A. De Vos in his previous work in understanding social role behavior in Japan (1973c). It is a conceptual framework that has evolved out of analyses of the Thematic Apperception Test in different cultural settings. It has been applied to analyze the persistence of a Korean ethnic identy within a Japanese society that has sought to obliterate any separate identity on the part of Japanese citizens of Korean ancestry (Lee and De Vos 1981).

REFERENCES

Balzer, Marjorie Mandelstam. 1991. "Doctors or Deceivers? The Siberian Khanty Shaman and Soviet Medicine." In *The Anthropology of Medicine; From Culture to Method.* Lola Romanucci-Ross, Daniel E. Moerman, Laurence Tancredi, eds. Pp. 56-84. South Hadley, MA: Bergin and Garvey.

Balzer, Marjorie Mandelstam. 1993a. "Shamanism and the Politics of Culture. An Anthropological View of the 1992 International Conference on Shamanism, Yakutsk, the Sakha Republic." *Shaman* 1(1):71-96.

Balzer, Marjorie Mandelstam. 1993b. "Two Urban Shamans: Unmasking Leadership in fin-de-Soviet Siberia." In *Perilous States; Conversations on Culture, Politics, and Nation.* George E. Marcus, ed. Pp. 131-164. Chicago: University of Chicago Press.

Bruner, Edward. 1976. "Some Observations on Cultural Change and Psychological Stress in Indonesia." In *Responses to Change: Society, Culture and Personality*. George A. De Vos, ed. Pp. 234-252. New York: D. Van Nostrand Company.

Crandon-Malamud, Libbet. 1991. "Phantoms and Physicians: Social Change Through Medical Pluralism." In *The Anthropology of Medicine; From Culture to Method*. Lola Romanucci-Ross, Daniel E. Moerman, and Laurence Tancredi, eds. Pp. 56-84. South Hadley, MA: Bergin and Garvey.

De Vos, George A. 1973a. "Some Observations of Guilt in Relation to Achievement and Arranged Marriage in the Japanese." In *Socialization for Achievement: The Cultural Psychology of the Japanese*. George A. De Vos, ed. Pp. 144-146. Berkeley: University of California Press.

De Vos, George A. 1973b. "Role Narcissism and the Etiology of Japanese Suicide." In *Socialization for Achievement: The Cultural Psychology of the Japanese*. George A. De Vos, ed. Pp. 438-485. Berkeley: University of California Press.

De Vos, George A. 1973c. *Socialization for Achievement: The Cultural Psychology of the Japanese*. Berkeley: University of California Press.

De Vos, George A., and Hiroshi Wagatsuma. 1966. *Japan's Invisible Race*. Berkeley: University of California Press.

Durkheim, Emile. 1947. *The Elementary Forms of Religious Life*. W. Swain, trans. Glencoe, IL: Free Press.

Erikson, Erik. 1968. *Identity, Youth and Crisis*. New York: W. W. Norton.

Haley, Alex. 1966. *The Autobiography of Malcolm X*. New York: Grove Press.

Kardiner, Abram, and Lionel Ovesey. 1962. *The Mark of Oppression*. Cleveland and New York: World.

Lee, Changsoo, and George A. De Vos. 1981. *Koreans in Japan: Ethnic Conflict and Accom modation*. Berkeley: University of California Press.

Ogbu, John. 1978. Minority Education and Caste, the American System in Cross-Cultural Perspective. New York: Academic Press.

Romanucci-Ross, Lola. 1966. "Conflits Fonciers a Mokerang village Matankor des iles de l'Amiraute." *L'Homme* 6(2):32-52.

Romanucci-Ross, Lola. 1977. "Hierarchy of Resort in Curative Practices." In *Culture, Disease and Healing*. David Landy, ed. Pp. 481-487. New York: Macmillan.

Romanucci-Ross, Lola. 1983. *Conflict, Violence, and Morality in a Mexican Village*. Chicago: University of Chicago Press.

Romanucci-Ross, Lola. 1985. *Mead's Other Manus; Phenomenology of the Encounter*. South Hadley, MA: Bergin and Garvey.

Romanucci-Ross, Lola. 1989. "The Impassioned Cogito; Shaman and Anthropologist." In *Shamanism: Past and Present*. M. Hoppal and von Sadovsky, eds. Pp. 35-42. Budapest-Los Angeles: Istor Books.

Santayana, George. 1936. *The Last Puritan*. New York: Scribner.

Sapir, Edward. 1968. "Contributions to Cultural Anthropology." *International Encyclopedia of the Social Sciences*. New York: MacMillan.

Valiers, Pierre. 1968. *Negres Blancs d'Amerique: Autobiographies Precoce d'un "Terroriste" Quebecois*. Montreal: Parti Tris.

Author Index

Subject Index